C. RAJAGOPALACHARI

Role in Freedom Movement

mdian Freedom Fighters Series—20

C. Rajagopalachari
Role in Freedom Movement

S. R. BAKSHI

Anmol Publications

ANMOL PUBLICATIONS
4378/4B, Ansari Road, Daryaganj,
New Delhi-110002

C. Rajagopalachari : Role in Freedom Movement

ISBN 81-7041-433-4

PRINTED IN INDIA

Published by J.L. Kumar for Anmol Publications and Printed at Sangita Printers, Maujpur Delhi-53.

Preface

In the long-drawn political struggle for freedom of our sub-continent, the part played by C. Rajagopalachari is most significant. At a young age when he was struggling hard at Salem to build up his legal practice, he came in touch with Mahatma Gandhi with whom he worked like a disciplined worker of the Congress. He was arrested and convicted several times and faced the troubles in the jail with smile on his face. He held several offices and discharged his official functions with meticulous care. He was Chief Minister, of Madras Province twice, Minister in the Interim Government, Governor of West Bengal and Governor-General of India. Besides he was the founder of the Swatantra Party. Indeed he was a very fine speaker, a prolific writer and an independent thinker.

The themes dealt in this work are his early career, political ideology, social philosophy, Congress, War and the Raj and an assessment of his personality. Besides I have given the glossary, chronology and the bibliography at the end of these chapters.

I have consulted the research material from the Nehru Memorial Museum and Library, Sapru House Library and the Indian Council of Historical Research Library and feel much beholden to the authorities of these institutions for affording their academic support to me during may researches.

S.R. Bakshi

Contents

1

Early Career

Rajagopalachari was born on 10 December 1878 at Torrapalli in Hasur Taluk of Salem district of the Madras Presidency. The family traces its origin from the Srivaishnava community of Brahmins. His father, Chakravarthi Iyengar was the Munsiff of Torrapalli. He was very keen to impart the best possible education to his son. Rajaji had his early education in Hosur. Later on, he joined the Central College, Bangalore. He took his B.A. degree in 1897 and was sent to Madras to study law. He was awarded the Bachelor Degree in Law in 1899, at the age of twenty-one and commenced his legal practice at Salem.

He was married when he was a student in the Law College. As a lawyer, he it did not take him much time to be a prominent lawyer in his region. His income increased day by day. He, now, began to take part in the socio-political activities of his region by addressing several meetings attended by both educated and uneducated people. He was also in touch with the national leaders like Mahatma Gandhi, C.R. Das and others. At this point of time, he began to attend the annual sessions of the Indian National Congress where he represented as a prominent delegate from the Madras Presidency.

He was very humble in his statements. He did not make a show of his capabilities. Once he opined thus: 'I have no experience in governing a country. I have some experience in conducting cases in courts. That experience is of no use in governing the country. The habit of speaking for a party is of no use in administration. My twenty years' experience as a lawyer at the war is of no use to me'.

He also did the editing work of *Young India*. The also launched the programme of prohibition in 1928. Indeed his *Ashram* at Pudupalayam became a place of pilgrimage for several people of the region. The Khaddar depot was a useful feeder for the masses.

At the call of Mahatma Gandhi for Non-Cooperation Movement, he at first swore not to enter the courts. He also pulled out his two sons in college, according to the boycott of schools and colleges programme, with the help of Mahatma Gandhi, he organised the All-India Spinners Association. Allied to it was the Khadi Board. He also established an Ashram to propagate the Gandhian ideology. He asked the people around him to spin Khadi.

He was one of the signatories to the famous manifesto of October 4, 1921, declaring that it was the duty of every Indian soldier and civilian to sever his connection with the British Government and find some other means of livelihood.

At Salem he made himself busy in public and literary work. He was one of the founders of the Salem Literary Society and very often attended its meetings and participated in the deliberations. Thus he developed a new social and political ideology which had deep linkage with the life of a common Indian. He did not believe in the caste barriers. He even recommended scholarships to the promising untouchable students.

He was a modest person and lived a simple life. He was a staunch believer in the *karma* theory. He has been called a true *karma yogin,* doing his duty as was assigned to him. He indeed was a practical man and firmly believed in action—an action mostly for the welfare of the masses of our country.

He was a very fine writer. He wrote Tamil books on Socrates and Marcus Auerlins, and in English the Mahabharata, the Mayana and upanishad and fables and short stories. His commentaries on the Bhagwat Gita are regarded as outstanding on the subject.

In the following years, when the Swaraj Party became the dominant wing of the Congress, Rajaji devoted himself to the constructive work such as Hindu-Muslim unity, eradication of untouchabilitity, the Swadeshi movement and prohibition.

He was also instrumental in evolving the Yervada Pact between the representatives of the Hindu conference and those of the depressed classes.

2

Political Ideology

C. Rajagopalachari was in his mid-thirties when he came under the influence of Mahatma Gandhi who came back to India during the second year of the first global war. In 1915, Gandhi happened to tour all the regions of India in order to understand the socio-economic condition of the masses of India. Rajaji found in Gandhi a leader who could lead the millions of his nation towards Swaraj. He himself joined the first Non-Cooperation Movement and the Civil Disobedience Movement. Besides he spelt out his political ideology through his speeches and writings. He gave up his legal practice when Gandhi gave a call for the Non-Cooperation Movement. He also showed his resentment at the promulgation of the Rowlatt Legislation which had greatly demoralised the people of the Punjab.

ROWLATT LEGISLATION

The Government Explanations Answered

Mr. C. Rajagopalachari has issued the following noteworthy reply to Government resolution dated 14th April 1919 regarding the Rowlatt legislation :

The Government of India complain that the character of the Rowlatt Legislation has been much misrepresented in the present agitation, and that the intensity of the popular feeling against the legislation is due to such misrepresentations. Government has taken action to meet the agitation by issuing its own literature "to explain the very great value of this legislation to all peaceable and law abiding persons in this country." !

Whatever the merits of this agitation against the Rowlatt Law may be, one just victory has been already achieved, in that the Government has realised its duty to appeal to the people at large to obtain their consent to an enactment, though after the event it may be. This is a success of no mean constitutional importance; for it may well be claimed that the Government has in this for the first time acted as if it were constitutionally responsible to the people. All that we yet want is that the appeal to the people should be before the legislation and not after.

The point most strongly urged in the Government explanation is that the law can have operation nowhere except where there is anarchical crime prevalent. We answer that this would have been a really protective clause, if any legislative council or other body responsible to the people had the power to decide this. Under the Rowlatt Law the provisions come into force as soon as the declaration is made by the Executive Government that in their opinion there exist such crimes or movements tending to such crimes. The declaration is not subject to any test or appeal or veto of the legislature. On what insufficient grounds such operative formulate can be uttered would be apparent on an unbiassed consideration of the circumstances, under which a state of open rebellion has been recently declared in order to bring martial law into operation, though all the riots were practically completely quelled even before such declaration. The manner in which the Press law has been worked throughout India, and the ease with which the deportation regulations have been utilised, do not create any confidence in the unfettered discretion of the Executive in matters relating to political crime.

It is said that the first part of the Act merely provides for the speedy trial of certain grave offences. No one objects to speedy trials, provided they are not hasty: but every one objects to the Executive Government, who is the prosecutor in the case, to have power by its own unappealable order to bring any case within the jurisdiction of a Special Bench which can exclude the public and try without jurors or assessors.

It is said that in the second and third parts provision is made "for preventive action against persons suspected of revolutionary or anarchical crime." "Preventive action" is to put suspected men in prison or under other restraints, without trial according to law. Whatever language Government may employ, it means imprisonment without trial : and the people cannot be very misguided in objecting to such legislation. The Local Government's executive order arresting and confining persons suspected by it is final, and there is no appeal to law. The Government explanation lays stress on the point that such orders are to be made only in the case of persons suspected of anarchical or revolutionary crime, and assures us that the provision need cause no fear or apprehension to any person other than the revolutionary or anarchist. Government in effect tells people that in such cases courts are not necessary, and that they may depend on the Executive Government's decisions without enquiry as to whether men are innocent or not. It assumes that innocent men can never be suspected or misunderstood by the Executive Government. As long as Government does not suspect you, you are safe; but when it suspects you, or rather when it declares it suspects you, you are no longer free, and the protection of the courts is taken away. Whether a man is innocent or not can only be decided by trial. How then can the executive declaration be a protection.

The statement that the terms of the Act definitely exclude its use in any case not falling within the definition of anarchical or revolutionary conspiracy is delusive; for there is no remedy open to any man or woman who is proceeded against under the Act and who is not guilty of such crimes. The word of the Executive is final, and there is no appeal to any court on the ground that the case is not one of anarchical or revolutionary crime.

The provision as to the investigating authority which is to examine and report on the cases in which action is taken under the Act is of no consequence. This investigation is done in secrecy, without the man charged hearing the evidence, cross-examing the witnesses, or defending himself by counsel. Further the report is not binding on the Government. It is no wonder that such a safeguard is considered a sham and a delusion.

It is claimed that no, unusual or extended powers have been given to the police. When men can be interned, deported and imprisoned without appeal to courts, on the mere executive order of Government, it is vain to contend that there is no increase of the powers of police officers, on whose *ex parte* reports such orders are necessarily based. To what extent the Executive Government gets within its sole jurisdiction powers which according to the Constitution should vest in judicial tribunals to that extent the police undoubtedly get increased powers.

The Government desire it to be understood that they will protect all well behaved citizens. In the vernaculars of the country Sirkar means the Government as well as the Courts established by law. But here the protecting Government is only the Executive Government, and not the courts of law. May not the people claim that just and independent tribunals should protect them against the assaults of an irresponsible Executive ? Even if the Executive Government were responsible to the people as in democratic countries, that responsibility alone is not deemed in those countries to be adequate protection, and courts are constituted as the supreme authority in matters affecting the freedom of person and property. How much more necessary then, is such protection, in a country where the Executive Government consists of an irresponsible bureau of salaried officer ?

Let it be clearly understood that we would oppose such

legislation vesting in the Executive Government the absolute right to suspect and imprison without trial, even if the Government be democratic and purely Indian, and not bureaucratic and foreign.

We invite the Government to answer these difficulties truly and fairly, and enlighten the people on the merits of the agitation.

SOME OBJECTIONS TO SATYAGRAHA

(By Mr. C. Rajagopalachariar)

Some people imagine that the practice of civil disobedience is likely to lead men into a general habit of disobedience of law endangering peace and good order in the state. This apprehension can be felt only by those who have no practical experience or mental realisation of Satyagraha, and who make calculations and portend consequences ignoring certain of the essential elements of the movement. If the movement of civil disobedience is accompanied by violence or hatred, it may be taken for granted that it cannot for one moment succeed and that any government be it the present bureaucratic form or any future administration commanding the resources of the State, can easily and at once put it down with a strong hand. One need therefore have no anxiety in respect of the evil consequences of spurious passive resistance movements. For a civil disobedience movement to succeed or command respect and attention it has necessarily to be conducted strictly on the lines emphasised repeatedly by Mr. Gandhi. There can be no violence or hatred or untruth. Every person actively taking part in the movement will, have to develop an extent of purity of thought, word and deed and self-restraint, which guarantees for the society and the state of which he is a member, that he will not be a danger to its peace or order, but on the contrary will be a source of strength and elevation of general morals. Those who are incapable of that self-restraint which is demanded by Satyagraha will, far from being led to disobedience of the law by the example of Satyagrahis, be deterred from it by a contemplation of the suffering and difficulties undergone by those in the movement. Thus neither by themselves nor through others will those who adopt Satyagraha endanger peace and order in Society.

Another apprehension felt by some people who wish to see representative institutions developed in this country and real administrative functions transferred to them, is that the spirit of passive resistance, encouraged by success against certain obnoxious laws made by the present government will not stop there, but will rise to manifest itself on every occasion, when any body of perons can combine for trifling or selfish ends to get rid of any rule or law whatsoever passed in the general interest of the community; and this, too, more easily when the functions of government are transferred to the people of this country and their representatives; that thus the inculcation of the theory and practice of Satyagraha is opposed to the success and progress of self-government in this land.

This again is an objection arising out of ignorance of the essential features of Satyagraha. The first lesson of the experience of Satyagraha is a realisation of how difficult it is for those swayed by selfish motives, successfully to practise Satyagraha even for one day. Satyagraha is not mere disobedience. It demands courage and the spirit of sacrifice of the highest order. A just cause is in the nature of the thing an essential requisite. Those who have undergone the actual experience of Satyagraha and its difficulties will be the last persons to advise or undertake it on slight and insufficient grounds, or hastily and without trying all other methods of remedying any great and serious wrong. In fact it is in this very feature that the superiority of Satyagraha lies. Protests and demonstrations can be organised by interested or prejudiced classes against every measure even though it may be just and for the good of other classes. But Satyagraha can be undertaken with any degree of success only for just causes. No one would sacrifice and go to person while many may go to a meeting and pass resolutions for unjust or slight causes; even if some one did it out of ignorance no one would be moved by it. Satyagraha is a weapon in the hands of both parties in a struggle. It is the one mechanism for the remedy of social wrongs which contains within itself its own checks and adjustments. Just as, or perhaps more truly than, in physical warfare the more powerful party ultimately wins, in spite of temporary results to the contrary, in the warfare of Satyagraha the forces which may for sometime gather round the unjust cause drop off by the very nature of the warefare and the just cause always issues triumphant.

There are the chief arguments of those who raise their hands in horror at the proposal of civil disobedience. What course of action do they themselves suggest? If they deprecate Satyagraha, they must stand for one or other of three things, continuing a lifeless agitation in which they themselves have no more belief, total resignation to evil, or violence. Stated thus, every one would reject all the alternatives; and then, in truth, only Satyagraha remains.

CIVIL DISOBEDIENCE AND DISTURBANCES

(By Mr. C. Rajgopalachariar)

Sufficient time has now elapsed to take a dispassionate view of the disorders in the Punjab and other places and to apportion the blame therefor. How far outside causes such as Afghan, German and Bolshevik intrigues had anything to do with them we shall not now discuss. We shall simply state that we are not prepared to believe such theories without any proof whatever worth the name. In any event we shall confine our remarks to-day to the undoubted internal causes of the outbreak.

It is commonly stated that Mr. Gandhi admitted that clever revolutionaries conspired secretly and took advantage of the Satyagraha movement and organised the disorders. Stated in this general way, it is absolutely unwarranted by what Mr. Gandhi said. He has long ago made it clear that his remark about clever men inclined to violence was only about

Ahmedabad disorders, and had no reference either to revolutionaries or to the Punjab. It is unfortunate that what Mr. Gandhi said has been twisted and misapprehended and made the basis of statements of such responsible authorities as even the Secretary of State.

It is right to connect the Satyagraha movement with the disturbances? This question is answered in the affirmative by some who therefore deprecate resumption of the movement in any shape. To us this imputation seems wholly unjust. It arises out of a fallacy to common in political and historic discussions conducted in a party spirit, viz., *post hoc proctor hoc*. The men who attribute the disturbances to Satyagraha ignore altogether the general political situation in the country and look with a narrow eve at only the new factor, and believe that anything is attributable to it. The best way of examining the matter would be, for a moment, to divest ourselves of all in as connected with Satyagraha, and to imagine for ourselves the state of the country if Mr. Gandhi had not even thought about the passive resistance movement.

No one can maintain for one moment that there would have been no discontent in the country but for the civil disobedience movement. The Rowlatt legislation, the Muslim question, the economic distress, the feeling of bitterness in consequence of the material disappointment of hopes of a great measure of political emancipation after the close of the war and other important causes of acute discontent would all be there even if Mr. Gandhi had not started any movement. To crown all, the deportations in the Punjab would have taken place none the less, at the instance of the strong Lieutenant-Governor. A point is reached in the psychology of all nations, when if constitutional agitation is widely felt to have been worked to its fullest limit, and yet fails to bring about remedy, an outburst becomes imminent. It is only a question what shape this explosion must take. Such a bursting point was reached when the Rowlatt legislation was passed amidst the surrounding circumstances indicated above. Now if civil disobedience had not been thought of at all, what would have been the programme of politicians and leaders ? There would have been certainly strong protests, huge mass meetings and great popular excitement all the same. The acuteness of feeling together with a sense of dispair would still be there, and we venture to think that upon the deportations the outbursts would have taken place just as they did now in spite of Satyagraha. In fact, we may be at liberty to state that the effect of Satyagraha throughout the country was rather to moderate the resentment by giving definite hope through peaceful work, where otherwise it was blank despair. It gave a self-reliant and dignified line of action, where otherwise the only alternatives were an impossible submission, or violence.

We wish to emphasise one more point. It is a poor understanding of Satyagraha to mistake the events and the programme of the sixth April or the thirtieth March with Satyagraha proper. The meetings and fasts observed on that day though prescribed and undertaken by the Satyagraha leaders, were not by themselves either Satyagraha, or passive resistance. In the Punjab where the outburst took place, passive resistance had not been begun at all, and it is idlė therefore to talk of Satyagraha as having been in any way directly or indirectly connected with the disturbances in the Punjab.

The tiller of the soil ought not to be neglected. The best intellects arose from the tillers of the soil—Tiruvalluvar Kamban, Ottakuthan, and Auvai. The greatest men were born of the humblest class of people, not of the upper classes. The upper classes are living on other's labour and do not look upon labourers as their benefactors. There is awakening among the people. According to Varnasrama Dharma one at the top must always be there and one at the bottom must always be at the bototm, and he must have his thin gruel, scanty clothing and must work day and night and cannot have a share in the profits of the field or other concerns. That has been the deception practised by the people. A certain class of people are untouchables but their productions are touchables

False interpretation put upon Varnashrma Dharma has been the bane of the country. The lower classes have not had the courage to question the correctness of Varnashrma Dharma. Owing to contact between the East and the West there has been a change.

We are today assembled representing all classes of people, demanding their right to be treated as human beings. This is an achievement of which we are glad. This is only a beginning and we have a long vista before us Labour should be represented in the Legislative Council. Their representatives should be either appointed or elected. The big trader, manufacturer and landlord would look at the question from a different point of view. I am sure that the Goverenment of Lord Willingdon would be solicitious about the condition of labourers. His Excellency has indicated his sympathy by the appoiniment of Mr. Paddison as Labour Commissioner. Mr. Paddison is a tactful and sympathetic gentlemen and knows Tamil and Telugu and studies labour questions and would be intermediary between the employer and the employee. I am sure Lord Willingdon's Government will do more to give a status to labour in this country. Labour has been long despised in this country. Government should lay down rules in recognition of Labour Unions.

Most of the apitalists are objecting to outsiders taking part in much Unions. For some time more, outsiders who are educated men should be allowed to be the guides of these illiterate men who are pressed by hunger. I don't think outsiders who have some in the Country would give the labourers any bad advice that would land them in difficulties. We find strikes all over the country. Strikes are less frequent in Madras on account of these Labour Unions. If there were no labour Unions and if there were no educated people at their helm, strikes would have been more frequent. Labourers in Bengal and Bombay are going to have some representation in Legislative Councils. Why should not the labourers in Madras have the some privilege and why should they not be content with their position ? The labourer in Madras is more liberal in his views and more loyal. These people deserve to be treated with greater consideration by the employer, European or Indian. I know what mirasdars and Zamindars are. The village labour is in a far better condition than the labourer in town. I do not know much of Tanjore but I may say generally that village labourers get more wages then labourers in Ceylon or anywhere else. They get 8 annas a day and get also something to eat in the villages, whereas in Ceylon and other plantations they get only 5 annas. Their prayer is that it may be raised to 8 annas. A women labourer in plantations gets only 3 annas. Labour demand is that women should be treated as human beings. Now let me say a few words in Tamli to make labourers more powerful more virtuous, and more affectionate towards each other.

At this stage the European visitors rose to leave the hall. Before doing so Mr. Robertson, on behalf of the Europeans present at the meeting thanked Mr. Kesava Pillai having expressed his views in English for the benefit of persons like them who knew English alone, and said they were all glad of the message given by Mr. Kesava Pillai to the workmen. If they kept to that message, he added there would be no trouble between European employers and the workmen.

Dewan Bahadur Kesava Pillai said "Let us be humble partners in the art of making money', and thanked them for their presence.

Resolutions Passed

Mr. C. Rajagopalachari moved the following resolution in the all India Labour conference in 1920.

1. (a) This Labour Conference while welcoming the recommendations of the Joint Committee to extend the franchise to include a proper proportion of the urban wage earning classes, expresses its grave suprise and dissatisfaction at the official

statement recently made implying that the benefit of the recommendation is not to be extended to the City or Presidency of Madras.

(b) This Conference considers that a minimum qualification for franchise of Rs. 15 income per month by wages may be fixed for the urban wage-earners.

(c) This Conference recommends that all factories coming under the purview of the factory law should be required to furnish to the elctoral officers lists of persons employed who have earned for six months continuously Rs. 15 or more, to facilitate the proper registry of such wage-earners in the electoral rolls and that other employers may be supplied forms for sending similar lists.

He said that there was no use of one or two members of the council taking up the cause of labourers, but every member sent to the Council should have the deepest interest of the labourers at heart. They would think of the labourers only when the latter had the privilege of voting. If Bolshevism was not to enter this land, law should be so framed as to adequately represent the interests of labour.

Mr. Kumaraswamy Naicker seconded the resolution and Mr. Subramania Sastriar of Arni supported it.

The resolution was unanimously carried.

From his Solitary Cell

Here is a titbit from C. Rajgopalachari from Vellore Jail :

"I guess you have not started for Bardoli and Anand yet. I am allowed to write one letter a month and to receive similarly one letter a month, and am completely shut out from all politics, news and newspapers. What an ideal condition which I know you are envying !

"The greatest common measure between thoughts, words

and what the jail authorities would allow and what I need write to you at all, it but little.

"It took me till now to get rid of the boils. I am now quite free from the trouble. It must horrify you to learn that I willingly underwent five injections of vaccine for these boils.

"My asthma persists, though by keeping my stomach light I hold the upper hand over the enemy. I have gone down from 104 to 98 lbs. but that does not matter.

"Your eyes would flow with delight if you saw me here in my solitary cell spinning not as a task imposed by a tyrant faddist, but with pleasure. Between spinning and beautiful Ramayana I have been spending practically the whole of the time left me by the agony of eating, washing of dishes etc. The spinning wheel I have is a real beauty. It is a live companion and younger brother in my cell.

"This Ashram is very much less congested than yours at Sabarmati and I wish more people understood the real advantaged of this retirement and discipline."

This is a curious Government. The same law is supposed to reign in the country and yet what is a crime in Bengal is not a crime to Madras. And the treatment in a Madras jail is not the same as in a U.P. jail. George Joseph in the Agra jail has all the comforts and privileges including newspapers, Rajgopalachari in Vellore jail must live in solitude and have no newspapers. Rajgopalachari does not mind the deprivation of newspapers. I know that I would esteem it a privilege to be without any, but difference in treatment is obvious. Rajgopalachari's loss of flesh is a more serious matter. This, of course, may not be due to want of nourishing food but if the solitary cell is anything like I know, it must be almost death to an asthamatic patient. When you are locked up in a cell you are in a box with a few holes for just enough ventilation to keep you alive. There is little light and no cross ventilation. The air in a short time becomes thick and foul with your own exhalations. And you are doomed to rebreathe your own omissions. The least that humanity demands is that C. Rajgopalachari should have, if he has not, all the fresh air he can get day and night.

Mr. Rajagopalachari

We are glad that Mr. Rajgopalachary having completed his term of imprisonment for three months has been released from the Vellore Jail. We hope he returns to his own field of activity like a giant refreshed. Many a crucial problem is awaiting his attention at this artical moment. Madras will no doubt occupy him primarily. But we fear he cannot any longer confine his activities to Madras alone. He will not find India the same country as he left her three months ago. Most of his friends, co-workers and associates in Madras are in jail and new workers have taken their place. The voices of the great provincial leaders of the Punjab, U. P., Bengal and Andhra have been hushed through their imprisonment. Lastly, and to crown all, has come the conviction of Mahatma Gandhi which was the least unexpected, and probably long over due. Mr. Rajgopalachary knows, and it would be perhaps presumtuous for us to remind him, that the cutting down of the tall poppies would not have the effect intended. India has a reserve of life and energy which is inexhaustible. As in the past so in the present, her vitality is perennial; but she represents a distinct type of existence in the history of the world. She would be going as young and fresh as ever, although she is so old, if only we know how to tap the sources of her peculiar life and energy. Mahatma Gandhi having discovered the sources of her real strength, has made her march with giant strides within the brief space of a year and a half. We have only to follow in the steps of the great master. By an incessant—application of the principles of Truth and Non-violence in the field of politics, Mahatma Gandhi has shown to us and to the world which way the road to salvation lies. As one of his trusted lieutenants, Mr. Rajgopalachary will have an immense burden to shoulder. We hope God will give him strength and vision to help to steer the national bark along the right and proper course.

My Great Disappointment

Judge Broomfield said to Mahatmaji when he stood before him as prisoner : "It will be impossible to ignore the fact that you are in a different category from any person I have ever tried or am likely to have to try. It would be impossible to ignore the fact that in the eyes of millions of your countrymen, you are a great patriot and a great leader. Even those who differ from you in politics look upon you as if man of high ideals and of noble and of even saintly life."

These beautiful words falling from the lips of an apparent enemy led India to rest in the belief that dispite the exigencies of warfare, the soul in man had triumphed over the brute and that the officers to whom Mahatmaji's body was to be entrusted according to the sentence would realise their privilege. We believed that the Superintendent and the Jailor of the prison that was to hold Mahatmaji within its walls would feel proud of this great charge and carry out the punishment not in a spirit of revenge or pettiness, but in a noble spirit. We had reason to hope that the punishment that was voluntarily sought and accepted by Mahatmaji in double atonement of the sins of our rulers as well as all the crimes of the people who had misused the strength to which he had opened their eyes, would be carried out in a spirit of worship and not that of the Jail Mannal.

But our hopes have received a rude shock. Devadas, Mahatmaji's youngest son, and I, who were at our respective posts of duty and, therefore, had not the privilege of being present during the great trial, went to Poona on the Ist of April and applied to see Mahatmaji in accordance with the rules as to interviews of prisoners. In a few minutes as we were at the gate looking through the bars, my heart leaps as I saw the old and familiar source of inspiration and joy. The frail form clad in a single loin-cloth jumped into the Gate

Passage from inside through the wicket door. He was immediately led up the stairs into the Superintendent's Office Room and we were called in. As was right and proper according to the code of official dignities and prestige, the Prison King, the Superintendent, was in his throne; and the prisoner was kept standing all the time during our talk, which on account of the Superintendent's justification and explanations and the Jailor's interruptions, took longer than we had expected.

We had a peep into the truth, and it was disappointing in the extreme. The curse of vulgarity and ignorance rendered ugly what otherwise would have been the most beautiful thing in the world. We saw at once that the Superintendent and the Jailor of Yervada had failed to realise their great opportunity. They had not the eyes to see what the cultured Judge of Ahmedadad had seen. They did not see that they were honoured with the privilege of being custodians of a man greater than the Kaisar, greater than Napolean of St. Helena, greater than the biggest prisoners of war, a man of world-value, one whose fellows in history and companions in Heaven will be Buddha, Socrates and Jesus and others of that class. Mahatmaji's jailors cannot claim the ignorance which had blinded the persecutors of Jesus or Socrates, for times have so far changed that even during the lifetime of the great Indian seer, his worst enemies have understood and explained to the world his purity of purpose and his greatness. The crime of the people to whose charge an indifferent government has entrusted him is all the greater. Food Mahatma has. The little bread goat's milk his body wants is no doubt given to him. They give him also two oranges a day as it was notoricns, be lived mainly or buit. They may even improve the quantity and quality when they learn by and by what he was all these years used to. They have not given him his own bed, but make him sleep on regulation jail blankets without a pillow. We will presume they will now give him even a pillow. His solitary cell has ventilators. He can use the verandah during day time, though at nights he has to sleep is the little space locked in with a commode. The food, air and water that the animal functions of his body require, he no doubt has, or they will soon be supplemented adequately. Even otherwise, the body will adjust itself after perhaps some trouble to the conditions laid down. But what grieves us is that we saw indifference and blindness where we had believed there would be full recognition of their great duty. The human soul is not recognised by the jail code. But we had expected Government would not leave it in this case to the poor jail officials to find out their duties towards their great prisoner from the articles in the Jail Manual.

We know that Jail single-cells are constructed for condemned murderers and recalcitrant and dangerous felons. But if necessary, it is not too much for a great and powerful Government to build afresh to find suitable prison accomodation for one whose life and self-inflicted punishment are things standing in a category apart altogether from the Jail Manual. All prisoners should be locked in at night; but, surely, Government ought to be able to find a verandah for Mahatmaji to sleep in as he has been all through doing after his pleurisy, barred and locked if they think it necessary to prevent his escape ! He is asked to petition and obtain orders from Government to have even his own religious books. He is not given such human companionship as even ordinary prisoners have. Such simple imprisonment is indeed worse than hard labour.

The whole story is sad and disappointing. But what is the thing to be remembered ? Our great leader's indomitable spirit cannot be broken by such or even worse treatment. About that all may be certain. But it is a severse test of our strength and our faith. Anger would be a fatal outlet for the resentment which the nation must feel at Government's indifference and pettiness. Bestraint all cost must be our watchword now. Otherwise, the great Sacrifice would indeed be fruitless.

A grim determination to clothe India in white Khadi and silently organise the nation into a disciplined army of Non-violence is the only worthy form which our great resentment should take.

C. Rajagopalachariar

Government contradicts

I have just been shown the following note issued by the Director of Information, Bombay :

> Misleading and a certain respects entirely untrue statements regarding the treatment of Mr. Gandhi in Yervada Gaol have appeared in certain newspapers. The following note gives the facts :
>
> "Mr. Gandhi is given precisely the same diet to which he was accustomed when he was free, namely, goat's milk, bread, oranges, lemons, sugar, tea and raisins. He brought his own raisins to prison with him which he used until they were finished and a fresh supply was provided for him by the jail authorities. It is untrue to say that he is locked in at night. He has separate quarters of his own, one cell to sleep in and the other to work in during the day. The sleeping cell he is allowed to keep open at night. Half the yard is reserved for him to exercise and the space is ample for the purpose, as Mr. Gandhi has stated to the authorities or several occasions. Mr. Gandhi has not asked for any newspapers and but regnect in the allowed to retain some of his private books was granted as soon as it was made. A pillow, in addition to the usual bedding, was supplied when it was asked for. A commode for use at night was placed in the cell on medical grounds for the benefit of the prisoner.

It should be added that Mr. Gandhi has been seen by the Inspector-General of prisons on several occasions and has each time made no complaints, but on the contrary, expressed himself as completely satisfied with the treatment he is receiving. Moreover, on the occasion of the interview which some of Mr.

Gandhi's friends had with him and of which distorted accounts have appeared in the press, Mr. Gandhi distinctly stated that he did not want his prison life discussed in the papers, but only that it should be stated that he was quite well."

The article 'My Great Disappointment' was in type before the above was received in the *Young India* Office. It is a satisfactory feature that the Government have paid attention to the matter so speedily. But to speak the truth, I did not expect that the Director of Information would stoop to such evasion as I see in this Note. I assume the reference is to the facts elicited from me by the *Bombay Chronicle* representative and published on the 3rd inst. I am charged with having made misleading and untrue statements. Let me take the facts one by one.

"Mr Gandhi is given precisely the same diet to which he was accustomed when he was free, viz., goat's milk, bread oranges, lemons, sugger, tea and raisins."

It was stated distinctly by me that goat's milk and bread were given. I stated also that he had two oranges a day (which is insufficient in quantity but I avoided this aspect of the matter). Mr. Gandhi does not take tea. There must be some mistake here, which is, however, immaterial now. As for the raisins, I repeat what I have already stated that the Superintendent noted the request only at the interview and said he would give them.

"It is untrue to say that he is locked in at night . . . . the sleeping cell he is allowed to keep open at night."

I assure the public that Mr. Gandhi was locked in at night and that the cell in which he slept was *not* allowed to be kept open at night *till the time of my interview*.

The Superintendent and Jailor discussed this matter with me at some length and so, there can be no mistake about it. I shall be glad if Government since then have allowed Mr. Gandhiji to sleep in the Verandah as he has been accustomed for so long, and which I believe is necessary for his health. But the Director of Information, if he gave dates, would have to admit that this was done only after my interview. The evasion is perfect. "It is untrue to say that he is locked in at night." perhaps now; but it was quite *true* upto the Ist of April when I saw him.

"He has separate quarters of his own."

Here also it is a clever evasion to make the privation of human intercourse look like a privilege. Is Mr. Shankerlal Banker who was sentenced with Mr. Gandhi allowed to see or live and sleep with him, or any other prisoner for that matter ? Let the Government make it clear that Mr. Gandhi is not compelled to suffer absolute scelusion.

"Half the yard is reserved for him to exercise."

Here too it is a reservation, not a limitation."

"Mr. Gandhi has not asked for any newspapers."

This is truly a wonderful statement to make. The Superintendent and Jailor were both particularly persistent in refusing all private books, even though they may be purely religious and as for newspapers, none was allowed. Here too the Director evades dates.

"A pillow in addition to the usual bedding was supplied when it was asked for."

Note the double evasion here. When was the pillow given? Had he one during the ten days he was in Yervada Jail till I saw him ? Did not the Superintendent raise objections even during my interview, when I expressed painful surprise at their having allowed no pillows ? Again, what is "usual bedding"? Is it Mr. Gandhi's own bedding which a prisoner undergoing simple imprisonment is according to my understanding of even Jail code entitled to ? The Director evades this question.

"A commode for use at night etc."

When ? After my interview, but the Director's note is silent. The Director's note is silent again as to interviews and letters. It is desirable that this matter as well as that of the enforced seclusion from all fellow prisoners, are all made clear without evasion or equivocation. We have all no doubt that Mr. Gandhi will express himself 'completely satisfied' with any treatment; but this does not in his case absolve a civilised Government from its duties. It is true that Mr. Gandhi told me that he did not want his prison-life to be discussed in the papers. But I told him he should trust my judgment in the matter. I consider it my duty to state the truth in a matter of such public importance and could not find my way to suppress or evade. It may not be easy hereafter to obtain interviews or correct information and we may have to rely only on such evasions as I see the Director of Information of Bombay has been guilty of (and he adds insult to injury by charging me with having made misleading and untrue statements.)

Treatment such as I found after thorough cross-examination of Mr. Gandhi as well as of the Superintendent and the Jailor, has given us an insight into the spirit of the whole thing. Details do not matter. Subsequent mending in this or that trifle is not what we are concerned about. The evasive note issued in reply to my statements and the bold charge of untruth on the top of it do not improve the position.

C. Rajagopalachariar

In this connection, we might inform our readers that only today the copies of the *Navjivan* and the *Young India* which were sent by our office to Mr. Gandhi have been returned to us marked "not accepted."

Manager Y.I.

OUR WORK DURING THE HALT

Mahatmaji has ordered a halt and has asked his non-violent army to utilise the time gained to increase its fighting efficiency, by solid work of organisation. In a war of violence, the capture of a general by the enemy would be a fatal blow. Many among us being new to the science of Mahatmaji's non-violent war, and familiar only with the principles of wars of destruction and gunpowder, are grieved over the arrest and imprisonment of our beloved leader and consider it a fatal blow to our movement. On the contrary, what in a war of violence would rightly be deemed a reverse, in a war of Non-violence has just the opposite effect. It is clear that the principles of a war of Non-violence must be in vital respect the exact opposite of the principles of a war of violence. Consequently, the Government being guided by a totally inapplicable body of rules would take action which, instead of hurting or hindering us, morally speaking would on the contrary be more likely to help us in developing our moral powers of resistance, through a greater capacity for loving sacrifice and suffering. The loss of a general in a compaign of gun-powder and steel would be the severest blow that an army could sustain. In our campaign of Non-violence, it is the opposite. It strengthens and spreads more extensively the determination to suffer, which is our ammunition; it creates self-reliance, which is our simple drill; it increases the power of love, which is the basis of all non-violent discipline. Above all, the indomitable spirit of the imprisoned saint climbs over the prison walls and is still with us to guide and help. Therefore, the halt that has been ordered should be quickly utilised to the fullest advantage.

The immediate duty of Congress workers is :

1. To create throughout the country a net-work of non-violent organisations, enrolling as large a number of members as possible and as quickly as possible.

2. To collect donations for the Tilak Swaraj Fund on

which all Congress activities of the year will be a charge.

3. More than all, to make the use of Khaddar *universal.*

At Bardoli and Delhi, mass civil disobedience was suspended; and individual civil disobedience also has been practically suspended, if not by resolution, by the weighty advice of Mahatmaji. The reason for the suspension was insufficient discipline and strength of organisation. Whether it may become necessary to resume civil disobedience of either type will depend on the future; for the compaign in favour of Non-violence and Khaddar in the opinion of our great Leader, if prosecuted throughout with unabated zeal is bound to lead to victory—the goal of Swaraj. But it is clear that if it becomes necessary at all, we shall not be able to undertake it unless we lay; the necessary foundations of non-violent discipline and organisation. It is a noteworthy feature that the common people have understood and realised the importance of following Mahatmaji's advice that before we proceed further, we must consolidate our organisations. It is, therefore, expected that if leaders and workers throughout the country harness themselves to this work, there will be no want of response on the part of the people to carry out the parting wish of Mahatmaji in regard to Congress work.

There should be an enrolment of members in each unit who by their quality and numbers will be able to control and direct the activities in that area in the chanuels laid down by the Congress without error or deviation, and prevent not only apathy, but also indiscipline and violence in any shape.

A specially and carefully selected body of volunteers must be brought into existence in every area who will carry out in letter and spirit all the pledges which they have to sign under the resolution passed by the National Congress which is worth repeating here in extenso :

With God as witness I solemnly declare that :

1. I wish to be a member of the National Volunteer Corps.

2. So long as I remain a member of the Corps, I shall remain non-violent in word and deed and shall earnestly endeavour to be non-violent in instant, since I believe that as India is circumstanced, non-violence alone can help the Khilafat and the Punjab and result in the attainment of Swaraj and consolidation of unity among all the races and communities of India whether Hindu, Mussalman, Sikh, Parsi or Jew.

3. I believe in and shall endeavour to promote such unity.

4. I believe in Swadeshi as essential for India's economic, political and moral salvation, and shall use hand-spun and hand-woven Khaddar to the exclusion of every other cloth.

5. As a Hindu, I believe in the justice and necessity of removing the evil of untouchability and shall, on all possible occasions, seek personal contact with, and endeavour to render service to, the submerged classes.

6. I shall carry out the instructions of my superior officers, and all the regulations not inconsistent with the spirit of this pledge prescribed by the Volunteer Board or the Working Committee or any other agency established by the Congress.

7. I am prepared to suffer imprisonment, assault or even death, for the sake of my religion and my country without resentment.

8. In the event of my imprisonment, I shall not claim from the Congress any support for my family or dependence.

In the enrolment of members, it must be clearly understood that every one who accepts the Congress creed is entitled to be enrolled, and neither civil disobedience nor Non-co-operation is a necessary part of the creed, but only the attainment of Swaraj by all legitimate and peaceful means.

The enrolment of members for this year is not only necessary for carrying on normal Congress activities, but it also will be in its numbers the nation's answer to the arrest and imprisonment of Mahatmaji and to the threat of 'hard fibre.'

The collection for the Tilak Swaraj Fund must be vigorously proceeded with in order to successfully carry on the Congress programme. Unless the nation taxes itself, it cannot achieve the great object it has set before itself. A study of the resolutions already passed by the Working Committee and the A.I.C.C. from time to time would show how every local purpose can be served through this fund and at the same time how the central fund has been used for giving relief to local Congress finances.

In order to encourage the principle of provincial autonomy and to induce efforts to make each province self-supporting, the Working Committee has recommended that only 5 p.c. of the provincial collections should go to the central fund instead of the 25 p.c. as in the past. While the T.S.F. Collections will go on throughout the year, the Working Committee has passed a resolution that the 18th of every month should be observed as a day of sacrifice and prayer so long as Mahatmaji is kept away from us and that every person should offer his actual income on that day as his contribution towards the Tilak Swaraj Fund.

While we have made much progress in developing the Khaddar programme, it must be admitted that we have not yet fulfilled our great leader's expectations. Even as he went away from us the one word on his lips was Khaddar. His faith in the spinning wheel as the one invincible weapon of Non-Violence which will purge us of our sins of untouchability, idleness and apathy to words national affairs and will bring us prosperity, peace, unity and freedom, was at its maximum, when he cheerfully retired into prison, leaving all the national affairs in our hands. Let us be true to his faith and see that every man and every women who have faith in the nation and affection for the saint who guided us and whose indomitable spirit continues to guide us, shall pin his or her faith on Khaddar alone as a symbol of the nation's determination to be innocent and free.

C. Rajagopalachariar

THE KEY-STONE

By far the most important part of the Nagpur Sub-Committee's Report is where they make general observations on matters of principles. The difference between our school of thought and the other is not in mere detail. In our opinion, it serves no good purpose, if vital differences be ignored and a patched up agreement is arrived at over details. After two years of joint labour and most cordial effort at agreement on both sides, the two schools of thought remain as far apart as ever. Dr. Moonje and men of his school of thought hold, as we hold, that Swaraj is the only panacca for all our wrongs and grievances. But they do not believe in emphasising on Non-violence or self-suffering or on any other moral principle as a means to that end. The aim of the Congress is worldly. So, they say, let there be no religion or morals introduced in our programme. Our policies and programmes, they hold, should be governed only by considerations of expediency and practicability. To expediency in the best sense of the term there is no objection; and to practicability there can never be any objection. But the object is by these formulae to exclude religion and morality. Here lies the main issue.

Religion and morality have, we believe, a place in everything, in commerce, in art, even in science, certainly in all human activities, including politics. The success, so far achieved by us under Mahatmaji's guidance, is entirely due to the introduction of religion and morality into politics which had hitherto been thought to be solely governed by the principle of expediency. Mahatmaji's priceless contribution to politics in India and in the world is the introduction of the moral principle of non-violence. Non-violence is the key-stone of the structure we have raised. To take it down is to pull the whole structure down. The Nagpur Sub-Committee sees the importance of "a firm and cordial unity between the different religions and races inhabiting and owning India as their "motherland." Yet it fails to grasp the key to the whole situation. If we put non-violence in the back ground of national life and policy, there can be no trust, no safety and no unity among the different religions and races.

The suggestion of the Nagpur Sub-Committee that we should have all the Congress programme, except the creed of self-suffering, would be like a man approving the whole of Islam, but asking to be relieved of its inconvenient system of prayer; or, like one accepting marriage without the inconvenience of its restraints; or like one accepting military life, but pleading to be relieved of the liability to serve in the front. Even as prayer is the essence of Islam, as restraint is the essence of matrimony, and as readiness to give up life is the essence of military service, so is Non-violence and self-suffering the essence of the Congress programme. It is only by accepting the essential restraint and privation that the other active parts of our programme get strength and effectiveness.

The Sub-Committee appears to understand by non-violence mere abstention from violence. In this, it is greatly mistaken. Non-violence is a great deal more than a mere negative. It is the method of love and peace as opposed to hatred and anger. It is this important and active principle which the nation accepted, when it accepted Mahatmaji's leadership. Is the policy impracticable ? Certainly not, not more impracticable than the policy of honesty or of trust or of fidelity, which we still teach our boys and girls to follow as good practical principles of conduct, though we know that universal honesty, universal trust and universal fidelity are unattainable except in the millenium.

The fact of the matter is that Dr. Moonje and some others are where they had stood before, not changed. They believe in hitting back, in diplomacy, in demonstration, in fighting in the law-courts and in fighting in the councils. They have not yet realised that in love there is a stronger weapon than hatred, that in deplomacy, they are more than matched by their adversary, that agitation has proved futile, that law-courts are but instruments of the Executive and that obstruction in the councils is co-operation of the finest sort.

The last point deserves fuller notice. The question of entering the Councils is at the bottom of many a difference. We entirely agree that no fetish should be made of any item of the Congress programme, and that the national movement should be allowed to take shape in varied channels. If people desire to enter the Councils, in order to oppose bad measures and support good ones, help the making of precedents and conventions and try to achieve liberal amendments of the Government of India Act, in fact, to work the Reform Scheme, if not exactly like moderates with full faith in it, but making the best use of it though thoroughly discontented, we have no quarrel with such men. But they would no longer be non-co-operators. They would frankly be co operators, and we never want to prevent any one co-operating who sincerely hopes to help India that way. What, however, is proposed in some quarters, or at least what is commonly understood when entry in the Councils is suggested from non-co-operation quarters, is that the legislative Councils should be used for obstruction, i.e., obstruction of all work, good or bad, as Mrs. Das put it. A careful study of the Government of India Act would show that it is so framed that serious obstruction of this sort is not really possible. When we enter the Councils, we go there to exercise either our legal powers or our moral influence. The legal powers are strictly limited and, if exercised merely for obstructing the administration, will be much further reduced. Moral influence cannot be acquired or retained by people who set themselves to obstruction, pure and simple. Much help by co-operation, either direct or indirect, is a necessary preliminary for any moral influence or power outside the legal constitution. If obstruction is immoderately persisted in, there would be absolutely no moral influence whatever, and nothing to prevent the legal powers against obstructive tactics being fully utilised by government. So sooner or later, obstructionist nationalists must face the dilemma, i.e., either to save their own moral influence become co-operators and moderates, or indulge in obstruction, but become impotent and entirely harmless. We need hardly refer to the divisions that will split our ranks as soon as such a dilemma presents itself. So long as we are pledged to Non-co-operation, we should recognise that non-violence is the key-stone of the principles on which our Movement rests, and abstention from Councils is the key-stone of the super-structure.

C. Rajagopalachariar

WHY KHADI FOR CIVIL DISOBEDIENCE

A question was raised by the Secretary of the Bengal Khilafat Committee on the right of the provinces to declare Civil Disobedience, irrespective of progress in Khaddar. Where an intolerable situation is created by interference with the elementary rights of association and free speech, and the magistracy issues orders making normal Congress work impossible, the Provincial Congress Committees have the power under the Delhi Resolution to organise Civil Disobedience to meet such a situation. In as much as this would be a purely denfensive measure to protect the elementary rights of citizens, why, it is asked, should it be necessary to satisfy any preliminary self-imposed condition such as the universal use of Khaddar. We do not need to wear Khaddar in order that we may claim the right to eat food, drink water, sleep or offer prayers to God. It is argued, therefore, that Provincial Committee should not be limited by the Khaddar condition, when they are satisfied that Civil Disobedience is necessary to protect such elementary rights. The answer lies in the meaning of Khaddar. It is admitted that non-violence is an essential condition for organising Civil Disobedience, even in such urgent and purely defensive cases. However justifiable the cause, however fundamental the rights infringed, without non-violence, no disobedience could be organised within the Congress programme. The Khaddar condition is really a part of the non-violence clause. We are firmly of opinion that so long as the Congress leaders in any area are not able to universalise the use of Khaddar, in that area they have failed to obtain that control over the people, which is a necessary condition for the maintenance of true non-violence in that area. Non-violence is not mere present abstention from violence. It is a positive state of mind, in most cases implying a change of heart and life, truly and conclusively proved by the wearing of Khadi and the turning of the Charkha. It is not assured by mere oral statement. When the leaders of any place assure the Working Committee that they have perfect control over the people, and that they expect the latter to carry out all their orders from time to time, it is an assurance which carries no conviction, if they have not so far succeeded is inducing the people to wear Khadi or spin. It is not unreasonable that a certain standard of concrete proof should be demanded before taking a very grave step.

A GRAVE WARNING

In spite of much protestation and equivocation, it is increasingly clear every day that a section of the Press both in England and in India are feeling intensely anxious over the Hindu-Muslim unity. Their disappointment at the steadiness of the Hindu support of the Khilafat claim, and the Muslim support of the agitation for immediate Swaraj, and their eager desire to see disunion and division among the two great communities of India are but thinly veiled. In Government policy, there is a frankly avowed reversion to the old policy of favouring the Muslim element, but it is so obviously a camouflage, unaccompanied by any sincere attempt on the part of England to bring about a Turkish settlement such as the Indian Mussulmans want, that no one can be deceived by it. Indian Mussulmans are asked to be satisfied with the excellent intentions of the Government of India. The very hurry in publication of these intentions is too obvious a race with the determination of the British Cabinet not to carry them out. Meanwhile, those Mussulman leaders who are believed to be responsible for the extreme demands of the agitation in India are to be removed from the scene, dividing them into two classes, one for prosecution and imprisonment, and the other for invitation to England for a prolonged education in diplomacy.

We cannot be too careful in guarding the secred bond between the two great communities. The two things of the greatest importance in our movement are non-violence and Hindu-Muslim Unity. During Mahatmaji's stewardship, we had an ever-watchful and long-visioned master, guiding, guarding warning, chastising, and helping us as occasion demanded. We have now to help and watch over ourselves. Too much caution cannot, therefore, be exercised by us. We should perserve inviolate the principle of non-violence in thought, word and deed. During Mahatmaji's separation from us, purity of thought and word has to be more carefully guarded than ever before, so that we may not lead ourselves and others into the path of error. Hindu-Muslim Unity also,—which is a short phrase to indicate the unity among all the communities that claim India as Mother land,—should be preserved in thought, word and deed and when we are sheep without our shephard, if we should not make sad mistakes, we should be more watchful over thought and word than ever before.

It has sometimes been asked, what should the Hindus do if the British give all that the Mussulmans want in respect of the Khilafat. If such a thing should happen, Hindus should hail it as the happy consummation of their desires and as their greatest victory. It is impossible to imagine that the Mussulmans after victory in the greater struggle would give up the lesser struggle for Swaraj. For the Swaraj objective is comparatively a small thing by the side of the Khilafat demand, which, though unimpeachably just and proper, is in effect as Sir

Valentine Chirol put it the other day, a claim not merely for managing our own affairs, be to shape the policy of the Imperial Government on a great question of international policy which concerns the whole Empire. Success in the Khilafat agitation is success in attaining for India a status really higher than Dominion status. If the Mussulmans after restoring the Khilafat with Hindu aid agree to live in an India not fully free, and give up the Swaraj agitation, i.e., if the impossible should happen, surely even then, Hindus can fight their battle alone, and with a moral strength inconceivably greater than before.

Let us not forget the firm basis of the creed of non-co-operation and non-violence, viz., faith in the essential goodness of human nature; and let us serve without looking for a return. Hindus should place themselves in the position of the Mussulmans and ask themselves whether under the circumstances, they would leave their brethren to fight their own battle. They should not imagine that Mussulmans would be less patriotic or be less responsive to be promptings of human nature.

C. Rajagopalachariar

MUCH THE BETTER FOR HAPPINESS

The demand for individual civil disobedience is becoming irresistible. Before this is read, the All-India Congress Committee will have met at Lucknow and decided on this question. The operations of the Government against the non-co-operation movement are taking intolerable forms of interference with the fundamental rights of citizenship. There are increasing signs everyday that the restraints against courting imprisonment laid down at Delhi and the injunctions issued by Mahatmaji as his own considered opinion are straining the loyalty of Congressmen to the utmost. There is a point beyond which, in times of revived national life, the strain of interference by the Government with natural and elementary rights cannot be borne. Apart from any constructive plans for the attainment of freedom, the sheer force of repulsion will operate to drive men into the prisons.

The secession of the Plebeians is a very early historical example of organised non-cooperation. The services and the co-operation of the Plebeians were necessary to the Patriciana of Rome, in peace as well as in war. In such a state of things, it was seen that a bloodless revolution could be effected by the swift and sharp method of withdrawal in a body. In a small state like what Rome was at the time, secession in a body to the neighbouring sacred mount with a determination to live apart till satisfactory terms were offered, was the natural form which the principle of peaceful non-co-operation took. The *Hijrat* recommended by Islamic tradition is also based on the same universal principle. If any Mussulman is not at liberty in any state or country to follow his religion, he is recommended to withdraw himself from that state to some other country where he can enjoy the liberty of his faith without interference. As industrious and honest citizens are a strength to all societies and states, such withdrawal acts as an effective deterrent on interferences with their liberties.

Withdrawal to a different country as an answer to tyranny or injustice is a difficult remedy in the state of society in which we are living in India. It is impossible to find suitable places for emigration in the present conditions of the world, and the hardships involved in movements of large bodies of citizens are well-high insurmountable. It is true that under compulsion, even in the present day, such movements of large bodies sometimes take place, as the happenings in Eastern Europe and Asia Minor show. But to people in India, such a remedy is practically impossible. There is, however, a substitute to which the actions of the Government are naturally driving the people. The movement to fill the jails is often misunderstood to be a trick to embarass the administration. Rightly understood, however, it is based on the same principle of secession. If in modern times, it is difficult to find a suitable country to emigrate to, there are places set apart by the Law within the hostile State itself, into which those who feel that they cannot honourably remain as limbs of the State or Society can withdraw themselves. The prisons are places into which oppressed people may, without having the country, retire in order to free themselves from voluntary surrender to wrong, and to withdraw their services from the state or society which oppresses them. No civilised state can function for long with a large number of its honest citizens thus acceding from it and retiring into its prisons. Enforced work in the prisons cannot be a substitute for the free co-operation of honest citizens, which is the very life of a state.

Individual Civil Disobedience is an act of the highest moral significance. In proportion to the purity and intensity of the motive that drives one to it, is its efficacy. In its purest form, it is an act, the spiritual value of which is strong enough to dissolve the corruption of a whole state or civilisation. It is essentially a religious act. It is not a thing to be done in a spirit of bravado or of mechanical party discipline, when it is almost worthless, "Swaraj for my country is what I want, but between remaining out without Swaraj and prison-life, much the better for my happiness is the latter." Every one who feels thus is fit for individual civil disobedience; and if feeling thus, our best man and women surrender themselves to arrest, their fetters will be the trophies of true Swaraj.

C. B.

DANGEROUS DOCTRINE

The practice of good and sincere men is often better than their theory. Mr. Bapat's appeal to the people of Maharashtra on the Mulshi Valley struggle contains many statements about Satyagraha, which would have surprised the inventor of the term, if he had been free to read them. India teems with examples of the perversion of good ideas, which should be warnings enough. In the new and all-amending definition of Satyagraha which Mr. Bapat gives in all receipt Mulshipets pamphlet he includes the very opposite of Satyagraha. "When group is opposed to group and all possible Satyagraha efforts by the party of justice to work a psychological change in the opposing party fail miserably, then arises a case where the restriction of non-violence may be justifiably removed and what is called pure of shuddha Satyagraha may be tried." Removing the restrictions of non-violence, that is to say, adopting the methods of violence, there would be nothing left of Satyagraha, which after that would be a pure misnomer.

The basis of Satyagraha is self suffering, which again is based on the force of Truth. Physical force is rigorously excluded; for when once such force is called in, the party that has the larger force on his side wins and not necessarily Truth. It is quite a different question whether it is justifiable to use physical force in a just cause. Many systems of Dharma allow it; but Satyagraha has no place for it. The Satyagrahi knows that love and not retaliation, nor the hatred born of the use of brute-force, can ever end a quarrel. According to him, the right to use physical force cannot accrue so long as human judgment is not final. Physical force can achieve a temporary victory in unjust as well as just causes. Even where one is conscientiously convinced that one's cause is right and uses brute-force in support of it, inflicting injury on others, it often turns out that one's judgment was wrong and the injury inflicted was undeserved. The beauty of Satyagraha is that it can never go wrong. Self-suffering is bound to win when the cause in just. Where it is unjust, it automatically fails by its own inherent weakness, but it will have caused no harm to any one but oneself. There may be some incidental and unavoidable injury to others involved in the methods of Satyagraha; but the real objective is not this, and it should be always avoided or reduced to the minimum. The psychological change in the party doing wrong is not sought to be attained by any loss or injury inflicted on him, but rather by the inherent force of one's own suffering. The Satyagrahi believes that human nature is essentially good and must respond to suffering, and his persistent appeal to the natural force is based on this faith. It is a great mistake to believe that the success of Satyagraha is to follow from the injury or loss caused to the wrong-doer. It is this misapprehension that leads to many an erroneous plan in the name of Satyagraha. Injury may be unavoidable, but to the extent that it is caused, it is a source of weakness and retards the effect of Satyagraha. In proportion to the elimination of injury to the opposing party, the suffering undertaken by oneself avoids hatred and anger, and the effect of Satyagraha is accelerated.

The struggle which the Mavlas are engaged in is from all accounts a just one. But it is one demanding the exercise of all the moral strength of which the resisters are capable. Unless the methods employed are kept absolutely free from all taint and impurity, the results will be disastrous. It is necessary, therefore, that those who guide and advise the registers should strictly guard the fundamental principles of Satyagraha against all misinterpretation and misunderstanding.

Mr. Bapat's extension of Satyagraha may be nothing more than an attempt at philosophical synthesis. But we cannot be too careful in the conduct of great and severe struggles in keeping within the strict limits of non-violence, the fundamental condition of success in Satyagraha. When Satyagraha was started at Mulshi in April last year, Gandhiji wrote :

> "The duty of the Satyagrahis is written in letters of gold. There can be no Satyagraha in an unjust cause. Satyagraha in a just cause is vain, if the men responsing it are not determined and capable of fighting and suffering to the end; and the slightest use of violence often defeats a just sense. Satyagraha excludces the use of violence in any shape or farm, whether in thought, speech or deed. Given a just cause, capacity for endless suffering and avoidance of violence, victory is a certainty."

C. R.

A FUNDAMENTAL ERROR

Judging from what is often spoken and written, one might think that the difference between Mahatma Gandhi's plan of action and the bomb-throwers is that while the latter believed we could be saved by killing Englishmen in India, the former believes that we will achieve our salvation by injuring them in their trade or by making their lives uncomfortable without directly, causing physical injuries on their persons. This conception of Mahatma Gandhi's doctrine is, it should be needless to say, radically wrong Again, it is believed by many that the only difference between Mahatmaji's method and the old constitutional method is that while the latter consisted in begging and protesting and raising a big noise, the former is based on hitting and embarassing—only no physical weapons should be used. This, too, is a vitally erroneous conception of Satyagraha. The fundamental basis of Mahatmaji's doctrines, as well as of his plans, is that the law of life is love. Human nature, he holds, must respond to love. Hatred, ill-will, tyranny and crietly are all deviations from the natural law. To put things in the right path, we have only to apply the force of love. If another does you wrong, bear the injury yourself and return good-will. The suffering should be all yours; then, the opponent's heart will melt. The only embarassment intended by Mahatma Gandhi is the pain arising out of the constitution of human nature on the sight of a fellow bring's suffering which is called sympathy, or *Hamdardi*. This is the energy on which Satyagraha is based, no energy as true and as potent as electric energy generated in a power station.

If any person does not accept this basic doctrine that every human being is essentially good and must respond it you only know how to reach his heart and undertake suffering, returning good for evil, then there is no common ground between that person and Mahatma Gandhi. There is no use believing that we follow Mahatma Gandhi simply because we go to the prison or strike work, or close shops, or wear Khaddar or withdraw from practice or boycott schools or disobey laws, as and when he directs. All these acts have two effects. In so far as they injure the other party they are unavoidable incidents and to that extent cause anger or ill-will and retard the attainment of our goal. In so far as they bring suffering on ourselves and bring home to the mind of the wrong doer that we undertake that suffering on account of his wrong, they are Satyagrahi processess leading to the purication of the wrong-doer. Our aim and object should be to reduce the evil arising out of the former incidents by special efforts, and increase the letter to the maximum degree attainable.

The best way to attain this is by developing good-will in our hearts while we offer non-cooperation or civil disobedience.

The erroneous conception of Mahatma Gandhi's programme pointed out above is at the basis of many of the suggestions for improvements and modifications of his plans which have therefore been rejected. It is also at the root of much of the hostile criticism of his work, from friends as well as enemies. It is enough if a flagrant instance or two are pointed out. Mr. Bapat suggested in a pamphlet that Satyagraha should include the use of physical force and the causing of injury to persons and property, because, he said and perhaps truly believed, that Mahatmaji's non-cooperation is a media-causing injury to the Government and Englishmen. Again, one often bears at Khaddar meetings descriptions of the prospect of hungry and dying families in Lancashire as if that would give joy to our hearts. If Mahatmaji heard such propaganda used in the cause of his Khaddar, he would shudder in pain and anguish of heart. Again, counter-offensives and retaliations by way of mass civil disobedience are all talked of, as if the secret of civil disobedience were the tactical blow or a modified form of violence; forgetting that the essence of civil disobedience is the suffering undertaken and not embarassment and that the latter should in fact be reduced to the minimum and the former to the maximum in order to produce quickest effect.

C.R.

CONSTRUCTION BUT NOT COOPERATION

The *Indian Social Reformer* advises Congressmen to go into the Councils and "work there as well as outside to advance the Bardoli programme which is the only programme before them."

It may be true that the Bardoli Programme is the only programme before non-cooperations, but a programme should not be confounded with, or be carried out at the sacrifice of, principle which is of far more vital importance. How does the *Reformer* propose that we should work in the Councils to advance the Bardoli Programmes ? Are we to attempt to get laws passed to further Swadeshi, e.g., by protective measures and subsidies ? Are we to get the Government to recognise national schools ? Shall we get laws to compel the admission of the depressed classes to public schools, wells etc. and attempt to abolish untouchability by legislation ? Are we to work in the Councils for the absorption of panchayats in the judicial system? To attempt to state how the other items in the Bardoli programme could possibly be advanced by entering the Councils would amount to burlesque.

Except in the one matter of temperence, attempt to advance the Bardoli Programme by the influence or the power we can acquire by entering the Council's would be a self-contradiction. The constructive programme has its value in the effort and in the self-reliance it involves, and should not become an end in itself, to be attained anyhow. We could not, for instance, agree to the removal of untouchability or to effect the boycott at foreign cloth or to carry out any of the other items of the Bardoli programme by the use of force or by intimidation; no less can we agree to attain these objects by giving up non-cooperation.

Non-cooperation is not to us a "Dead Caroase" nor do we think it is on its "funeral pyre." It is yet the living principle of our politics and will continue to be so as long as it is true that our own cooperation is the measure of our degradation, and that rigorous self-reliance is the only antidote to the process of emasculation that has been going on. For causes known to all and needless to repeat, Mahatmaji suspended the aggressive activities of our movement but it would be a grave error for any one to suppose that non-cooperation has been given up and social reform has replaced it in the non-cooperator's programme. There is a whole world of difference between social reform on the non-cooperative plan and carried out for the non-cooperator's ends, and social reform carried and effected, with the aid and by the compulsion, of a system with which we should abstain from cooperating. If one believes honestly, as non-cooperaters do, that cooperation in the councils will prolong the question of the present system and therefore add to the degeneration of the nation, then, it is his duty to carry on the Bardoli Programme unaided by the powers attainable through the councils.

C.R.

CORRESPONDENCE

Within or without the Empire

Sir,

I am an Indian—a refugee in Japan. I am not sure whether it is not the height of impertinence for an insignificant, humble being like me to join issue with you, or for the matter of that, with most of the Congress leaders, on a subject on which you all are regarded as, or at least supposed to be authorities, having spent much time and money in the study of political philosophy as propounded by the English writers. As an Indian and as one who tried in the past to serve Mother India in his own way and who hopes to continue his work in future, although along different lines, I, however, consider it of paramount importance to address you these few lines in order to get a clearly definite expression of your opinion on a vital question.

In the *Young India* of August 3, 1922, (page 321), you reproduced under the heading "The Mentality of Free

Nations" an article from an Australian Labour paper passing, rightly, a severe criticism about Mr. Sastri's mission, and remarked therein : "It is no wonder that the attitude of Australian workers is one of disgust towards an Indian who accepts the subjection of his country to foreign rule, *what it is sought to be kept up not by consent* but by the force of military power . . ." Now I would respectfully ask you to let the Indian people know through the columns of your paper if there is a single instance in the whole world of a foreign rule kept up by the consent of the governed. For a free and full growth, complete freedom is absolutely essential not only for human beings but also for animals and plants even. The domination of one by another is in natural and contrary to the highest impulse of human nature. No people on earth can consent to be governed by another people. It is an anomaly and except in English political literature this phraseology, i.e., to maintain foreign rule with the consent of the governed, cannot be found anywhere else in the world. There can be either Freedom or the opposite of it—Slavery. There is no midway. If you and other venerable leaders want real liberty for India, you must be prepared to sever all British connection, and must announce to that effect. On the other hand if it is the object of the Congress not to exert for complete independence but to endeavour to better India's lot within the Empire and to ensure her more humane treatment at the hands of her conqueror by securing Home Rule, which, in other words, means the perpetuation of her present position of a slave, the Congress leaders should say so plainly. It certainly does more harm than good to adopt an unnatural course, as implied in your remarks about foreign rule with the consent of the governed.

I have had a talk on this subject with many Americans and Japanese, some of them being authorities on international laws. They just simply cannot understand what the Indian leaders mean by Home Rule or status of equal partnership within the Empire. Australia and Canada can have real-freedom within the Empire for the sole reason that they are peopled by the same British race and have the same customs, manners, traditions, religion and language. They are quite right and logical when they claim the Empire as their own. But the case of India is quite different. She is a conquered country inhabited by people of completely different customs, traditions, religion and language. For India to desire to remain within the Empire is to acknowledge herself as a slave. Freedom and slavery cannot go together. If India wants freedom, she must completely sever all connections with Britain. Of course, she will be at liberty to conclude a friendly alliance with England but that should be done as between equals, between two sovereign states. If she wants Home Rule or status of equal partnership within the Empire, it cannot mean anything else than that she desires to perpetuate her serfhood.

Tokyo, Japan. Yours truly,

September 21, 1922 *Rash Behari Bose*

[The question raised has been many times answered by Mahatmaji and I can add nothing to what he has written and said on the subject. The Congress creed is perfectly clear. It contemplates a breaking of the British connection if for full national development it becomes necessary. It desires to retain that connection if we can rise to our full height with it. I admit that there are two great impediments for Swaraj within the Empire. The equality which we claim for Indian citizens in the Commonwealth appears to be a fatal impediment, if we judge from the obstinate conduct of the white Colonies of the Empire, and the constitutional impossibility of Imperial interference in such matters. If this spirit of inequality continues, it means separation. The other great impediment arises out of the peculiar situation of India. While Canada, Australia, New Zealand and South Africa may have no foreign politics different from Britain, India cannot but claim that the Commonwealth should not drag her into wars with Turkey or the Mussalman states of Asia or use her resources to humble them. This claim may or may not be capable of being granted to India as a member of the Commonwealth, but on it depends the possibility of her remaining in it. The idea, that India can never have real freedom within the Empire for the sole reason that the people of India have not the same customs, manners, traditions, religion and language as the other components of the Empire, is as erroneous as the common notion imparted to us in Government schools and through English books that because the people of India are divided into a number of communities with different customs, religions, languages etc., they can never become one nation or hope to be a free people. If South Africa and its Boer people could accept the domination of the Empire and attain to quality and full freedom in spite of differences in language and nationality, it should be also not impossible, though of course harder, for India to enjoy similar freedom and equality within the Empire.

So long as there are wars in the world, alliances and *enientes* are necessary, and no single nation can stand by itself. Why should free India reject the readymade bond of friendship in which she finds herself if it means nothing dishonourable or detrimental ? With the two impediments pointed out above solved, membership in the Commonwealth will mean nothing more than an honourable alliance.

C. R.

Mahatmaji's Bold and Clear Path

The following is the text of Mr. Rajagopalachariar's speech delivered at Nagpur :

It is really a wonderful thing that a man, in the southern corner of this country should be heard by you with patience as such a late hour—that this vast audience should wait to listen to me knowing that I am compelled to speak in a tongue which they cannot understand. All this wonderful magic has been wrought by one man who is now in prison. He united together all the languages and religions of India. In other countries they have only one language and one religion : but here we have many languages and many religions, but let us hope, one heart. I have heard the legend attributing particular characters to different provinces but I have found in my travels that at bottom all is one. The whole country from the Himalayas to the Cape Comorin is as strong as ever in its affection for and loyalty to Mahatmaji. The people may have fallen in their standard of action but certainly there is no change in their sympathy for his movement. The great population of our country is like an ocean. Just as the ocean retains the same normal level inspite of its waves our people retain their affection towards Mahatmaji.

Government's Challenge

Yet I have to remind you to-day that Mahatmaji has been imprisoned twelve months ago. You have read the history of India. I too have read it and let me tell you that the last three years are the most glorious in that history for the last thousand years. Mahatmaji started this glorious career in our history and it is now in your power to being it to an inglorious end or to continue it. When Mahatmaji went to prison he went in the full confidence that the 300 millions of his countrymen will act as one man and there will be no differences. He wrote at that time that he hailed his imprisonment with pleasure because the world would have an opportunity to see that the people of India stood on their own legs. He was glad for the opportunity to disprove the charge that it was the mere influence of his personality that was guiding them. Mahatmaji declared, when he went to prison, that the people would carry on the work. The Government imprisoned Mahatma Gandhi and said "we will now easily subdue the people." Which will you prove to be the truth ? If we do not perform our duties, if we hear speeches and forget them the next day, if we do not put on Khadi the Government's word will be true. There is no use in our being tall and strong men and women if at the first attack we give in. If you told any man coming from some remote part of the world that the country holds within its boundaries 300 millions of men and women and that it has been possible for an alien Government to imprison a man loved by all these, he would not trust his eyes and ears. He would be bewildered to know that for twelve months we have been eating, drinking and making marry. If you only cast yourselves forward to the time where we shall have finished our brief periods of life, and our children would look behind to our own achievements, you would realise that they would be ashamed of their forefathers. I know that many a brave boy and girl, when they come across a passage in our history telling us how our forefathers fled from a battlefield hang their heads in shame and wish they could draw over the passage a black line and deface the passage so that nobody may read it. In our sloth and neglect we are writing indelible records of shame and degradation which our own children will have to draw a black line across.

(Here the speaker dwelt briefly on the forthcoming anniversary of Mahatmaji's incarceration.)

Still Time

We have lost much time but we have plenty of it yet if we only use it. Government has locked Mahatmaji in prison but we have the keys in our own hands. It rests with us to use them. If the Government opens the prison gates and lets him out what would be the reason ? If it were certain that we were as weak and powerless as we appear to be; that we were worthless and that Mahatmaji would be of no use to us; if it felt that the movement is dead beyond recovery, Government would let him out tomorrow. But the Government is under no such delusion. We are glad that Government still thinks that we will be a great source of danger if Mahatmaji is let out. We must open the prison gates ourselves.

Become mad after freedom

This movement that has been started by Mahatmaji can never die until we reach the goal. If we take any backward steps the people may stand it for 2 or 3 months, but we are bound to have soon to revert to the bold and clear path of Mahatmaji. Because it is the only way to revive the health of the nation. So long as the people remain clever and not mad, so long will they be governed as they are row. We must change the manner of our thought and action. When Sita was lost, Rama did not rest patient, but went mad and thought of nothing but her recovery. Damayanti too became mad when she lost Nala. Is not our freedom dear to us as Sita and Nala to Rama and Damayanti ? But I forget that by years of slavery we have lost the very use of freedom. As a blind man does not know what light is and as a deaf man does not know what music is; we do not know what freedom is. Like birds born inside a cage, we do not know what is to fly in the air and greet the Sun. A man came to give us back that lost sense of freedom. We have neglected that man. People who have forgotten how to pray to the unseen God make an idol and offer their prayers through it. We are unable to understand freedom but there is Mahatmaji through whom by our sacrifice we realise and worship Freedom.

What is the examination to which the country will be subjected during the next two months ? We have to proclaim to the world that we all stand for the Congress. Just think for a moment, if after this speech of mine, to-morrow you all enrol yourselves as members this year what will be the effect throughout the country and on the Government ? Yet this is so easy that you can perform it with the short space of an hour. If only the necessary forms had been here and volunteers could go out among you; you would gladly sign your names and pay the four annas. I hope to-morrow you will flood the Congress office and enlist in large numbers.

"Do Your Duty"

Let us forget the country, for a moment; let us forget for a moment that we are citizens of a nation fighting for freedom. Would you not have signed a monster petition praying for the release of Mahatmaji if it could secure our purpose ? I am sure you would have. But such a step to-day would be a disgrace. I want you to express your passion to free Mahatmaji in a brave and noble manner. I want you to formulate a petition of a very different kind—a petition of brave and solid action. If all the adult population had realised this duty, Mahatmaji would have been set at liberty long ago. I want each one of you not to think of what others think or do not think, or do or do not do, but individually you do your duty. Do not continue in the habit of saying "This country is doomed. It will never rise to do its duty", but look to yourself each individual. It is your religious duty. As you go to a temple and each one individually among a multitude of worshippers, offer prayers, and speak to your God, you are required to offer prayers in the form of sacrifice at the altar of freedom.

The Congress is also in need of funds and it cannot be expected to keep the movement alive without funds. It is the only body that is fighting for Swaraj. Within these two months we have to give twenty-five lakhs. This is the minimum required for the work to be done. Do you know how much the Government have budgeted for their expenditure this year ? The amount is in so many croses that I may well leave out a few. They want 200 crores of this year and we are to pay it. The Congress asks not for a hundred crores, not ten crores, not even one crore but just a quarter of a crore. If you divide the amount among the various provinces and districts, you will find that Nagpur has a very small share which even one honest merchant here can pay. But it is neither good nor proper that one person should pay. All of you must contribute your share to it. It will show your undaunted loyalty to the Congress and trust in it. Unless we help the Congress how can you expect it to bring Swaraj. Before the 18th of March I beg that each of you should pay your mite and induce your friends to do like-wise. Your very waste-money for a month would be enough to fulfil your quota. What for instance, you would pay for tabacco to injure your health in one month would be more than the sum required of Nagpur.

The Crore well Spent

So many ask, "What has happened to the one crore subscribed the year before last ? Even if you yourself do not believe the charge contained in the question, I want you to be able to answer it. It was spent to give political education in the course of one year to a country which had lost, the sense of freedom. With this one crore Mahatmaji was able to make his country, 2,000 miles long and 2,000 miles broad, reverberate with the cry of Swaraj. If you only would look to the Government records you would see how many crores were spent to give you a worthless education—an aducation which taught a few of you to read and write and that too not well but which killed your spirit of independence. What it failed to achieve during the course of so many years and with many crores of rupees Mahatmaji achieved with this one crore in one year. Any other nation would have given many times the amount for the object achieved. Friends, tell those who talk about this crore that it was spent thus. But there are other things also which the crore has achieved. Put your hands on your khaddar shirts and coats and you will see what I mean. It is due to the crore that we are all wearing Khaddar to-day. If you had not worn Khaddar, crores of rupees would not have been lost to Lancashire and saved for India. Two thousand million yards cloth went out of Lancashire's Indian trade last year. We are told that 500 millions per year have been lost permanently. Even if it had not been due entirely to Khaddar. I say the crore was well spent. If Lancashire could spend a crore and get back the trade it would readily do it. I want you to tell me whether in view of this, in your opinion, the crore was well spent or wasted.

I want you to endorse this assurance by paying twenty-five lakhs again to keep up the institution which is responsible for carrying on the movement. You will have to do it in any case before the close of two months. But I ask you to do it before the 18th so that you may have something to offer at the altar of Mahatmaji's memory on the anniversary of his imprisonment. If any volunteers come to you, I ask you to receive them well. Take them to your relations and friends and make their task easy and pleasant. Do not argue over differences of opinion. There is no time for that. The Congress has accepted the challenge which the Government has thrown. If it fails before the 18th it has time up to the 30th April. If we fail to fulfil this quota, the Government may well deride us and look upon us with contempt.

One thing more before I sit down. Great sacrifices are demanded only of a very few. From all others I crave active sympathy and help. I am sure you will not reject this demand of mine for I know that as long as an obscure man like myself can come in the name of the Congress and convene such a great meeting there is hope for the country.

Worse than Jallianwala

We wonder if the people can find time out of their daily worries—arising out of the general atmosphere of inertia in most parts of the country, and out of the divided counsels and the nauseating sectarian squabbles that poison the national life of to-day, we wonder if this worried public can find time to follow other happenings in the country. If they did, would they sit still stricken with inertia ? Do not the Sikhs and the Mussulmans and the Hindus in the Punjab, if not in other parts of India know anything of the little tragedies enacted in the Punjab, if not in broad day-light as in the Jallianwalla or Guru-ka-Bag days, at least within sufficient knowledge of the ever-vigilant Shiromani Gurudwara Committee ? The chroncile published daily and hourly by this Committee reveals a reign of unbridled lawlessness which no amount of council controversies or Shudhi activities can overshadow. We reproduce here some out of the numerous crimes perpetrated in that unfortunate province.

Press communique No. 432 says : "On 20th February another 500 Akalis are reported to have been transferred from Attock Jail. Mr. Saint G.A. Beaty of the Guru-ka-Bag fame was specially requisitioned from Rawalpindi and placed in charge of the operation. On the arrival of the first Jatha of

100 Akalis at the gate of the Attock fort jail, 2 Akalis who happened to be there greeted them with 'Sat Sri Akal.' This evidently was too much for the nerves of the gallent Police officer. He first treated the erratic couple of Akalis to a generous shower of hunter cuts with his own saintly hand and then ordered his equally gallant subordinates to throw the Akalis into the Indus. No sooner was the chivalrous order given than obeyed. Propelling them by sheer first-pushes the policemen took the submissively non-violent Akalis to the edge of the river bank and there hesitated for a minute. A *Nimakhalal* Sub-Inspector at once reminded them of their promise to unquestioningly obey orders and commanded them to carry out the saint's bidding. The unresisting Akalis were dumped into the river and got their clothes drenched. As they swam back to the river bank, they were ordered to be shut up in the fort and the order was obeyed then and there."

We have reproduced the note verbatim, which if we take out one or two needless adjectives seems to be free from exaggeration.

There is communique No. 433 which is full of tales of draggings and pullings by *keshas*, and kicks with boots by the Superintendent of Police, Milltan. "Prayer books and extracts from the scriptures were forcibly taken away from the Akalis by the Superintendent of the jail and trampled upon by the constables. All this was serenely watched by half a dozen officers present on the spot." And still more from the same communique; "There is hardly any water-tap that is in working order and yet steps are not taken to repair them. Cries of "water" continue proeeeding from the grinding mill cells even during night."

Here are a few samples of lawful lawlessness indulged in the course of realisation of fines. A zaildar, and some policemen went to the house of Bhai Santoksingh, who was sentenced to 9 months' imprisonment and a fine of Rs. 150. His mother was not in the house. "They broke open the locks and took away every thing they found."

(Comm. No. 437)

Bhai Tehlsingh son of Mian Singh was sentenced to 3 months' simple imprisonment *without fine.* "Yet a sum of Rs. 100 has been realised from the property of Bhai Hazarasingh who has nothing to do with Bhai Tehlsingh. Bhai Hazarasingh has got land on contract from Bhai Surainsingh, nephew of Bhai Tehlsingh."

(Ibid.)

Bhai Kartarsingh *alias* Ajitsingh of village Kasail was sentenced to 2 years' imprisonment and a fine of Rs. 100 by Lala Amarnath magistrate. "He was released on consideration of age. Recently a fine of Rs. 200 has been realised from him on the basis of a warrant issued against another man of the village named Bhai Ajitsingh who was sentenced to 9 months' imprisonment and a fine of Rs. 200".

"What surpasses all", says Communique No. 438, in this comi-tragedy of fines is the case of Bhai Hazarasingh, son of Bhai Jhandsingh of Narli, District Lahore. He was arrested under section 108 in the early days of Guru-ka-Bag affair and was sentenced at Kasur to one year's imprisonment. It is strange that on 3rd February a warrant was issued from the court of Mr. Banwarilal, Magistrate Amritsar for the realisation of a fine of Rs. 150 from Bhai Attarsingh. All the lambardars and watchmen of the village testified to the effect that he had never been sentenced at Amritsar, and yet a second warrant was issued on 25th February. Not satisfied with this a third warrant bearing the same name is said to have been issued from the court of Nawab Aslam Hayat Khan, Magistrate Amritsar to realise a fine of Rs. 200."

Here is the harrowing account of the indignities and cruelties perpetrated on Bhai Randhirsingh in Nagpur Jail. Having refused to hold out his hands, he was deprived of the privilege of cooking his own food, of his clothes, turban and shoes.

Bhai Randhirsingh resolved to go without food. "For about 8 or 9 days", the chronicle records, "Bhai Randhirsingh was without food and then an English officer began to apply all sorts of cruel methods to force the Bhai saheb to take food. This Englishman after trying to thrust the food into the mouth of the prisoner with the help of filthy abuse came to apply fisticuffs (sic) and kicks. The helpless prisoner cried out to a policemen who was looking on, but he did not help. Bhai Randhirsingh complained to the Superintendent but it was of no avail. Then the Jailor and his assistant came with a few others and tried to apply anema simply to disgrace and trouble him. He protested saying that he had no complaint about digestion, that he had nothing inside him. But without listening to him the thing was done after knocking him down against a wall, which made him insensible. Next day they threatened to insult his religion if he did not submit. They threw him on the ground and securing him with handcuffs attempted to feed him with milk with a rubber tube. His mouth was forcibly opened, and it was not until a few teeth were broken that some milk could be forced in." This was thrown out, with the result that his *keshas* and beard were pulled and after "being kicked and beaten he was left half-dead." And so on and so forth until a member of the jail committee is on a visit, and things change for the better.

It should be observed that all these communiques are only signed by the General Secretary Gurudwara Committee, Amritsar. No successful attempt has yet been made to contradict them. It is useless to say anything more on happenings which may be said to be of daily occurrence. The people may be dead enough to put up with this. But surely Nature is not so dead.

Behar, the province which had produced Babu Rajendra Prasad, was beautiful to see. We may well judge a tree by its fruits. The unfaltering faith and the consequent strength mark this province out. Some of the districts have such a number of strong and brave workers that it is no wonder that in village organisation this province stood first.

We were somewhere near Mokammah Ghat. The train stopped at a station and as usual there was a crowd round our compartment. An old woman, dressed in clothes that showed that her daily lot was hunger and hard work, made her way to our compartment and got in. She went straight to Devadas, "Is this Mahatmaji's boy ?", she asked, and with a mother's hands she stroked his head and caressed his face after placing her gift for the cause at his feet. Even the rustic crowd was moved at the scene. "Is Mahatmaji kept in jail by the Government ?" she asked of the son, and burst into an imprecation. Of course she knew about the imprisonment already. But she wanted the actual provocation to find outlet for the word of anger. She left the carriage having given Rs. 1-0-6 for the fund; it was all her savings probably for many a weary day.

C.R.

MR. RAJAGOPALACHARIAR'S SPEECH AT PATNA

Below is the speech that Mr. Rajagopalachariar delivered at Patna on the 21st instant :

> "Till yesterday we spoke at various places looking forward to the celebration of the great anniversary. Now we have come to the other side of the hemisphere, leaving behind the light that has led us so far. But we all know that the sun will continue to give light whether it is in front of us or behind us. Whether we look forward to fulfilment of duties or look backward to the promises and pledges we have made, our action must be guided by our resolve. Till yesterday we all looked forward to the anniversary to remind us of our duties. To-day I want you to remember the pledges you have given, to help you in the work you have undertaken. I do not think that a race noted for keeping its pledges and promises as the Hindu race will not fulfil them. We are a nation known in the times of the Greek travellers as a nation that did not want any document or agreement to keep its pledges. We never needed any witness for our promises. We are a nation

which called the sun and the moon as our witnesses. I, therefore, feel that till the goal is reached we should keep fast to our pledges. The anniversary was not an ordinary demonstration. It was a proof of the grim determination of the people to carry on the struggle. Never before in the history of any country, had any nation expressed its grim determination in the manner you did on the anniversary day. There were eyes keenly watching whether the movement was really dead or whether there was still fire burning in the ashes. The statesmen and military commanders that governed India are keenly watching us. For they are able to perceive the strength of the struggle more than Indians themselves. A movement inaugurated by a great military commander like Mahatmaji can only be understood by other great military commanders like him. Government knows that they must keep Mahatmaji in jail though everybody swears that the movement is dead and that it is perfectly safe to release him. The Government knows very well that it is not dead and that it needs only to be strengthened. Even a child knows that if the movement is dead there can be absolutely no harm in releasing Mahatmaji. But Mahatmaji is still in jail and that is sufficient proof that the movement is not dead or weak. Even in your own province of Behar and Orissa there is a partial confession of this truth by the Government. One of the members of the Government said that the Government was not dead but was simply disorganised. So long as the patient is not dead it is in your hands not only to cure him but to make him strong. The duty of a doctor is greater when he is told that the patient is alive and can very well be saved. Therefore it is our first duty to look to the patient. There can be no better news than that a member of the local Legislative Council asked the Government to release all political prisoners, and that the Government refused to do so. The request of the councillors to release all the political prisoners, however pleasant to the weakminded, was a confession that the movement was weakening. For apparently, they thought, the Government would be safe if these prisoners were released. But when the Government refused to concede their request it showed that it was not safe to release the prisoners.

I remind you of your duties and their fulfilment. I ask you, first, to look to your organisations and put them on a strong basis. Every Congress Committee, whether in a village, in a district, or a sub-division, must stand as strongly as the Government organisations. Our duty is to see that even as a Thana or any other Government office is strong in its place so our Congress Committee should be. All the talk of the weakness of the movement is due to one and only one reason as we could see everywhere in our tour in the country. There is no faltering in the loyalty of the people. There is no want of affection on the part of the masses towards the Congress. Wherever we went we found the same absolute faith in the Congress amongst the masses as existed before. There was no feeling of disappointment or despondency amongst the thousands of people whom we met, wherever we went. Some of the workers were disappointed and not the people. On examination, it will be found, that the chief cause of the despondency among the workers is due to their having come to the end of their material resources on which they were depending so long. You know what a siege means. When an army surrounds a fort, it does not fight with the men inside the fort. It simply stops food and water being taken inside the fort and thus compels those inside the fort to surrender. Likewise poverty has beseiged our workers and we are disappointed and despondent. Government knows its battle and is simply waiting for poverty to break workers' patience. But all know that if the people resolve to be generous, the movement will be up again and Government will have to fight a grim battle. If your brothers were imprisoned in a fort and if they were about to surrender to the enemy, I ask, will you not take food and water to them ? The majority of the workers hail from classes which do not know what poverty means. They are now feeling the pinch of it and are ashamed of begging. Their silent patience is now coming to an end. And unless you come to their succour, the movement may break down. If you want your organisations to be strengthened you must realise your duty and come forward with money. Your brethren the thousands of workers are ashamed to beg. But we stand here shamelessly to beg, because our country is so poor. It is not begging, my friends, it is taxation, if only we had Swaraj. But because we have no power to govern ourselves taxation becomes begging. You must know how Government is begging for two hundred crores from the country. They are begging this sum to-day of the members of the Legislative Assembly. Of this 200 crores that they are begging, more than 60 crores is for spending over the army which is kept to govern this country. They are not only begging, but are preparing to raise a loan because begging will not suffice. When Government is prepared so shamelessly to beg and to raise a loan why should we not beg ? It is not the workers that are begging of you. It is the Congress that begs this sum of you. It is in your hands to look upon your workers as beggars or as tax-collectors. If we had liberty, if we were a free people, these beggars should have gone to you as tax-collectors.

In any free country every tax is a voluntary donation. It is only in a slave country that taxation becomes involuntary payment. The day you learn to tax yourselves voluntarily that day you will be near the gate of freedom. I have sufficiently explained to you, I think, the necessity, the urgent necessity, of collecting money; and I hope all will cooperate with us to make this Congress organisation go on.

I know that there is a strong temptation to know the accounts of the income and expenditure of last year. I know that every time, the Congress wants money some mysterious person comes out with the condemnation of past years' expenditure and immediately we find leading articles in some newspapers about the danger of any further payment. But I hope you will not sit down as auditors and spend your times in book-keeping while you are fighting an enemy. If you have spent one crore you have achieved an amount of work which could not have been achieved by spending even hundred crores I would ask of any businessman how many crores he would spend in advertisements to hit Lancashire to the extent our movement has done. I would ask of proprietors of any tea estate whether they have spent more or not to push on their sales in this country. If I had to give a contract of advertisement for Khaddar, I think, I shall have to spend more than one crore to achieve what we have achieved within one year Khaddar means 60 crores and to spend one crore for the spreading of the knowledge of Khaddar which will save us sixty crores is too little even from the business point of view. Any military ruler will say how much he will have to spend for gaining the affection of thirty crores of people. And to spend one crore to spread disaffection among them is nothing. Leaving alone the merchant's and commander's points of view, I ask if one crore of rupees is much from the point of view of a social reformer, for what has been achieved in the matter of removal of untouchability and cementing of brotherly and cordial relations between the different communities ? I ask further if one crore is too much for giving political education to the people who have been sleeping so long ? Government is engaged in giving literary and political education to the people and how many crores has it spent ? But with what result ?

Has it been able to achieve the result which the one crore of rupees has achieved ? With one crore Mahatmaji gave political education from which Swaraj will spring like a plant from the seed. This crore, therefore, has done so much work within such a short time. As to the accounts, I would ask you, to look at them and audit them after we have achieved Swaraj. You may bring all your leaders to book and confiscate all their property. But in the meantime I want you to act up to the solemn promise you have made. Your first duty therefore is to unite your pursestrings and bring life to the desponent. That alone will be enough to make the heart of the Government beat quicker. I hope, before we disperse, you will have given whatever you have with you, as a symbol of your love, affection and loyalty to the Congress and the resolve to make good the solemn promises made by you. I do not think that you have all assembled here to listen to me and then go home and think later. I know that you have not brought much with you.

But I want only a symbol of your affection. As for national resolve you have had sufficient sign and proof of it. Men and women have come forward each with a rupee at least which perhaps is more valuable to him than thousands to others. If we want Swaraj our organisation must be strong. We want men loyal to the Congress. The Congress has not been enrolling members this year in such numbers as it did last year or the year before last. It is necessary to enrol more members if you want to show that your affection for Mahatmaji continues to be the same as before and if you want to show that the Congress is a living organisation. I know it was thought once that it was not necessary to enrol members. It was considered that every adult, male or female, was a member of the Congress whether he paid four annas or not. Although I also thought like that I consider that the present rule to enrol members should continue for some time more. And it is necessary to have such members in large numbers. It is not right that we should allow Mahatmaji to be in jail, by not doing such a little work as the enrolling of members. It may be too much to give a rupee; but I ask, is it difficult to give four annas and show your love for the Congress and Mahatmaji ? Or are you so confused with arguments of parties, I ask, that you do not know whether you should be members or not ? There are volunteers waiting to register your names and I hope you will register in large numbers.

April 30 is fixed for the fulfilment of the Gaya programme as to men and money. Wherever we go we find that the work of enrolling volunteers and collecting has just begun. I hope you will realise your responsibility of completing the programme by the 30th of April. Otherwise the solemn promise made at Gaya will remain unfulfilled. I hope the people of Behar will not wait for me and Rajendra Prasad to ask them for it. And you will have to give your quota by the 30th of April. If we fail in this, it will again open the period of controversy and then some more time will be wasted. If you want to be saved from this criminal waste of time you must fulfil your share. This year again you will have to put a number of men into prison so that the people may not go to sleep. If you do not do that your work will be tenfold more difficult next year.

We have got to put men into prison to continue our glorious record. We have to put our heroes in jail to show that we prefer jail to slavery. We have to put our brethren in jail to show that ours is not a mere gambler's desire for Swaraj, not the reformer's desire for reform, but it is a dying man's desire for life. Like a drowning man's struggle to get to the shore, like a thirsty man's desire for water, like a hungry man's for food, so must our desire for Swaraj be. But you may ask, 'Are we really drowning'? Why then I will tell you this. I do not know whether we are all drowning. But it is a fact that that our Budget showed a deficit of 100 crores during the last 5 years. Since the war began our debts have increased by 300 crores. We all know that 270 crores were spent not in irrigation or any other productive project but absolutely on unproductive things. I know that for the last few years the Government which was called paternal was spending more than it was able to get from the country. But I ask why should this nation spend more than it is able to get ? Because it spent every year 60 crores over an army which would not have been necessary if we had Swaraj. Then people would not have lived in fear of Government and Government in fear of people : and there would have been no necessity of spending this 60 crores.

If they required an army for defending themselves against invaders they would have trained the people left them to defend their country when there was any necessity. That is a fortunate nation which has no need to keep a standing army. But if it is not done so, it is because the Government thinks it will not be able to exist. That is why the Government has to keep an army and the people have to tax themselves for it. That is why the poor man has to pay more for salt, sugar, and matches than what he can afford. Are you not convinced that we are all drowning ? But reason will not convince us. It is only the instinct of freedom that will save us. Never before did any nation know of such a clear weapon as the one which Mahatmaji has given us. If you do not want to allow this weapon to rust you must keep it active. We have no fear of Behar, united and sympathetic as it is. I believe that Behar will lead the movement in future. I am not flattering. I judge the tree by its fruit such could leaders as Behar has produced be possible if the people were not so. I hope you will fulfil your quota of men and money soon to-day or to-morrow. I wish to remind you again that you should not go away from here with any money that you have with you. I have no shame to beg of you. But it is not we that beg. It is your country and mother, your future Government, that is begging of you.

Unworthy Squabbles

The following paragraphs are called from Mr. C. Raja-gopalachaiar's speech at Ajmer :

We are here in the centre of the present so-called struggle about the conversions. This struggle I tell you is not really a struggle between Hinduism and Islam at all. It is not possible that in these days of mutual understanding of each other's religion there can be any real struggle between Hinduism and Islam. The greatest truth which Hinduism teaches to its followers is that all ways lead to the same heaven. There can be no possible doubt over this point in the mind of any one who has studied the Bhagwad Gita. Indeed, as I understand it, it is wrong for a Hindu to go and interfere with any man's religious convictions, and I do not think that in these days when Mussulmans have better understood Hinduism that they bear the same attitude towards Hinduism to-day as they once bore towards idolatry in general.

The present disturbance is, as I understood, due to the

consciousness of weakness, of each party in its own mind, and not really to love of religion. The Hindu is afraid that he is politically weak and the Mussulman is afraid that he is numerically weak and hence these mutual attempts at gaining numbers. How can we increase our strength by mutual adjustment when all our strength is wanted against a common enemy ? While the Hindu believes that he will become stronger than the Mussulman or the Mussulman believes that he will become stronger than the Hindu, both fail to see that they are weaker before the common enemy.

As far as I have seen in my experience it is not possible really to convert a Mussulman to Hinduism or a Hindu to Islam. It is only possible to convert people who are doubtful and who are not a strength to either religion.

I know also that no force or fraud is being used. For I know that our beneficent Government will prevent force. As a matter of fact we imagine we are working under strength of Hinduism. But really, we are working under the shameful guarantee of peace which the police station gives us. We take license from the police station that we may go to breach our religion and that our brother thought he is angry may not come and be at us. It is under that sort of license that we have to breach. It is true that we do not take license in writing but every act that we do is really done under such license. On any day the Magistrate can serve us with a notice that in such and such a place we cannot go to preach Hinduism. And on that day we are bound to stop preaching our vaunted Hinduism. So also any Mussulman preacher who goes to make Mussulmans of Hindus goes under such license from the Government, and when any Government Magistrate thinks fit he may also be stopped from preaching his religion.

If we tried to get Swaraj by force we might be afraid of force and therefore minorities should be afraid of majorities. But we are training ourselves in a discipline which makes the numerically weak as strong as the big. The weakest of our communities will be able to enforce its influence on our society under Swaraj. Not even the scavengers need despair but they will be able to command terms under the Swaraj Government. If we ask seven crores of Mussulmans not to be afraid of twenty crores of Hindus, is it not a shame that twenty crores of Hindus should be afraid of seven crores of Mussulmans ? If twenty crores of Hindus are afraid that 7 crores of Mussalmans may become 8 eight crores, I am afraid, I cannot conceive of such a nation being brave and able to rule India. It is merely a confession of weakness, and not real political effort. What is the history really of true religion ? It is a history of sacrifice. But secret political quarrels do not make up religious efforts. Where do you get most encouragement from for this work of Hindu Muslim dispute ? That will indicate to you the real couse of encouragement. This Government has succeeded in setting Mussulmans quarrelling with Hindus over posts and offices, in the Punjab. You do not really get help from people who are bent upon religion but from people who are oul really for posts. I appeal therefore with all the earnestness I am capable of, to my friends and leaders here not to go on with this quarrel.

I am told by some that Mussulmans do not care for Swaraj, but only care for the Khilafat. But if you were true politicians you should know that the Khilafal question is greater than Swaraj. Swaraj is only the right to govern India, but Khilafat is the right to control England in its foreign affairs. Is if not a greater thing to have Swaraj and control over foreign affairs than to have Swaraj only ? We cannot get Khilafat restored before we get Swaraj, because the Khilafat is greater than Swaraj. If we are able to alter the treaty between England and Turkey it follows that we rule ourselves. Some people believe that the Khilafat question will be closed with the Angora treaty and that thereafter the Mussulmans will give up the fight for Swaraj. This is really because we Hindus are ignorant of the Khilafat question. What is the Khilafat question ? The most important thing is the freedom of Jazirat-ul-Arab. It is true that nationalist Turkey might be forced to agree to a treaty. But Islam in India cannot agree to a treaty unless Arabia, Palestine and Syria are free from non-Muslim control. And that will be done only when India is strong enough to wrench Swaraj from England. I ask therefore my Hindu brethren not to be nervous about these matters. After we get Swaraj I promise you a fair field for all tournaments and wrestling. But now the enemy is seeking to enter the *akhada* and help one against the other. If we want really to wrestle we must first make sure to buy our *akhada*, that *akhada* is Swaraj. Let us therefore first finish this first duty and than look to other things.

THE COMING SLAUGHTER

Would to God that He gave us more wisdom and less ambition ! We desire to 'strengthen' Hinduism. And after our latest efforts, today Hinduism is weaker than ever it was during the last few years. Hinduism has lost the support which it had secured from Islam by sacrifice and love, and has earned the positive ill will of thousands of Mussulmans. We had been silently winning convert to the universal creed of love, the vital part of Hindu Dharma. Islam in India had begun to look on old animosities and misunderstandings as ugly dreams of a night that was over. It had begun to identify itself with the single truth. Never before was a more successful silent conversion. But now in trying to win a few men to the forms of Hinduism, we have lost or are fast losing all our previous conquests of the spirit. Gaining in form we are losing a thousands-fold in substance.

We seek to save the cow. But the vision of the coming slaughter is before my eyes, and who can say that we have not been the cause of it all, by our foolish pride and our mistaken attempts to strengthen ourselves. We may have plans of our own. But the moist eyes of thousands of dumb creatures led to slaughter not as symbols of sacrifice, but in anger against us during the next ID will turn their piteous gaze at us; and if we have a conscience, we would feel their silent reproach.

We will have to admit before the Father of all that it was we that brought them to torture and death by our unwisdom and uncalled for arrogance of creed. We indulge in hatred and we suffer; but the unfortunate cow suffers more. If we wake up not soon, our folly will flow red with cruetly.

Why do I reproach only the Hindu folly, and why do I not point my finger of complaint at the Mussulman for his lapses from the right path ? Because I am not so pure, I am not so strong as I must be before claiming to chastise him. I am a Hindu and have a claim and birth-right to speak harshly (in love) to my Hindu brethren. But the man who had by his love and sacrifice and work earned the right to chastise all without distinction of creed or race or community is a prisoner in a solitary cell and India cannot have him in her hour of need.

Unless God give us the courage and the wisdom to see the truth and be led by our peerless leader from inside his prison, breaking down by our loyalty and our affection the bars and gates erected by cruel authority———.

C. Rajgopalachariar

WE CANNOT SUBMIT

I cannot understand the contention that the resolution adopted by the All India Congress Committee does not violate the principle embodied in the resolution of Gaya Congress in regard to boycott of Councils. It entirely nullifies the Gaya Congress resolution, whose primary purpose was to defeat the elections of this year. The mandate of the Congress was a positive direction to effect the boycott. On the other hand the Committee's resolution if accepted would make a boycott impossible. It actually recommends a course which will result in the country voting for candidates on the ground that they are Congressmen. The Committee's resolution is therefore in flat defiance of the Congress. The present Working Committee has issued a statement that the mandate of the Congress, maintaining the boycott of Councils, remains untouched. It is futile to claim that the Congress resolution remains untouched, when every step is taken to make it a dead letter. To curry the mandate to the people, propaganda was absolutely necessary. I think the resolution of the Congress and the All India Congress Committee's compromise cannot stand together except by casuistry. All Congress-men and Committees have to decide whether they will accept the All India Committee's decision or the Congress resolution. I feel that we should prepare and give effect to the Congress resolution, it is not enough merely to stand aside. We must do our best to reaffirm the national rejection of the present system of Government by refusal to participate in the scheme of Reforms imposed upon us. I feel very strongly that if we accept the All India Congress Commitee's resolution there will be no programme before the country next December or afterwards, except consideration of amendments, to the Reforms Act drafted by the new Councils party. I therefore think it my duty to resist the All India Congress Committee's decisions and to ask the people to carry out the Gaya resolution. We have been taken from step to step in a downward course. The Councils party in the Congress did not content themselves with propaganda inside the Congress, but actually revolted. We were thus forced to accept the revolt as a fact and make terms with the rebels. Now in December we will be forced to consider, amend and adopt the Council programme of the rebel party. We must stop this downward career somewhere. We must reject the All India Committee's decision and choose to be loyal to the Congress. I can understand that some provinces on account of particular conditions prevailing, may not undertake the work of the boycott of Councils; but we cannot submit to a total reversal of the policy of boycott of Councils throughout India.

C. Rajagopalachariar

MONDAY

The status decreed for India in the British Empire is one which it is impossible for her to accept. India would rather be segregated as a whole from the Great Empire than allow her childern to be untouchables and helots in it. The Imperial policy has been made clear with brutal frankness by the South African Prime Minister. He has laid down a programme for not only preventing future Indian immigration but for mercilessly wiping out the existing Indian population by depriving them of political and municipal liberties, trade and property rights, and by locating them outside the towns. This programme, there is no doubt, will be carried out without serious objection on the part of the British Government and soon become the general policy of all the British Dominions.

The Kenya decision is the symptom of a great Imperial conspiracy for racial domination. It is a chastisemet and a warning from God for our faltering steps. There is no way but grim determination to sacrifice everything and to achieve freedom for India, as the necessary foundation and the first condition of honour and equality abroad. Every Indian irrespective of community or political party should join in the great demonstration on twenty seventh August.

A word to English merchants and traders. The suspension of business called for on the twenty-seventh August, is a non-party demonstration. Is it too much to appeal to every Englishman, who is on the side of India in this struggle, to demonstrate his sympathy and non-racial catholicism by joining in the general demonstration? From the earliest times Indian rulers allowed you perfect freedom to settle and trade among her people, and you are now here by reason of that same hospitality. It is your turn now to support our suffering children abroad and obtain for them the liberties they are asserting in the national demonstration, and suspend your business on Monday the twenty-seventh August, when the Indian baears will be all closed. It will be an achievement of good-will, worthy of your best traditions and a noble example to the whole Empire. It will make the struggle a truly religious and irresistible battle. On the other hand, if you keep your shops open and compel your employees to attend business in spite of the National *hartal*, the racial character of the Kenya decision will be emphasised and your action will support the White Imperialist policy.

The National *hartal* will be successful as a demonstration of Indian sentiment in spite of English traders in India keeping aloof. Your non-participation will be a defeat of those who still fondly build on Christ. But if even a few among you join, the cause of Religion and Truth will have triumphed.

C. Rajagopalachariar

MR. RAJAGOPALACHAR'S ADDRESS

Following are the extracts from the presidential address delivered at the Second Karnatak Provincial Conference, by Sjt. C. Rajagopalachariar:

> I shall not detain you with any lengthy address. I shall not attempt to exhaust all the topics that engage the public attention, and crave your permission to leave many things untouched. Obviously, late in November, with the coming sessions of the Congress approaching us fast, it is not necessary or advisable to take up questions that must find final solution only in the Indian National Assembly. We cannot, however, at a Conference like this, fail to give public expression to widespread feelings on some topics, at least as an indication of opinion which may be useful in shaping the decisions at Cocanada. But the main business of the Conference is to organise your Province for the work before you.

The Congress suspended propaganda on the Council boycott and permitted those who were convinced of the utility of entering the Councils to do so. This Compromise was agreed to as a necessary evil. We deliberately allowed this breach in the fortifications, but we should not let it widen into anything bigger. Respect and tolerance for difference of opinion is an essential feature of all Gandhian methods including Non-co-operation. We should not prevent any man from acting according to his convictions. The Moderates and other co-operators enjoyed this liberty, and the Swaraj Party too had the same liberty. But they wanted something more than respect and tolerance. The hold of the Congress and the Non-co-operation programme over the people was so great that they wanted on our part a suspension of action according to our own conviction, in order that they may have fuller opportunities to put their own beliefs into practice. Rightly or wrongly, for the sake of peace this was done. But we cannot be led further into a path which we are convinced is contrary to the essential principles of non-co-operation. We cannot permit the Congress to be identified with the activities of any group inside the legislatures. For the sake of peace we sacrificed a splendid opportunity to organise the most striking national answer to the Salt Tax, to Kenya and to Nabha. For the sake of peace we gave up the golden opportunity of confirming our hold on the voters and to educate them in the Gandhian principles. If we but compare the educative value of the boycott campaign of 1920 with what has been done by the Swaraj Party this year in getting themselves returned we can see how much has been sacrificed by us. But not to regret the past which cannot be recalled, and to turn to the future, let us not allow ourselves to be dragged into the counter programme any further. There is no doubt there is grave danger. We do not know the further programme of the Swaraj Party. They may wait till another general election for getting their full strength, or for the Congress to give up the Triple Boycott *in ioio*. They may join other members in the legislatures and try parliamentary methods from total obstruction down to co-operation-cum-discriminate opposition. They may join the Convention proposed by Mrs. Besant and await the fate of a newly drafted constitution. But the Congress cannot take any part, active or passive, in any of their proceedings. Unless this is rigidly laid down, the Congress would be led to a repudiation of the great non-co-operation programme.

The political situation has been taxing Congressmen to the uttermost point. The dynamic force of the great tide raised by Mahatmaji seems to have spent itself out. Ideals and methods which in the freshness of first promulgation by the great Mahatma roused surging reaction in the hearts of men, seem now by very reiteration to have lost their magic. Everyone wants something new and newer yet every day. The old truths fail to impress men. The great expectations and hopes that bnoyed up the spirit of the people at first and created an unexampled energy have yielded to a sense of disappointment and failure. Doubt and circumspection reign in the place of courage and hope. Knowledge and experience have made people wiser but also more apprehensive of failure and unwilling to act.

Our enemies whose first shock and surprise at the revolution aided our efforts and encouraged us to push our campaign on with vigour, have now naturally regained their stability and rallied themselves to a more effective defence against us. People thus feel that the Government is stronger today than they were during the earlier days of non-co-operation. The situation is in every way more difficult than it was in the first phase of our revolution. Mahatmaji himself found the difficulty developing, and was trying to meet it. No wonder that after he was taken away from us, lesser men find the problem difficult.

While on the one hand those who stand by Mahatmaji's programme are faced with this situation, the forces that never believed in the Gandhian method of suffering and non-violence have taken advantage of the inertia to reasert themselves. Men, who were compelled by the irresistible force of the national upheaval to adopt the Gandhian programme against their real political convictions, have thrown off the oppressive Spiritual burden, and are seeking to interpert and shape the programme into a form of political resistance more suitable to their own temper and convictions. The forms and shibboleths are retained but the guiding principle is different. Not love but hatred; not *ahimsa* but violence such as can be put forth; not self-suffering but cleverly organised embarassment of the enemy with the minimum amount of suffering one our part; this is the easy Satyagraha sought to be interpreted and practised by the new school of parctical non-co-operators. To these folk the basic law is that men is a non-spiritual being, essentially selfish and violent, who can only be compelled by pain and punishment to respect others; whereas the whole basis of the Gandhian method is a truth that men is essentially good and spiritual, and responds to love, not to fear; to sympathy, not to punishment.

The German Government too attempted to sustain Gandhism on a basis of hatred and organised emharassment without the life-giving Gandhian principle of love and suffering. They ordered non-violent resistance on a large scale. The Government supported the population and reduced suffering to a minimum. The attempt was gigantic and seemed near to success, but failed. German resistance was not Gandhian Satyagraha even as the very best mechanical engine is yet not a living thing.

Non-co-operation interpreted as mere political embarassment is far from Satyagraha, and is foredeemed to failure or relapse into futile agitation, pure and simple. You can no more set up non-violent coercion of this kind into a living force, than make a living man out of an electrified mechanism. Such non-violence will be nothing more than second-rate violence and will have to acknowledge its weakness. Only if we have the courege and the faith of Gandhi according to his own interpretation, can we organise his movement as an irresistible battle of the Spirit against the Devil. Suffering, maximum; love of the enemy, true and genuine, the love and pity that filled Christ's eyes with tears as he was led to Golgotha,—not suppressed hatred, finding legal and constitutional shape but feeding its endless vicious circle all the same,—without these non-co-operation and Civil Disobedience can be of no avail, indeed cannot live for long, even as political formulae.

In my opinion, the one and only way out of the present situation is the Constructive Programme, Back to Nagpur!

as Maulana Mohammed Ali beautifully put it. It may be difficult to light a fire with damp sticks. I do not know how many of you have had experience of the depression and the agony of lighting a fire with damp fire-wood. To work the Constructive Programme now is very much like such a process. But it must be done if the cooking is to be done and the household kept going. Other programmes may be easier to catch, may lock more glorious, may indeed be necessary now and then, but the first and the main work is this work of construction sketched at Bardoli. Even the Constructive Programme includes . more things than can be at once strenuously concentrated upon. I would ask people to norrow it down for the present in practical working and widen it with progress. Spinning in every house is the one programme I would ask you now to concentrate upon. That the Charkha means non-violence, means removal of untouchability, means saving the people from the curse of drink, means social service, means Hindu-Muslim unity, means the whole of Gandhian Reform, is not a mere figure of rhetoric but is actual realisable fact. The Charkha and active strenuous propaganda for establishing the doctrine of non-violence must be our programme. Do not speak, about the Charkha but actually spin and get people to spin.

Speak boldly, frankly and fully upon non-violence. Non-violence is losing the universality and firmness of conviction which Mahatmaji has secured for it. The assaults upon it are too many. We must re-establish it firmly upon the throne of the people. This is the great secret of Hindu-Musilim unity in India. The creed of non-violence alone can establish Hindu-Muslim unity on a firm basis. No committees of arbitration, no mixed panchayats will achieve much. Readymade panchayats for deciding disputes will only create disputes where none existed before. That is our experience of the establishment of courts and consequent increase of litigation. Allopathic tretment will fail here as elsewhere. The constant insistence and spread of the fundamental doctrine of non-violence is the only remedy and the only hygiene for healthy communal life and unity. We have been too long treating non-violence as a Gandhian idiosyncracy in an otherwise practical programme, giving to it a condescending toleration and nothing more. In truth, however, it is the bone of the whole programme, that which gives it strength to oppose the violence of the Government and the anarchy of the people, the most vital part of it, without which the rest will crumble to pieces. Peace and order are necessary for our movement. The essential implication of the Gandhian Revolution is that the Dharma of non-violence must be established as a substitute for the Tyranny which is now policing the country. If we do not work for this the tentacles of the existing Government will continue to hold us in its grip.

I have described the difficulties of the situation, and insist on what I deem to be the only right path before us. The difficulty of problem—the stalemate as some would call it—was only to be expected. Unless we won the whole war in our first campaign this second and more difficult phase was inevitable. It need not depress us. This nation wants freedom, will surely want tomorrow even if it is apathetic today; and when it wants freedom, it is bound to have it without doubt Our diffiulties are not in the methods we have employed being unsuitable or inadequate or in the strength of the enemy. It is only the subsiding of the hunger for freedom that makes work difficult. Let us attend to this mainspring of action. The rest will take care of itself. I am convinced that this great nation is bound to see its own good, to see that freedom is life, and that slavery is hunger, misery and death. I am convinced that for our freedom there is no way but the Gandhian way. I am convinced that the nation is bound to take it up tomorrow if not today, and reach its appointed goal, even if it puts it by for a while now. There is no need to feel depressed or sad. Nothing can be more foolish than the assumption that non-co-operation is dead. What is the meaning of the death of non-co-operation? Is it that not having achieved success by it, the Indian Nation will abandon it as a political weapon, or that the Indian Nation abandons the gold of freedom? Neither can ever be true.

I am certain that the Ali Brothers can revive the life, and raise the tide once more as of old. They can take the word of Mahatmaji and speak as with authority scourging the idle and the needless and giving hope and strength to the faithful and the diligent. They can transform the conditions, as no one else can.

I have not referred to many a topic but I should not close without a word about Nabha. Nabha is a belated recrudescence of Dalhousie-ism. People have been befooled by phrases like Sovereign British Government, Suzerain Power, Feudatory State, and the like. Indian Princes may be weak, may be deprived of their armies, may be controlled and emasculated by treaties, but in law they are free and sovereign like the Government of India. There are many little states in Europe now which are as weak as Hyderabed or Mysore or even as Nabha or Patiala. But a neighbouring Government does not go and claim the right to depose the ruling Government for maladministration This process is tolerable only in past history as one of the many worng things that made the British Empire in India, even like the forgery of Clive or the extortions of Hastings. But we cannot tolerate a repetition of it now when we are masters of our own time and its moralities. Whether Nabha voluntarily abdicated or was compelled, is beside the point. He was either forced or scared into abdication. Coercion of one kind or another is there. What kind, does not matter. If there was maladministration, the British Administrator has no greater legal or moral right than you or I to take charge of the State. We must see to it that the people of a State are the only tribunal entitled to dethrone a Rajah and they are the only authority entitled to elect a Board of Regency to govern in the place of a Sovereign dethroned for misrule. The Congress which stands for popular rights and liberties and whose function is to prevent encroachments upon these, must consider the British Administrator's in road into Nabha as but an act of unconstitutional violence and must help to resist it. The Sikhs are fighting it bravely, and when the call for general help comes, there can be no doubt as to our duty.

The battle has spread outside Nabha. War has been declared on the Gurudwara Prabandhak Committee, and the Akali organisation is sought to be crushed. The battle is accepted and India will stand behind the S.G.P.C.

In this connection I must deplore one capital departure from the principles which guided the Akalis hitherto and led them to victory. The Guru-ka-bagh fight was fought according to strict Gandhism without defence in Court and with faith in the efficacy of suffering. The engagement of lawyers and the offer of defence in the present campaign is a retrograde step. Guru-ka-bagh is a victory of Gandhism pure and unsullied. I know the object is not to save themselves from punishment but only to expose the Governmental misdeeds. But truth and suffering are their own propaganda. Defence and the doctrine of suffering are incompatible. Engagement of lawyers and non-co-operation are incompatible. The propaganda and publicity of cross-examination are a fatal substitute for the self-lustre of truth and suffering, even as Parliamentary obstruction is a fatal substitute for non-co-operation.

THE GREAT TEST

The Congress has given a clear and unqualified mandate for concentration on the constructive programme. It remains now to be seen whether the workers will be loyal to the Congress and carry out the mandate. The next few months are without any exaggeration a critical period in the history of our national movement. Success or failure depends on how we now respond. These few months will be marked by no excitement or demonstration; yet during this period we shall be put to the severest test. Will India really round the banner of non-co-operation again and show that steady work and strength which will at once render foreign domination impossible and plant Swarajya on unshakable foundations? This is the question upon the answer to which the history of our movement now depends.

Our workers, not the most cruel caviller will deny, have these four years stood the most trying strain bravely and patiently, with faith and courage and steadfast purpose worthy of the glorious motherland. Now will they be tried more sorely than ever. It pleases Him that rules nations that we should pass through a further ordeal to prove our claim to freedom. Our sufferings and privations are at breaking point. 'How long?' Is the cry of many a weary soul. Gladly would they welcome others taking their place in the struggle so that they might put their knapsacks down and rest their weary flesh for a time. But this cannot be. The last and greatest trial we must go through, and if it pleases God successfully.

Constructive work and nothing else now. Other things however tempting, however speedy-looking and attractive shall not take us out of the path of construction which the Congress with one voice has ordered. It is not without deep and anxious thought that such restless souls, spirits that thirst for freedom immediate and quick and would never count the cost like the All Brothers have asked in clear and unambiguous terms for concentration on the constructive programme. No distraction of any kind should be permitted to imperil the quick fulfilment of the programme. The courage of silent work should be given the fullest play.

"I am fed up with three years of politics. Let me go to my village. I shall take a Panchama boy into my house and sit at the spinning wheel. Let me go", said a weary fighter yesterday. "God bless you" said I, "it is the very thing wanted."

Sincere souls instinctively find the truth which logic and reasoning often fail to reach. Now is the time for every Congress worker to be an example to others like my weary friend. Select your village and splu all your time. Let the people see in your action the faith that is in you, that Swaraj shall be won through the charkha even as Bapu promised us. Sit in peace and spin. You need not go to the people, for the people will come to you. In your village you will verily see Swarajya building itself round you like King Arthur's palace built to music.

I look upon the Cocanada Congress as a Congress that opened the Charkha year—a year that will see Bapu's desire fulfilled. Ask no questions about the wage value of spinning, no querries about economics and politics, but get up in the morning and spin religiously for at least a half hour. Do this for the sake of Congress whatever be your politics, whatever be your day's task. To me this is the great message of the Congress that met and dispersed at Cocanada. Set up the Charkha. All the communities touchable and untouchable will gather round it. The sweet music of it will dispel all jealousies and all anger.

"Even if I fall in everything else," I remember the Master saying one day, "if I restore the ancient cloth of India to her people, I shall have fulfilled the mission of my life." Let us prepare this fulfilment as our great welcome to him upon his release from prison. C.R.

A Correction

I am reported in most papers to have said in moving my resolution at Cocanada that the Council boycott was alive and not dead, as in the case of schools and courts. A misplaced fullstop has altogether reversed what I said. I said that the triple boycott was alive and not dead. I pointed out that in the case of schools and courts, the boycott was there as long as we sought to maintain national schools and arbitration courts, though we suspended aggressive propaganda. I then proceeded to say in a new sentence, that as in the case of schools and courts even in respect of Councils the boycott was there, because dissociating ourselves from the Government Legislatures we sought to make the Congress a true and powerful national assembly.

An Appeal

Sisters and Brothers! You are aware of the proceedings of the Indian National Congress at Cocanada and the resolution adopted there. I know that many of my comrades were dissatisfied and thought that the resolution was not strong enough. I desire however to point out that the resolution is clear in respect of four matters: one, the immediate work before us is constructive work; two, the fundamental basis of our programme, viz. the triple boycott is affirmed; three, we have been just and fair to the Swarajya Party; four, we have secured essentials without sacrificing peace.

The Cocanada Congress has given a definite and clear lead to concentration on constructive work. Let us take it up and put forth immediate, sustained effort this year. Let us not allow doubts and disputations to take up our time and energy. The charkha is the one immediate programme. In the fulfilment of this one programme lies our loyalty to Mahatmaji. **C.R.**

THE DEBATE AT COCANADA

[The debate in the Cocanada Congress centred round the following resolution. Below are the speeches made by Mr. C. Rajagopalachari in moving the resolution and in replying to the debate.]

Resolution

This Congress reaffirms the non-co-operation Resolutions adopted at Calcutta, Nagpur, Ahmedabad Gaya and Delhi.

Since doubts have been raised by reason of the non-co-operation Resolution adopted at Delhi with regard to Council entry, whether there has been any change in the policy of the Congress regarding the policy of the Triple Boycott, this Congress affirms that the principle and policy of that Boycott remain unaltered.

This Congress further declares that the said principle and policy form the foundation of constructive work, and appeals to the nation to carry out the programme of constructive work as adopted at Bardoli and prepare for the adoption of Civil Disobedience. This Congress calls upon every Provincial Congress Committee to take immediate steps in this behalf with a view to the speedy attainment of our goal.

Mr. C. Rajagopalachari's Speech

In moving the resolution he said:

The Congress is determined upon non-co-operation. We have to decide what part of the non-co-operation programme we should work during the year, and in what manner we have to act under the leadership of Maulana Mahomed Ali during the next twelve months.

Constructive Programme

We all know what he wants us to do so far as he himself is concerned. He has told you already that we must concentrate on the constructive programme adopted at Bardoli not merely in policy, but in day today work, with strenuous effort. I therefore want you to accept that programme of work and if you do so, one part of the proposition that I place before you must be approved. You must decide upon carrying out the constructive work which is part of the non-co-operation programme.

A Declaration of Policy

Another part of the resolution which I place before you is a declaration that we still adhere to the principle and policy of the triple boycott. I must be brief and therefore go straight to the point. I want you to adopt the principle and policy of the triple boycott as inaugurated and enforced by Mahatma Gandhi. I do not want you by this resolution to adopt the triple boycott in the sense of going the platforms and immediately and aggressively calling off lawyers, school boys and councillors. We must keep that principle, as understood and enforced by Mahatma Gandhi, as the basis of the constructive programme. This foundation of the constructive programme is necessary to be declared once again because I feel that the atmosphere in the country has been disturbed by what we have been talking and doing regarding the Councils. That declaration of policy is the reaffirmation of the Congress policy as inaugurated by Mahatma Gandhi and forms the second part of this resoulution.

Delhi not Disturbed

Another part of the resolution is a clear expression of our determination not to undo what we did at Delhi or to disturb those who acted under the Delhi decision. It does not mean that we adopt that policy for the future. It only means that we do not disturb what has been already done. These are the three things that form this resolution. I have given them to you in the order of their importance according to my opinion.

Avoid a Battle

Another important consideration I must place before you for adopting this resolution in the form in which I have placed it. It is that the resolution will be supported by Mr. Das and his friends from whom we have had the misfortune to differ. Why does he give his support? Because he does not want a battle now, but simply wants you to accept facts as they are. He does not want you either to adopt his programme or to reject it. He recognises the fact that the Congress has the same policy today as it had before.

I don't think I need add anything more, except a few words with regard to the alternative resolution you have before you on the agenda paper. I want to know whether you what a stronger resolution and to fight a battle for it with all its consequences, or whether you will have this resolution which contains the substance of what we want without the evil effects of a battle. I certainly prefer the latter. I want you to agree with the policy with which my name has always been associated

I want you to rely upon yourself and not upon others in carrying on your work. But we ought to do nothing to prevent other people from assisting us. You might take from me that even where union is not possible we might at least avoid the aftermath of a bitter war. If we proceed with work and forget the passion for war we might get even union. I shall not detain you further but proceed to read the resolution in English. Mr. Venkatappiah who will follow me will read it in Telugu.

(Here he read the resolution in English.)

Duty of Provincial Committees

I don't place before you a more complete and detailed programme of constructive work, because in the present state of want of homogeneity in India each Provincial Congress Committee will have to consider what particular items are more urgent and necessary and possible. The detailed programme of work will have to be considered by the Executive of the Congress in consultation with each P.C.C. But one thing is clear that we give a mandate to the Executive to concentrate their attention on constructive work and work out the details. The words and phrases of this resolution have been thoroughly threshed out in the Subjects Committee and that Committee has recommended the resolution in the form in which I have proposed it. I want you therefore, as a National Asssembly of men intent on business, to accept this resolution without further doubt or discussion. Some persons ask me whether this resolution contains a ban on the Councils. We do not ask the Councillors to go out of the Councils. It is for them to go out if they like. What was decided at Delhi remains without being extended or reduced by a single inch or fraction of an inch.

Mr. C. Rajagopalachari's Reply to the Debate

Mr. Prakasam was saying to you that dissociation from legislatures would mean dissociation from our friends who are in the legislatures. I do not agree. Like Dr. Subrahmanyam I say we have nothing to do with the legislatures and we should not look to them for help; but we have not come to say, we ought not to say, that we dissociate ourselves from the gentlemen in the legislatures. We never say that even as regards the Government member therein. We ought to dissociate ourselves from the institutions not the men. I am really surprised at the misinterpretation—phobia. I put the proposition in a clear way. I claim the utmost right of dissociation from the legislatures in this resolution not only from Councils but also from courts and schools. It is quite another thing for me and the Congress organisation to decide whether we will take an aggressive propaganda or not in the future. Mr. Das seconded the proposition without any speech or word; do you think that Mr. Das is not one who would claim his own interpretation if there was room for misinterpretation? Still there were speakers claiming that the amendment was the non-co-operation resolution and that my resolution was the expression of the death of non-co-operation. I am surprised that men who stood by me faithfully and with the conviction of their own judgement could imagine that to-day I have signed a warrant for the death of non-co-operation. Without asking for any explanation they condemn my resolution in that manner.

Pandit Sunder Lalji's whole speech was this and nothing else; and my friend Ramaswamy Naicker's Tamil speech was also this. Let me assure you that I accept almost the whole of the amendment to which they give their support, but my complaint is that they give the go-by to the Delhi resolution. That is why I cannot accept the amendment. We may claim the maximum faith in the programme of non-co-operation. But how can we ignore what we did at Delhi? We must either have the courage to move a resolution rescinding and cancelling that resolution of Delhi or we must accept it and place before the Congress today a resolution that we reaffirm the old triple boycott. What we say is that we do not cancel the Delhi resolution. but our future policy and programme continues to be the same. Comment was made on calling the Delhi resolution a non-co-operation resolution. Dr. Pattabhi Seeta Ramayya's whole speech was based upon this single word non-co-operation.

I tell you that because the word non-co-operation is there my position is stronger and safer. Why are you afraid of the Delhi resolution? It is because you say it is another form of non-co-operation. If it was not a non-co-operation resolution why should you be bothered about the Delhi resolution? But if it was a non-co-operation resolution, is it not your duty to say that in spite of it our policy is the same as before? Can anybody say that the policy of triple boycott which we affirm is not the triple boycott inaugurated by Mahatma Gandhi but the triple boycott as inaugurated by anybody else. We reaffirm the policy of the triple boycott as interpreted by Mahatma Gandhi. Not that Mr. Das or any of his party accepts that interpretation as correct, but they say they would not fight us over it here. He accepts the fact that you and I are committed to that policy and continue to be committed to it. If you want to accept Mr. Das's interpretation you must join the Swarajya Party. You won't do it by accepting the resolution. Speaker after speaker gave a lurid picture of the difference between the Swarajists' programme and the old non-co-operation programme. Take it from me that if you vote for the proposition I have moved, you may sleep soundly with the knowledge that you do not accept the Swaraj Party's programme. You confirm the policy which we had before the Delhi decision. But you assure our friends who differ from us that what was done in Delhi is not to be undone now. If we want to keep the prestige of the Congress we must maintain the integrity and the unity of the institution. We ought not to undo what we did with open eyes unless there is grave reason for it. There would have been grave reason if we were prepared to take up now an aggressive triple boycott programme. But what you want is not an aggressive whirl-wind programme but only a foundation for your constructive work. I remind the speakers that an aggressive whirl-wind constructive programme would be out of place now.

The subject of boycott of bye-elections was also introduced. A boycott to be effective must be impersonal. Boycott of a particular bye-election would be as ludicrous as a hartal in one of our streets when all the other streets are open to traffic and trade. Boycott of bye-elections would not be useful to the nation. Let us not therefore bother about bye-elections and let us leave it to the Congress organisations to decide such things from time to time. Let us now decide about principles.

When I moved the proposition to you I dealt briefly and only with general principles. Details ought to be left to Committees and it would be impossible to consider here the lagal language, etymological and other aspects which were introduced by the oppossers of the resolution. I am sorry I was compelled to enter into some of them in reply. One word more. Fear of misinterpretation is born of weakness and must be put aside. If you believe me there is non-co-operation in all its force in this resolution and there is authority and mandate for constructive work. That is what we want for the year. I beg of you therefore to give your acceptance to this proposition and reject the amendment. If we commit a mistake thereby, mistakes can always be corrected. Let us go according to our present convictions. (Cries of Mahatma Gandhi-ki-jai.)

PREPARE FOR BAPU'S RELEASE

It is easy to buy foreign cloth; as easy as it is to commit any other crime;—but we may not therefore commit the crime. Self-restraint has a pleasure of its own, which can be realised only by those who exercise it. It may be somewhat difficult to find the Khaddar that suits the particular purpose for which I want it. The breadth may be less than what I want. The length of the *dhoti* or the *saree* may be more or less than the requirements of my case. More than all it may be much thicker than I would like it to be. It would be temptingly easy to find the exact dimensions and quality in foreign cloth; the more so, because my wants and my tastes have been themselves built on the foreign supply. Even after everything else is settled more or less satisfactorily, the price would certainly point again to the foreign article as cheaper.

Let us learn, however, to stand all these temptations. We should remember that if we can afford it, the costlier stuff may indeed be the cheaper in the end. Even if the beauty and the durability of good-hand-spun do not appeal to us, let us remind ourselves of the source of the cloth we buy, the families to whom the money that we pay goes. If but we think about it, the faces of the half-starved women and children of our peasantry should appear before our mind's eye as we go shopping. If I buy a yard of Khaddar, the money I pay goes to help such a family to make both ends meet and to struggle against debt and economic bondage for some time; to give hope and shed light where darkness and despair ruled and to encourage those who have taken to spinning to continue to spin.

"Gandhi is in prison. Nobody cares for my yarn now," many a sister has said to herself; and many a wheel which lived and sung in joy for a brief time in the great days of 1921, has gone into melancholy silence again. Every yard of Khaddar that you buy rouses a fresh wheel from sleep and gives hope to a poor and unfortunate sister in the village. Khaddar is certainly cheaper, if all this is taken into account, than foreign cloth that may cost a little less.

The choice we make when we buy cloth has far—reaching effects. It is not merely a question of size, colour or thickness. The right choice automatically sets the wheel moving and the flow of yarn from the poor woman's family to the weaver going. It we make the wrong choice, it adds to the weight of the chains that bind the half-starved families to poverty and bondage, although it may give better dividends to some rich mill-owner here or abroad.

Khaddar is the only wear for thoughtful and good people; all other is, if not positively wicked, at least thoughtlessness and indifference. Let us strive this year to make Khaddar universal. If we do, as day follows night Mahatmaji will be with us again; and what is more, on his face will blossom a joyous smile of sacrifice and work that fulfilled their purpose.

Every good family should have at least one Charkha at home. Every girl should learn and practise the simple art of spinning. Boys and parents cannot better occupy their leisure-moments than at the family-Charkha. Reader, if you are finding time to read this paper, surely you could find a few minutes for doing something better, something which Mahatmaji is silently wishing you should do, all the time he is in jail deprived of liberty for our sake. When he comes out, would you not like to stand blameless before him? That is why you should at once get a Charkha and spin. This year the Congress has resolved that we should make up for all lost time, all past sins of omission. We should revive religion and prayer. The very best prayer, the very best religious service, besides being the most valuable national service, is a half-hour at the Charkha before the day's work, and before the day's eating and drinking. The buslest lawyer, the busiest merchant, the most bookish student and all girls can certainly find time for this.

I cannot hope that these words may reach the village folk, or even more than an infinitesimal fraction of the reading towns-folk. But I may beg of all that read this, to tell others and more than that, to set an example to others. It is the duty of Congress-wokers to carry out the resolve of the Congress a by taking the meassage of the spinning wheel to the villages and to put forth unceasing effort to make every home adopt the Charkha as an extra child on behalf of Bapu. Let us try with all our might this year to attain a standard of fulfilment of our programme that will bring united mass action within actual view. The Spinnnig Wheel is the Key of the situation in every way. Is there a braver or more restless spirit than Maulana Shaukat Ali? And he has, not without meaning, accepted a chief place in the Khaddar Board.

The Constructive Programme is identical with the spinning wheel. All the other items really flow from it in natural sequence. If we take care of the Charkha, all else will automatically shape themselves around it. **C.R.**

Spare Hours

Mr. C. Rajagopalachari's appeal to the students printed elsewhere deserves the careful attention of all students not merely of national schools but also of Government schools Scholastic non-co-operation like every other had a touch of violence about it. Hence the gulf between the boys and girls belonging to national and Government schools. As a matter of fact there should be no such gulf. Mr. Rajagopalachari's suggestion if adopted will serve a double purpose. The adoption will bridge the gulf and provide a means beneficial to the nation of utilising the spare hours that students get during vacations. The advance must be made by non-co-operation students. They will not only thereby not surrender an iota of their principle but they will actually emphasise its non-violent and therefore vital part. There need be no despair if the advance is rejected. The suitor may feel sure of success, if it is fellowship that prompts the advance.

VACATION THOUGHTS

For Youths in Schools and Colleges

In a few days you will all be free from the toil of your school and college studies and the anxieties of having to prepare for examination, and will enjoy a long vacation. Some among you will continue to remain during this period in big towns but a large number among you will go back to your homes in the villages and smaller towns. My appeal is intended for you all, but I urge it especially on those who will spend this long holiday in rural parts. Some of you may have sacrificed a great deal, and others done but little work for the Congress cause uptil now, but during this vacation there is a splendid opportunity for you all to help the National movement.

The Sacrifice Asked

The work of the year is Khadhi, and my appeal to you is that you should utilise your leisure time during the long vacation to help us in the Khadi work. This will not entail any sacrifice on your part nor any change in your plans for the future such as you may have chalked out and for which you are preparing. It will only involve a little physical labour, which the weakest among you can do without detriment to any literary studies or other occupations in which you may engage yourself.

A Little Cotton

The essentials of the Khadi programme are very simply stated. Every family that can afford it should keep a little cotton of its own. A Madras maund (25 lbs.) of cotton is the family standard. If spun into yarn this will be more than enough to make all the clothes which the family, including women and children, can want for a whole year.

A Few Minutes Daily

The spinning of this quantity of cotton is easily done in the course of six months if the members of the family sit each but a few minutes at the wheel, giving between them all two hours every day. It can safely be asserted that there is no family but its women, girls, boys and even the men can afford to spare out of their waste-hours this much time daily between them all.

An Hour's Carding for a Week's Spinning

The cotton has to be prepared for spinning. If a young man sits at the carding bow for about one hour any day, he can in that one hour prepare cotton enough for the entire family's spinning for a whole weak. If a young man sets up a bow during the vacation, he has time not only to learn the art, but also to card and prepare slivers ready for spinning for the whole year for his family in the course of these two months, if only he sits regularly for an hour a day at the bow. If the cotton is unginned stuff, the ginning of a maund of cotton in an ordinary hand-gin, one of the simplest of household tools, will take but an inappreciable time. The seeds will be good food for the cow and the cotton is ready to be carded. If ginned cotton is procured, this part of the work is saved.

Carding the Key-stone

The Key of the whole programme is carding. Our efforts at spinning have hitherto found their greatest obstacle in the difficulty of procuring carded cotton. Almost any one can be induced to spin if you give well prepared slivers and a good wheel. Wheels stop working because carded cotton is not regularly available. Attempts to get prefessional prinjaris to card cotton and sell the slivers from the Congress offices are bound to prove costly, irregular and unsatisfactory. If there is one cause more than another for for the apparent set-back in spinning activities among the the leisured classes, it is due to the carding difficulty. Like spoon-feeding, supplying livers to spinners, is not a healthy method of stimulating growth. This difficulty [is however only apparent. If tackled properly it disappears at once. Carding should become an ordinary accomplishment of young men. It is here that you can do yeoman service during this coming vacation.

Most Easy

A young man can learn the art of carding in a day or two. A middle-sized pinjan can be easily hung up in any room and as already stated, a young man can learn and practise and also finish the actual carding and slivering of cotton for a whole year's use for his family if during this vacation be gives but one hour in the morning every day at the bow.

A True Story

It was nearly three years ago that I brought a carding-bow

from Satyagraha Ashram along with one of Maganlal Gandhi's big charkhas. The charkha became an active member of the family. But the bow, after some vain attempts to set it up went to a corner in the lumber room. There were slivers which a friend had supplied and this was more than enough for the spinning that went on. A Congress Committee borrowed the carding bow for some time. I don't know if it was useful there, but it was soon returned and it went again to the lumber room and thereafter was forgotten. My young friend S.G. of the Ashram came here last year, and I asked him if he could set up and work a carding-bow. "Oh yes", he said. But after inspecting a local bamboo shop, he said there were not green bamboos such as he wanted, and we gave it up and forgot the subject again.

This year Shivaji, Vinobaji's brother accompanied me when I returned home from the Khadi tour.

"Can you set up this bow?" I asked him one day.

"Oh, yes" he said. And this time I was more active and got the two or three strips of good bamboo and strings that were wanted. It did not cost us quite four annas, and more than half an hour's labour. The carding-bow was installed.

Shivaji examined the tune of the gut like a veritible musician, shook his head and took it out and restrung it. It was quite ready.

"Where is the beater?" I asked. We searched for it, but it was not to be found. Either the Congress Committee forgot to return it with the bow or it was mislaid somewhere else. Subbiah, my typist, would not brook delay but went to the town and returned in the evening with a new and beautifully made beater and a pound of cotton to start work. He boldly sat at the bow and after a few preliminary awkward blows, and warnings from Shivaji, he pulled along well enough. He soon got tired as all enthusiastic beginners at any game do. My son young Narasimhan stepped in. I smiled, for I thought the lad was too weak-limbed a boy for such work. But to my astonishment he went on all right. The thing proceeded regularly after this. The unmistakable music showed that the hands were deft enough and the young men not idle. Subbiah proudly came to my room on the second day with a neat paper roll containing quite a decent quantity of clean white slivers. "Really", I asked, "Did you do this?"

"Yes", said he. "It is quite an easy affair". The third day my son came with a still larger roll of slivers. It was delightful.

"The problem of spinning is solved", said I.

And so it is, reader, for every one can easily learn this simple art of carding and place the Charkha so to say on an independent and unshakable basis.

You become an independent centre of work.

The Tamil Nadu Khadi Board is arranging to open a colony where young men can stay without any expense for food or lodging and learn all about carding and spinning. They will have to work industriously in this colony but the result will be as Mr. Santanam, the Provincial Khadi Secretary puts it that every one of them becomes an independent centre of Khadi work. If you set up a bow in a room in your hostel, you can on Sundays card enough cotton to distribute slivers for all your friends and neighbours for the whole week. Every hostel could become a veritable centre of active Khadi work absolutely standing on its own legs.

Yarn spun can easily be made into cloth. You can easily find a weaver for your yarn. If it is thick it can be made into coating, towels etc. If thin enough, it can be made into dhotis. The best yarn should be made into *sarees* for the womenfolk. If you cannot find a local weaver, the Provincial Khadi Board would be glad to arrange the weaving for any one who has yarn, provided there is sufficient yarn given at a time, say 5 lbs.

Your Quota of Service

This, then in the true Khadi Programme in which you can give your quota of service. If you learn carding, you substantially solve what has hitherto been the hardest past of the problem. You qualify yourself to be a worker of the first class and by your example, wherever you are, you do immense service to the movement.

There are other lesser things you can do; you can speak to men and women and induce them to wear Khadi;—of course you can do this only if you are yourselves exclusive devotees of Khadi. You can hawk Khadi. You can collect funds for Khaddar work. But all this is not such valuable service as your own carding and spinning. **C. Rajagopalachari**

A CONDITION OF CONGRESS MEMBERSHIP

The All India Khadi Board has issued an appeal that every Congress member should have at least one spinning wheel working in his family. This appeal only re-expresses the expectation with which Mahatmaji had organised the new Congress membership. One of the main objects of the Congress organisation is the production and substitution of hand-spun Khadi for all other cloth. Membership in any organisation is meaningless unless it carries with it active assistance and cooperation in the chief function undertaken by the organisation. It is not merely an army of passive sympathisers that we seek to enrol in the Congress Register. We may assume that the whole of India is sympathetic and there is no need to register names. It is only if there should be something more in membership, namely, assistance in the life-activity of the organisation that there could be any meaning in the enrolment of oneself as a member. It follows, therefore, that every member must, in order to consider himself as such, regularly give a portion, however small it may be, of his own or family's time to the making of land-spun. He must wear Khadi and help in the production of Khadi. The Khadi movement is so conceived that every man and woman can do his or her bit for it. Every one that spins regularly helps in the production of Khadi.

No person who has not a charkha working regularly in his home can deem himself a Congress member. Difference of views there may be in other matters, but in this programme of revival of Khaddar, there is no doubt or difference, and no person can truly claim to be a member of the Congress, which works for the universalisation of spinning, unless there is a live charkha under his own care and protection. It would be a false pretence to be going about as a Congress member unless one fulfils this primary condition of membership. The mistaken notion that only a few "workers" are to do Congress work, and that the members are a mere body of sympathisers, should be got rid of. Every member is a pledged worker. It would be ridiculous for a member of a Temperance Association with a negative programme of abstention from drink, to indulge in alcohol simply because he is only an ordinary member. No less inconsistent is it for enrolled members of a great organisation, with a positive programme of making every family spin, to remain without spinning themselves. During this Gandhi Month, every one should hasten to set himself right in this respect. The Charkha is the *yajnopavitam* of Congress membership, as essential as the sacred thread is to the Brahmin.

The programme of work this year centres round Khadi. On the one hand, if we do our duty by Khadi, it is more than enough for all the purposes we have in view. It will rid the nation of the political, social and economic evils that are sapping its life. On the other hand, if we fail this year to complete our Khadi programme, we shall have proved ourselves hopelessly unworthy of any ambitions of speedy nation-building. The Khadi Board Deputation assures us that the atmosphere is ready and that every circumstance is favourable. No one should imagine that his own small efforts would count for nothing. The humblest example and work are certain to bear copious fruit. Not a single day should be lost now but he who has a charkha at home should see that it is set in working order, he who has not should procure one immediately; and everyone should wear Khadi at once. C.R.

THE ROOT-NEED

The long expected and oft-postponed speech of the Secretary of State was made in the House of Lords on Tuesday, week before the last. We are neither satisfied nor grieved. Indian affairs stand just where they did before the speech was made and before the present Government came into power. Beyond this summary, there is nothing in reality to say.

But there are a number of observations the incident suggests. They are academic, but it is the fault neither of Lord Olivier nor of ourselves; they are the automatic product of the atmosphere of unreality with which current politics is invested. That Lord Olivier made a speech which it was impossible for Lord Peel to have made may be conceded; also that it contained some of the common places and superstitions of Indian politicians. But that does not mean much. The reason is obvious. The present Secretary of State is a member of the Labour Government; Lord Peel belongs to the Conservative Party and is the descendant of a famous Conservative statesman. The Fablan intellect is different from the Tory. There was no bullying in the speech of Lord Olivier. The passage about Mr. Gandhi for instance was charming, and we shall certainly not quarrel about the deprecatory clauses about the consequences about his teachings. Lord Olivier being an experienced administrator did not commit the mistake into which Mr. Henderson fell and very nearly lost his election, the mistake of forgetting that he was a minister.

But when all this is conceded, what is there left in the sphere of action? For, after all, politics is concerned with action whether as art or science. We suggest, with all respect, that of action present or in the immediate future, there is not a trace. We do not say it to taunt the Nationalists in the Assembly or the Swarajists out of it; but the truth is that the Round Table Conference on which they reckoned as the very foundation of Swaraj in the future finds no acceptance at the hands of the Secretary of State. The Royal Commission on which the Liberals founded their hopes has been rejected with an equally dubions gesture. We are left with Sir Malcolm Halley's promise of a departmental enquiry. There is nothing in this which may not have come from Lord Peel himself. For, in the natural course of things, the statutory Royal Commission is due a few years ahead and there is nothing strange in the initiation of attempts to get the materials ready for the Commission. In saying that, we do not dismiss from our mind the hint that the Cabinet in consultation with the Government of India will soon devise measures to get into contact with the better mind of India. That may or may not be; it is yet a thing of the future. It is the speech of the Secretary of State that is our pre-occupation now, not what the future holds. God will take care of that.

The explanation of this remarkable phenomenon, of a Labour Minister proving in action the very counterpart of a Tory, is painfully simple. But it is by no means part of the convinced presuppositions of the movement for national freedom. But the matter is clear beyond the shadow of a doubt. As far as India is concerned, fear, cupidity and high honourable pride are not affairs of party; they are of the very texture of national being. There is nothing in the vital facts of Imperial Government in India which can be disposed of in terms of party. India is a national interest of England (perhaps there is none other which is greater) and can be dealt with only by common political consent. That was how the Morley-Minto Act was passed; that was how the Montford Reform came into operation. Whenever in the future also, it becomes the business of Parliament to undertake Indian business, the same procedure is sure to be followed. We make a present of these obvious considerations to our fellow-countrymen who believe that the accession of Labour to power means the end of our troubles or absolution from our work.

There are some questions that Lord Olivier askes in all innocence, or perhaps he is not so innocent as he will have us believe. He asks us how exactly we shall get on if Swaraj came suddenly in the night, what we shall do to fight the invader from outside, to hold our own with the Moplah inside our borders. We are quite as anxious as he is, and there is no responsible man but is exercised in his heart of hearts about them. But we are not going to be scared by the prospect of responsibility. India solved these problems in the days of her freedom and is continuously solving them even today. Aryans, Greeks, Scythians Afghans, Persians, Turks and the embattled tribes of the West have been so many episodes in her history. Our fathers battled with them when there was need, made friends when there was need; but the course of the great life went on uninterrupted. Malabar and Arrah and Saharanpur were ripples, angry ripples, in the calm waters of her being. Whatever it is the business is ours, and our children's. They will not be unworthy of their ancestors.

The truth is no more than this, and let it be added, it is no less. Whether Lord Olivier means business or no, India can mean business only on one condition. What she decides will be the final decision for her, not what England decides. There may be an infinity of difficulty in ascertaining her mind; it may be through a Royal Commission or through a Round Table Conference, or it may be through informal conversations; all this is detail. But when India has had her say, England must be prepared to accede to her demands. As long as successive Secretaries of State refuse to recognise and if necessary reconcile themselves to this root-need, there will be no peace in this country.

But if Khadi is not only to deal a blow but also to organise the nation for self-government, if it is to be the constructive agency that will transform a moribund mass into a living people who can give non-violent battle to arbitrary rule, and also rule themselves peacefully, Khadi has to be organised on a co-operative self-contained rural basis. The spinner, the weaver and the weaver should be neighbours all acting together. Then will Khadi be truly a part, and the chief part of national construction, and Shankarlal Banker's tour will be fraught with great results for Khadi and for the constructive programme generally. The people cannot give Mahatmaji's prison-Chela a better welcome everywhere than by setting the charkhas a turning before he arrives to see them. C.R.

THE KHADI BOARD ON TOUR

Mr. Shankarlal Banker, Secretary of the All India Khaddar Board, with other members Sjts. Jamnalalji and Maganlal Gandhi have now been for some weeks touring in Andhra Desha and Tamil Nad. From there they proceed to the north. They are carrying home to the masses the message of Mahatma Gandhi and the spinning wheel. They wish to impress on all, those living in urban as well as in rural areas, the Khadi Ideal—the ideal of *Vastra-Swatantrya* (Self-sufficiency). They want the people not only to increase their capacity to produce Khaddar but also to make all necessary arrangements for the consumption of that increased output as far as is possible by the producing areas themselves. They desire that men and women should out on their own Khadi locally produced, and not send it off to neighbouring provinces taking it away from the reach of the vast mass of the poor peasantry. The following speech of Mr. Shankarlal Banker at Madras gives succintly the subject matter of what they have been saying to the people:

> The last session of the Congress called upon the country to take to the constructive programme. The carrying out of this programme is essential, if the country desires to offer Satyagraha. And as Satyagraha alone can help us in this struggle we have to make up our minds to carry out this programme throughout the country. The main plank of this programme is Khadi. Mahatmaji has repeatedly told us that true Swaraj can only come through Khadi. Khadi alone can develop those qualities in the people that can really lead us to the realisation of true Swaraj. Khadi stands for simplicity of life. It alone can discipline the nation by making it industrious and self-reliant. Khadi

alone can help us to build that national organisation which can lead us to the attainment of our goal. But this Khadi cannot be the commercialised product that we find it at the present day. There must be a different ideal behind it. That ideal can to a certain extent be expressed by the term self-sufficiency. Influenced by this ideal the citizen will take to carding and spinning and use the cloth made from his own yarn to the exclusion of other cloth. In fact you have to pursue in the matter of clothing the same method which you pursue in the matter of your food. This may appear to some to be beyond the range of practicability. But to the people of Andhra and Tamil Nad it need not appear so.

Andhra Villages

In our tour we have seen some villages in the Andhra province where 90 per cent of the population are clad in Khaddar produced locally. The cultivator stocks his cotton, the cotton is spun in his home and the Khaddar cloth is woven by the local purchaser. He does so because he finds that the cloth thus produced is cheaper and more durable. I must admit that here, the political consciousness is not the operative factor. But if the cultivator would realise his power, he will find, that this policy would really present to us the ideal we want to follow. But elsewhere I have seen this ideal worked out and there it is the political consciousness that is the operative factor. I say, therefore, that it is feasible if we are only determined to work it out.

Urban Areas

But some of you may ask if that is so even in Urban areas My answer is that it is as fessible there as in the villages. I will attempt to illustrate what I have said by an example. There is a clerk living in a suburb of Bombay, within an hour's run of the city. He works ten hours a day at his office. Two more hours are taken up by travelling. Still he finds time to spin and spin religiously. He stocks cotton and carde it himself. He also spins and weaves his own cloth. He learned weaving in his leisure hours, and not only does he weave for himself but he is able to weave for neighbouring spinners too. What a clerk in Bombay, who has very few spare hours, is able to do for himself should not certainly be impossible of attainment for town dwellers all over. So the ideal of Vastra-Swatantrya can be worked up to even in big cities.

What Mahatmaji Does

In this cannection I therefore wish to tell you what would be the message of Mahatma Gandhi—I say would be because he has really given us no message. I asked for a message, but he would not give any. But he said "You had better tell my people what I am doing here." I understand that it is because he felt that his words failed to reach our hearts. It is a matter of shame and grief for all of us. I shall however tell shortly what he is doing there.

He is spinning in the jail four hours a day. If his health permitted he would spin the whole day. He has learned carding also in jail. One might say he has nothing else to do in jail. But it is not so. He has got a hard day's work before him. He studies Urdu in order that he might be able to carry on conversation and correspondence with Muslim friends in their own language. He is also studying Vedas, Upanishads, and the Geeta. Because he wants to understand thoroughly the Islamic mind he is also reading the Koran. I can tell you he is studying harder than a student would do for his examination. And yet he has time for spinning. He has granules in his eyes. He had to be operated twice for that. This troubles his vision too. Still he would not give up spinning. He would not take his meal unless he spins a certain quantity. He does this, I understand in order that his message may be more effective than it has been till now.

Our work

If we therefore really want to carry on his work we must follow him. We must take to Khadi and hand-spinning. He wants hand-spinning to be universal. We have now to organise ourselves for realising that ideal. We have to carry that message to the ryot in the innermost part of our country. We have to help him in every possible way. We must be able to supply.

COMMON ELECTORATES

The agreement over the common electorate proposal is a great achievement, which alone may suffice to give lustre to Mr. Srinivasa Iyengar's regime as Congress President. Reactionaries and persons interested in keeping up the almosphere of communal discord may still oppose the proposal. Whatever may be the result, that such a proposal has been influentially supported is one of the most note-worthy triumphs of good sense in recent times. There is nothing so effective as a long rope for people to learn lessons. The wisdom of the exclusivists has been given a full trial and found by all to be most damaging in result. That way lies no hope for the nation or any community for that matter.

Voluntary forms of untouchability are no better than that enforced variety which is known as a blot on Hinduism, Untouchability is an evil not only when it is a social bar between high and low caste, but also when it takes the shape of a political bar between two components of a population that must live together for good or evil. Though not imposed by ancient custom, but invented by modern politicians, the system of separate electorates is a form of untouchability. Untouchability is bad socially; so also is it bad politically. In both cases both sides suffer.

From exclusive and separate electorates to a joint electoral roll is a great advance. There may not be inter-communal confidence enough yet for men to give up the divisional idea altogether and to accept complete identification with other communities. An easy path-way to personal position and power which communal exclusivism opens out to fortunate members of a minority community is yet too much of a temptation for individual ambition to resist in the larger interest of national growth. But any step in advance is in itself to be welcomed. We must wait patiently, for all the lessons to be learnt. The full course of affliction must be gone through for truth and good sense to triumph completely. Wisdom learnt that way is burned into us and will be permanent.

Let us, then, not be impatient. When men get really to govern themselves through their representatives, when our democratic institutions are not as now mere clubs of the pushful, but real institutions responsible for the happiness and misery distributed among the people, the latter, i.e., the governed, will see that there is no particular advantage in having men of this or that persuasion to manage their affairs. They will then see that it is more important to put good and able men in charge and that a man of one's own caste or faith, if bad or foolish, does terrible injury, not to be compensated for by the consciousness that a member of one's own faith or caste is enjoying power.

Even if seats are still reserved for particular communities, there are distinct advantages in a joint electoral roll. Candidates, both Mussulman and Hindu, will come forward whose conduct has obtained the approbation of Mussalmans as well as Hindus. Those who have set the one against the other community must lose the votes of the one or the other, and cannot hope to win the majority of votes in a joint electorate. It will gradually bring men to see that the path to political position and power lies through broad-minded and non-sectarian activities and true service, and not by playing to communal passions and prejudices. Every aspiring public worker will see that narrow interpretations of patriotism serve to diminish one's opportunities for being chosen to render public service.

It may be thought that even if we have joint electorates, men will go on working up communal prejudices and appealing to voters on the basis of caste or religion, privately, if not publicly. This cannot long continue, for anything done on a large scale cannot but get known and bring its consequences with it. Some may try to secure the votes of a solid mass of voters by appealing to communal patriotism and may thus successfully defeat rival candidates working on more difficult and non-sectarian lines. This may be so as long as there is a paucity of candidates. But as time goes on, the natural result of opportunities afforded will be that a number of candidates will come forward from the same community, and they will perceive that in the competition among themselves he who by his non-clannishness secures votes from the electorates of both communities, has an advantage over one who plays to religious or sectarian prejudice. This will tend certainly in course of time to lead the activities of public men in the right direction. Let us therefore hope that all men of far-sighted patriotism will support the principle of communal electorates. This is not merely a phase of the working of the present Montford reforms or a question only for the Royal Commission for the revision of the Reforms but is a substantive principle affecting the permanent fate of India. It is a step towards Swaraj.

FOREIGN PROPAGANDA

Before the non-co-operation movement, Indian political activity largely consisted of propaganda in Great Britain. A great deal of money, comparatively, was spent on it and was considered well spent. When Gandhiji took up the guidance of our national affairs there was a change of outlook. A grasp of the essentials of national strength was the first result of his programme and it marked all our political thought at the time. We understood the natural laws that governed the sanctions needed for the non-violent enforcement of national demands. An almost exclusive spirit of self-reliance was the natural consequence. The cultivation of favourable opinion in foreign parts including Great Britain was valued at its correct worth and distinct efforts to that end were practically given up, and opposed vigourously whenever the question was raised. So intense was the work in India and so marked were the results that the tables were soon turned, and instead of Indians going to do propaganda in Great Britain and foreign parts, India attracted numerous foreign visitors; and the British Government was forced to undertake counter-propaganda in foreign parts.

In India itself the Government had to give up its self-confidence and organise its own propaganda among the people in order to resist or at least postpone the effects of the national upheaval.

With the stoppage of aggressive non-co-operation, however, there has been a reversion in Indian thought. Slowly but steadily the cry for foreign propaganda is gaining volume again. The internal situation also namely, the difficulties in the way of united national action, has naturally led people to turn to easier outlets of activities abroad. To those who still hold to the creed of non-co-operation and who look to emancipation only from within, his turn of the national gaze and energy to East and West is a symptom of growing weakness and a cause for anxiety. The vision is bound to be clouded and constructive efforts are bound to be prejudiciously affected by the growing tendency to this diversion. Not only does it divert attention but some of the best workers will be drawn bodily into this channel of pleasanter though futile work.

Pre-non-co-operation foreign propaganda was mostly propaganda in Britain. But one of the permanent results of the efforts of these eight years is loss of faith in Britain. The last vestiges of faith that stuck to the British Labour party have been also destroyed. The present harking back to foreign propaganda is therefore not for propaganda in England, but for the cultivation of contacts and friendship with other foreign nations. We are told that it is very desirable to develop intimate association with the German and Russian people. We are told that the Latin races of Europe present a favourable field for propaganda. France, Italy, Spain and Portugal are mentioned. Even Scandinavia is not forgotten being important neutral soil. We are told again that the need of the hour is to link India up with other countries suffering under like imperialistic exploitation. We are assured that the hope of India is a federated Asia rising against Western domination. This change of attitude in regard to foreign propaganda had naturally its echo in the proceedings of the All-India Congress Committee where foreign affairs dominated the atmosphere, and many resolutions were adopted calculated to form a basis for international friendships.

It would be narrow-mindedness, indeed and show us to be lacking the spirit of culture and humanity to refuse to have dealings with other nations if we were better circumstanced. But what would be civilisation and culture and broad-mindedness under favourable circumstances would be mere helplessness under existing conditions and would lead to nothing beneficial. Friendship with other nations can grow and be beneficial only if as in personal friendships it is not cultivated on the mere expectation of advantages all on one side. If we seek honourable friendship with others there must be something for us to give them while we seek something from them. If we are in effect truly unable to help others and only ask for something at their hands it would not conduce to mutual esteem; nor can a healthy alliance grow. If we are able really to help others, it must be by a supreme effort of national assertion which can and must, if well directed, produce far more marked results at home. The nations, whose friendship we go to woo, must find something to learn or something to gain from close association with us. If we have going on amidst us some movement of dynamic value, some revolutionary effort or some great constructive activity worthy of copy or study on others' part, we would be seeking friendship on honourable, if not equal, terms. But we cannot be ever living other on the capital of our ancient culture or on the history of the Gandhian movement.

The link of mere friendship of slavery is not likely to be a real or useful bond. Why do we turn to Russia, China or Turkey? It is not simply the greatness of the past history of these nations that attracts us. If that alone were offered we would hardly be interested. But it is because we believe that there are great movements now going on in those countries which furnish matter for useful study or admiring observation, that some of our people go to those countries. Similarly if we seek international friendship with such nations, we should have something to offer to them of value. Otherwise we would only be beggars and should expect to be treated no better.

But then, it may be said, this is to ignore world politics. There are wars coming on. The nations of the world are ever seeking to subvert one another's plans, and India is an important piece on the board. We are not so helpless internationally as we may be internally in our own affairs. This needs clearing up and plain talking. Are we in for a war and the formation of alliances with those likely to fight England, or do we expect other countries to go to war over us? If the powers abroad go to war, they do it with gunpowder and ships. Are we ever likely usefully to participate as a nation in such war? Is it contemplated that India and other slave nations in the East may enter into a treaty, some time in the future, to rise in revolt helping each other against the common foe? Is India to expect, under any contingency arising in a world-war, to render active assistance to a belligerent power against England? What, to put only one argument, is the chance of our ever achieving anything in this way? Is it practical politics of the remotest kind, disarmed as we are?

We do not want arms, it may be said: we can do a great deal by passive resistance. The only weapon in our hand in non-co-operation with the British Government during a war or peace. Here we come back to the old position. The Indian fight against England if it is to be by non-violent means depends entirely on its own strength and can never be converted into an international affair. In a non-violent struggle it is not easy, if at all possible, to obtain any material help from abroad. It must be conceived and organised and fought only on a basis of complete self-reliance.

Non-material moral help we can get from foreign countries. This we shall do not by any propaganda foreign or domestic but exactly in the measure that we do solid constructive work and develop internal strength.

[I have no desire to start any hot controversy over the

question of foreign propaganda, but I publish the foregoing as it summarises the views of many workers who hold them in no sense weakly because they do not express them in public. If the pure non-co-operation of 1920 is not witnessed on an extensive scale at the present moment, it is most decidedly going deeper with some and everything that is happening today in the land goes to strengthen their belief. But they cannot make themselves felt by being vocal in season and out of season. On the contrary they feel that they serve the cause of Swaraj better by observing silence where they cannot serve by speech and helping humbly and actively wherever they can.

M.K.G.

3

Social Philosophy

In the long political career for more than seven decades, C. Rajagopalachari developed a social philosophy which indeed became a mission of his life. He showed much interest to under socio-economic measures for the development of the weaker sections of our society. He attended to the development of education, discipline among students, of orphanages bhoodan, rural service and several other aspects of human life. He did succeed in many ways in his noble efforts. He launched the prohibition campaign and exhorted the people not to drink. This he did through his writings, speeches and a chain of devoted workers who would propagate his social ideology.

DUTIES OF STUDENTS

Have you ever noticed, my young friends, how the bullocks which are yoked to a cart behave? They keep their eyes on the driver who has the whip or stick in his hand and they also keep them on the road. The eyes of the bullock do *Ashtavadhanam*. The bullock watches the slightest movement of the driver's stick, and at the same time watches for any trouble on the road, as well as going forward. Now our future democratic governments will have to emulate the vigilance and the *Ashtavadhanam* of these bullocks, the drivers being the newspapers and public opinion, both of which have got sharp goads in their hands. If the Ministers keep their attention on nothing but the driver and his tricks they will miss their footing on the road. We two-legged animals can manage to go straight. The bullocks not only have four legs but have to keep all four of them going in unison and perfect co-operation with one another —rather a difficult task. Try to walk on all fours and you will soon see how uneven your gait becomes.

Now a Cabinet consisting of many Ministers, which is like an animal with many legs, is rather a difficult thing to manage. Do not envy the lot of Ministers. Do not think their task is easy and that they are possessed of a prize. They are just bullocks tied to the cart with a driver behind, goad in hand. Newspapers are very busy and sharp-tongued, while the Ministers have to stick to the road marked out by Mahatmaji and other leaders. They have to make progress and to achieve something in the way of more happiness for the people. I do not think, after this description of mine, you will envy the Ministers. Pray all day and all night that you will not become Ministers, but that you will remain freelance journalists. Then you can write anything you like. Ministers are generally very unhappy people, but you can make them happy by co-operating with them. It is you young students, who will have to bear the burden in the coming years. We have lighted the torch and handed it over. You have to carry it.

Now tell me whether you mean to go on strike now and then, or whether you will continue preparing to be good citizens of the land without a break. Will you take over the question of whether a teacher is to be transferred, dismissed or promoted, and go on a small hunger-strike, which I know you will not maintain for more than three or four days? You will want somebody or other to send you a telegram: "For God's sake give up your hunger-strike," and then you will stop it. I have come here to tell you that I thoroughly disapprove of hunger-strikes. I do not want students to go in for any form of strike. The responsibility for managing is on Government, on the Department concerned and on the Professors and Principals. The business of students is to train themselves to become citizens without break and without interruption. Whether the methods followed are wrong, you cannot judge. Whether the professors are not competent, you cannot judge. The sin is on their heads if they go wrong, but your duty is to go on with your preparation without a break. Freedom having come, democracy having come, the only problem hereafter is to become good citizens.

You cannot become good citizens if, during your youth, you begin to think of other people's problems. The citizen in a good State always thinks of his own duties and not of the errors committed by other people. Mysore has become part of the Indian Union. Do not imagine that the responsibility of the people of Mysore has been diminished thereby. It has increased. You have to look after Mysore, as well as the rest of India. Patriotism, is a mere word unless you realise the full meaning of it. Patriotism consists hereafter in work—honest, co-ordinated work. It does not consist in shouting or singing songs. To realise patriotism you have His Highness the Maharaja as a symbol. You cannot realise God if you reject the idol which you have always associated with God. The Maharaja symbolizes all the duties which citizens should remember and fulfil towards the State as a whole. The more complex the State becomes, the more necessary it is to have a symbol of that kind.

Democracy all the world over has set up various symbols. Look at me. Why am I Governor-General? Constructive patriotism in Free India requires a symbol as Head of the State and you must look upon that symbol, whether it is made of brass, wood, clay or human flesh. with awe, devotion and love. I have claimed this incidentally for myself but my main purpose today has been to claim it on behalf of His Highness the Maharaja. I want the students of the Maharaja's College to look upon their college as their mother and the Maharaja as their Father. Let me tell you that if you regard your symbol properly, and genuinely, everything will turn out well. You cannot be loyal to His Highness the Maharaja and commit any offence, private or public. Loyalty to His Highness, like loyalty to His Majesty the King for the British citizen, will protect the citizen in all his duties and in all his efforts on the road of patriotism. He is the symbol of patriotism in Mysore, and freedom having come, our loyalty has to be all the greater. Otherwise freedom will go to pieces. It will dwindle and deteriorate into intrigue if you do not keep your devotion to His Highness at a high level.

India is free. Somebody has to be Governor-General. There is nothing very great in somebody becoming Governor-General. Being the first Indian to occupy the place. I must make you feel somewhat like a crowd that watches the mango trick performed by a juggler. From out of Free India, an Indian has come as Governor-General and you are all exhilarated. I too am exhilarated by the feeling that I am able to command so much affection from you all. Your affection is to me simply a symbol of the complex thing called patriotism. I want all you students to remember your duties towards the State. Do not pull a long face over it. Do not become melancholy. The task is easy, because it is natural. You are the children of the land and the duties are natural duties which you are bound to perform if you are straight. There is no difficulty about it. Try to cultivate an outlook of joy towards everything. Do not try to recapitulate in your drama, or play, or song, all the troubles through which we have gone. We cannot live an old tragedy hereafter. We have to live on the prospect of joy and happiness. As an old man. I bless you all. Do not allow yourselves to be wicked, whatever the provocation may be. Thank you very much.

EDUCATION AND PERSONALITY

Primary education, whether it be reading, writing or arithmetic, or learning through work or through joy, whether the child be soaked in symbols and inured to bewilderment and pain from the earliest period of his life, or be allowed to deal with things, so that there is little difference between play and work and finding joy in both, whether we call our method Project

Montessori, or Basic or any other dear name, the education of our children must be planned so as to suit our present conditions, for obviously we cannot change these in order to suit our pet ideas. If you sit down and apply common arithmetic to your plans and to the national income on which you must ultimately draw for their execution, you will find that most plans go to pieces in the process of calculation, and that, in sheer desperation, you will have to put your head ostrichlike into the sand, and refuse to see what is before you.

Elementary education is perhaps not very relevant to our function today, though it is not altogether unconnected with it. What *Samskriti* or culture can we hope to conserve if our children are not brought up well and wisely? In spite of all the processes of unsettlement and the reform and reorganisation of society in India through Acts of Parliament and Welfare movements and associations, those threads of essential labour, on which the nation's life depends, have fortunately been kept unbroken by family tradition. Most children still assist in the work of their fathers and mothers and learn the family trade without school or institute and learn it well. Farmer, carpenter, cobbler, sweeper, smith, weaver, shopkeeper, cart-driver, all these millions of humble folk, unconscious of the ambitions and the ideologies of bigger people, carry on as if nothing were happening and so we live on. We may build our castles in the air with impunity, because the real house we live in down below has been maintained by the humble and the unlettered, unmindful of our endeavours at a higher level. The food is grown, the cloth is woven, the sheep are shorn, the cows are grazed, the shoes are stitched, the scavenging is done, the cart-wheels and the ploughs are built and repaired, because, thank God, the respective castes are still there and the homes are homes as well as trade schools and the parents are parents, as well as masters to whom the unaspiring children are automatically apprenticed.

Under these conditions, which no one but a mad man would disturb, what is the plan we ought to follow in the elementary schools we have established and are adding to? Shall we force all children, that is those we can lay hands on, away from a family apprenticeship to the trades of their parents, and compel them to spend their time in the schools we have set up—and we know just how efficient they will be with all our efforts—and make it impossible for them to learn the trades of their parents? They cannot learn them satisfactorily later on in life, nor can we hope to teach them in the schools which we are obliged to set up through hurriedly trained-teachers. The thought alarms me, for I see only too clearly the mischief that must result from such a step. Perhaps I am needlessly afraid. Quite a number of children may escape our tyranny, in which case their old system of familly apprenticeship and traditional occupation will continue despite our efforts.

How can we reconcile our laudable aim of spreading education with the need for continuing traditional occupations and family apprenticeships? I am a moderate man, a man out for healthy appeasement of all kinds, and so I venture to suggest to the crusaders for compulsory primary education whether we cannot be content with three days in the week for schooling. During those three days you may do with the children just as you like. But give them a chance during the other four days to work with their parents. Let us see what happens. There would thus be an insurance against error. We shall, so to say, advance, while keeping the communications in the rear intact. Those who do not have to follow the trade of their parents, or whose parents distrust them for parasitism, or for government service, or for competition and gambling of various kinds, may use the four free days in any way they like. The humble folk will use these four days for training in the family occupation and schooling will occupy the other three days, which I think should be quite enough.

This would double the capacity of our schools and our teachers, for it would mean they could take two sets of children in the week, leaving one day off for rest from labour.

The financial problem would be greatly eased by this

arrangement and the pressure of symbols and word-building on the tender brains of the pupils would be less. The four days off would give time for recuperation and would furnish an opportunity for the boys and girls to assimilate and to apply and to benefit from the schooling. Indeed I think this would bring about an all round improvement both in the quality of the instruction and of the assimilation.

So much for primary education.

The colleges in India are full to over-flowing. At the beginning of every academic year there is a great scramble for admission, matriculates putting forward claims and counter-claims on all possible grounds, including caste and community. Judged from figures, our universities must be declared to be completely successful. Yet it must be confessed that almost everybody is certain that the universities as they are today are unsatisfactory. Professors, students, members of our Parliament, the general public and various Public Service Commissions, are all agreed that the stuff manufactured in the universities is by no means good enough. The demands of the States are not met, although as far as numbers go there is no question of insufficiency. There is, however, deplorable inadequancy in quality.

Democracy's claims and all-embracing pretensions notwithstanding, sound leadership is the fundamental of national achievement and it must come from the products of our universities. We cannot seek for it elsewhere. From time to time, a revolutionary leader or saint may appear as by a miracle in the history of a nation and reshape its affairs and its character. But the day-to-day work that is required for the steady evolution of progress depends on a continuous supply of leaders who can manage men and guide the affairs of a people, and this does not belong to the realm of miracles. We want, not one, but thousands of men of character in the thousands of districts throughout the country. It would be no exaggeration to admit that the gap between the needs of the times and the quality of the supply from our universities, is a yawning gulf.

The men and women who come out as graduates have to learn everything and personality has still to be shaped after they obtain employment. This is most unsatisfactory when the burden and responsibility of the public services have increased beyond the wildest imagination of the previous generation of our public men. The most important equipment that a young man must get before he leaves his university is personality, not learning, but character. Unfortunately the atmosphere of our colleges is far too much vitiated by intellectual and moral confusion for anything like this to be attempted. There is not that guidance available which is essential for the building up of personality in the young men and women who study in them. Their brain power is of a very high order and a tremendous quantity of learning is put in, but the essential stuff is wanting. The explanation offered is that there is so much intellectual and moral confusion in the world around them that this is reflected in the universities. But is it enough for universities to reflect outside confusion instead of making up for it? The function of the universities must be to reform, not to represent society proportionately but to do something to restore moral values and intellectual orderliness where there is anarchy.

I once again emphazise, that the universities must give the nation the leaders, teachers and administrators who are required in this complicated age to fulfil the duties devolving on the State and to guide society in its cultural life. Folly must be replaced by reasons, passion must be put aside in favour of reflection, ideals must be installed where caprices govern, in fact principles must prevail, not opportunism. All this cannot be accomplished for us through some mighty miracle. It is the function of universities to produce the young men and women who will be able to find joy and fulfilment of spirit by guiding the people up this glorious mountain path.

The young men of today are the sport of random and confused thought that finds expression in ephemeral printed matter of whose undependability even the victims are not unaware.

In the great experiment which, in the evolution of her destiny, India has undertaken to make in our generation, there is nothing more unfortunate than the present state of our colleges and universities. They were planned and built in a past generation and it is no fault of theirs if they do not suit our times, and have not gained, but rather suffered, by the revolutionary technique that was evolved for the speedy attainment of freedom.

Had our philosophy and our culture, which formed the great bulwark which protected India through past ages been intact, the mischief arising out of the inadequacy of our universities might have been of relative unimportance. If our Vedantic culture had been kept alive, not in scholarship alone, but in the hearts of men and in their deeper understanding, no deficiency in school or college education would have resulted in serious harm. Unfortunately, this ancient inheritance has become a rapidly diminishing asset. Little of it I fear is left now. Otherwise we should not be witnessing the vast quantity of greed and selfishness that have made the aims of our National Government so difficult of achievement. The discipline and restraint and the sense of moral values which Vedantic culture implies, have been almost completely jettisoned by the steady and unrelenting educational plans pursued during the last fifty years, which, alas, did not furnish us with anything in place of the old inheritance that was thrown overboard.

All learning should develop personality, otherwise it is worthless in every sense. On the other hand, if this aspect of university aims be kept in mind, every variety of study will be rich in fruit. Be it science, technical training, economics, history, law, domestic science, or whatever else it may be, it would—each one of these—be an ample field for making a boy or girl a leader of men, provided that, along with intellectual equipment, the development of personality received attention.

I am not unaware of the difficulty of providing moral training. We cannot get the right type of personalities to live and move among the youth gathered in the universities, whose very lives and deportment, without direct instruction or the compulsion of discipline, would be an inspiration. We get teachers who are vastly competent in every other respect, but the greatest reluctance is generally felt in introducing anything in the scheme of school or college education which may be mistaken for denominational religious teaching. One must recognise the validity of the reasons and apprehensions that lead to this, but we cannot afford to exaggerate our fears and rest content with doing nothing.

The crisis is far too real and grave. We cannot take a simple negative attitude on account of our hesitations. I feel that there is a way to achieve our object. A comprehensive scheme for the creation of opportunities to study and understand various religions and philosophies, including that which goes by the name of classical humanism in the Western universities, namely, the thoughts of Greece and Rome, would, taken together, furnish an atmosphere and an incentive which would enable our boys and girls to seize the truth and to assimilate the culture and philosophy of our own land, without any exclusive or direct effort organised for that purpose. The indirect approach may achieve that which cannot be directly undertaken. Let our boys be encouraged to interest themselves in the literatures of Christianity, Judaism, Islam, and the classics of Greece and Rome. Then, without being asked to do so, they will recapture the Vedanta for themselves, for it is still available for recapture by anyone born in India and who is blessed with enlightened pride.

When straying from the studies prescribed for me when I was young, I read Bunyan's *The Pilgrim's Progress*, and chapters in the Old and New Testaments of the Bible, and later I acquainted myself with the thoughts of Socrates, Marcus Aurelius and Brother Lawrence, and although no one incited me to it, the joy and reverence which these things induced, turned me towards the *Upanishads*, the *Gita* and the *Mahabharata*. All spiritual search is one and God blesses it wherever and by whomsoever it is done. If I am today a devout, though very imperfect Hindu Vedantic, it is no less due to my contact with some of the sacred books of other people, than to the contemplation of what our own great ancestors have left us. Not by total exclusion from all religious and spiritual thought, but by an all-embracing acquaintance with and appreciation of spiritual thought of all kinds, shall we be safe and shape ourselves properly.

I have said all this believing it to be somewhat relevant to this occasion. I congratulate Mr. Munshi and all his good and eminent co-workers and associates of the Bharatiya Vidya Bhavan on their splendid achievement, of which the opening of this new mansion is an additional landmark of progress. I feel much honoured in having had something to do with it, however symbolic.

May the labours of the Vidya Bhavan in the cause of culture find their true fulfilment.

SOCIAL SERVICE

That which can be done by law, administrative orders or force, may be left to Government. But a family requires not only a father but a mother. Just as a family is guided by the authority of the father, and by the indescribable force called the mother's affection, which is also necessary for the happiness of the family, in a State, without trying to make the analogy too perfect, all the social service organisations conducted by well-intentioned men and women and especially women, are in the position of the mother. The poor people in the country, those who are oppressed and those who are at a disadvantage, require not only laws, regulations and monetary help, but a mother's affection, in the first place to soothe and in the second, to relieve distress. These things cannot be done by Government organisations.

Even if all the social organisations were to be clubbed together into an official federation and an expert honorary non-stipendiary officer were appointed to look after it, the ways of

Government would not suit a problem which requires something other than mere orders and regulations. For the solution of it demands affection, and for that reason every government in the world, even including that most perfect of all governments in regard to social affairs, the Soviet Republic, depends upon non-official voluntary service of a kind such as the one under whose auspices I have the privilege of speaking today. There may be Government help. The Governor's wife may be the moving spirit in it. There may be grants, there may be inspection and so on, but the moving force must be the urge in the human mind to help people in distress, the urge that I began by speaking of as a mother's affection.

No one is more aware than I of the fact that it is not possible to help everyone who is in distress by means of voluntary social service. We just touch the fringe of the matter. As our Indian proverb says, it is a drop of asafoetida in the ocean! Still, asafoetida is required in our preparations, though we use very little of it. I do not, therefore, want you to make light of voluntary effort. It is true that the Secretary of a voluntary organization may be dressed in beautiful clothes. It does not mean that her heart is not equally dressed in pity and sympathy. I am aware of the general criticism that is made of fashionable women who help the poor. It may happen that a Collector's wife may be very charitable while a poor man's wife is not. Poverty does not necessarily make people charitable. I do not blame the poor. But is it not right that we should encourage sympathy and charity to become the fashion? Let us then make it fashionable in truth. There is no necessary connection between ragged clothes and a fondness for social service. The moral is only this. Let us not make light hearted comments and by so doing discourage people from undertaking social service. Everyone is entitled to seek an outlet for the urge of affection which God has placed in every human being—sometimes it may be suppressed, sometimes it may find free expression. Therefore all these organisations require the encouragement of the newspapers, of public men, of Government and of those individuals who pass comments on others without doing anything themselves. All these things are necessary and I am very glad to know that in Free India there will be more and more of these organizations.

Do not think that social service work was a peculiarity of old Government House manners. Let me tell you that the new Government House will go on doing the same thing and that every man will do more hereafter in that direction than he ever did before. Our new Government in Free India will want the services of the existing and even more. It will require them to work harder and they will be bound to do so. Look at this organization. It was doing plenty of work before, but after the 15th of August it increased its work, widened its scope and took in more people. The Dewan Bahadur is not a fashionable young person hovering about Government House. Why has he joined this organization? Because that is the urge of the New India. Almost everyone will join this organization. Let all the organizations, the aim of which is to be charitable and to help people in their difficulties, work together. I am here, friends, as the official representative of Free India's new Government, to say that all these social service organizations are most welcome to the Government, and that everything possible will be done to help them in their work.

PROFESSIONAL SOCIAL SERVICE

I must confess I have been truly puzzled by the proceedings to-day. A lot has been said about the history of the institution and I have been thinking all the time of its future and what it is going to do hereafter. If anything could be smothered by too many influential people being in it, this institution must have been smothered long ago. I cannot understand, and rather dread, too many influential people at the top trying to produce results in the direction of social service.

When good men and women endeavour to achieve something, they deserve all our good wishes. I am here in my capacity as an individual and have accepted your invitation only in that capacity and not as Chief Minister. I will therefore, warn Mrs. Clubwala and her fellow intriguers that they will not succeed in committing the Government because of my presence. The fact that your request for grants, recurring and non-recurring, has been turned down should have taught you how unwise it is to reply on the smiles of princes and governments (laughter), and made you determined to work by yourselves, and to rely on yourselves. If you succeed, Government will come to your aid; but if you depend on Government, you may not succeed.

The promoters of this institution have entertained a number of students for training in Social Service. But I know what the students have in their minds. They want employment. If the promoters of the institution have raised such an expectation, they should fulfil it. No doubt there are number of institutions which want personnel trained in social service with a good university education. This is what might be called professional social service. Perhaps this is a contradiction in terms according to old-fashioned ideas; but it is a reality now. There are now young men and women who have come forward to serve as employees of social service organisations. I have no doubt that they will make themselves useful by doing social service. I am also sure that the institution will train them well for the work and get them posts worthy of their efforts. That however depends on the institutions which absorb them. There are a number of institutions which are called government institutions but which really are social service institutions. It is the fashion these days for governments pressed by the people to take on all kinds of work. Government have thus taken up co-operation, women's welfare, rural and medical service, etc., all of which I will call social service. The Government will need the services of young men and women for discharging these functions. I hope you will succeed in inducing the Public Service Commission to recognise the diplomas awarded by the institutions and I, for my part, will help you in your efforts in this direction, provided diploma-holders are well trained. It is not necessary that appointments to Government departments on the social service side should be limited only to the older people, advertised for usually. These positions might be opened to diploma-holders also. But that will depend on how the institution works, the staff it employs, the type of students you take in and the way you get through the training. It will take some years to judge these things. But I hope the training here will be good and the course neither too long nor too short.

The masses of this country though illiterate, are otherwise educated. They know the value of cleanliness, good behaviour, tidiness and all the other things that may be preached to them by trained personnel. Even those who dwell in the dirtiest of slums in Madras City know the value of cleanliness, that it is good to keep one's person, dwellings and surroundings clean. But they do not have the wherewithal to do it. All the efforts of social workers should therefore be to remove the difference in resources, to make a more just distribution of the resources of the country, to spread things a little wider, so that everybody may have a little of what there is. This effort is real social service.

In the old days, the very old days, it was the custom for people to be very charitable. Those who possessed something felt it was their duty, and they felt real pleasure, to give away what they had. They felt that to give was a greater pleasure than to possess or receive. Possession gave pleasure to the miserly; receiving gave pleasure to the active; but to the charitable-minded, giving gave much greater pleasure. The pleasure was greater still if the giving was done at a little sacrifice. This realisation however has disappeared these last many years. People have taken to thinking that giving is folly, that they should receive, possess and keep and that if at all charity is to be done, it should be in an organised way. As an old-fashioned man, I regret this development and I am rather worried about it. It is said that indiscriminate charity encourages pauperism. That is the beginning of the process I have referred to. We began to dislike private charity and now we have gone to the other extreme. There is almost no such thing as private charity now. That is my regret.

Somewhere in between these two extremes, we should find the golden mean. We should not be indiscriminately charitable as we used to be in this country in the very old days. But there is something very valuable in personal and private charity which is lost in efforts made by organisations such as we have in view, requiring employment of trained personnel, etc. What we should aim at is that we should catch hold of people who are well off—young men and women belonging to rich families—and attract them to social service and train them for it so that they can go into the houses of the poor and use their trained knowledge and their resources in the service of the poor. That will bring great success to social service work. Training people who merely wish to get employment will involve finding resources elsewhere for social service and depending on associations, governments. Governor's and Minister's wives and so on (Laughter).

All this is good in the absence of anything else. But thinking it out fully in the context of our country, I would rather that we try not to advertise for graduates, double graduates and other such men but catch the interest of the rich, persuade them to send their boys and girls for training, make them charitable-minded, get them to undergo a special training for social service so that they might use their wealth in the proper way in the service of the poor. I am sure we will not fail if we make such an effort.

I have known quite a number of young men and women of wealthy families who have gone into the Communist fold. When one examines the psychology of that phenomenon one will find that these young men and women are tired of their parents' ways and wealth and want to serve the people in another way. Personally I do not think that way is good or right. Instead of allowing the boys and girls to go that way we should draw them into social service institutions and train them to utilise their superfluous patrimony for the public good. They could be encouraged to spend their time and resources in a manner which would also please their parents. We will thus be able to remove the difference in resources among people and make the culture and knowledge of our country blossom forth. Professional social service is something which I dread. That is the point I want to emphasize. It is a contradiction in terms and nothing that is a contradiction will succeed.

I once again extend my good wishes to this institution and hope that Government with its welfare programme will find work for the people trained here. I have seen similar efforts in Bombay and elsewhere. Pupils there reach high standards and then they want to be sent to foreign countries for further training and on return at *Dharma* at the Prime Minister's place, for getting some new departments opened. That way, I think, is to tackle the thing from the wrong end. But even that way, I give my best wishes. I hope you will find employment for the boys and girls you train. I would advise you not to take in too many students, but select boys and girls of the right temperament—charitably minded, sympathetic and compassionate young men and women—who will put up with disappointments in life. Unfortunately, the system of education here is hard to change. It is so efficient that it cannot be changed. A bullock cart can be made to go in any direction at any point of the road, but a train can go only a particular way on rails. May be, a time may come when these trainees will be chosen in preference to others. I promise that if I should get to be in charge of the welfare services, I will do what I can to employ these young men and women.

TO WOMEN

I want you all, irrespective of creed or community, to help to establish goodwill among the communities in India. Men have quarrelled and have ruined the country. Women alone can save the country by undoing all the wrongs that have been done by men during the last few months. You have no hatred towards one another. If among you, you create a feeling of sisterhood, men will automatically become friends. To whatever class or community you may belong, keep your hearts pure and do not allow hatred to lodge there. Keep goodwill fresh. Work actively to create and increase this goodwill in other people's hearts also. Trifling though it be, our daily behaviour has a great effect on the cultivation of goodwill. Do not neglect little acts of courtesy. If all of you will exert yourselves for a few months to re-establish goodwill in India, everything else will follow. This is your particular work.

Nothing will come right in the evolution of the world unless you work hard in positive service to the State. Let all women restore goodwill in India by determined work. Equality of rights will come to you like a ripe fruit, without your asking for it. Women have served India nobly during the last few years and that is why they have now risen to the extent they have. Have not women risen to a higher level than that at which they were in, say, 1920? How did they attain to this? During these twenty-five years, women have served and suffered alongside men, and put in hard work in equal measure with men. So they have automatically risen to the level at which they now are. During the next few months or years, your work will bring you equality, whether men pass their codes or not. I do not object to any measure that you want.

You may change all the codes. But our temperament and our national culture will still govern everything. That is the unchangeable law. Therefore, ultimately, what we have to change for the better is not laws but the culture of the country. Men must learn to respect women and not to treat them as born slaves. The individual man must be taught to have consideration for his wife. With all due respect to our legislators—and I have been one of them—these things are not changed by law, but by culture and education, so that it is to them we must attend. That is why I ask you to be teachers. Nothing else will save womanhood, except having women teachers everywhere. Fight as strongly as you can that women shall become the teachers of boys also. There is no reason why you should not monopolise such work, because it is the mother who is most fitted to teach. I do not believe in the notion that in boys' schools men must be the teachers and in girls' schools women.

Women should be teachers in all schools—boys' as well as girls.' Then culture will change rapidly and education will progress and all rights will come.

ORPHANS

It gives me very great pleasure to have done something here in the way of helping orphans. Those who have nobody to look after them must be looked after by some institution. Those who do anything for orphans and who give alms to the poor buy tickets for heaven. In all religions this is prescribed and believed, and there is no difference on this point. We may pray in different languages, we may kneel in different ways, but all religions teach that we should help orphans and thereby get nearer to God. I have therefore every reason to be proud of the privilege you have given me of laying this slab and thereby promoting the cause of charity and of help to orphans.

All orphans to whatever community they may belong are my children and the children of my successor heads of the State of India. It does not matter what caps or shoes or trousers they wear, orphans are the same. In one way orphans are fortunate. Let them not imagine that they are miserable. They are looked after by a great State. Governments teach children to be good citizens. May all the orphans who come under the protection of this orphanage be good citizens of India.

I do not know whose inspiration it was, but it has given me great pleasure that on the day on which I have laid the foundation-stone to memorialise Mahatmaji's teachings in Queen's Gardens, I am laying the foundation-stone for an orphanage under a Muslim organizations. I am not so good a beggar as the illustrious father of my interpreter (Pandit Govind Malaviya). I cannot beg lakhs and crores of rupees and build a big University. But may I be enabled to see that this stone that I have laid will have bricks over it and that an orphanage will be established.

At the place where I laid the bricks over Mahatmaji's ashes they sang a song which said that Iswar and Allah were the names of God. That song was sung by Mahatmaji thousands of times before he died. He did not pray as we pray, but very sincerely. Most sincerely he sang that Iswar and Allah are the names of God and he prayed that men may be blessed with good sense. He has prayed so often that we may perhaps be allowed to hope that his prayers will bear fruit, and perhaps we may also believe that that is why we do not quarrel with one another now. God seems to have turned His face towards us and I think we shall not quarrel with one another hereafter. Though I am Governor-General, let me tell you this—let governments quarrel but let us not quarrel. Let all the quarrels be confined to governments, and let men and women, brothers and sisters, love one another.

My best wishes and blessings to the children that are in the orphanage and all those who will hereafter come to the orphanage. If I send you some orphans when your orphanage is ready, do not refuse them admission! I thank all the members of the organization for giving me this privilege and this opportunity of speaking to you. It gives me great pleasure to see you all assembled here without distinction of caste or religion, and helping me to perform this function. May this grace of God continue for all time.

RURAL SERVICE

May I, at the outset, congratulate the new graduates on their success in the examination? I am told this course is a very difficult one, that the period of five years is too long and that there are too many examinations each year. You have in all, to clear fifteen hurdles before being qualified to cure people. A technical and professional course by its very nature must be difficult, and one has to satisfy the examiners thoroughly before being certified as competent for professional work. You will not gain anything by making professional examinations easy or cheap. The glory of Madras, if I may say so, consists in the high standard maintained by the University of Madras.

(Cheers). I am glad that you young people here accept here this proposition. The University maintains the standard, very probably against the wishes of the students. But I would deprecate any attempt to bring pressure on the University to lower the standard and thus cheapen the degree and generally reduce the quality of service rendered by various professions. I am not quite sure whether such attempts are made in regard to all examinations. But I have no doubt whatsoever that the medical men that come out of the Madras University, whether they be physicians, or surgeons, have always rendered a good account of themselves and the hospitals and medical institutions in Madras have gained world-wide reputation. I am confident that the graduates who have been declared successful this year will also keep up the standards.

It is not enough if you secure passes, and even good passes at that. You will have to maintain your study right through your life. Medical education is not completed when you get a degree. Though I am a layman, I know enough being constantly attended upon by doctors. Medical education does not end with college education; every year in practice you should keep your knowledge growing and study the results of research made by other people on various matters. I hope all the new graduates will find suitable employment quickly. I know you will get plenty of work provided you do not want fees. There are a lot of people who want your services, but they are not able to pay the fees.

So far as improvements to the College are concerned, the Health Minister and the Finance Minister will look into them. I can only guide you. The Finance Minister can only work within his limits, while the Health Minister can make recommendations. However, the Government must have the capacity to pay for all these things. There appears to be some confusion about the proposal to run a shorter course. It is a fact there is much difficulty in the supply of medical practitioners for service in rural areas, and Government have been anxiously considering what they have to do in order to meet the difficulty.

It is easy to say that we want high quality. It is not easy to get in sufficient numbers, dectors who possess that quality and also are willing to serve in rural areas. Therefore, it is for that reason that we are attempting to produce some less qualified medical men—but adequately qualified to work in the rural areas—and for sending up difficult cases to major institutions where they could be better attended to. I think we should not sacrifice the requirements of the rural areas merely at the altar of high standard and equipment.

After all, all those who are qualified to practice under the present regulation are not quite so much up to the mark as one imagines. There are degrees of qualification even among those who graduate. If we desire to equip all rural centres with fairly good medical practitioners, it is not necessary that the entire lot should be subjected to various written and oral examinations. The result is, we have to consider the alternative. If we do not do so, the places of qualified medical practitioners will be taken by quacks, ill-educated compounders and others who cure some and ruin the health of others. There will be a vacuum and nature will not allow it and patients will like to take medicines from any one, be he an astrologer, an ordinary compounder or a yogi. I have just received a letter from one of my friends that a yogi held out hopes of curing his son's illness if he was paid Rs. 128 in advance; my friend has asked for my advice. This yogi is a big fraud. The police have been set on him and they did not succeed in getting him arrested or even when once arrested, in being hard on him. Our policemen are very kind-hearted people. But it is no good being kind-hearted to criminals. Our policemen are soft-hearted. They might sometimes bear arms but they are part of us. One of our brothers might become a policeman; on that account, he cannot suddenly become hard-hearted. Now this Yogi is far too rapid for the policemen to chase and has been going quickly from place to place.

That is why I say that if we do not send decently qualified people to rural areas, their places will be taken up by dangerous people. Persons who are refused admissions in the Medical Colleges and who are intelligent enough to read and understand things, and be of service to others, should be chosen and trained in a shorter course and sent to serve in rural areas. The more serious cases, they can send to the practitioners in urban areas. It is suggested that if conditions are improved in rural areas, doctors will be willing to go there, after taking their degrees. If conditions are improved in rural areas, then those places will also become towns. Then many of you will go there, no doubt. The main thing you all want is to earn money. It is not the rural conditions that deter you from going to villages. If you are sure of a salary of Rs. 500/- per month, never mind the conditions in the villages, you will go there. But money is not available there. People in the rural areas are poor and they cannot find money to run their families and also pay for doctors. Of course, people in the rural areas are now getting a slightly better wage and as such may be paying a little more for medical aid, but they cannot pay what the medical men expect and which I would like you to get. Therefore, do not blame us if we decide finally to put forward a moderate and quick programme and send qualified people. We may take a fairly lower degree of qualification for admission. And if we do that, do not tell us, 'you have gone back to the old L.M.P.' or that the unification has been destroyed. We want to have cheaper medical practitioners only in the sense that they come without much cost. It is not imposible to make the course less expensive. My own view is that book-reading and written examination should be avoided and practical training should be given just as you find in other technical courses where workers and other practically illiterate persons learn their work and do their job well. The rural medical practitioners, whom we want, will neither be actually illiterate people nor necessarily graduates. If they are intelligent people; they can probably make more money than the medical practitioners in towns. The Government is therefore still examining this proposal. The problem of rural poverty and rural medical service is as difficult as a disease like cancer. But I hope we will be able to do something.

I would like the young medical graduates to serve first in the villages. If you find you do not like to continue there, you may later go to towns. You should, when called upon to treat a patient, first listen patiently to what the patient has to say about the disease. It will help you to diagnose the disease correctly. You must keep an open mind and not follow always the text-book method. Don't think that money is everything. The Hindu scriptures lay down that you should perform your duty faithfully and earnestly without looking for any return. It has been stated in the scriptures that to whatever profession one belongs, one should consider one's duty far more important and essential, never minding the money part of it. If we do our work, that itself will be worship of God.

You belong to a great profession, a rising profession. You also belong to a State which has attained great glory all over the world for the standard of work. May you all live up to that reputation and tradition.

GRAM-KALYAN

The concept of the community project is based on the faith that *gram-kalyan* can be brought about by the joint efforts of the public services and the people if properly co-ordinated and directed.

During the next three years, there will be pilot plants of *gram-kalyan* in a number of places throughout the country. The essential principle of this plan is the gospel of work. All the people of the area must be persuaded to work in close and intelligent co-operation with the public servants and technical officers placed in that area. The community projects are pilot-plants of the idea of Bharat *Gram-kalyan*. The scheme will be implemented in selected places over three years. Thereafter it is expected that the work will stand on its own merit, and will be a model and an incentive to people in other areas, showing them the true and only way to happiness, namely, through work—manual work—the use of the body and intelligence with which the universal mother, Nature, has endowed us. The gospel of work was taught by Sri Krishna in the Gita. It was the theme of all Gandhiji's teachings through spoken word and writing.

When work is done by a group of people for the good of all, the task becomes a joy in itself. The assured fruits of work in the shape of water or food or a transport facility or a sanitary amenity is one thing, but in the association of one another in a task, over and above the material result, there is a joy issuing out of it like the *amrit* that issued from the ocean when the Gods churned it. This joy can be felt only when men actually work together. Weavers weave each for himself; but when they all meet in the *Pavadi*, the warping ground, and each works for all, there is a festive atmosphere and a joy which even outsiders can see at the place.

The first thing to be achieved in *gram-kalyan* is the production of food, good nourishing food, and enough of it.

The *Taittiriya Upanishad* taught the gospel of food production long before the present age of deficit.

annam bahu kurvita tadvratam
na kancana vasatau pratyachaksita tadvratam
tasmadyaya kaya cha vidhaya bahvannam prapnuyat

Make plenty of food. This is a vratam, a sacred duty and a pledge. No one, who comes as a guest, should be sent away unfed. Therefore by every means available *yaya kaya cha vidhaya* make and keep plenty of food.

But man wants not merely food for his body. His intelligence and spirit require help and guidance for growth and happiness.

The programme of *gram-kalyan* includes improved agriculture and reclamation of all available land, the utilisation of all local resources and the making of good feeder roads to facilitate transport and so link up all the villages of the area more closely together. But it also includes education, sports and entertainments.

The Projects include the provision of facilities for the fuller education of working children and vocational and technical training for those who have no family craft to follow. Again, what is necessary for the betterment of the health of the area will be attended to, especially in the matter of good drinking water and the proper disposal and utilisation of human and animal waste. In Nature's wonderful workshop, as Marcus Aurelius wrote down in his meditations—and the same thing was sung in the Upanishads in other words—all waste matter is reconverted by Nature into something fresh and useful. There is nothing that decays but is again ready to be re-made into fresh living substance. Everything is food for something else and man's skill consists in utilising this great law of nature and making his environment clean and tidy. Waste is wealth if man knows how to assist Nature, that is to assist himself.

Special attention will be given to what is woefully lacking at present, viz., proper medical attention for those who need it. The development of cottage and small-scale industries to absorb all those who now over-burden the peasant families is an important part of *gram-kalyan.* Efforts will be made to bring into being satisfactory housing conditions for all classes of people suitable for their work and in accordance with their way of living. Sports and community entertainments of a healthy, simple but exhilarating nature will be organized for men, women and children. More joy comes from an hour's good play than out of a purseful of money.

There are about sixty centres of this nature in India and in Madras six centres of *gram-kalyan* pilot schemes have been located in various parts. All officers of the Government will help to carry out the plans and in each district there will be advisory committees of disinterested men who will take a keen interest in the work for its own sake. Each project area will be divided into three blocks for co-ordinated development, each block comprising of 100 villages and a population of approximately half a lakh.

Success will depend on the spirit in which the people work and the officers guide and assist. It is not a gift from Government to the people. It is a plan of work for all the people including the officers of Government and the members of the Legislature, a plan of work for happiness wherein there is no fear of failure or disappointment, and wherein there is much joy, the like of which inspired men in olden days and which in recent times has almost been forgotten. The revival of this joy in working together and for the community's sake is, indeed, revival of life. It is a project of revitalisation of the community. It is called by the prosaic name of community project but it is *gram-kalyan*, a festival of Lakshmi.

DOCTORATE IN SYMPATHY

As I rise to speak, I have not yet overcome the physical exertion of giving away the prizes (Laughter). Not only was it a competition in various academic subjects, but the audience seemed to consider it a competition in the shaking of hands (Renewed laughter). There was a variety of impressions on my own hand. It was practically an examination I held among all the prize-winners as to who created the best impression upon me. Some were shy, some were expert and some were middling. This indicates a difference in temperament also, the brightest boy being generally very shy. But the medals given are so many that I wonder why medals have not been prescribed for music, singing, etc. I hope, Father Principal will before next year, institute a prize in music also.

You young men of the Loyola College are the most fortunate amongst the students of Madras because you have a beautiful hall. It is a grand possession; it must have cost a lot of money. I wish we had more such halls built for us by our forefathers because things were cheap in those days. I admire the courage of those who laid the foundation and had schemes for halls of this kind. Nothing less than the courage of the organisers of the Loyola College could have thought of and achieved this big hall. But as the Principal has observed, it is not a mere hall. It contains a world of 2500 souls—not 2500 bodies but 2500 souls. It is a great charge and I am lost in admiration of the unmarried gentlemen who have taken charge of so many children (Laughter). Without any practical experience of looking after even small families, they have plunged into this enormous task of looking after this huge family. But they have done it very well. I must say they have continued to do well throughout the years and I have been filled with admiration for their efforts.

There are many colleges in Madras—some of them managed by the Government, some by committees and some by Missions. But amongst these there is no doubt that this college has good reason to be proud of its history and the maintenance of order and discipline (Applause). I am pleased to see that the applause for this started from the students' end instead of the teachers' platform. It is only when we ourselves like, appreciate and are proud of discipline that the discipline will be of good quality. Otherwise, discipline will only be organised fear and nothing else. From the report that was read by the Principal and the prizes in gold and silver that I have given away, I see you have done very well in learning and emulating one another's achievements. When you are in any difficulties, you will get inspiration from these medals you hold. But among the 2500 souls, only a few got medals. I wonder if meal-giving is a good system at all. It does encourage the recipient to greater endeavour. I hope that those who did not receive medals will not mind the fact but will carry on with their studies because more medals are waiting for them than could have been won in the college. In the world, I have often seen that the medalists have not done very well (Loud laughter). I will tell you why I say this. I never got a medal (Renewed laughter). Do not worry about not securing a medal. When you get a medal, it is a very good thing. If you do not get a medal, it is a better thing still. Do not exhaust your energies in the college. Reserve some energy for the world beyond and you will get lasting medals there.

The Principal spoke of plans for more hostels and buildings. All those who leave this institution and secure good jobs must send part of their monthly savings to this college. It will do them good when they come back for a reunion of old college boys to see how their money is helping to expand the college in every way. Whether it is big or small, you should send your money to your own mother. I am sure that the principles inculcated in every college under careful guardianship will have already created this desire among the students and my appeal might be quite superfluous. You should be proud of your college. You should also contribute to the maintenance of that pride. In that case a day may come when the number of old boys will be so large that the Principal will not think of Government contributions at all.

Your Principal appreciates the difficulties of the under-paid Professors and appealed for generous help so as to make their lot a better one. This the Principal has done when he himself and his colleagues are content to earn a petty amount all their life time, without any prospect of a large salary. For, I think, that is the motto of the Society of Jesus. While the Principal, without thought of himself, was speaking on behalf of the unpaid Professors, I was all the time thinking how far the example of the Fathers of the Society of Jesus was influencing the students who left this college. Unless some of us at least make up our minds to live the lives which the Fathers here live like simple poor folk, the poor unfortunate country cannot bear the burden. The Principal spoke about the requirements of the college, the expenditure on staff, housing of the people, tuition fees, etc. If you make a rough calculation of these, you will see what a large sum is spent on each one of you, how the universities and colleges of this country spend a great deal on each one of you. Who is to pay for all this? The country, in the end, must pay for everything. If you have really earned your medals in Economics and Commerce, you can make a calculation of what the meaning of it is in terms of the burden on the people. These are no doubt excellent institutions. But can they support such institutions in growing numbers and keep them growing and prosperous? That is why I say that the burden is very heavy on the poor people of this country. We should take into account the average earning of the people and the amount of contribution they can possibly make to the national enterprise. You will then see that it is not altogether wrong on my part to think of this as a terrible vanity. We have lived in a particular atmosphere, isolating ourselves from the people of the country and we think entirely in our own isolated atmosphere. We think we should have these very necessary and very beautiful things. But what about the maintenance of them from below? There comes the vanity I have referred to. Unless a mircle changes the condition of the people, they will not be able to do proportionate justice in this country to themselves, as they seek to do to some of the people.

It is quite easy to give college education to a select few and it is also quite easy to give very good secondary education to a select few. It will be possible to build beautiful laboratories, in each of which 20 persons can do research. If you take the magnitude of the nation and the number of poor students, then you will understand why I speak in this language. I am only explaining why I sometimes feel greatly depressed when I contemplate on the method of it all. I do feel greatly depressed because the desire is so great, the eagerness is so large, but resources are so limited. I have said exactly what I feel. We should hope for the best. The responsibility lies on the young men to realise the realities of the situation and to make the utmost use to the knowledge they have acquired, the utmost use of the time they have spent here in order that they might lift the nation outside to something which could be decently co-ordinated in colleges like this.

You should compare your condition with those outside the college. The children outside are just like ourselves when we were young. Can they ever hope to come up unless we do something very great for them? The students must ask themselves, "Are we helping people forward. To what use am

I putting the knowledge I have gained. Do I waste my time or do I make full use of it?" There is no joy except when one serves others.

This is an institution that has grown up in the growing inspiration of Christ. We, in India, know how to venerate teachers throughout the world and I hope all the students of the Loyola College will remember and venerate the inspiration which gave them the education. It is religious impulse that has created this institution. If you wish in your lifetime to grow into anything great, useful and good, remember that you should also act under the impulse of religion. Religion is not knowledge. Religion is a feeling. The fundamental feeling is the one called sympathy. Unless you develop that high-grade feeling called sympathy in English, nothing will be achieved. If you harden your hearts from youth and refuse to sympathise, then you will grow into a monster or worse, into a piece of stone unorganic stuff. If you cultivate the art of sympathy, you will grow into something living and so help our country to grow up. That is what I call religious impulse. You all read the scriptures of Christians. In olden days, Hindu students used to walk away with those prizes and I hope this practice continues even now. You will find what I have said in the Bible. The sympathy I have referred to is what is called love or charity. It is this you have to develop, not mathematics or physics or science alone. I want you all to get a Doctorate in Natural, Spontaneous Sympathy and keep it with you throughout your lives.

TO MALAYAN STUDENTS

I am glad to be in the delightful company of young men and women who are so cheerful and industrious, who are learning something here in India and hoping for a big future for their country Malaya which they consider a country worth working for and living in. From the way in which you, who differ so much from one another, seem to like one another I can see that you have already solved your problem of heterogeneity. You feel united as one already. I have come to the conclusion that all of you are bright, cheerful, intelligent and smart people and that you care nothing at all for differences of a religious or racial origin.

I feel sure that the people of Malaya will soon achieve their independence. In fact, they are independent already. They should not lay too much stress on their dependence. We in India committed the same mistake in thinking we were dependent on the British while all the time British people were depending on us. Similarly, British depended on the Malayan people and not the Malayan people on the British. So, they are really independent and politically, they will be so soon. When you get political independence, do not quarrel among yourselves—Malayans, Indians, and Chinese. Any one who lives there and is fond of that country should be recognised as a citizen. Only such an independence will be worth having. There are many free countries in Asia, but Malaya alone will be in the position of a Switzerland in Asia, composed of people of many races but living as one solid nation. I hope you will set an example to Asia as Switzerland set an example for Europe. Do not make too much of these differences of language and other things.

The Malayan language is remarkably simple, free from many of the grammatical hurdles of other languages; this makes the work easy for both the teacher and the taught. I would advise you to stick to that language. Then you will have no trouble in that beautiful Switzerland of Asia. Malaya will be as good as Switzerland, if you are intelligent, united and patriotic. If you work together without any differences you will be greater than your great neighbour India. You are young and I am confident that you will make Malaya independent, great and prosperous. You must also learn to be happy and the secret of happiness consists in being happy under difficulties. For that you must cultivate, while young the spirit of cheerfulness.

There is no need for you to go to England or other foreign countries for your studies. You can come to Madras for your higher studies because the educational institutions here are good. I do not believe in sending our boys to outside countries for higher studies. Very often they do not return alone (Laughter) and sometimes they also learn a few worng things. Students from Malaya can come to India and can also treat this as their own land. I will see to it as will my successors that their applications for admission in colleges are not rejected Their presence will be an education for the students of this country.

The percentage of Malayan people involved in the present troubles in Malaya is very small. The trouble in Malaya is the historical consequence of what happened there. It will soon die out. It has attracted a certain type of gangsters and being young and adventurous, they think that it is worthwhile carrying on. Even after Ireland attained freedom, the Revolutionary Army gave trouble. Similarly, the Bengal revolutionary gang continued for a long time. The revolution habit will continue even after the purpose is achieved. It will take some time for that habit to disappear. I am sorry that some Tamils were hanged apparently for nothing at all. But there is no need to get alarmed or vexed about it.

I am happy to see that the President of your Association is wearing national dress for this occasion; it is good to cultivate this external symbol of unity. I hope that all of you will adopt your national dress on such occasions. Singapore is a good name and you should not give it up even after you are politically free. People from India will have to go there for trade and other purposes, and like Ceylon, you should not start saying. 'Do not come here'. The whole world is going to become one ultimately. Nations of the world have got themselves entangled in one net or another from fear. They will ultimately become one. The atom bomb is so terrible that nobody dares to use it. Hereafter there will be no war because the atom bomb is there. They have gone back to cold war and so abuse one another. Let us give our hearts to one another, let us be happy in each other's company. This is the secret of happiness in this world.

Happiness comes out of cheerfulness, kindnsss and gentleness. That should be the aim of educated Malayan behaviour.

ART AND THE CHARKHA

It has given me great pleasure to visit this exhibition. I have seen very good pictures that have been drawn and explained by living artists. It is not often that one gets the chance of seeing a picture and also the artist who has drawn it. I have learnt a good deal here this evening. We often offer worship to pictures and idols without understanding them. You have seen Nataraja or Kali-mata dancing. We do not know what it means, though the meaning must be there in any case. It is the most beautiful conception of posture that artists have ever conceived. The image of Nataraja, of which the original is found in a temple in South India, is known all over the world from the work of artists.

To my mind the meaning of the dance is that when God dances, everything happens in the world. The recent events in the Punjab, which we have reason to bemoan; the celebration of a marriage, the loss of a dearly-loved husband, the signing of peace by the big powers—all these happen when God dances in one way or another. So, therefore if anything unfortunate happens, we should neither weep nor lose heart, but remain courageous and think of it all as God's dance.

Anyone who can produce a good picture is worthy of our respect. Knowing the sacredness of his profession the true artist only produces good pictures. Pictures can do great good and also great harm. Every picture is Saraswati, and obsence pictures are a crime deserving of capital punishment. Our minds are bad enough—we need no assistance from bad pictures to make them worse.

I am very pleased to see spinning-wheels in action. Indeed we cannot celebrate any birthday of Gandhiji without the help of spinning. I have seen the window of a martyr spinning away in a manner which indicated expert knowledge of the craft. In her personal bereavement, which is difficult to forget, spinning must be a great consolation to her. Other people's words of wisdom carry neither conviction nor consolation; it is only our own work that enables us to forget our sorrows.

Talking of spinning leads me to the charkha, of which a part, and that the most important, has gone into our national flag. The wheel represents continuous action, uprightness, and justice. It comes to us from the greatest law-giver of India, Asoka. And the Asoka of our time is Gandhiji. This birthday is specially important to all of us who revere Gandhiji, because it marks the achievement of freedom which was his greatest achievement, but the achievement of goodwill and peace and harmony among all men.

MEDIUM OF INSTRUCTION

We have been told that the die was cast in favour of Bengali twenty-seven years ago. This decision, though taken in 1920 has not yet fully been acted upon and English continues to be the medium of instruction in the University.

The English language sits on our thoughts, even as this academic robe sits upon me. This robe may be beautiful and it may sometimes serve to protect you against the weather, but it is on the whole an inconvenience; in the same way, the English language may be beautiful, but it sits heavily on our thoughts and does not let them grow, or move about freely.

I should like to remind the graduates and the elite assembled here of the very fine argument that has been put forward by the Vice-Chancellor with regard to the foundations of a University. He adjured us not to think architecturally in such matters. He was right. Education does not rest on its foundations like a brickwork structure but grows like a living tree. The University gives the lead to the High Schools and the High Schools to the Primary Schools, very much like a tree ramifying from the stem upwards to the branches. That is how living things grow and yield. The University is the stem, High Schools are the bigger branches and Primary Schools are their offshoots.

It is also very hard to change an order of things that has prevailed for a long time. For instance, it is not easy for members of the I.C.S. to write administrative notes in Bengali all at once. I am not to be understood, however, as pleading for the 'go-slow' methods of the I.C.S. I am simply urging 'go-fast' methods on the Universities. I want you to adopt your mother tongue as the medium of instruction in the University of this Province. And I urge every University to adopt this formula.

There are to-day about a dozen important languages in India. Larger estimates are occasionally given, mainly in order to frighten us into thinking that India is just a big museum. But indeed even if India were a museum, with all its splendour and its variety, we should regard it as a grand one. Apart from that, the main languages we have in India are just about a dozen. That is to say, (1) Hindi, (2) Urdu, (3) Bengali, (4) Marathi, (5) Gujarati, (6) Kanarese, (7) Tamil, (8) Telugu, (9) Malayalam, (10) Assamese, (11) Oriya and let us add English to this list also. Each one of these dozen Indian laguages is the mother-tongue of not less than a crore of people —some of them of many crores.

In accordance with what prevails in Europe, each one of these languages is important enough for a separate state and a separate University. Now, therefore, each one of our great big Universities should, instead of all blundering in the same manner, recognise, by agreement or by tacit consent, the mother tongue of the area as the authoritative medium of University instruction. Accordingly, Banares may have Hindi, Ahmedabad may have Gujarati, Poona may have Marathi, Osmania may have Urdu and Waltair may have Telugu, Annamalai may have Tamil and Bombay and Madras may continue English, if they like.

English can and should be kept as a second language because

of its importance in international communication. By all means give English the importance it deserves, but please do not make it the medium of all instruction.

A University is not merely an organisation for the calling of Convocations and the manufacture of graduates. It is the fountain-head of culture and the inspiration for all those whose life-activities are to be guided in a cultured and civilised manner. It was, therefore, not an accident that under the old administration Governors were made *ex-officio* Chancellors of the various Universities in India. It was recognised that administration was intimately mixed up with education and the Governor was therefore placed at the top of the University as Chancellor *ex-officio*.

Till now, education in India has been no more than a slave's accomplishment. The education that will be imparted in India from now onwards, will be for a different purpose. It will no longer be that of a slave or servant but will hereafter be directed towards equipping our boys and girls to be citizens of Free India.

DISCIPLINE

In the course of his report the Rector has quoted high authority for the maintenance of discipline in life. Discipline is difficult and the atmosphere all round us is not favourable for its maintenance. It is easier to study and pass examinations than to control oneself and observe vigilant self-restraint, and that is why whenever anyone speaks to students, emphasis is laid on the need for discipline. Discipline is, as I have said, difficult to maintain. You will forgive me if I say that the difficulty is increased by the hesitation of those who are responsible for giving advice. Even here you will have noticed —if the Rector will pardon my saying so—how the language demanding enforcement of discipline is sought to be put in the months of other people than in that of the Rector himself. Friends we need discipline; I ask you to be disciplined.

May I take this opportunity of saying, plainly and firmly, that principals and professors of colleges must talk plainly and firmly to those who are in their charge and tell them—'We want discipline, otherwise we shall have nothing to do with you.' This must be clearly said and not put on to the shoulders of others. I do not mince matters. I tell you exactly what I feel. If principals and professors talk plainly and firmly and without hesitation, I know that the boys and girls who are my brothers and sisters, will understand them and follow their advice. Let there be no beating about the bush.

We should talk plainly to one another, though we need not be so brutal as the German Professor. I tender this advice to principals and professors because I have faith in our boys and girls. Were we not disciplined from time immemorial? Are we not born of the wombs of those who were resolutely disciplined, the descendants of the Munis and Rishis of the past?

Discipline was never more necessary than now, when, as the Rector has put it, we have entered on a new era since August 15, 1947. We have begun a new era in which nobody is responsible for us but ourselves. If we do not work hard and behave in a disciplined manner, our state of independence will be worse than our state of dependence. Independence is a mere context that we have achieved, a state of our environment, but the substance of Independence has yet to be gained by our own deeds. Must we not work to produce? Must we not study to learn? Must we not learn to behave well?

Therefore, friends, let us keep our ideals before us. Let us now unloose the reins, but hold the horse firmly and direct the chariot in the right direction. I shall not detain you any longer. I thank you very much for giving me the courage to talk plainly to you.

ALCOHOL AND FATIGUE

[A correspondent from Bihar writes to say that alcohol is

good for miners, as it is the cheapes and the easiest way to relieve fatigue. I was under the illusion that, thanks to Gandhiji's vigorous campaign for prohibition of over more than a generation this dreadful ignorance and killing superstition no more existed in India. Reformers in Bihar and elsewhere should see that this wrong belief lingering among the masses, and the classes even, is removed. The following is taken from Shri C. Rajagopalachari's *Indian Prohibition Manual*. It will dispel the wrong belief that people like the Bihar correspondent ignorantly harbour in their minds. —M.P.D.]

Some persons fancy that a little strong drink nourishes them and enables them to do their work. The best medical testimony declares that alcohol has quite the contrary effect. The hardest workers in fields, in factories and in mines, soldiers marching, and well-known athletes have all testified that better work can be done without strong drink than with it.

There is no nourishment in beer, toddy or wine. There is a trace of substances that may be called food in these drinks, but there is more nourishment in a few grains of rice or wheat than in a gallon of beer or toddy. The amount of poison in the drink far exceeds the small trace of nutrition dissolved in it. People fancy that there is nutriment in fermented drinks, because the alcohol deadens the feeling of hunger, which is a very different thing from being food.

The fact that toddy is drawn from the palm tree, or that wine is made from grape-juice, or beer and whisky from grains, should not make us believe that these drinks have the nourishing or other good qualities of the fruit or the grain. The alcoholic ferment alters the whole character of the thing, making poison out of food. The sugar which was food has been split by the ferment into two totally different substances, viz., alcohol and carbonic acid.

There is hardly one reputable scientist today who could be induced to assign any food value to alcoholic drinks.

Intoxicating drinks do not impart strength. They take it away. The action of alcohol is to lessen muscular power. This is the opinion of the best doctors and experts.

In a statement issued in January 1918, Surgeon-General Evatt, Sir Alfred Pears Gould, Sir Frederick Treves, Professor Sims Woodhead, Dr. Saleeby, and a large number of Indian and British physicians of repute and with good experience of Eastern conditions, testify to the fact that even a moderate use of alcohol, opium or other narcotic drugs "is harmful, especially in tropical countries like India. They are of no avall permanently to relieve physical and mental strain."

Alcohol does absolutely nothing to remove the cause of fatigue. It deadens the power of appreciating the result. If its action be frequently sought in this respect, deeper draughts are called for.

The temporary relief, exhilaration or feeling of strength obtained by the use of alcohol is just like the relief, or feeling of possession, obtained by borrowing from a relentless usurer. You are much the poorer for it.

Brookes, World champion tennis player, said: "Now, when I am more or less at the end of active athletics, the message I give to all young men desirous of attaining their highest efficiency in any line of sport is, "Do not touch spirituous liquors.',, W. T. Tilden said: "I am convinced that tobacco and alcohol do not refer here to the idiot who smokes all the time or attempts to drink all the liquor he can get. I refer to the moderate smoker and moderate drinker, if there are any. Both tobacco and alcohol are absorbed into the system, and in time have an injurious effect." Jeck Dempsey said: "I am a total abstainer and have always been one. I am opposed to spirits in any form for any young man who desires to compete in sport."

THE MADRAS EXPERIMENT

All the Congress Governments are committed to a policy of complete prohibition, and all have begun the experiment in right earnest and in their own way according to the circumstances in their respective provinces. The Madras experiment has been on since October 1st, 1937, and it is being conducted with the vigilant care and the thoroughgoing way which characterize everything that is associated with the name of the Madras Prime Minister. The enforcement was in the hands of the police working under the District Magistrate and the District Superintendent of Police assisted by a Prohibition Officer and a special Development Officer. The results of the experiment achieved so far have been noted in detail in his latest report by the Collector, Mr. A.F.W. Dixon, who was in no way pre-possessed in favour of the experiment. In his long report of sixteen foolscap typed sheets, he has in no way overdrawn the picture. He notes the large increase in the number of palmyra trees tapped for sweet toddy, as also the evident risk of their being tapped for fermented toddy if there was not the necessary vigilance; he also notes a few cases of smuggling of *gānja* and opium, and says that, without non-official help, it will not be possible to put a stop to smuggling; he also says that illicit distillation is being kept under control and appears to be going on only on a small scale and in a very secretive manner; he notes to some extent a tendency to drink methylated spirit and asks the District Medical Officer to write a Tamil leaflet describing the deadly effects of drinking the spirit; also an increase in gambling arising out of the attempt by former drinkers to relieve the boredom of the evening hours; but notes on the whole that "as month succeeds month without general signs of a deterioration in the situation, the chances of ultimate success become rosier."

This much regarding the success of the actual working of prohibition. When he comes to the effect of prohibition on the lives of the people, he notices a definite improvement all round and summarizes the large mass of information received from various resources and also his own personal impressions in about six sheets. Suffice it to say here that this is the deliberate conclusion he has arrived at as a result of his own impressions on observations:

> "Viewing generally the effect of prohibition on the lives of the people, I am convinced, after 3 months' experience, that prohibition is proving a great boon to the poorer classes in the District. Leading as they do a hand-to-mouth existence, they simply cannot afford the expensive luxury of drink which used to reduce the small earnings of the labouring classes to a miserable pittance, quite insufficient for the proper maintenance of a family. Drink brought misery into the homes of many thousands of the poorer classes in this District, misery in the shape of domestic unhappiness, insufficiency of food and crushing debt. Already in thousands of homes in this District conditions have changed to a remarkable extent. Domestic brawls have ceased a sufficiency of food is available, and the grip of the money-lender has relaxed. This has happened within a short space of four months. If the Act continues to be enforced not less effectively than it is now. I anticipate a great and permanent improvement in the material well-being of the peasants and labourers of this District."

Let us see how much these good results have cost. Said C.R. in his Budget Speech:

> "The net cost of Prohibition for the last six months of the Financial year 1937-38 will amount to Rs. 13,19,000 made up of Rs. 13 lakhs loss of Excise Revenue and Rs. 51,000 cost of additional police and special officers, offset by a saving of Rs. 32,000 on the excise staff previously employed in the District." Who will say that the moral and material results do not far outweigh this cost? Apart from individual cases here is a case of the moral effect of prohibition as applied to a mill area affecting 2,000 workers. Whereas these workers were irregular and inefficient before prohibition and night brawls were a regular feature of the area,

the workers have now become, regular and more reliable, the brawls have now ceased, machines are better looked after, "production increased and expenditure decreased. The outturn has actually doubled. Women were sickly, dirty and clad in rags. Now every woman has two or three *saris*, most of them have petticoats, and 50 per cent wash daily. Their financial position has improved, they have redeemed their jewels, which they mortgaged due to extravagance. Children are better clad and cleaner. Dwelling houses have improved and lights have been introduced into houses which were formerly unlit."

The United Provinces Government have also set about the task in right earnest and their experiment, like the Madras one, has several features which might be copied in other provinces... ......Too great an emphasis cannot be placed on the Excise Ministers of different provinces getting into touch with one another, comparing notes and trying in their own provinces the measures that have been tried with success in other provinces.

SUPPORT HANDLOOMS

I have taken up a few minutes of All India Radio in order to make an appeal on behalf of the lakhs of families who are still engaged in what made India famous throughout the world in the old days, viz., the noble crafts of weaving. The cottage handloom industry flourishes to-day as well as it did in ancient times and the fingers of the weavers are as deft today as ever they were. There are more looms today than there were in the old days. There was no competition whatsoever in ancient days, but to-day there is a giant competitor in the shape of mill-manufactured cloth which has copied the handloom and like an ungrateful child seems to kill the mother. The handloom weavers of our State are some of the best craftsmen in the world. Is it not a great pity that they are suffering and their families are starving on account of want of purchasers of their cloth? Should men go and buy mill-cloth leaving the handloom weavers in distress? I have no hesitation in assuring everyone that the cloth produced on the handloom in our State is as good cloth as any textile of that class produced by machinery. If it is a question as to whether one should buy mill-cloth or handloom cloth, I have no hesitation in making my most earnest appeal that you should prefer the handloom cloth and feed the families of the handloom weavers who follow an honest and noble occupation.

In spite of many decades of competition handlooms have survived. The mill industry with plentiful capital and a strong organization for production and distribution and for propaganda, has not been able to kill the handloom, thanks to the fly-shuttle and to the traditional skill of our weaver families. The handloom has maintained its own against the mill and is not only not dead, but is quite able to supply plenty of cloth, and very good cloth and cloth which is attractive enough to suit the tastes of consumers of real good taste, both men and women I am sorry the dyers by using cheap dyes have brought the reputation of handloom cloth down. Our people are very fastidious and particular about colour and it was criminal to let cheap dyes ruin the weavers' market.

No mathematical calculations or economic doctrines can be a substitute for human happiness where numerous families are concerned, who follow a traditional occupation based on family apprenticeship. The State provides no workshops, no training centres and no educational facilities. Everything is provided in the little cottage of the weaver and in his family life. No call is made on the State for land or capital or training institutes or supervision. This national asset we should not lose or allow to be destroyed by neglect.

My appeal on behalf of handloom should not be understood to be a letting down of Khadi. A social welfare movement should not deteriorate into an obscurantist denominational doctrine or metaphysics. The weaver prefers to use mill yarn. Let him do it. For it enables him to produce enough to maintain himself against the competition of the weaving mills. Khadi is also handloom cloth. The appeal on behalf of the handloom is automatically an appeal on behalf of Khadi also.

Let any weaver buy any hand-spun yarn that might be offered for disposal and made available to the weaver. If it is good cheap yarn, he will buy and use it up. Let him mix it as he likes with such yarn as he finds it necessary to use. Let us leave the matter entirely to the skilful weaver who knows his business. Let him adjust his materials and his requirements. Only, let us insist that he should not call his product by the name of 'Khadi', if he has used mill yarn or mixed mill yarn with hand spun. If he does not tell people that his cloth is pure hand spun, we need not put obstructions in the way of his normal weaving business. Both hand spun yarn and mill spun yarn may be woven on the handloom and the cloth is handloom cloth, though not Khadi or called by that name.

I earnestly appeal to every one to patronize handloom cloth wherever it may be available and for every purpose for which it can be used, in preference to mill-cloth. We should help the weak. We should save the handloom weavers and their families from starvation. We can make everything we wish out of handloom cloth, provided we pay a little attention.

No subsidies and other helps can come up to the help that the public can give. Ultimately any subsidy can help only if the public will buy. If the people decide to help the handloom weaver and buy his cloth which is both durable and decent our handloom weavers need not be unhappy. One out of every twelve families in our State is a weaving family that desires to maintain itself on honest labour and seeks to clothe the people for a very moderate wage. The children are brought up in the family craft without any assistance from the general public or the State. A part of the house is the workshop and family life is not broken up or endangered as in the case of factory work. A self-respecting and self-supporting section of the population of the order of six millions appeals to you and the appeal cannot be rejected. Buy handloom cloth whenever you want cloth. Do not let mill-cloth printed and made up to appear like handloom cloth attract you. Do not be deceived by such imitations. It would be a crime—deliberately to prefer the imitation to the real hand-woven cloth.

Freedom and political rights must rest on occupational balance. Political freedom cannot but break down if we neglect the foundations of national life. Every twelfth person in our State is a weaver. Do not let him starve.

CLOTH-MILL *vs.* HANDLOOM

[The following report of a Press Conference addressed by Shri Rajaji on September 8 at Madras is taken from the *Hindu*, Madras, of 9-9-'52].

"The question of reservation of the manufacture of *dhotis* and *sarees* to the handloom industry is not a question of yardage, but of human families whose care is the obligation of the State Government and therefore, of the Central Government", stated Mr. C. Rajagopalachari at his Press Conference today, reiterating the justice of the stand taken by the Madras Government in this matter.

"My demand on behalf of the handloom weavers that *dhotis* and *sarees* should be entirely reserved for this cottage industry" the Chief Minister said, "has been opposed publicly by the Minister for Commerce and Industry, Government of India, during his short stay in Madras. This opposition is welcomed by the mill-owners of Bombay and Ahmedabad and the piecegoods merchants here. Some persons have been much concerned over the personal aspect of the matter. It is not necessary for anyone to come to our assistance in maintaining our mutual goodwill and friendship. Mr Krishnamachari has said enough about it.

Only Sound Solution

"We are entitled each to defend our policies. I am convinced that this reservation, as I have proposed, is the only proper, just and economically sound solution for the conflict that has risen between the unprotected handloom industry and the long-protected mill industry. We are concerned not with private feelings, but with the merits of the handloom cottage industry and its present position arising out of its dependence for yarn on the mill industry and the competition of the mills in a field which was entirely the monopoly of the Indian handloom all through the ages up till recently. The mills have plenty of scope to produce cloth that could be tailored and could be used otherwise, *Dhotis* and *sarees* are peculiarly Indian and could give adequate employment to the five million people engaged in the handloom industry. The total number of people engaged in the weaving section of all the mills in India would be much less than one lakh of workers. Actually, it has been calculated that they would be only 60,000. The number of men, women, and children depending on the handloom in Madras State alone is, I think, five millions. The question is not a question of yardage, but of human families whose care is the obligation of the State Government and therefore of the Central Government also.

A Practicable Compromise

"I am afraid the Union Minister made some error in his statistics; but nothing much hangs on that argument. You may take it that the mill production is round about 4,000 million yards per annum. The handloom production may be taken to be round about 2,000 million yards per year, most of which are *dhotis* and *sarees*, whereas mill production of *dhotis* and *sarees* has not been even upto 50 per cent of total output. *Dhotis* and *sarees* have been a good field for exploitation for mills only in recent times. I would call it pilfering of pattern from the handloom, to which the mills are not entitled. Considering the under-employment prevailing among millions of handloom weaving families, who cannot switch over to any other employment such as a handful of people in England or Scotland could manage to do, it is really ridiculous to talk of the handloom weavers of India going over to other occupations. It really amounts to a policy of allowing one million families in Madras or three times that number all over India to be wiped out of existence. This will not happen. Human beings do not allow themselves to be wiped out. Problems will be created in the meanwhile which Governments will not be able to solve peacefully. I wish to avoid this and have suggested a fair and practicable compromise which could be smoothly worked.

Industry Cannot Be Allowed to Die

"We cannot allow the handloom industry to languish and die. That is the equivalent of the policy underlying certain statements made on this subject. It is absurd to go abroad for marketing the handloom cloth instead of providing for handloom weavers what is due in their own country within whose social conditions and tastes and manners, their avocation has grown. It has been stated that there will be a cloth famine if *dhotis* and *sarees* are reserved for handloom cottage weavers. This is a groundless apprehension. A few months ago, the Handloom Weavers Society in Madras had Rs. 4 crores worth of *dhotis* and *sarees* on hand which they could not dispose of and which they wanted the Government to buy. Does this indicate a cloth famine?

"If any one says that people took to handloom on account of a boom, it would be quite wrong. Nobody takes to handloom weaving unless he is to that avocation born. No one can learn to weave crores worth of cloth simply by way of speculation. It is because he is a weaver by birth, and is trained to do it from his early infancy that he weavers cloth. The mills with their machinery and paid labour and their extra-ordinarily strong organization can produce 4,000 million yards of cloth other than *dhotis* and *sarees*, which can be used up for all requirements against nudity and which can also be exported and easily marketed abroad.

A Deepavali Gift to Weavers

"The whole of the argument against my proposal arises out of want of imagination. I do hope that the Minister at the Centre will make up his mind and induce mill-owners of India to make a Deepavali gift to the handloom weavers this year. It will be a memorable step towards peace, stability and prosperity, and God will bless it and make it fruitful".

The Chief Minister was asked whether the public could afford to bear the high cost of handloom cloth. He replied: "The public and the weavers have a way of adjusting themselves. The public cannot bear the starvation of the weavers either".

When he was asked whether it was not a fact that mills reserved a certain percentage of their output to *dhotis* and *sarees* at the request of the Government, the Chief Ministers said that when the Government asked for that, they could also demand the stopping of production of *dhotis* and *sarees*.

Replying to further questions, the Chief Minister said that the Madras Government and the Union Minister had discussed this subject and were entitled to discuss and consider further all its pros and cons. Probably, the Union Minister allowed himself a little loud thinking when he was put the question by businessmen. "Then is no question of my replying to Mr. Krishnanachari. I was presenting my case again because the public have been disturbed over a trifle. Whatever the Government may do or may not do, the Government here or at Delhi, let us buy only handloom *dhotis* and *sarees* for the next Deepavali and not any *dhotis* or *sarees* made of mills".

NOTES

"Mahatma"

Four handsome volumes of this biography of Gandhiji by Shriyuts D.G. Tendulkar and V.K. Jhaveri have already come out. They give an year-to-year account of Gandhiji's public activities, with copious extracts from his writings, speeches etc. They also abound in photography interesting cartoons, and facsimiles of some of Gandhiji's important writings. The writers seem to have for the present restricted themselves in giving a factual narrative without their own comments thereon. Possibly they propose to do so after completing the whole factual life-story.

The volumes will be important for students and producers of smaller biographies of Gandhiji and as a reference book to trace particular subjects. Being in the form of a *de luxe* edition only they are too costly (being Rs. 25 per volume for ordinary workers and small libraries. But they should certainly be found in the collections of the rich and in large public libraries. I hope they are finding their patronage wherever the English language is spoken and Gandhiji is died through English. The fourth volume brings Gandhiji's narrative to the end of 1938.

Wardha, 1-9-'52

K.G.M.

Utter Pradesh Land-Gifts

Till the 13th of this month the figure of hand gift in Uttar Pradesh is 3,10,068 acres. The number of donors is 11,842. Of the land received 7,590 acres were distributed among the landlord.

A GREAT FOUNTAIN OF AMRIT

An angel has gone back to his place. Grief is Gomtibehn's and for the rest of us left behind. For him the peace that was his right has been awarded. How and why should we grudge it? Let us bear our grief in prayers and humility.

Tears alone befit the occasion, words fail to express even in part what feelings even do not fully express.

Gomtibehn knows how great Kishorlal's affection was for me, Lakshmi and Devadas. We have lost a great fountain of *amrit* in him.

I did not realize that it was fact and not an ugly dream when I read the news. I had to read it over again and look round so as to accept the fact as fact.

My love to all who grieve.
Madras, 10-9-'52 C. RAJAGOPALACHARI

TRAINING FOR HAPPY HOME

[Shri Rajaji is our venerable wise old man of India today. Whatever he speaks is always refreshing and has a ring of rare originality and affectionate wisdom, chastened by age and experience, profound learning and deep meditation. The other day at Madras he was called upon to address the All-India Home Science Conference which was having its second session in that city. In his unique simple style he gave to his audience some plain home truths which are worthy of attention. Home Science is a new Art in our college studies, I think, imported from America. It is fast on its way to becoming fashionable in educational circles. It is therefore well to go into it. It seems it is taken for granted that this old art of home-keeping is a science and is meant for girls. Is it so? I thinks the art is good for boys as well. Much of this subject will, on examination, be found to be useful to us irrespective of our sex. The following is reproduced from the report that appeared in *The Hindu*, Madras, of September 24, 1952.—M.P.]

Among the many things that confused a person like me who belongs to an older generation', Mr. Rajagopalachari said, 'was the holding of such All-India Conferences.' It seemed to him that by such conferences, they were trying to make a very big country a small place of compressed size. They wished to have All-India conferences for everything conceivable. He thought that the limit was reached when somebody proposed an All-India Children's Conference! He could not understand how all the children could be brought together or the few brought together could be made to represent the whole of India. Home Science was again a matter concerning every home and they wished to have an All-India gathering to discuss principles of running homes which were different from one another and of infinite variety. So he would congratulate the adventurous ladies and gentlemen who had organized the conference.

Asking the gathering to forgive his ignorance of the subject, Mr. Rajagopalachari said that "now all culture, especially home culture, in India has been raised about four feet from the old level". The old level was on the ground. They sat on the ground, ate on the ground, and taught on the ground. Now, they slept on a cot and dared not sleep on the ground. They ate from a table and sat on a chair. "In fact, we do everything four feet above ground level. That is the great difference between the old culture in which I was born and the present culture for which you are preparing through Home Science classes in secondary schools and colleges". Saying that he was not joking, but only expressing "a universally applicable truth", Mr. Rajagopalachari observed that today even the fire-place was four feet above ground and they cooked either standing or sitting on a chair. "Do not go away with the impression that I do not like change. I like change. But let us not imagine that we have lifted the whole of India by four feet. We have raised only a few families to this extent. The older home science was practised entirely on the floor and it wold be some time before you can fit the new science into it."

Science of Family Happiness

Nobody would imagine that Home Science was "taught", simply because one learnt laundry work or some cooking, Mr. Rajagopalachari said. Home Science was a much bigger thing, "It is the science of family happiness. It includes quite a number of subjects." Good cooking, good house-keeping, and things like that by themselves would not make a family happy. "You must learn how to marry and live a married life. That is true Home Science. Home is made by married people and children and the science deals with that subject. Please remember that Home Science is not preparation for a profession or a trade; but it is preparation for marriage". They might imagine that he had said something funny or the laughter might be the natural reaction to mention of marriage. "I am telling the plain truth here. Home Science is it conceived for helping young people to live a good married life and make the home happy."

Pointing out that training in courses like this was utilized by people to become teachers in such courses, Rajaji observed that, in this manner "most of their attempts in this world got amputated". They prepared a number of young people to serve as teachers in the very process without getting to the end of the training, namely, getting homes filled with mothers who knew how to make a home happy. Rajaji said that what he wanted was that the aim of the Home Science curriculum, whether in the secondary school or in the college, should be to deal with the science of happiness in the home and education should end in "a practical application of what they learn to the homes to which they go."

The first thing a girl should learn, Rajaji observed, was how to make her husband happy and her children happy. Most college girls easily lost their temper. The loss of temper was due to strain—the strain of too much study for the purpose of passing examinations. He would warn young girls that "married life will involve greater strain, more even than the examination-life you are going through. You must know how to control your temper and how to speak the truth. When speaking the truth to one you love and for whose feeling you care, truth must be soaked in affection."

Mr. Rajagopalachari pointed out how strain made husbands lose temper when speaking to their wives and wives when speaking to their husbands, and said that the marital loyalty preached to them would enable husbands to bear with the temper of their wives and *vice versa*, but would not make for happiness or positively for joy in the family. They might be able to iron the cloth especially when they were provided with a four-feet high table. But it was difficult to iron out the wrinkles on the husband's face. For that, they required an attitude of piety and self-control. All this was Home Science. These were aspects of the science which were difficult to teach. That was why he said that Home Science supplemented in certain respects what they had to learn generally. They had to learn self-control, kindness, affection and very many other things from literature and poetry. Thus what they learnt as Home Science was not the whole of Home Science. A truly scientifically trained young man would learn to work with very little apparatus or sometimes with no apparatus. Similarly, the Home Science must be capable of being practised without electrical switches and tables. "You must know how to get down from the fourth potential to a lower potential", Rajaji concluded.

MESSAGE OF THE NEW 'KURUKSHETRA'

Journals of particular organizations have a tendency to become printed self-flattery, which bores the ordinary reader whom we wish to interest in us.

Any number of shadows do not make substance. Any number of desires do not make an achievement. What produces is work. Desires are good, but they must be urges from within and by being prevented from exhausting themselves in expression, made to create pressure. Recording and printing that we wish to do this, we wish to do that, we plan for this, we plan for that—is suicidal. The record must be only of what we have achieved. Let us avoid finding pleasure in and cultivating a taste for drum-beating and trumpet-blowing. It is no substitute for work.

A certain foreign style has been alluring us and destroying our old tradition of *maun* and quiet service. Am I running counter to the general stream? I am sorry for that, but some one must warn.

Not advertisement, not beautifully illustrated journals, not noise and self-praise, but manual work will save us from shame and disaster.

Our loving mother is Earth, the mud that is waiting to be embraced. It will give us everything we want, if we work at it. Work, hard work—down at manual level. Decentralize and do not over-departmentalize. Let there be no supervisor except the internal watchman. This is the message of the new 'Kurukshetra'.

Madras.
Shri Jayanti Day

[*Kurukshetra* is the name of a magazine started by the Community Project Administration (C. P. A.) of India as its monthly organ. The article reproduced above was the message Shri C. R. sent to the Journal at its inauguration. It tells the C. P. A. in a few beautiful words what people generally tell and talk to one another about such Government ventures in publications. These very often slip down to talking more about themselves than actual achievements. The example of 'Grow More Food' during the last five years must be noted here. There was a plethora of paper propaganda consuming scarce paper more than producing any more food. Such 'printed self-flattery' is more often an eyewash than real report of things done. It would be interesting to know how much Government spends after photos etc to bring out 'beautifully illustrated journals' and advertise small little things casually or ceremonially done once in a while and not as a constant *yajna* that is really wanted. It would be as well Government' stopped such really unnecessary and no way helpful expenditure after self-advertisement or 'printed self-flattery'. Work is its own propaganda and the surest at that; that must be enough for us.

BAD EFFECTS OF TODDY AND BEER

I have just read in the course of a report in the Press of the Prohibition Week celebrated in Bombay that Dr. Jivraj Mehta has referred to and refuted a nutritional claim made on behalf of toddy by Prof. Julian Huxley.

Some 24 years ago I read an article signed by Prof. Julian Huxley referring to the enzyme and B. Vitamin content of beer and toddy over and above the admittedly harmful content of alcohol. This was not a plea for alcohol but a plea for something that supplied B. Vitamin although it contained alcohol (4 per cent in the case of beer and 8 per cent in the case of toddy is the alcoholic content). When I saw this in 1931 I immediately got into touch with Col. McCarrison, the illustrious nutritionist, who was then working in our country. He authorized me to say what I thereupon printed at page 25 of my Prohibition Manual which I quote below, as my book is now out of print:

> "It is sometimes claimed for beer that it contains enzymes, and is therefore good; and similarly that toddy contains Vitamin B and is therefore useful. In non-technical language the enzyme in beer is the malt that was in it, and the Vitamin B in toddy is nothing but the yeast in it. Enzymes are secreted by cells in our bodies, if we keep them in healthy efficient activity. Yeast Vitamin can be readily obtained in many ways without having to consume alcohol for it. Col. McCarrison, our best expert in nutritional research, has stated: 'To drink beer in order to ensure efficient enzyme action in the body is as unnecessary as to drink toddy in order to ensure a sufficient supply of Vitamin B.' "

Having said this, now let me say all about it as it may be useful at this juncture.

Alcohol has a degenerative effect on the structure and functions of the human body, especially on the brain cells. The higher centres of the brain are the first to suffer under alcohol. Self-control is one of the highest functions of the brain. Alcohol weakens this. Many persons recognizing this fact consume a large quantity of liquor as a preliminary to the commission of crime.

The impairment of reason and judgment by alcohol is well recognized. The drinker is not able to value events properly. A light affront or a trifling matter may appear to his unbalanced judgment a matter of great gravity. Alcohol incites the baser instincts of combativeness and licentiousness. These effects are mistaken for courage and increased vitality.

The first result after the consumption of a small amount of alcohol is a heightened sense of pleasure and wellbeing. It is this that gives alcohol its power over men. Alcohol diminishes the feelings of hunger and weariness and sends an increased flow of blood to the skin causing a feeling of warmth. Its first and apparent effects are stimulating. But real effects are to depress the nerves which fail to register true conditions. It blunts sensibility. It causes dissipation of heat by sending the warm blood to the surface. The depressant effect of alcohol upon the higher centres of the brain produces a lessening of restraint and a lowering of standards and a slackening of checks upon the animal nature. This is the reason why speech becomes readier. Confidence grows as efficiency declines.

The first effects of stimulation of alcohol is like the increased pace of a horse when the reins fall away from a drunken rider's hands. The brain and the nerves correspond to the rider and the reins; the muscles of the body are the horse. Energy is let loose and, therefore, soon exhausted.

Dangers

A famous British physician, Dr. Saleeby, wrote in April 1926: "All first-hand scientific students of alcohol from Sir Charles Sherrington, President of the Royal Society, and Sir Humphrey Rolleston, President of the Royal College of Physicians, downwards are agreed that alcohol from first to last in health and in disease is not a stimulant as mankind had so long believed but a narcotic. It mocks us as a stimulant, because simply it narcotizes control, and lets loose and therefore exhausts our reserves. Why reserves? We have known for a generation that alcohol paralyses the white cells of blood, which are the defence army of the body."

Alcohol inflames the throat and the lining of the stomach. It hinders digestion, by coagulating foods and precipitating solutions. It permanently dilates the blood vessels, inflames the tissue of the liver, poisons the heart-muscles, and causes accumulation of fat therein. It prevents proper nourishment of muscles by robbing them of their oxygen. It hinders the functions of the mind by paralysing the delicate cells of the brain.

Alcoholism is a term denoting acute alcoholic poisoning. It occurs as a result of overdoses taken by habitual drunkards. But there is a disease, sub-acute alcoholism, from which the habitual taker of moderate dose suffers. The symptoms are carelessness of dress, habits, desires, welfare and family affection which are all subordinated to a craving for drink.

Prof. John Hay of Liverpool University has written: "It is not properly recognized by many people that the alcoholic patient, or even the moderate drinker, has his resistance to infection lowered by his alcoholic habits." The British Board of Education syllabus has it that "alcohol lowers the resistance of the body to disease."

Sir Victor Horsley, the great English doctor about whom the British Medical Association passed a resolution, when he died in Mesopotamia in 1916, that the nation owed him a debt of gratitude, presents the following tabulation of the diseases caused solely or in part by the use of alcohol:

Diseases due to alcohol alone: Acute alcoholic poisoning; acute mania; delirium tremens; chronic alcoholic insanity; alcoholic epilepsy; alcoholic neuritis; nevalcoholic paralysis.

Diseases of which alcohol is frequently a determining or contributing cause: Pharyngitis; arterio-sclerosis; gastric catarrh; increased susceptibility to inflammation of the lungs; congestion of liver.

Contributing cause: Pharyngitis; gastric catarrh; congestion of liver; cirrhosis of liver; fatty liver; albuminuria; Bright's disease; gout; glycosuria; inflammation of the skin; functional disorders of ovaries and breasts; dilatation of heart; fatty heart; arterio-sclerosis; increased susceptibility to inflammation of the lungs; consumption; chronic dyspepsia; dilatation of stomach; bronchial catarrh; increased susceptibility to the inflammatory diseases of the eye; epilepsy; melancholia; hysteria; dementia; idiocy; sun stroke, erysipelas; blood-poisoning; tubercle; syphilis; diphtheria; cholera and lead poisoning etc.

No Nourishment

There is no nourishment in beer, toddy or wine. There is a trace of substances that may be called food in these drinks, but there is more nourishment in a few grains of rice, especially if not over-polished, than in a gallon of beer or toddy. The amount of poison in the drink far exceeds the small trace of nutrition dissolved in it. People fancy that there is nutriment in fermented drinks, because the alcohol deadens the feeling of hunger, which is a very different thing from being food.

The fact that toddy is drawn from the palm tree, or that wine is made from grape juice, or beer and whisky from grains, should not make us believe that these drinks have the nourishing or other good qualities of the fruit or the grain. The alcoholic ferment alters the whole character of the thing, making poison out of food. The sugar which was good has been split by the ferment into two totally different substances, viz., alcohol and carbonic acid.

Tonic Wines?

Dr. Robert Hutchinson, physician to the London Hospital, wrote about tonic wines: "The use of these wines can on no grounds be recommended. On every ground their manufacture and sale should be strongly deprecated by the medical profession."

The Select Committee on Patent Medicines appointed by the House of Commons in 1914, after a thorough investigation came to the following result embodied in their report: "There can be no doubt that many persons acquire the drink habit by taking these wines and preparations."

The Committee exposed the claims of these preparations to contain nutrition by its finding that alcohol cannot contain meat extract in solution and that any medical man desiring to administer meat extract would do so without mixing it with alcohol.

Some people believe that alcoholic beverages help digestion; on the contrary alcohol injuries the digestive organs. Alcohol hardens food, whereas for digestion food has to be softened. Alcohol weakens the gastric juice by precipitating the pepsine in it. Alcohol deadens or stupefies the delicate nerves of the stomach. This is the cause of the false relief obtained by the use of alcohol when there is pain in the stomach. This leads to no cure, but to worse forms of the complaint. Rest for the stomach and a change of diet are what is wanted in such cases. Alcohol leads to inflammation and injury of the stomach glands. Alcohol injuries, besides, the heart, the liver, the kidneys and the lungs.

MY SCHEME OF ELEMENTARY EDUCATION

The present Madras Government have given up my scheme of half-day schools. My plan was based on the conviction—which was confirmed by educational officers of highest rank and experience—that three hours attendance was quite adequate for the purpose and would leave nothing out of the present elementary school instruction. But the crude arithmetical notion that whole-day schooling would give double the advantage that could be got from a half-day school prevailed and my scheme has been scrapped.

Education has been confounded with preparation for soft jobs and has ended in becoming a process of mass disablement in a stupid gamble generating all the bad qualities that go contrary to social co-operation. Seeing that schooling has brought Government posts and soft jobs to a large number of boys belonging to the upper maddle class, it is thought by a fallacious process of reasoning that if every child got that kind of schooling, every child could get such jobs and positions. This is of course impossible. The futility has already been amply demonstrated and the frustration will grow with accelerated pace. But jealousy destroys reason. The good is made to look bad and the bad appears to be very good.

To anyone with an understanding of the mind of the child it is revolting to see children of tender age shut up in the school-room practically the whole day. And what an unloveable person sitting there in charge all the time! There is a sham of an interval in the hot middle of the day which is mostly taken up by walking the distance from school to home and back. It is revolting, again, to anyone with a moral sense to see one teacher pretending to 'educate' two and even three standards simultaneously. The waste of time involved in keeping a child shut up through the entire working day for four long years is terrific.

The whole thing is a vicious circle of fraud, waste and dreary oppression of children and it goes by the name of elementary education.

A stupid notion has been propagated among uneducated families that education at all stages is a job-producing mystery and that it is quantitatively increased by the number of hours the child spends in the school. The idea is that if school-going gives an advantage in the new world, it is doubled by doubling the hours, and cut down by half if any one reduces the hours!

To the Montessorian principle that through the child's interest and pleasure the mind of the child should be drawn out and the Gandhian principle that not mere manual activity but useful work is the proper medium of instruction, I felt that we should add the principle of communion with the current life of the village. This is of course the opposite of education as contemplated by those who despise the child's family life and contemn his surroundings and whose concern is how to get the child away therefrom.

The Pestalozzian principle of teaching through muscular sense is not the same as the Gandhian method of teaching through work. Mere muscular activity has not the value or meaning of real work. Work has a social meaning which mere activity has not. Making a pot or stitching a shirt or weaving a towel or even preparing the clay for the potter or sweeping the floor of a house or tidying up a workshop is something over and above mere manual activity. Doing something useful is a chapter in real life and a lesson in social co-operation.

The exigencies of the situation as well as the desire to emphasize that the work in basic education is only a medium and not concealed child-labour, led to the running of basic schools with old style literary teachers very imperfectly trained in some craft. Plenty of money is spent on them to enable them, after a brief and imperfect course, to function as craft-teachers. I have no faith in these made-up teachers of crafts. I believe that this has led to waste of money and has served greatly to discredit the Wardha Scheme itself. I am convinced that more can be silently learnt from an illiterate craftsman who lives by his craft and who knows it from 'A' to 'Z' than from a literate imposter who looks upon what he has learnt as a qualifying course for himself. Indeed, the status and respect that the illiterate farmer or craftsman would attain in my scheme is itself a social gain and an education in citizenship for the children who otherwise get to believe that school-going children are a different caste from the cobbler or the village blacksmith or weaver or peasant.

There will be difficulties to be faced in every new system, but we may not discard all proposals for that reason and stick to a bad system. We must clarify our basic ideas and find ways to overcome such difficulties as come in the way. Do we want primary education to be a gamble in which most of the entrants lose all and gain nothing, or shall we make it a training for citizenship? This is the fundamental question to be answered.

CANCER

Some honest physicians and statisticians boldly gave out their view that from a study of figures they felt that cigarette smoking was one of the main causes for the occurrences of cancer among otherwise healthy men and women.

Now cancer is a terrible disease and men and women, naturally, are averse to taking any chances with it. When the above opinion was published there came a quick and accelerating drop in the consumption of cigarettes.

The cigarette trade is a highly organized business and it is an all-world trade that has absorbed a tremendous amount of a capital and human energy. The "rash" announcement of scientific apprehension about cancer was not to the taste of the cigarette trade-bosses. The mischief however had been done and it took some time for the trade to open its eyes and deal with the matter. But not much time was lost—soon everything necessary was done and now, doctor after doctor, some of them not very famous otherwise or known for medical or hygienic research, are one by one coming out with small communications which secure attractive space in the daily press of all countries. The daily press is always in an awkward position with advertising businessmen.

It is now pointed out by men with medical degrees attached to their names:

1. That cancer is caused by several other causes besides cigarette smoking.

2. That it has not been conclusively established that cigarettes cause cancer.

3. That quite a number of cheerful people have resolved to continue smoking cigarettes in spite of the medical opinion recently published, even those who have won running records and the like.

4. That it is possible the mischief is due to the paper and not the tobacco, and cigarette manufacturers are philanthropically busy improving the quality of the paper; etc., etc.

Now these and other informative points are set up against the adverse medical opinion. It may be interesting, but who wants absolute proof that snake-bite is fatal before desisting from playing with cobras! Most men and women do not like to develop cancer, either immediately or later on in life, and they prefer not to take a definite risk in the matter. Trade is for human happiness. It will not do to ask people to take risks with health for the sake of trade.

(Reproduced from "Alert", Jan.-Mar. 1955)

VAANARA VILAAP

[The ban on export of monkeys has been lifted as transport conditions have now improved: A Health Ministry news-item].

Know you not what they'll do with us
In whose hands in callous cruelty
You trap and place us for a little pelf?
If you are tired of your cousins dumb,
And you think our number robs you of your food,
Send us to lethal chambers
Or shoot us down among our jungle trees.
O give us sudden death, but do not make
Victims of us for tortures inconceivable,
More horrid than any disease
That man has earned by his various sins.
Have the tears of dumb creatures
No power now to move your hearts?
Put us not in a hell, crueller far
Than any Sita's enemies could devise.
We cannot speak the tongues of men
But the gods do hear and understand.

We did not grow to be quite like men,
And may be it was well we didn't
And we remained the innocents we are.
O stop this sacrilegious crime
On the heroes of your sacred book,
This cruelty on the nearest cousins that science
Has found for humankind.
Foul not the ancient river of faith
That waters still your land
And makes you worthy of some attention
In the world of armed and greedy men.
Think you the tears of these dumb cousins of yours
Have no power for a curse or that misfortune
Cannot touch you now that science has progressed?
Or that you can help the world
With knowledge got through execrable cruelty?
'Tis true Ramachandra rules not now:
O thoughtless ones that ride your cars
Up the imperial way in Indraprasth
And sit on your little thrones in the red secretariat,
You rule the affairs of an ancient people
Through whose veins still runs
The noble blood of compassion,
Whose pious eager ears drink still
The music of Tulasi and great Valmeeki,
And their undying voices give
Solace and hope to agitated souls.

Gandhiji on Religion

God and therefore religion are fundamental necessities for normal healthy life—to the individual as well as to nations. Here in this book the reader will find Gandhiji speaking from his heart on various occasions in the course of thirty years of the maturest period of his life. What a modern man who did very great things thought on the subject of God and religion cannot fail to be instructive to educated men and women in these difficult days.

"We the human family are not all philosopheres. Somehow or other we want something which we can touch, something which we can see, something before which we can kneel down. It does not matter whether it is a book or an empty stone-building or a stone-building inhabited by numerous figures"; so wrote Gandhiji, defending temple worship in the background of other prevailing religions. "Hindu Dharma is like a boundless ocean teeming with priceless gems. The deeper you dive, the more treasures you find," said Gandhiji.

Any one who desires to understand what sort of a man the Father of the Nation was, must read this book. One may not want to learn anything about religion that is not in our Shastras or in other religious books. But here is a facet of the mind of a great man we love and to whom the nation is grateful. It has a value over and above a book of religious instruction.

Madras, 11-4-55 C. Rajagopalachari

BHOODAN—THE MOVEMENT OF COMPASSION—I

[Shri Rajaji presided over the 3rd Sarvodaya Sammelan of Tamil Nad on June 4, 5 at Tiruturalpoondi. The following is from the summary of his speech in Tamil on the first day. His concluding remarks on the second day will be given in the next issue. The summary is adapted from the report of the *Sarvodaya* of July, 1955].

We have achieved freedom. We have now to build up our strength. For 150 years we lived as slaves under British rule and for about 1000 years we enjoyed no freedom. Today we are a free bird liberated from its cage. It will take long before we could establish ourselves.

Sarvodaya—Happiness for All

The next step is to strive for our prosperity and happiness. Sarvodaya is the way. Sarvodaya is not a *Potti Udaya* (rise by competition and conflict). It is the means through which all can become happy. Purity of mind and heart is the fundamental basis of Sarvodaya. It is the absolute rule. Every one and all should try and become pure at heart. No Government can achieve this by its law and regulations.

Sarvodaya—Not an Institution

We should always bear in mind that Sarvodaya is not an institution or organization. There can be no president or secretary or a committee for it. It is not a Trust or a Math. Is there any institution for the enforcement of such rules of conduct as the mutual affection between father and children, love between the master and servant, to offer food for the hungry who comes to your door, not to utter falsehood etc. etc. etc.? Similarly there can be no organization for Sarvodaya.

Sarvodaya is a Way of Life

Sarvodaya is a way of life. Welcome addresses, reading of meassages, loud-speakers etc. which I see before me now in this gathering, make me doubt whether Sarvodaya has become an institution. If it takes the form of an institution, with president, secretary etc., it means it becomes dead. For Heaven's sake don't make it an institution. Let it remain always a movement to guide the people to follow Dharma.

Sarvodaya and Land Problem

Sarvodaya includes all that is good. Gandhiji was ambitious to see that every one became good and for that he placed this ideal of Sarvodaya. Sarvodaya takes within itself all constructive activities. Any such activity, if left out or omitted by others, the Sarvodaya workers have to take up and fulfil.

Land problem is a tough one. Landowners will not easily agree to willingly surrender their rights for others. Hence Bhoodan work is not an easy task. People may easily part with cloth or money for the aske of others. But when it comes to the question of land, they will certainly hesitate.

Bhoodan—Not a Struggle

Bhoodan movement is not a fight in the sense of a struggle. *Dan* and fight are contradictions in terms. In *dan* there is no place for force or violence which are in fight. This basic difference the workers should well grasp and remember. Such words of intimidation as "the Government will bring in land legislation which will certainly take away land from you, so you better leave it off now as donation to Bhoodan" amount to compulsion. The workers may well understand that such methods spoil the cause and will kill the work.

Land—The Basic Need of Life

Every one should have the basic needs of life. It is against Dharma that some should suffer and others may enjoy. Can it be ever imagined for any one to claim ownership over air and water and to demand money to part the same for others' use? Like air and water, land also is a basic need for human existence. It is on land that food is grown. Any one keeping it as owner, excluding others and saying that he will part with it on payment of money value, is wrong. This wrong has crept in somehow or other and the poor had to suffer so much. To undo this wrong is Bhoodan movement. The tiller must get the land, just like a thirsty man receives water to drink. Land problem is not a new one. It is a very old one and requires a cautious approach for its solution.

A Hard Case

Many, through righteous means and by their hard work and suffering, have acquired possession of property. Many are now in possession of the same through their predecessors who earned them through similar means. Imagine the case of the wife and children of an elementary school teacher in possession of an acre or two of land. The teacher who worked for 35 years, saved a thousand rupees—one or two rupees every month—and bought this land with the hope of maintaining the family in his old age, and he died leaving the same to the family.

Suppose a Bhoodan worker goes to them and says, "To keep land with you on which you do not toil, is exploitation. Don't lead a life of exploitation." They will certainly retort by saying, "Your very demand to give up the property which is earned by our hard suffering throughout our life is itself exploitation. Now you are the real exploiter." Hence the problem is a long standing complicated one. On it Government and others also are bestowing their attention. Some want legislation. Others advise nationalization first. 'The landlords won't give up possession of their own accord. So take it from them by force by creating conflicts', so say yet others.

Bhoodan—A Dharmik Approach

Our country has an ancient culture and tradition. We have got our own ways to solve our problems. The Sarvodaya method is that way. A man who sees others suffering, feels the pain. He feels compassion. It is our ancient Dharma that makes us feel it is our duty to help the suffering and feed the hungry. Bhoodan movement is that same Dharmik approach to solve the land problem.

Zamindari was abolished through legislation and the Zamindars are angry against the Government. The Rajas voluntarily relinquished their States. So the Government is sympathetic towards them. Gift is a free and voluntary act. The socialists are for land legislation. And the communists demand not only legislation but more than that and say that in case it is not done, they will use force. The ends for both are the same. But Sarvodaya desires to reach it through the means of *dan* (gift). This is what is known as Bhoodan movement. It inspires compassion in the hearts of people. The feeling of compassion for each other is personified in Bhoodan.

Don't be in a hurry to get things done. Government can hurry up things. At certain times they may happen all of a sudden. For instance, if in a village a certain person freely and voluntarily gives land, that act may immediately influence others to come forward and offer lands. Bhoodan is a movement of the world.

Land Repels Irresponsible Owners

There are many poor peasants in our villages with good experience in agriculture, who really desire to engage themselves in it. If they are given lands, production will increase. It is reported that in the North in some places whole villages were being offered for Bhoodan. In some places such things may not happen. Conditions vary from place to place. Hence it becomes our duty to act according to the particular conditions of each place and also in a way which will make the people happier. Able young men inspired with the feelings of compassion and love should come forward to join the work and persuade the landlords to give away the extra lands with them. They who possess lands know the difficulty to maintain them. They who have more than what they need find it still more difficult to manage. It is said in Tirukkural that land, if not properly cared for and maintained well, will repel its lord as the neglected wife behaves to her lord who proves irresponsible.

Caution and Care Needed

With caution and care the movement has to be carried on. There is the danger of violence creeping in if quick and easy results are expected. Enlightened good men with *bhakti* in their hearts should come forward and do the work.

Land Distribution

Distribution is indeed a difficult job. I would suggest that it may be done at the place as and when the gifts are received, Care must be taken that the new owners do not develop in them also the same kind of attachment that is found among the present landowners. Government's help may also become necessary for distribution work. Land should be distributed among the deserving, experienced and enthusiastic peasants. It should also be given to those who have already bulls etc. with them for agricultural work.

[Continued from the last issue this being Rajaji's concluding speech on the 2nd day of the Tamil Nad Sarvodaya Sammelan.]

This Conference is held for the Sarvodaya movement which includes the various constructive work programmes inspired and initiated by Gandhiji. Khadi workers and Harijan sevaks have dwelt on their programmes. In all these group meetings the main theme of discussion was Bhoodan and how the constructive workers could speed up it progress.

Bhoodan and Other Activities

One feels a sort of monotony in any service that he is engaged in after some time and hence desires to join another. But one should concentrate all his attention on the one work he has taken on hand whatever it be. He should always have that one and full objective alone before him. He must focus all his attention on it. He should not allow his attention to be distracted from it whatever be the things that are happening around him in the world.

Gandhiji was insisting on this concentration and all constructive work was done in that way. He was telling Harijan workers not to court imprisonment. It does not appear quite proper if these workers leave these great activities and join Bhoodan.

It is good to aspire to do good things. Bhoodan is an important programme. It is true that workers desire to join it, because it is a Dharmik movement which will save the world. But such programmes of work which a great leader like Gandhiji thought so necessary for the good of the nation, should not be given up because they have become old. Even though old, these programmes have not lost their importance.

Khadi and Harijan Movements

The objectives of Khadi work and Harijan movement have not been yet achieved. These movements will die if they are not efficiently carried out on right lines. It is impossible to start a new any activity that is ruined. Therefore such kinds of constructive work as are accepted as important by the people should not be given up. Such of the workers who are not useful to the particular work, so also the extra hands, can leave and join another. But persons who have worked true and hard and proved absolutely indispensable for the successful working of a movement should not leave it.

When a worker leaves one service, he should consider well why he should leave it and then only decide. He should examine within himself whether it is disgust or hurry that prompts him to do so. If he feels that by his leaving it, that work in which he is already working, will not suffer in any way, then he can leave it. But those who function as pillars in big movements should not leave them. With fear and hesitation I place this suggestion before you. You may consider well and decide for yourselves.

In Bhoodan movement it is not the number of workers that counts; it is the character and quality that is important. Not because too many people come to persuade, the landowner gives. And the landowners in our country are able and clever. They are influential also. Only those who have strong influence and good character can prevail upon them to voluntarily part with land. An ordinary Khadi worker, because he has left that work to join this work, can hardly persuade one to give land.

Untouchability movement has now got the force of law behind it. We have to continue the work to convert the minds of the people and it will help the Government. The desire to get things done with speed and hurry will create situations which may require the help of the police. The police way is not the workers' way. They should approach the people and try to covert their minds by slow degress.

The Two Influences

Influences are of two types. One is that which the words

of good men command and the other is the power of the people in position. Good and well-baked bricks are essentially needed to construct a good and strong house. In the same way non-violence is absolutely necessary for the success of this Bhoodan movement. On deep analysis I find that the objective of this Bhoodan movement is the revival of the sense of Dharma in men, which they have now forgotten. An individual can possess property, but he should hold it as a trustee for the benefit of the people. Gandhiji wanted this form of trusteeship.

The Real Objective

It will be violence to distribute property through legislation. Those who have received land today will certainly produce more in the coming years. Increased production will make all people happy. The objective of Bhoodan is to secure through non-violent means the right for the poor, experienced agriculturist to cultivate and produce.

Unity Consciousness in Villagers

Those who do agricultural work must get lands. This movement will succeed by itself if all the people in the village are made to feel that they are all one. The major effort of the workers should be to achieve this unity consciousness in the villagers. Going round the villages with loudspeakers in jeeps and broadcasting high slogans will not help things much. The elders should be invited to help to create the desired atmosphere. They should be slowly persuaded to donate lands moved by compassion and love. The whole world is watching this movement. The question is not merely receiving land from one and distributing it to others. The objective is the creation of the real mental transformation in the people which will make each to do his Dharma. If her land problem is solved through love, India will shine as a guide to the whole world.

PILGRIM'S PROGRESS DAY BY DAY—III

Surrounded on all the sides by the green hills, even in the hot days of May, and presenting attractive and charming sight, the Pilgrim is marching ahead day in and day out, collecting land and whole villages in Gramdan.

Hearty Welcome Everywhere

At several places on the way to Sundhi Dhamini, he was accorded a very hearty welcome by the Kandhas, the Adiwasis in this area. Their language is different from that of the Sauras another tribe amongst the Adiwasis. They welcomed Vinobaji with the usual slogans but had their mark of originality also. They played music on flutes about two and a half feet long. The sweet tunes of the melodious Durga Raga filled the atmosphere and also attracted the attention of Vinobaji.

On reaching Sundhi Dhamini, we were informed of the sufferings the people had there undergone during the famine four years ago. The village was then on the point of extinction. About a dozen did breathe their last. It must be said to the credit of the constructive workers that timely help was provided and the tragedy was averted.

Spirit of Fraternity

The villagers who were addicted to wine and freely consumed beef have since been successfully persuaded to abandon these evils. They have accepted a new mode of life which is simple and unaddicted. Inspite of their bad habits of food and drink, however, their association was never a risk even to the lady workers who worked amongst them. They lived in their midst free from all fear and in the most familiar way. The villagers built for them a tidy shade in which we, the *padyatris*, have camped. Vinobaji was much impressed by the way these Adiwasis had fared in the famine. He witnessed the spirit of fraternity in the atmosphere.

In his prayer meeting that evening Vinobaji expressed his deep sympathy for all the agonies of life they had undergone during the famine and congratulated them for the way in which they collectively faced the tragedy and got it over also successfully. He then told them: "It is but in your interests that you join this movement of Gramdan because the famine has already taught you what common group life can achieve."

Gramdan—Its Fourfold Advantages

Vinobaji then explained in details the fourfold advantages of Gramdan, viz., the economic, the cultural, the moral and the spiritual. Continuing he said: "If the people are properly educated regarding the advantages of Gramdan, I have not the slightest doubt that there will be no village left in India that will not surrender its entire land in Gramdan."

Economic Revolution

"The first advantage of liquidating ownership over land and converting the total land into one unit is that it will help to increase the village wealth. Crops will be properly planned by the villagers themselves who will also decide about the quantity of the produce to be disposed off or otherwise. Joint deliberations in the direction of agricultural improvements will be possible. Government assistance or any other external help, if and when necessary, will be easily procurable. *Individuals will not be required to incur any debts.* This is all a subject matter for an independent volume. In short, Gramdan will facilitate village planning and will help to make life contented and happy. To use the modern phrase, it will achieve economic revolution."

The Cultural Aspect

"Next, when the village becomes one family, mutual affection would be deepened and life would be full of bliss. By sharing suffering decreases and happiness increases. The village as a whole will be transformed into heaven when people will participate in each others, joys and sorrows or gratifications and affictions.

I am certain that one day in the future this B.C.G. will be declared as of no value and given up by the world of scientists and forgotten. As the Health Department of the Government of India is throwing its great weight on the side of this unscientific adventure, the rejection will take time. Meanwhile the children and the finest section of them all over the land are being deliberately infected on a mass scale with a variety of one of the deadliest living bacilli known to man. Some among the most eminent men of science have expressed their grave doubts as to what the bacilli introduced in the human system may be capable of becoming and doing in the course of time if not at once. The risk is aggravated by the immense number of persons thus affected and by the unavoidable chances of contamination in a hurricane mass campaign.

The stated object of the mass campaign is to prevent the occurrence of clinical tuberculosis among children. In the first place, the statistical data generally given for mortality among young people from tuberculosis in India are not real statistics but only inferentially deduced conclusions. In the next place, the disease never has occurred or will occur in an epidemic form, so as to justify mass injection with a poison not by any means fully proved to be harmless. Again, the claim put forward for the vaccine is an admittedly undependable immunity and that, too, only for a couple of years. Taking all these into account, one must come to the conclusion that the campaign is thoroughly unjustifiable.

One of the worst incidents of a mass campaign is the ceaseless effort by men whose words carry weight, to rouse a dread of the disease in the vast majority of people. Fear considerably reduces the power of resistance among those who have hitherto coped with dormant infection. Another general consequence of the campaign is the neglect of other measures such as would go far towards real control of tuberculosis.

I am not against modern 'western' therapy or modern

science. B.C.G. has nothing to do with modern western medicine. In fact, it is more akin to the principle of homoeopathy than to what is generally known as modern medicine. It proceeds on a creed very similar to that of homoeopathy, namely, that diseases are to be dealt with by the administration in mild forms of the very things that produce the disease. The difference is that the homoeopath does not introduce what multiplies in the human body, but the B.C.G. man introduces a large body of living multiplying organisms, which never leave but are intended to remain forever in the body of the person vaccinated.

Informed readers have to forgive me for devoting even a little space to this, namely to point out that the B.C.G. vaccine is not a cure for anything. The claim is that it may serve as a preventive in some cases and for a brief period of time. I need not have had to say this but for the fact that I have met quite a few respectably educated men who ask why I oppose something that is proposed to relieve sickness! B.C.G. does not relieve any sickness. It is not intended for it.

Quackery is bad whether it be modern or of the time-honoured variety. It is easy to deal with the latter type but modern quackery is difficult to cope with, as it absorbs for its purposes modern medical terminology and methods of procedure.

"A lie which is all a lie
  may be met and fought with outright
But a lie which is part a truth
  is a harder matter to fight."

A principle is discovered which is not universal but it is sought to apply it to cases, where it cannot be applied, and exposure of error is resisted. B.C.G. is an extension of the principle of immunity underlying the artificial introduction of the very same virus or bacilli that cause the disease, with the object that the human body may be stimulated to produce a defence, as it is observed to do when catching the infection in the normal way. The extension of this principal to tuberculosis is wrong because it is known that tuberculosis infection does not lead to the creation of any defensive antibody in the system. But struggling against this hard fact and insurmountable objection to the application of the pasteurian method of producing immunity, the B.C.G. protagonist proceeds to depend on the mere allergy or hypersensitivity created by the introduction of the poison, as a substantial defence against infection and asks us to accept all the unknown risks of the injection for the sake of this allergy, even which admittedly lasts only for a couple of years. The ultimate argument is merely statistical which, according to the best appraisers, as will be seen, is inconclusive. Mere figures of inoculation done, without any well-confirmed observation of results as regards immunity, do not form a valid statistical argument beyond proving the energy and resources at the back of the operating organization.

This is what I respectfully say, is the quackery involved in B.C.G. I am not a medical expert. But my conclusions are not based merely on my *a priori* fears and doubts, but on the definite pronouncements of most eminent and illustrious medical men of the civilized world. The Indian medical men that have been recruited by the Health Ministry to conduct and speak for this campaign, the biggest among them, are not as eminent as any of the medical men, on the basis of whose observations and opinions, I have come to the conclusion that this mass campaign of inoculation with live tubercle bacilli is wrong and must be given up.

Newspapers are not all of them very willing to oblige one who opposes a Government—sponsored campaign with large space, even though the subject be of utmost general importance and though the object be to reach truth and not the furtherance of a particular administrative or political policy. Even when they are generous and willing to publish written criticisms or the reports of speeches dealing with the subject, they are necessarily unable to find space for publishing all the authorities that may be quoted or referred to. This booklet is intended to make up for this. I have here collected and present to readers a few important statements of eminent medical men. I have reduced my own remarks to the minimum that is necessary to explain the relevance of the extracts.

WHY I OPPOSE B.C.G.—FIVE REASONS

I

Extract from the first paragraph from a preliminary assessment of B.C.G. vaccination in India prepared by the WHO Tuberculosis Research Office, Copenhagen:

> "Assessment of these programmes (of B.C.G. vaccination carried out under the auspices of WHO and UNICEF), would obviously be desirable in terms of how much tuberculosis is being prevented; but this would be a long range task—too difficult and too expensive to be feasible, and it may never be known how much these programmes have contributed to the fall in tuberculosis which is observed to be now going on almost everywhere."

After this confession, the memorandum proceeds to state that:

> "the more modest task assumed is the assessment of the technical procedures in use in the campaign, not so much to document what has been accomplished in the past but to obtain guidance for the work of the future."

On this point, the following observations are made:

> "The allergy produced by the mass vaccination campaign in India appears to be not only variable but in average very much weaker than the allergy resulting from natural infection. Indeed for many groups it is well below the level considered desirable.
>
> "No single factor has been found to account for these

results.

"Improvement of the vaccine by exposure to light could only be a contributory factor. The marked variability of the campaign results suggests that some factor connected with the handling or application of the vaccine is involved."

II

The basis on which the whole scheme of B.C.G. rests is that the allergy referred to above amounts in some way to a protective immunity however limited. The following is an extract from Topley & Wilson's *Principles of Bacteriology and Immunity*:

"Even if we admitted the beneficial effect of B.C.G. vaccination, which we are not prepared to do, we should still have to decide what value it is likely to be in practice...Calmette himself advised re-vaccination at 3, 7 and 15 years of age. If re-vaccination is not performed, the immunity—if any—resulting from the primary vaccination will probably wear off in a year or two. If, on the other hand, it is performed, there is a danger of setting up in a tuberculin-positive patient an acute allergic reaction, which may have serious results."

III

The following is an extract from a letter received from a lady whom I do not know personally:

"I have just read your booklet on B.C.G. vaccination. If I had read this some months ago, I would not have allowed my two girls aged 6 and 2 to be given B.C.G. It was when the Nilgiris were being covered 4 or 5 months back. It is only from your writings in the papers that we understand that the period of immunity is only two years. This fact I am sure is never mentioned in the blaring loud-speakers of the B.C.G. vans. If the public knew that the immunity is for such a short time and that re-vaccination is not advisable nobody, would get their children vaccinated with B.C.G."

IV

The following is an extract from a very recent letter from the United Kingdom Health Ministry:

"......As you will see we have gradually extended the scope of our B.C.G. vaccination scheme, but until the present Medical Research Council trials to test its efficiency are completed—and an interim report may be published in the near future—we still have no accurate estimation of its value —we have no intention of expanding our vaccination programme at the moment."

V

The following is an extract from a letter written by Dr. R.C. Webster in the *Lancet*, March 5, 1955:

"Prof. Heaf (Feb. 12) says that 'there is strong evidence that B.C.G. increases resistance against tuberculosis infection, although statistical proof is difficult to obtain.' He admits our ignorance of allergy and immunity in taberculosis, but he also says 'these acknowledged advantages of the vaccine are sufficient to justify its use.' Are these advantages so generally acknowledged? The fact that the vaccine is readily administered and cheap is not so very important: the fundamental question to which we do not known the answer is whether a positive skin reaction is really very important in immunity to tuberculosis. After all, we have other diseases in which positive skin reactions occur, but I do not know that it has been suggested that they mean immunity......Are we really justified in asking parents to submit their children to injections which may in a significant proportion of cases produce unpleasant local reactions and have a risk, however slight, of causing general disease, when we have really no sound knowledge of its good effects?"

Madras, 7-8-'55

"B.C.G. DAY" OBSTINACY

To

Editor, *Harijan*,

I do not wish to repeat all that I have been so earnestly saying and writing on this subject of B.C.G. Vaccination. An announcement has been made that February 20 will be an All India B.C.G. Day. It is a pity that the Health Ministry of India refuses to yield to reason and persists in pushing this useless vaccination which has been practically rejected by the American health authorities. The U.K. Health Department is still investigating and its special committee has not yet thought fit to issue its long-awaited for report in spite of Dr. Benjamin's optimism about it. Dr. Carol Palmer has recently and publicly supported I.N.H. oral administration as better than B.C.G. or at least as good. Why should this live bacilli injection be persisted in by the Health Ministry of India when Dr. Carol Palmer himself has expressed himself thus?

It is well known that all those or almost all those that get a fatal or serious attack of T.B. were "positive," for years before the appearance of clinical T.B. The aim and object of B.C.G. Vaccination is to produce artificial 'positives'. How can an artificial 'positive' condition do what the normal "positive" condition has not been able to do so far, viz., to prevent clinical T.B.? Something is better than nothing. But something useless is not better than nothing, in dealing with the human body. It is a pity that Smt. Rajkumari Amrit Kaur is obstinate in this as she has been in the export of monkeys for being tortured with artificially injected diseases.

4-2-'56 **C. Rajagopalachari**

4

Congress, War and the Raj

Undoubtedly Rajaji meticulously participated in deliberations of the several sessions of the Congress. His arguments on various political issues from the Gaya session onward had deep linkage with Indian nationalism and freedom struggle. In fact he argued fearlessly and was heard with attention and respect. Soon he captured the attention of no less a leader than Mahatma Gandhi.

PROCEEDINGS AT GAYA

The sitting lasted for two hours only. Four resolutions were adopted. These are the last four in the above list.

On the Committee assembling on the next day, December 24th, Mr. Rajagopalachari asked for leave to move a resolution to reaffirm the principle of non-co-operation on the lines accepted in the previous Congress sessions.

The President immediately expressed his wish that the motion may be deferred till after the Presidential address.

A member asked if it was a mere express on of a desire on his part or a definite ruling. The President replied it was his ruling.

Mr. Rajagopalachari moved that No. 7 of the resolutions relating to Council entry be taken into consideration.

The President said he could not allow it for the reason already stated by him with reference to Mr. Rajagopalachari's first motion.

After a passage-at-arms between some members Mr. Vallabhai Patel moved for adjournment of the Subjects Committee till after the President's address. This raised several points of order which was finally settled by the President's ruling that he had got every right to arrange the order of business as he thought desirable and directed that the resolutions in the draft programme be considered in the order in which they appeared on the agenda.

Dr. Ansari then moved the first resolution on the agenda paper (see p. 850 No. 1).

Dr. Ansari moved the resolution in an Urdu speech detailing at length the circumstances under which the C.D. Enquiry Committee recommended the boycott of British goods.

Mr. C.S. Ranga Iyer seconding the resolution said that commercial jealousy was rampant in Europe and that it should be exploited in the interest of India to injure British Trade as much as possible, as boycott of British goods was necessary to bring the British to their knees. Several amendments were then suggested but discussion turned generally on the question of boycott or no boycott on principle. Dr. P. Sitaramayya opposed boycott as they were not formulating a method of retaliation. Mr. Harisarvatama Rao said that the resolution should be deleted altogether as it was opposed to the non-violent creed of the Congress, for boycott involved hatred. Mr. Aney of Berar reflecting the Marhatta view made a lengthy speech supporting boycott. Mr. S. Satyamurti supported the resolution. A few more speeches were made after which closure was moved. The President declined to apply as he said he intended to close the debate when members who had sent in their names had an opportunity to speak.

Mr. C. Rajagopalachari

Mr. C. Rajagopalachari opposed the resolution He said, he was aware there was a considerable body of opinion who in other matters accepted his views but were not prepared to agree with him in this question of boycott. He told his hearers that Mahatma Gandhi was opposed to it and if he were present in their midst, he would certainly oppose any suggestion of boycott of British goods. As opinions were divided very sharply the speaker did not propose to advance any elaborate arguments. He desired the assembly to take the common sense view. If the resolution was accepted under the authority of the Congress it would interfere with the constructive programme in Khaddar, whether might be the reservations that might be made in that matter. Those who manufactured mill cloth and others who imported foreign cloth would take advantage of the resolution and impede progress in Khaddar. If they should carry forward successfully any aggressive programme, it was absolutely necessary to ensure the atmosphere necessary. That depended upon the extra care in their action as well as in their feeling. Even supposing there was no personal hatred involved in boycott, the necessary amount of work that should be done in successfully carrying out the resolution would certainly interfere with getting the atmosphere essential for any legitimate aggressive propaganda. Again the whole country would know that Mahatmaji was against boycott. Did the country after his arrest stand by him or not? The Government contended that as Mahatmaji had been taken away his followers were unable to work. They contended on the other hand that even without Mahatmaji they could go on with the work. The resolution was the real test. If they proved to the world that the hold Mahatmaji had on them before his imprisonment did not exist to-day in the same strength as before, because he was not there to lead them, the cause of Swaraj would without any doubt be weakened. The responsibility was very heavy on them. They must restrain their feelings and conserve their strength by rejecting the resolution.

After a few more speeches the meeting adjourned.

DECEMBER 25TH, 1922

The Subjects Committee continued sitting at 9 o'clock on the 25th Dec. and finished discussion on boycott of British goods by 11-30 A.M. All amendments except the substitution of the words "within the next two months" at the end of the resolution for "as soon as possible" were withdrawn. Dr. Ansari accepted this time-limit amendment and the resolution as amended was put to the meeting.

Mr. Stokes was one of the speakers in support of the resolution. He said the question was not whether boycott implied hatred or retaliation. He entirely repudiated the suggestion. The only standpoint from which they should view the resolution was the future of this country. For winning Swaraj he believed boycott would really help the country. After all, what the resolution proposed to do was to refer the question to an expert Committee who would be most competent to decide what goods should be boycotted and how the boycotted goods could be replaced.

Mr. Abhyankar

Mr. Abhyankar made a vigorous speech supporting the resolution. He regretted that adjournment of the Subjects Committee was not granted and that opportunity could not be had for deciding upon the most reasonable and acceptable interpretation of the term Non-violent Non-co-operation. He expressed regret because they had reached a stage in the political discussion when they could not proceed further unless they understood what exactly non-violence meant. If boycott was held to militate against non-violence, he should then say that non-violence was running amock. Love and hatred were counterparts of the same thing. If they loved 'Punaya', they must hate sin and if they loved Indian goods, they must hate

British goods. Boycott of British goods did not create any hate against British people. In the words of Mahatmaji boycott did not create contempt or hatred, but only disaffection and, if they were ture to themselves, they could not have any affection for British goods. It might be that Mahatmaji was against boycott of British goods. In their loyalty to Mahatma they should not be less faithful to themselves and to the country, for, after all, Mahatma was for the country and not the country for Mahatma. He appealed to the meeting to consider the proposition calmly and cooly, without trying to soar when they could not flutter in regions of spirituality and 'puritanism', and take a practical view point on this important question of boycott.

Mr. D. Gopalkrishnayya, in supporting the resolution, said they were boycotting many things and more boycott was implied in the resolution of non-co-operation passed at the previous Congress though that word did not occur. Therefore there was no question of hatred involved in it and the expression was only a matter of taste.

Mr. Srinivasa Iyengar

Mr. S. Srinivasa Ayyangar made a lengthy speech commending the resolution to the acceptance of the Committee. He had understood Mahatmaji to say, Mr. Ayangar said, that non-violent Non-co-operation in the Congress was a political creed. Satyagraha was a different thing. Some of the Non-co-operators in Congress might be Satyagrahis, but the Congress itself was not committed to that creed. The only question before them was duty to the country. Patriotism and national interest required that they should launch on a campaign of boycott. He was absolutely unable to say that it was either irreligious or dishonorable.

A number of others spoke including Messrs. Rajendra Prasad, Zahoor Ahmad, Siva Prasad Gupta and Dunichand of Ambala, when the President asked if the movers of the different amendments desired to press them. All amendments were withdrawn, except one, and the following is the amended resolution as finally read by Dr. Ansari:

"The Congress accepts the recommendation of the Civil Disobedience Enquiry Committee with regard to boycott of British goods and resolves that the question be referred to a Committee for a full report as to what British goods may be successfully boycotted and the places from where such goods may be easily obtained and that the said report be submitted to the All-India Congress Committee meeting within the next two months."

A division was taken with the result that 146 voted for and 129 against.

The Committee then adjourned.

The Congress opened its Session on the 26th. (For the Presidential Address and the Address of the Chairman, Reception Committee, see before).

2nd day's Proceedings of the Congress

The Congress met on the 27th to pass five resolutions.

After expressing condolences the following resolutions were put from the chair and passed, the entire audience standing.

"This Congress places on record its grateful appreciation of the services of Mahatma Gandhi to the cause of India and Humanity by his message of Peace and Truth and reiterates its faith in the principle of Non-violent Non-co-operation inaugurated by him for the enforcement of the rights of the people of India."

"This Congress places on record its profound appreciation of the services rendered to the National cause by all those brave citizens who have suffered in pursuance of the programme of voluntary suffering and who, in accordance with the Congress advice, without offering any defence or bail, served or are serving various periods of imprisonment, and calls upon the Nation to keep alive this spirit of sacrifice and to maintain unbroken the struggle for freedom".

"This Congress records with pride and admiration its appreciation of the unexampled bravery of the Akali martyrs and the great and noble example of non-violence set by them for the benefit of the whole Nation."

Mrs. Sarojini Naidu then moved the following resolution:

"This Congress congratulates Ghazi Kamal Pasha and the Turkish Nation on their recent successes and further records the determination of the people of India to carry on the struggle till the British Government has done all in its power and removed all its own obstacles to the restoration of the Turkish Nation to free and independent status and the conditions necessary for unhampered National life and effective guardianship of Islam and the Jazirat-ul-Arab freed from all Non-muslim control."

Mr. Naidu in urging the resolution for acceptance by the Congress said that those who accused them of narrow patriotism or blind and bitter local patriotism would find a refutation of those accusations in this one resolution which carried them as a united body across the seas to extend the hand of fellowship to those indomitable Turks who under the leadership of Ghazi Mustapha Kemal Pasha had broken once for all the bondage of Asiatic peoples. In congratulating Mustapha Kemal they were congratulating the Turkish Nation and the embodied soul of Turkish honour. They were also congratulating and honouring themselves by assuring the indomitable. Turks that the people of India would continue the struggle till the enemy of the Turkish Nation, the British Government, whether in India or in England, had removed with its own hand the obstacles it created out of its own passionate desire of crushing the very Soul of Islam out of the Christian continent. They pledged themselves to the uttermost in this way so that their ultimate peace might be the peace of Asia and deliverance of Asia from bondage. But they were assuring the Turkish Nation not merely of their determination to continue the struggle till Turkey became an independent Nation, till all those Koranic injunctions were fulfilled and till spiritual supremacy of the Khilafat whose seat is the capital of the Turkish Nation was saved, and further more till the Jazirut-ul-Arab was free from all non-Muslim control. The Muslim people should have full and unbroken and unchallenged control over the graves of the founders and sustainers of Islam. Therefore, in the name of the people of India, she pledged to the Turkish Nation their assurance of the bond of love and fellowship, that while there was the menace of one single non-Muslim hand and the shadow of non-Muslim control to that sacred Island where the revelation of the one God came to the Dreamer in the desert, and who tending His camel received from the heavens the illumination of that central truth of Democracy that all men were bound together in a common brotherhood, they (Hindus), would continue the battle and would be doubly bound to sustain the honour of India because the Islamic brothers were in small minority in this land. Mrs. Naidu further assured that Islam would not die so long as there was a single life in India, to die for its freedom and if rivers of the blood must flow before Islam could be free, then it would surely be the confluent blood of Hindus and Muslims (applause).

Mr. G. Harsarvothawa Rao in supporting the resolution said that if there was one religion which was alive to-day it was Mahomedanism and therefore the triumph of Mahomedanism was the triumph of spiritual life and in the life hereafter. From that point of view, the success of Kemal Pasha was an event which would be writ large in the history of the world. Standing as the disciple of Gandhi and for non-violence in supporting this cause he said: "But my belief of the supreme necessity of 'Satwa' does not rule out of this world other methods of achievement. My belief in 'Satwa' is only the belief in the best and highest method, but there are other methods, human methods, imperfect methods, which may not ultimately be supreme methods but all these methods are legitimate and may be used by those who have to struggle for liberty. (Hear, Hear.) I think therefore that this question of non-violence does not enter in congratulating Ghazi Mustapha Kemal or Turkey."

AN AMENDMENT

Mr. Shiv Prasad Gupta moved an amendment substituting the word 'foreign control' for words 'non-Muslim control'. As soon as Mr. Gupta came to the rostrum he bowed before the photo of Mustapha Kemal in whom he read the spirit of Liberty which would spread all over the East and liberate the subordinate nations. He reminded the audience that the Congress stood for Liberty and they were all worshippers in the temple of Libertv. He did not want to see any nation ruling over another. He would like to see the British leaving India to-morrow. The same feeling would make him oppose France ruling over Germany and the Turks ruling over Arabia. His amendment would therefore have the effect of declaring that the Jazirat-ul-Arab should not be under foreign control even if such control was that of another Muslim Nation, and that the Arabians should be their own masters.

Babu Bhagwan Das seconded the amendment while Hakim Ajmal Khan strongly opposed it. The latter said that Islam enjoined upon all Moslems to keep the Jazirat-ul-Arab free from the hands of all non-Muslims. For this purpose it is necessary that the power of defending it should be sufficiently strong to ward off and successfully defend it against the invasion of all non-Muslims. He would like liberty for all nations but if the Government of Arabia was left to itself it would not be able to defend the country from European nations whose warships frequented its shores and it would again fall in the hands of one non-Muslim power or other. The question as to whether Arabs would enjoy autonomy within the Turkish Empire or independently should be left to the Arabs and Turks to settle between themselves.

ORIGINAL MOTION PASSED

Mrs. Naidu replying pointed out that it was part and parcel of the Khilafat question that the Arabs should owe allegiance to the Khalifa.

Pundit Motilal Nehru came to the rostrum and put the amendment to vote. Cries were heard from remote sides of the pandal asking as to what the resolutions and the amendment were. Pandit Motilal thereupon explained in land voice the difference between the two propositions and when votes were called a number of hands were raised in favour of the amendment. But the majority were against it. The original resolution was passed.

SUBJECTS COMMITTEE PROCEEDINGS

27TH DECEMBER 1922

The Subjects Committee at its sitting on the 27 December gave a prolonged consideration to the resolutions on the Council question, over ten in number. Besides the resolutions of Pandit Motilal Nehru and Mr. C. Rajagopalachari, the following is a list of the other resolutions proposed. Discussion in the strict sense there was not, but resolutions were moved and seconded with brief speeches from those responsible for them.

Mr. Jamnadas Mehta's resolution was in the following terms:

> That in view of the Report of the Civil Disobedience Enquiry Committee this Congress is of opinion that Congress-men should contest the elections on the issue of the redress of the Punjab and Khilafat wrongs and immediate Swaraj and make every endeavour to be returned in a majority.
>
> It is further recommended that in view of the new Councils assembling early in January 1924, the Congress session of

1923 be held during the first instead of the last week of December and the matter be again brought up for final decision by the Congress as regards the policy to be pursued by Congress-men in the Legislative Councils.

The following is Babu Bhagwan Das's resolution:

While this Congress believes that substantial progress in the constructive programme is the surest way of again training the people in the art of local self-government and is the indispensable foundation of a stable Swaraj and is the necessary preparation for the successful carrying out of mass civil disobedience as the final weapon against the common enemy, viz., the irresponsibility of the bureaucracy, and while it thinks that sufficient steady, patient, plodding work has not been done by the Congress organisation towards the realisation of the constructive programme and therefore insists that more work should be done along this line by all workers at the same time, this Congress sees that there is a considerable body of opinion in the country which in the present conditions strongly favours the contesting of elections to the official councils, though there is also another very considerable body of opinion to the effect that to do so for mere obstruction and wreeking or for any other purpose is doubtful in principle and not likely to succeed in practice and, therefore, taking into account all the circumstances, this Congress thinks it a legitimate and permissible line of work, for such members as are convinced of the goodness of its principle and policy, to contest elections, provided that Congress funds shall not be used this purpose.

Mr. Sen Gupta moved his resolution which ran thus:

Whereas this Congress is of opinion that civil disobedience is the only weapon left to the people of India for the redress of the Punjab and Khilafat wrongs, and for the speedy attainment of Swaraj and whereas it is necessary to bring about a more effective boycott of the Councils, non-co-operators should contest the elections to the councils but shall refuse to take the seats when elected.

Mr. Srinivasa Iyyangar's resolution took the following form:

This Congress once again places on record its fixed determination to continue the programme of Non-violent Non-co-operation with greater vigour than hitherto in the manner indicated below and in such manner as each province may determine, till the Punjab and Khilafat wrongs are redressed and Swaraj is established and the control of the Government of India passes into the hands of the people from that of an irresponsible co-operation.

Whereas notwithstanding the fact that the majority of the electors in the whole country abstained from voting at the council elections of 1920, many Indians allowed themselves to be elected thereto and did not resign their seats inspite of their being so advised by the Nagpur Congress, with the result that, though the new councils do not represent the country, they are used to consolidate the power of the present system of Government in India which the Congress has resolved to put an end to.

The Congress earnestly advises, with a view to render the boycott of councils more effective than it was in 1920, all electors to vote for Congressmen, who shall, when elected absolutely, refrain from taking their seats in the Councils.

Mr. A. Rangaswamy Aiyengar had a resolution in his name to this effect:

In view of the fact that opinion is sharply divided on the question of entry into council, this Congress resolves that, as in the case of the boycott of law courts and schools, all activities in connection with the promotion of the boycott of councils be suspended pending the completion of the constructive programme in order to start some form of aggressive civil disobedience and that in the meanwhile those Congressmen who desire to seek election may be allowed to do so.

Mr. S. E. Stokes' motion to delete the preamble from Mr. Nehru's resolution on the ground that the statements contained in it were open to question was accepted by Mr. Nehru.

Mr. Babu Ram moved to refer the boycott of councils for final decision to a special Congress to be held three months hence.

After all these motions had been moved, Pundit Madan Mohan Malavia made a brilliant address lasting for nearly an hour. He spoke very feelingly about Mahatmaji's imprisonment and the futility of the work which the A. I. C. C. was doing outside when Mahatma was inside the prison. He considered that the best way of proceeding forward was to enter the councils solidly and using that weapon to break the citadel of the bureaucracy. He attempted hard to persuade the members who were for obstruction or postponement to take his view.

THE VOTING

Immediately after Pandit Malaviya's speech a desire was expressed to proceed to voting without further speeches.

The President consulted the wishes of the assembly and the majority were in favour of it but as it was already late it was agreed to adjourn the meeting till noon next day for the voting.

28TH DECEMBER 1929

The Subjects Committee met at 1 o'clock on the 28th and carried on a discussion on the Council question till 5 when the resolution and amendments began to be put. But it was not until after nearly 4 hours that the result of the voting could be announced. Considerable time was devoted to the interpretation of the decision of the Jamiat-ul-Ulema against Council entry.

Hakim Ajmal Khan, Dr. Ansari, Mr. Moazzam Ali, Mr. Sherwani and Mr. Zahoor Ahmed were the principal speakers and the general opinion seemed to be that, even though the Ulemas' resolution could not be taken to be a 'fatwa' the fact that learned Moulvis and divines had taken a certain definite attitude in respect of Council entry must have a very considerable effect on the Muhamadan community though it might not carry the same weight with Hindus.

Hakim Ajmal Khan interpreted the Ulemas' decision as leaving open the question of Council entry being religious or otherwise. He thought that it was not a 'fatwa' in the absence of a unanimity among Ulemas.

Dr. Ansari said that the decision of the Ulemas might not be a fatwa, but as 70 members of the Jamiat-ul-Ulema had come to a conclusion against Council entry, Muhammadan voters would not go to the polling booth, despite the best efforts of candidates. As a practical proposition council entry was out of question. Moreover the expenditure of money, time and energy in contesting the elections was not worth the game.

Messrs. Sherwani and Zahoor Ahmed differed from Dr. Ansari.

END OF DISCUSSION

The debate closed at 5 o'clock, when voting was proceeded with. There were 11 months on the paper. Mr. Nehru's motion was taken to be the principal resolution, while others were treated as amendments.

Mr. Rajagopalachari in moving his motion as amendment to Mr. Nehru's main proposition did not make any speech but merely contented himself by explaining one or two technical points.

Mr. Vallabhai Patel of Ahmedabad who formally seconded the motion also made no speech.

PRESIDENT'S QUESTION

Before it was seconded by Mr. Vallabhai, the President called upon Mr. Rajagopalachari to show cause why his amendment should not be rejected as it negatived the main resolution which it proposed to amend.

Mr. Rajagopalachari explained that the question was whether boycott should be from within or without. A mere finding of the former one way or the other left the latter point still unsettled and this Congress must regarded it as its imperative duty to give a lead to the country on a question which was engaging its attention.

The President observed that he was not convinced by the argument of Mr. Rajagopalachari, but would admit his motion as amendment and that it would be voted upon prior to the last amendment.

After all other amendments were withdrawn three motions remained of which Mr. Srinivasa Iyyangar's resolution of contesting elections and not entering Councils was given the precedence. The votes stood 139 against the resolution and 107 for it.

When the result was telegraphed to thousands of visitors outside the pandal eagerly awaiting the decision of the Subjects Committee, it was hailed with shouts of "Mahatma Gandhi-Ki-Jai" but this outburst of feeling was only a prelude to the jubilation and satisfaction with which the majority of delegates in Congress camp received the news of the final result two hours later.

Mr. Rajagopalachari's resolution was then pressed to a division. Voting in this case was finally announced as 203 voting for and 87 against the resolution.

THE DIVISION LIST

The following are details of voting for the resolution:

For:—Tamil 19, Andhra 23, Kerala 3. Maharastra (Poona) 7, C.P. (Marathi) and C.P. (Hindustani) 4, Sindh 8, Assam nil, Gujerat 11, Karnataka 12, Bengal 25, U.P. 14, Punjab 17, Behar, 28, Berar nil, Delhi 3, Bombay 6, Ajmeer 3, Utkal 11 and Burma 9.

Against the resolution:—Tamil 4, Andhra nil, Kerala 1, Maharastra (Poona) 8, C.P. Marathi, 6, C.P. Hindustani 7, Assam 2, Gujerat 1, Karnataka nil, Bengal 15, U.P. 18, the Punjab 13, Behar 1, Berar 5, Delhi 4, Bombay, Ajmeer, Utkal and Burma nil.

Andhra, Gujerat, Behar, Bombay, Karnataka, Sindh, Ajmeer and Utkal all voted solidly for Mr. Rajagopalachari. Votes were more or less equally divided in Maharashtra, Poona, Bengal, Punjab and U.P. Berar was wholly against boycott. Almost all Mahamadan members are believed to have voted against council entry while lady members, of whom there were nearly ten, voted half and half. Four out of five Akalis voted against entry. A few members did not vote either way.

The Motion as Passed

The text of the resolution as passed by the Subjects Committee runs thus:

"Whereas the boycott of Councils carried out during the elections held in 1920 had destroyed the moral strength of the institutions through which Government sought to consolidate its power and carry on its irresponsible rule, and whereas it is necessary again for the people of India to withhold participation in the elections of the next year as an essential part of the programme of non-violent Non-co-operation.

"It is resolved that this Congress do advise that all voters do abstain from standing as candidates for any of the councils and from voting for any candidate offering himself as such in disregard of the Congress advice, and signify the abstention in such manner as the A.I.C.C. may instruct in that behalf."

Pandit Nehru's resolution was formally put and declared lost.

3rd Day's Proceedings of the Congress

The Congress held its third sitting at 2 P.M. on the 29th December. Attendance was as large as on the opening day because of the interest centering round the two most controversial issues on which the Congress had to record its verdict on this day, namely, boycott of British goods and advisibility or otherwise of participation in the next general election.

THE PROPOSITIONS

The resolutions and amendments of the Council question which appeared on the agenda paper were the same as those moved in the Subjects Committee with only this difference that Mr. Rajagopalachariar's proposition now became the main resolution and that of Pandit Motilal Nehru the main amendment.

Boycott of British Goods

The Congress discussed for full three hours the resolution on boycott of British goods and rejected it by a large majority.

Mr. Satyamurti moved the following resolution on the Boycott of British goods:

"This Congress accepts the recommendation of the Civil Disobedience Enquiry Committee regarding the question of boycott of British goods and resolves that the question be referred to a committee for a full report as to what British goods may be successfully boycotted and the places from where such goods can be easily obtained and that the said report be submitted to the All-India Congress Committee within two months next.

"Resolved further that the Congress programme regarding Khaddar and the boycott of all foreign cloth shall not be affected by this resolution and that the following gentlemen shall be members of the said committee:—Messrs. N.K. Sen, J.K. Mehta, N.C. Kelkar, Umar Sobhani and Professor Ruchiram Sahani."

Mr. Satyamurti said his resolution was modest as it did not contemplate the complete boycott of British goods because that was not possible. It was practical because it left it to a committee of experts to suggest what could be successfully boycotted. The resolution was only a supplement to the existing programme of boycott of foreign cloth and gave to the oppressed people of India one more weapon to use, so far as it helped them to achieve freedom, which was their birth-right. The resolution could also to some extent help in lifting the full now in the country and making life active. Moreover Labour in England, finding that an irreconciled India was making their future uncertain, would force the hands of the Home Government to come to terms with the Indian people. He did not understand the subtle and super-subtle doctrine of metaphysicians and psychological experts who expounded the theory that boycott of British goods would lead to hatred. "Does this Boycott," he asked, "involve more hatred than boycott of the Prince of Wales whom the English people loved with all their heart? Does it involve more hatred than burning of foreign cloth and boycott of the British Empire Exhibition?" There was no room for such sickly sentimentality of love or hatred. Hatred could not be manufactured nor regulated by resolutions or speeches in Congress. There was place for hatred provided that hatred did not contemplate or promote incitement to violence. "I do not," he continued, "condemn an Indian who refuses to love the nation,—not the nation which produced General Dyer, because foresooth he might have acted in a momentary impulse, but a nation which long months after Dyer's massacre colly collected 30,000 pounds and presented that money to the author of that massacre. This is surely asking me to be a superman, to be insincere and hypocritical." The speaker quoted the example of the United States and Ireland in regard to the boycott of English goods. "I want to get rid of this rule. This is a weapon which history has given me, and God willing, I mean to use it, hatred or love notwithstanding."

Swami Bhaskar Tirth seconded the resolution and said that it expressed the determination of India to stop the bleeding of India in order to keep alive Manchester. He did not like that England should starve and knew that mercy was doubly blessed but such mercy could be shown only when England knelt before India and begged for concession.

Mr. C. Vijayaraghavachariar opposing the resolution said, "I have come here to oppose this resolution on two grounds. One is that it is wholly impracticable and the other is, it is altogether undesirable. Much has been made of the argument that boycott of British goods is within the letter and spirit of Non-Co-operatior because there is boycott of foreign goods already sanctioned under the auspices of Mahatma Gandhi, and I venture to submit a greater fallacy has not been placed before you. There is a well-recognised principle in boycott of foreign goods, but there is no principle I know of, except that of revenge or mischief, in boycott of British goods (Hear, hear). Boycott of foreign goods is only another name for a policy of protective tariff. Because the Government of India is not "Government of the people, by the people, for the people", we are obliged to have recourse to boycott of foreign goods in the place of protection. It is recognised by all nations of the world and by text-book writers, the idea being to encourage native industry to the extent the prohibition of foreign goods would make the import of it altogether impossible or would diminish it in the highest degree.

Any controversy there might be between free trade and protection is mostly confined to a particular country. It is claimed that in England free trade is best. Some there are even in England who say that protection is best. The United States and other countries have adopted highly protective tariffs for the sake of manufacture and stimulation of their industry. That being so, I ask you to say that those gentlemen who have been party to the resolution already passed, namely boycott of foreign goods, can also resist this resolution. There is no inconsistency between the two. I am surprised that this argument is repeated both here and elsewhere in the press by the mover. Because we are required to boycott foreign goods for the sake of protection of our own industries now existing and hereafter to come into force, are we justified in asking you to pass a measure which will simply mean nothing but a feeling of vendetta and mischief?

In the report of the Civil Disobedience Committee the boycott of British goods is accepted, but no new principles have been enunciated. That the principle of boycott of British goods is different from the principle embodied in the boycott of foreign goods is quite clear. The resolution about boycott of foreign goods is already in Congress literature. Why then do they want a new principle? I say it is undesirable also for the reason that, in the case of boycott of foreign goods, there is a sacrifice imposed upon us by ourselves. In the early stages of boycott of foreign goods, consumers in India suffered. It might be that producers and possibly middlemen also suffered. This is a well-recognised sacrifice imposed by all civilised countries on the whole population in order that its manufactures and industries and its average wealth might be increased. That sacrifice is necessary in the interest of our motherland. In the case of boycott of British goods the effect will be that other countries will export more. They will increase their prices, because, if we deduct one great competitor like England from the market of India, we give other countries an opportunity to increase prices. Do you really believe that in order to carry out this policy of boycott the Congress will be justified in imposing an additional item of expenditure, so that it is mischievous alike to us and to England?

The people of this country to further this boycott would greatly displease the Labour organisation and Labour members of Parliament in England. You may say you don't care, but there are people who do care. The Labour party have become His Majesty's Opposition now. It is not fair that we should put forward just at this time a resolution, not useful to us economically except simply as bluff or bluster. Labour people are shrewd. They will soon find out that we are not well disposed towards them and they would dislike us. On the other hand if boycott fails, as it is bound to fail, all of them will laugh at us. Whether this is within four corners of Non-co-operation or not, people more competent than myself, the esoteric section, will tell you we should not cause feelings of hatred needlessly. In the case of boycott of foreign goods, it is not needlessly that we cause any feeling of hatred.

Mr. Rangaswami Ayyangar in supporting the resolution said that the Bible of the Britisher was his financial code. Anything that affected his income caused him grave concern. The proposed boycott was a political weapon which even Mr. Gokhale had blessed during the Bengal Partition days.

Mr. C. Rajagopalachari opposing the resolution, said: "I have come and stand before you to oppose this proposition after considering serveral times whether it should compel, by anything I might do, a division of the house over a proposition like this. I earnestly appeal to you to reject this proposal which has been accepted by the Subjects Committee. I consider that this proposal is a symptom of our weakness and will contribute to a growing weakness and will interfere with the programme of self-reliance that we have adopted. It is, I say, a symptom of weakness because we, instead of depending on Swadeshi, turn our thoughts to other nations in order to substitute things which we have been getting from England. If you don't wish to get anything from England it is our duty to manufacture it ourselves and not to turn away to Japan and create that domination for the future under which we have suffered already in our previous history. Why should we lay the foundations for future domination from other countries when we have sufficiently seen the evils of such neglect of self-reliance and the results of foreign domination? I beg of you, therefore, not to lay this foundation for future misery and never in anger do that which will afterwards be an evil out of which we cannot get out. I do not hope by anything that I am able to say to convert you. There is only one man who could have resisted the anger in your hearts and restrained it. I know the overpowering, the growing and accumulating wrongs, under which we suffer tempt us to this resolution, but we must restrain ourselves. We must restrain and convert that anger into something constructive, not merely to buy from Japan or America what we do not wish to buy from Britain.

I do not want to lead you to questions of philosophy or principles of Non-co-operation. Please dispose of this question on expediency only, if you like. We get from England a third of all the goods that we get from abroad in the shape of cloth and, so far as cloth is concerned, we have already resolved not to get it from England or any country outside as far as possible, and we are succeeding in that effort. We have sufficiently boycott Britain to the extent of a third of the total imports from abroad. Therefore in the Khaddar and foreign cloth boycott programme we have already before us a clear programme of the boycott of British goods. To that extent it is not a mere question of arithmetic that, if we boycott the remaining two thirds, we are adding to what we are now doing. It is question of intereference with our concentration effort. It is a question of leaving foreign importers from misleading the country. It is a question on turning away our workers from the one concentrated effort which has been proving successful.

I ask of you therefore not to divert the attention from this single idea of Khaddar. Mahatma Gandhi alone was capable of restraining your anger and converting it into concentrated constructive effort. When he is not amidst us and when he resisted the proposal for the boycott of British goods for so long a time, shall we in his absence turn our resolution from one to another? I do not appeal to you to do anything simply because he said so. It is difficult to resist your anger. Mahatmaji himself had stated that boycott of British goods is not to be confounded with boycott of foreign goods. He made clear that boycott of foreign goods meant swadeshi only and nothing else, but here the boycott of British goods is not a case of the part being included in the whole. Boycott of foreign goods means constructive efforts to replace foreign goods by our own effort. Boycott of British goods means "we reject British goods and can turn to other countries for getting those goods." It is not a thing which we would accept then. Please consider that the poor as well as the rich and every man, woman and child in this country is getting what we are boycotting. If we turn to other things, we turn only to particular classes for rejecting British goods. Are we likely to succeed? Is it a practical proposition?

It may be said that this question may be decided by a committee, but you are asked to accept a proposition wherein you accept a principle. Therefore we have to examine that principle and its practicability. I say, on the face of it, it is not a practical proposition and therefore you ought not to appoint this committee. If there had been no acceptance of principle we may pass it. If the committee is to go into the whole question why place it before the Congress? A committee like this the A.I.C.C. may appoint, but by placing this resolution you are asked to be committed to this policy. I ask of you not to be committed by this policy. Even Mahatmaji has said, in answer to Mr. Baptista in January last year, that even he would not be capable of restraining the feeling of anger that would be roused in a propaganda of boycott of British goods. Are we likely to be able to restrain the national forces which would be aroused in this propaganda if Mahatmaji himself felt that he would not be equal to the task. And why should we restrain this anger? As prudent men I think it is necessary because, with the programme of civil disobedience to be undertaken a little later, how can we afford to raise forces which we will not be able to control. As prudent men, not as a matter of principle, we should decide that this new difficulty and new anger ought not to be started now. I therefore ask you to reject this proposition. Friends who are whole-heartedly with me on other points are not with me in this. Therefore it ought not to be taken as a party question and should be voted upon as a practical proposition and on the strength of your own judgment.

Mr. Satyamurti replying to the debate said that he could not understand how India could suffer economically if, instead of the British, other countries supplied her with goods. He cleared not misrepresentation regarding the scope of the enquiry by the committee. It was to suggest places from where goods can be easily obtained and this also included suggestions for supply, wherever possible, by India herself. The political weapon with which they wanted to arm themselves would be only temporary till Swaraj was obtained. Labour in England would welcome it as ending the capitalistic system which was exploiting them as much as India. He deprecated the attempt of the opposition to drag a great name down for low, controversial purposes and declared that, however great his reverance for Mahatma Gandhi, he could not give up his inherent right of independent thinking. He commended his proposition as giving them an honest, clean, manly and political weapon in order to hasten the advent of Swaraj.

THE VOTING

At five after three hours' discussion, the resolution was put to the vote by show of hands. Hands against the resolution were in a large majority. The President declared the resolution lost. This announcement was hailed by shouts of "Gandhi-ki-jai." Division was challenged, and the President ordered counting of votes, but the confusion that followed and the unwieldly number of delegates and the desirability of proceeding with the next motion regarding councils seemed to have influenced the supporters of the resolution who withdrew their request for division and the decision of the President declaring the motion lost held the ground.

Thus the Congress took a very rare step, that of throwing out the resolution which its executive (Subjects Committee) had recommended it to adopt.

Boycott of Councils

The Congress then proceeded with Mr. Rajagopalachari's resolution which ran thus:

"Whereas the boycott of councils carried out during the elections held in 1920 has destroyed the moral strength of the institutions through which the Government sought to consolidate its power and carry on its irresponsible rule; and whereas it is necessary again for the people of India to withhold participation in the elections of next year as an essential part of the programme of non-violent non-co-operation; it is resolved that this Congress advises that no Congressman shall stand as candidate for any of the councils and that all voters do abstain from voting for any candidate offering himself as such in disregard of Congress advice and signify the abstention in such manner as the All-India Congress Committee may instruct on that behalf". He said:

"I need hardly tell you that this is a proposition which I commend to you with all my heart and in spite of any difference of opinion, to accept it with such overwhelming numbers as to make it effective in the country in spite of any differences of opinion in matters of detail. We are all agreed, I make bold to say, as to the ultimate object and also to the immediate steps in attaining that object, namely, effective boycott of Councils. Though there are differences of opinion as to how the boycott of these institutions will be better attained one way more than any other, we have agreed that this effective boycott has to be effected and attained. I therefore feel quite confident that, whether you accept one amendment or another our object is fairly unanimous and

I believe that after contesting, discussing and obtaining your vote on any amendment if this resolution is ultimately carried, you will attempt to bring about the object, that is, effective boycott of the Councils in the manner in which a majority of this assembly has decided upon. I am quite certain that, whatever differences of opinion there might be on the various amendments that might be proposed in regard to the form in which this boycott should be effected, I have no doubt whatever that the boycott will be an object which we will join to effect. I particularly commend to you this proposition, because I feel certain, and I believe that in most of your minds also there is no doubt, that the only effective way in which we can boycott the Councils is by boycotting the elections themselves. Unless we boycott the elections we shall not boycott the Council, for, if we accept the reforms, we thereby accept to a certain extent the prestige of these Councils. Our boycott is not merely to be a physical boycott of the Councils but it is the moral break-down of their prestige. If the destruction of the prestige and moral importance of Councils is our object, we shall lose it partly by accepting them in merely trying to fight them. Bhishma challenges me, my importance is accepted by Bhishma. Therefore, I say, this nation, this Bhishma of India, should not accept morally the importance of these councils and try to fight with them but rather treat them with indifferences. Treat the Councils with indifference, and that is the most effective manner in which this nation, when once it has resolved upon boycotting it, can boycott it.

Various forms of boycott have been suggested. One is, for instance, boycotting the Councils by standing for election, by paying homage to the electorate with with the Councils have been proposed to be worked by the Government, accept that electorate, get their mandate and then let the members who have succeeded in capturing the electorate not go in and take their seats. I can suggest to you another from. Let the members who have got the votes of the majority of the electorate get into the Councils and there not co-operate with the Government. There is yet another from. You can go and take your seat in Councils, but refuse to appoint your Ministers. Another method is, you can go in, appoint your Ministers and through these double representatives ask the Councils not to perform any function. One more method is to appoint your Ministers, ask them to accept office, but not to do anything which Government may ask them to do. Please do not enter into definitions but decide on the question as to which is the effective boycott which we, in order to further our programme may accept I do not think any useful propose will be served by attempting to boycott. In a House of this magnitude I can only express my views humbly though firmly, and ask you to decide for yourselves.

Here I say that if we disturb the atmosphere which we have succeeded so far in creating with reference to Councils and try a new experiment, we will have first of all to undo what we have done and then to begin afresh. What is the atmosphere that we have created? It is not a mere wax thing. Every body feels that we have successfully reduced the Councils to a mockery. Everyone knows that the Councils do not represent the people, but they are merely the mask of the Government. Government is executing its irresponsible will through these Councils and is prepared to execute it through one mask or another as long as we go on co-operating with Government in material ways. If lawyers, students, merchants, the army and the population of India co-operate, it does not matter in the least what mask the Government has. It does not matter what members are in the Council. The will of the irresponsible Government will go on manifesting itself. It does not matter if nominated members of Government sit there. It is only a mask. If there is any sense in the boycott of the Councils, the only thing that we have to do is to boycott it in the real manner. To compare this question with the other question, namely, that this Government is still carrying on its work, is a mere confusion of issues. Government will go on with its work even if the Councils are abolished and we must devise measures how to stop that process. So far as boycott of Councils go, we have done that. The world knows, this Government knows, and we know that our representatives are not helping the Government. It is only a false mask that is being presented as a representative Government. How to deal with this falsehood is a different question altogether. After the boycott of Councils is finished, we shall act, we shall show that it is a mask and we shall tear it to pieces, we shall non-co-operate truly, but, so far as boycott of Councils is concerned, we shall be helping to keep the mask alive so long as we try to go there one way or the other.

"DON'T CONFUSE THE ISSUE"

I beg of you not to be carried away by references to what we might possibly do by co-operating inside the Councils, so long as we are resolved on boycott. If and when we feel that we have given sufficient trial to the programme of Non-co-operation and that we can no longer carry of the programme of Non-co-operation, then it is right that we should discuss the question as to what miseries we can stop by going into the Councils. But so long as we feel that we have not given to this great programme a sufficient trial and so long as we feel that we have not achieved the purpose we intended during the short period of trial we gave the programme, we have to continue the trial, and so long as we have that programme, we cannot do anything which is inconsistent with it. Therefore the only question before you is whether this form of boycott is proper or not. If you find, on hearing the amendments that may be proposed, that any one of them is better form of boycott, even after I have replied, you are at liberty to adopt that method. There is no necessity to imagine that, though leaders are united in the object to be achieved, there will be any division in the sense in which a split of this organization is understood. Then the issue is confused. I beg of you not to confuse the issue by any of these considerations. We must believe that every one will act according to his conscience and that no misfortune will happen by reason of a mistake of an intellectual question. I therefore beg of you to direct your attention to one question only, as to what is best, what is wise, what is futile and what is useful, and decide upon that question (applause.)

All this stage th? House was adjourned till the next day.

Subjects Committee Proceedings

29TH DECEMBER 1922

The Subjects Committee at its sitting on the 29th Dec. passed Mr. Rajagopalachariar's draft resolution on Civil Disobedience. It reaffirmed the opinion of the Congress.

'That Civil Disobedience is the only civilised and effective substitute for an armed rebellion when every other remedy for preventing the arbitrary, tyrannical and emasculating use of authority has been tried.

"And in view of the widespread awakening of the people to a sense of the urgent need for Swaraj and the general demand and necessity for civil disobedience in order that the national goal may be speedily attained, and in view of the fact that the necessary atmosphere of non-violence has been preserved in spite of all provocation, it calls upon all Congress workers,—

"To complete the preparations for offering civil disobedience by concentrating their attention on strengthening and expanding the national organisation and to take immediate steps for the collection of at least Rs. 25 lakhs for the Tilak Swaraj Fund and the enrolment of at least 50,000 volunteers, satisfying the conditions of the Ahmedabad pledge by a date to be fixed by the A.I.C.C. at Gaya, and further empowers the Committee to issue necessary instructions for carrying the resolution to practical effect."

The resolution was adopted by a large majority, notwithstanding the obstructionist and hostile attitude taken by the minority.

Amendments were proposed for relaxing the conditions of the pledge, to fix the dates, to increase the number of volunteers and the amount of funds to be collected.

Plan of Work

The plan of work that Mr. Rajagopalachari suggested was contained in the following resolution placed before the Subjects Committee:

"In order to carry out the resolution of the Congress regarding the preparation for Civil Disobedience and the successful carrying on of the constructive programme, it is resolved that every delegate who has attended this Congress shall deem it his individual and particular duty,

(1) To start or put in efficient order at least 4 primary sabhas.

(2) To obtain the enrolment of at least 1,000 members for 1923.

(3) To collect, through his personal exertions and pay into the local district or provincial organisation, at least Rs. 500 for the Tilak Swaraj Fund.

(4) To instal at least 50 new charkas in as many homes.

(5) That every district shall have at least 100 Congress Sabhas in working order, and

(6) At least 100 volunteers enrolled in three classes as follows:

Class A.—A Civil Disobedience Corps of at least 40 volunteers ready for civil disobedience whenever called upon by the proper authority. Class B.—A reserve corps of service of at least 50 volunteers agreeing to serve in the prosecution of the constructive programme for a minimum period of 4 days in the month. Class C. A batch of a least 10 volunteers devoting full time in constructive work on such honoraria as may be fixed and paid by the local Congress organisations.

DECEMBER 30TH, 1922

On the third day the Congress devoted five hours to the discussion of the Council boycott resolution.

The discussion on Mr. Rajagopalachari's resolution reaffirming the existing constructive programme and opposing all proposals regarding Councils was continued.

Pundit Nekiram (Punjab) and Dr. M. A. Ansari (Delhi) supported the resolution. Both pointed out that a case had not been made out for changing the position take up at Calcutta and reaffirmed at Nagpur and Ahmedabad.

Dr. Ansari said he could not understand the camouflage of boycotting the Councils from within. He would rather welcome from the opposition an open confession that non-co-operation had failed and that the protagonists of Councils wanted to enter the Councils to utilise the reforms for the good of the country, but we could not conceive how the Congress could sanction a sheer waste of money and energy to return Congress candidates over and over again. They would get tired after two or three elections and would eventually have to leave the field again for the Moderates. And if they were not returned in a majority, what would then happen to "boycott" from within"?

BEGUM HASRAT MOHANI

Begum Hasrat Mohani said those who desired complete independence could not imagine the abandonment of Non-co-operation, but those who believed in partial independence could attain it even by working for a further instalment of reforms through Councils. She remarked that Mahatma Gandhi's mistake in opposing the motion for complete independence at Ahmedabad was responsible for the reaction now led by the pro-Councillities.

Mrs. Sarojini Naidu, in supporting the resolution, said that, though a woman, she was a soldier for Swaraj. While this Congress continued to take its stand upon their pledge as followers of Mr. Gandhi's doctrine of Satyagraha and Non-co-operation, so long would they continue to give allegiance to that ideal. She recognised that as times change and circumstances change, their policies must be readjusted and programmes altered, but until those policies were restated and the scope and functions as also the letter and spirit of new Non-co-operation clearly defined she must be loyal as she was, cling to her own Satyagraha definition of Gandhi's Non-co-operation and fulfil his ideal through the channel of Civil Disobedience rather than that of contest with the Government.

MR. SRINIVASA IYENGAR

Mr. S. Srinivasa Iyengar moved as an amendment the following proposition which was defeated in the Subjects Committee:

"Whereas notwithstanding the fact that the majority of the electors in the whole country abstained from voting at the Council elections of 1920 many Indians allowed themselves to be elected thereto and did not resign their seats inspite of their being so advised by the Nagpur Congress with the result that the new councils do not represent the country, they are used to consolidate the power of the present system of Government in India which the Congress has resolved to put an end to, this Congress earnestly advises, with a view to render the boycott of Councils more effective than it was in 1920, all electors to vote for Congressmen who shall, when elected, absolutely refrain from taking their seats in the Councils."

Mr. Iyengar said this motion was not a step in the direction of Council entry, but would give distinctly new orientation to the Non-co-operation movement in the direction of the destruction of Councils, at least to the extent of the elected part of the Councils. This was a business proposition representing a compromise between the two schools of thought which were now divided on this question in the Congress circles throughout the country. During the last two years, far from the opinion in favour of boycott of elections becoming consolidated, an appreciable percentage of those who unhesitatingly accepted boycott of elections in the beginning of the Non-co-operation campaign had come to think that it was necessary to change the direction. The fact that the Congress at Calcutta and Nagpur affirmed boycott of Councils by preferring a particular method which was then necessary should not weigh with them in rejecting this proposition. Speaking for himself he was not for entry into Councils and this opinion was due to personal experience in an unfortunate part of India and the experience of others in other parts of India. This amendment would keep in its integrity Non-violent Non-co operation in regard to Councils and at the same time bring round those who were opposed to them. Those who were of the view that they could enter the councils with a view to create deadlooks or work out the principles of responsive co-operation were willing to accept the amendment which was in the direction of making the boycott of Councils completely effective. "Our movement for boycott will only be effective if there is practical unanimity of opinion and if there is a policy of give and take. The minority is never diciplined by the majority and the majority which has power is seldom tolerant of the minority and the division cured by periodical compromise and by observing the principle of practical unanimity. The construction programme is by itself insufficient and Civil Disobedience cannot be immediately started in such a manner and on such a scale as to bring Government to its kness, and therefore I want you to boycott the Councils by capturing the electorate and thereby preventing co-operators from going into institutions which are used by Government for your destruction in the same way you boycott foreign cloth by picketting. Your duty is therefore to withdraw from Government the co-operation of that party without which they will not be able to get on. It is your duty to create unity and concerted action in the Congress camp. But there is now discord. How are you going to remove it? Will it be by the rule of the majority? I venture to say, "no". Let us not use the shibboleth of concentration upon any particular programme. This theory of concentration has been done to death. Let us not imagine that what Gandhi wanted was boycott of elections for all time to come. At that time the electors were not used to it. The Non-co-operation Party was not formed. Discipline was not there amongst them and there was no possibility of computing our chances of success. But to-day there is more discipline and we have understood, however imperfectly, the meaning of Non-co-operation and I therefore think the chances of boycott are far greater now than before. The most valuable and effective instrument for destruction of Councils is in this amendment which is a compromise between the two schools of thought. Show your spirit of compromise by your votes."

MR. C. VIJIARAGHAVA CHARIAR

Mr. Vijiaraghavachariar explained that of these contending motions, that of Mr. Rajagopalachari left the position as it existed now. Both Mr. Iyengar and Pandit Motilal fovoured contesting elections with this distinction that the former declared his intention of not sitting in the Councils, while the latter left it to the next Congress to state with what programme the elections be contested. He appealed to the delegates to vote on the merits of the rival positions taken up and not be led away by ideas of the fate of the Congress due to division in their ranks. The speaker prized the unfettered judgment of the Congress above all other considerations and believed that a nation which blindly followed a leader or leaders was heading for decay. Supposing they decided in favour of contesting the elections, desired Government at home may change the Statute at one night's sitting or the Government of India may change the rules, but if none of these happened and even if they got a majority, they had to face a provision in the Reforms

Act which had not existed in the previous constitution and which was extremely tyrannous. They authorised the Viceroy and Governors to dissolve the Councils as often as they liked without assigning any reasons for it. The Government may naturally be expected to retaliate by resorting to dissolving and tiring out both candidates and electorates.

Moreover Government would pose as martyrs before the outside world and would have its sympathy and would be able to propagate that orientals were not fit for the western method of Government. That course would then involve the use of mad and useless waste of money and time. There was no parallel in the history of the world to such a futile attempt. They should also remember that Government could do without Councils, that it was armed with numerous Acts to maintain law and order and collect taxes.

Continuing, he pointed out that the voters would be confused by a fundamentally different change and the change of direction would arrest the progress made in the mentality of masses by the Gandhi programme.

Mr. Vijiaraghavachari next referred to the reported intention of Pro-Council leaders to withdraw their active participation in Congress activities if the verdict went against them. He would regret if these leaders retired, but he asked Congress not to sacrifice its independent judgment for personalities. It should entrust itself to God and if an officerless regiment was led to victory by a private in France during the great War God would also help the Congress in ransoming the great cause.

MR. NEHRU'S POSITION

Pandit Motilal Nehru at this stage explained his position. He said he considered his own amendment more prudent than that of Mr. Iyengar as it was the Congress to decide after one year in the light of circumstances then prevailing as to what programme the Congress candidates should adopt, while Mr. Iyengar committed them to a policy beforehand. But as Mr.

Iyengar's amendment was put as a compromise and as he wanted to show that his own mind was equally opposed to entry in Councils, he would accept the compromise, provided the Congress so accepted it. Otherwise he would press his own amendment, which he considered the better of the two. He honestly believed that, comparing the result of the boycott at the last election his method was better to achieve the same purpose. It left him unmoved whether he was a leader or not. His love was for a clean weapon to attain Swaraj without bending before anybody and meant to pursue that end with full faith in Non-co-operation.

PANDIT MALAVIYA

Pandit Malaviya next addressed the house. His view was that the good of the country lay in entering Councils with a view to stop the mad course of repression which the Government was pursuing, to secure the release of Gandhi and other leaders, to force the hands of Government to effect retrenchment, reduce expenditure and lighten their burden as they were all tax-payers. Government was too stone-hearted to be moved by the sacrificing spirit which made them flood the jails. The speaker believed in giving battle by all weapons. He could follow whole-heartedly both the constructive and the Council programmes simultaneously. The boycott of Councils was part of a programme for the attainment of Swaraj within a year, but, when that year had passed without bringing them Swaraj, they must now change their programme. Pundit Motilal Nehru's amendment was, he thought, better than that of Mr. Iyengar in as much as it left a clear twelve months to decide what shall be India's programme at the end of that period and commended it for the acceptance of the Congress. Concluding Punditjee, referring to himself, said "Remember an old man's words. You will repent later if you reject them now."

MR. RAJAGOPALACHARI

Mr. C. Rajagopalachari then replied to the debate. He asked the Congress to remember that no great change from the present programme could be recommended by any but t e wisest and greatest of leaders. It was not possible for small men to ask the Congress to take a line different from what this house sitting at Calcutta decided after careful consideration. It was therefore natural that the biggest of leaders should now advise a change, but these leaders did not want them to decide the question except by their own judgment and they must use it whatever the result. The constitution of the Congress was so elastic that no difference of opinion could possibly lead to an undesirable split. The Congress might rest assured that they would not divide the country or divide themselves over any failure or error of judgment. The question about contesting elections was whether poor India could afford to spend money for putting forward candidates every time the seats were rendered vacant. One amendment amounted to a competition of intellect between the rule-making capacity of Government and the capacity of Congressmen to make the seats vacant and the other amendment amounted to a test of intellect inside the Councils as to how they could ever rule the decisions of Government and how still to maintain their position and great deadlocks. In both cases there was the contest of brains and such a contest was not going to bring Swaraj. He believed I that they had not given sufficient trial to the constructive part of the Non-co-operation movement which must therefore be carried on. They could not capture the electorate more effectively than by the constructive programme in villages. The method of contesting elections was expensive. Pundit Malaviya had said that if they went into the Councils they could get Gandhi released. The movement they suspended the Non-co-operation programme they had made an ignoble surrender and they could not hope to get Gandhi released.

After Mr. Rajagopalachari had spoken, the pandal was cleared of everyone except the delegates entitled to vote. The resolution was passed by a large majority, the compromise resolution of Mr. Iyengar being defeated by 1770 against 894 votes.

DECEMBER 31ST, 1922

The Congress met for its final sitting on the 4th day, December 31st, 1922 with about a dozen resolutions on the agenda. The following resolutions were passed.

LABOUR RESOLUTION

Mr. Dip Narain Singh moved:

"Whereas this Congress is of opinion that Indian labour should be organised with a view to improve and promote their well-being and secure to them their just rights and also to prevent exploitation of Indian labour and of Indian resources, it is resolved that this Congress, while welcoming the move made by the All-India Trade Union Congress and various Kisan Sabhas in organising the workers of India, hereby appoints the following committee with power to assist the Executive Council of the All-India Trade Union Congress for the organisation of Indian Labour, both agricultural and industrial:—Messrs. C.F. Andrews, J. M. Sen Gupta, S. N. Halder, Swami Dayanand, Dr. D. D. Sathaye, Mr. Singaravelu Chettiar and E. L. Iyer.

SCHOOL BOYCOTT

Mr. Rajendra Prasad moved:

"With reference to boycott of Government and Government aided and affiliated educational institutions, this Congress declares that the boycott must be maintained and further resolves that every province should be called upon to put existing national institutions on a sound financial basis and to improve their efficiency in every possible way."

BOYCOTT OF COURTS

On the motion of Mr. K. P. Sen Singha (Bihar) seconded by Mr. Srishchandra Chatterjee (Bengal) the Congress declared that the boycott of law courts by lawyers and liligants must be maintained and further resolved that greater efforts should be made to establish punchayats and cultivate public opinion in their favour.

CHANGE IN CREED

The next resolution related to a demand for change in the present creed of Congress. Mr. P. K. Mazumdar of Comilla (Bengal) moved:

> "That the ocject of the Indian National Congress is the attainment of Swaraj, that is, the attainment of complete independence without foreign connection by the people of India by all legitimate and proper means."

In the course of his speech Mr. Mazumdar said that the natural meaning of Swaraj was Swaraj or self-raj and not foreign or any other raj. Swaraj again meant complete independence. The time had come when every one should freely express his view on this question without being afraid of anything in this world.

Mr. C. Rajagopalachari in opposing the resolution observed that the present creed covered both the position, namely absolute independence and independence within the British Empire. Necessity for a change in the present creed would certainly arise if the position of Indians in other parts of the British Empire was finally decided to be impossible of solution. Indians might make absolute separation and independence as a possible condition of the solution of their difficulties, but that position had not yet been reached. There was also an attempt by some to change the methods of attaining Swaraj by altering the words "legitimate and peaceful" into "legitimate and proper". But Mr. Rajagopalachari continuing said, "The word proper' can cover more things than peaceful. I ask you to accept the position that peaceful means alone shall be tried by us and not as yet non-peaceful means".

Mr. Mozumdar replying to the debate appealed to those who were of the same view with him to declare their mind unequivocally. How long, he asked, were representatives of 30 crores to go on purifying their souls ? In his opinion unless they made their definition of the word Swaraj clear they could not proceed with their programme for achieving the goal.

The resolution was then put to vote and lost by show of hands amid cries of "Mahatma Gandhi ki jai."

PUBLIC DEBT

Mr. Rajagopalachari next moved the most important resolution of the day:

"Whereas by reason of the unjustifiable military expenditure and other extravagance the Government had brought the national indebtedness to a limit beyond recovery, and whereas the Government still pursues the same policy of extravagance under cover of the authority of so-called representative assemblies constituted without the suffrages of the majority or any substantial fraction of voters and despite their declared repudiation of the authority to such assemblies to represent the people; and

"Whereas if government is permitted to continue this policy it will become impossible for the people of India ever to carry on their own affairs with regard to the honour and happiness of the people and it has therefore become necessary to stop its career of irresponsibility.

"This Congress hereby repudiates the authority of the legislatures that have been or may be formed by the Government in spite of the National boycott of the said institutions in future to raise any loan or to incur any liabilities on behalf of the nation, and notifies to the world that on the attainment of Swarajya the people of India, though holding themselves liable for all debts and liabilities rightly or wrongly incurred hitherto by the Government, will not hold themselves bound to repay any loans or discharge any liabilities incurred on and after this date on the authority or sanction of the so-called legislatures brought into existence in spite of the national boycott."

MR. RAJAGOPALACHARI

Moving the resolution on repudiation of loans Mr. Rajagopalachari spoke as follows:

I do not think anything remains for me to tell you after this resolution has been heard by you, and the reasons for this resolution are incorporated therein. I can only detain you with figures. Within the last four years ninety crores of deficit have been accumulated by the present Government and they have got this money by borrowing repeatedly and by issuing unbacked currency notes. We are paying the interest on all these loans. Of course it may be said that this is due to the fact that we have not entered their legislatures and protested, but I say, whether you protest or not, you cannot interfere with the causes of this accumulation of debt. The causes are the military expenditure and our servility and the suspicion of every foreign Government as to the loyalty of its people. Unless we remove the causes the military expenditure is not likely to be reduced and the lngislature is not likely in the near future to get that power to interfere with that expenditure. I say Swaraj is the only remedy, but we have not attained Swaraj as rapidly as we intend to. We must in the meanwhile tell them that, even though we stand out of the legislature and allow the Government to govern by its own executive will, naked and unmasked, yet, when we attain the power we can not be responsible for the expenditure hereafter to be incurred. It may be said that it is a pompous claim that we make, but I ask you, do we have faith that we will attain Swaraj or not ? If there is any truth or honesty in our people, we must and shall attain Swaraj and, when we attain that, are we going to pay the debts which hereafter they might incur ? What has been incurred already will be a matter for adjustment when the final treaty between us and Great Britain shall be settled. There is no doubt we have the moral right to debt the British Nation and reduce that amount from our debt, but as to the future we shall now give notice to the people that those loans shall not be our liabilities.

I have already written on this subject. It may be said that there has not been sufficient discussion, if it is considered by any of our friends or leaders that there has not been sufficient discussion, I will leave the matter to the A.I.C.C. I say this because it was strongly pressed upon me before I came here that this is a resolution which should be further considered. I will leave it to the House to decide, but all the same let us give this warning to the people.

It may be also said that this will create suspicion among our own class who invest money. It cannot be so. What has been already borrowed we admit here and the only question will be whether Britain shall be liable when we take our affairs in our own hands. We therefore give clear notice to people outside and inside India that we shall not have the wherewithal to meet the wasteful extravagance which the Government is incurring in our name.

AN AMENDMENT

Seth Jamnalal Bajaj formally seconded the resolution. Mr. Vijayaraghavachari moved an amendment to refer the resolution to the All India Congress Committee. He said the question was a serious one involving the application of principles, not only in the matter of the domestic justice but also the principles applicable to International Justice on the decision of which they should stand or fall in the eve of the world. The question has not been very long before the public. It was only recently started and the attention of the people has not been sufficiently directed towards it. He appealed to them therefore to refer the question to the A.I.C.C., for consideration and report to the next year's Congress. It was one year no doubt but they were not going so get Swaraj in the meanwhile. Time was of no essence in this problem.

Mr. Rajagopalachari said he admitted that when this resolution was taken up by the Subjects Committee it was so late that a really full discussion of the pros and cons could not be had. It came however before the Congress after the Committee had accepted it. If, as he had stated already, they would accept Mr. Vijayaraghavachari's amendment, he had no objection at all, because he considered that the warning was there. If it was their pleasure that the resolution should not be disposed of in a hurry, let them accept he suggestion by all means.

A number of speakers spoke for and against the resolution, after which the amendment was put and lost, and, apparently to the surprise of many, the resolution was carried.

CIVIL DISOBEDIENCE

Mr. F. Abbas Tyabjee moved:

"This Congress reaffirms its opinion that Civil Disobedience is the only civilised and effective substitute for an armed rebellion when every other remedy for preventing the arbitrary, tyrannical and emasculating use of authority has been tried.

"And, in view of the widespread awakening of the people to a sense of the urgent need for Swarajya and the general demand and necessity for civil disobedience in order that the National goal may be speedily attained, and in view of the fact that the necessary atmosphere of non-violence has been preserved inspite of all provocation.

"This Congress calls upon all Congress-workers to complete the preparations for offering Civil Disobedience by strengthening and expanding the national organisations and to take immediate steps for the collection of at least Rs. 25 lakhs for the Tilak Swarajya Fund and the enrolment of at least 50,000 volunteers, satisfying the conditions of the Ahmedabad pledge by a date to be fixed by the All India Congress Committee at Gaya.

"And empowers the Committee to issue necessary instruction for carrying this resolution into practical effect."

He said that the only way of attaining Swarajya was by organising themselves for Civil Disobedience. This disobedience might at first be of individual character, but when once it was commenced it would assume, like a snow ball, a tremendous size leading to mass Civil Disobedience.

Mrs. Naidu in supporting the resolution in a spirited speech said that it was the first step in the preparation of men and munitions for the war of Civil Disobedience. She was sure that soldiers of Mahatma Gandhi would not let fall the pledge that they had given to an awaiting world while passing the resolution congratulating Ghazi Mustapha Kemal Pasha.

Mr. Basanta Kumar Mazumder, by way of amendment, suggested the immediate starting of Civil Disobedience under the direction of the provincial Congress Committees Messrs. Fazlur Rahman (U.P.), Sirish Chatterjea (Bengal), Raghuram Varma and others suggested some other amendments which were all lost and the original motion of Mr. Tyabjee was carried.

PRIVATE DEFENCE

Mr. Rajagopalachari next moved :

"This Congress declares that Non-co-operators are free to exercise the right of private defence within the limits defined by law, except when carrying on Congress work on occasions directly arising therefrom, subject always to the condition that it is not likely to lead to a general outburst of violence".

"Note:—Using force in private defence in grave cases, e.g. insults to religion, outrages on the modesty of women, or indecent assault on boys and men, is not prohibited under any circumstances."

Mr. Rajagopalachari explained that the resolution followed the recommendation of the Civil Disobedience Committee and was intended to please those who believed non-violence only as a policy confirmed to activities connected with the Congress. Moreover the definition given in the note showed that occasion on which it would be used did not generally come within the pale of political activities.

The resolution was put and adopted.

NEAR EAST SITUATION

Mr. Rajendra Prasad moved:

"In view of the serious situation in the Near East which threatened the integrity of the Khilafat and of the Turkish Government, and in view of the determination of Hindus and Mussalmans and other peoples to prevent any such injury, this Congress resolves that the Working Committee do take steps in consultation with the Khilafat Working Committee to secure united action by Hindus and Mussalmans and others to prevent the exploitation of India for any such unjust cause, and deal with the situation."

The resolution was adopted unanimously without much discussion, only the proposer making a short speech.

NEW AFFILIATIONS

The Congress adopted four more resolutions without discussion. Of these one granted the request far affiliation to Congress of the British Indian Association, Johannesburg, the Natal Indian Congress Committee, the Durban Indian Association, the Durban British Indian League, the Cape Town and Kabul Congress Committees. Of these the 4 associations in South Africa were authorised to send ten delegates to the Congress collectively and the Kabul Committee to send two delegates.

Mrs. Naidu then announced that Mr. and Mrs. Tyabji had

contributed Rs. 1500 for the Civil Disobedience Fund and Rs. 1500 for the Tilak Fund; also that the Tamil people living in South Africa had sent a cheque of £110 towards the Civil Disobedience Fund. Some more subscriptions were also announced.

NEW OFFICE-BEARERS

The services of Pundit Motilal, Dr. Ansari and Mr. Rajagopalachari, the outgoing general Secretaries, were appreciated and in their places were appointed Messrs. Muazzam Ali, Vallabhbhai Patel and Rajendra Prasad as General Secretaries for the next year. Seth Jamnalal Bajaj and Seth Chotani were re-appointed treasurers.

THE NEXT SESSION

The Congress accepted the invitation extended by Mr. Nageswara Rao to hold the next session of the Congress in Andhra-desa at a place to be announced later.

THANKS-GIVINGS

Mr. Deep Narain Singh, on behalf of the Reception Committee paid an eloquent tribute to the President for upholding the honour of the nation and conducting the proceedings with dignity and suavity. Mr. Das was, and would continue to be, he said, the pride of India. He also thanked the delegates, the gallant band of volunteers and the Municipality and District Boards of Gaya for their co-operation and support in the national cause.

PRESIDENT'S CLOSING REMARKS

Mr. Das in declaring the session closed said:

"I wish I could say that I congratulate myself and congratulate you upon the resolutions we have passed. Although I cannot do that, I thank you from the bottom of my heart for the patience and the wonderful manner in which you have helped me in carrying on the proceedings. That indeed is a matter of congratulation for all of us. Differences of opinion must arise in every healthy organisation or institution and although to-day I differ from the majority of the Congress, I have not given up the hope that a day will come when I shall get the majority on my side (Hear, Hear, and cries of "Deshabandhu ki jai"). I hope we have learnt now to respect each other's opinion with hope, in spite of what appears like a split, and I believe we are really united in more points than we differ (applause). But we are agreed on one thing from which nothing will separate me, and that is the speedy attainment of Swaraj. Although we differ on the question of programme, all of us are agreed in the principle of Non-violent Non-co-operation."

COCANADA, 31ST DECEMBER 1923

The Congress me on this day to consider the most important resolution of this session, viz., the Compromise Resolution. By this resolution the breach between the "No-changers" and the "Swarajists" or the Council-party, which was ever widening since the Gaya Congress a year ago and had but partly been repaired at Delhi, was now fully made up; and once more the Congress emerged at Cocanada as a united body of Nationalists, some to work through the Councils, others outside it, for the country's emancipation. The resolution is now famous as the Das-Achariyar Compromise, being a compromise between Mr. Das as the leader of the Swarajists and Mr. Rajagopalachariar, the leader of the No-changers. The opposition to the compromise was led by Mr. Shyam Sunder Chakravarty of Bengal who wanted not to recognise the Delhi resolution which, he said, was not a non-co-operation resolution at all, for it allowed permission to the Swarajists to enter the Councils, and there was nothing of non-co-operation at all in that idea. He had a very strong following and was strongly supported by many able non-co-operators who roundly accused their leader, Mr. Rajagopalachariar, of deserting their principles.

CONGRESS DEPARTMENTS

On the Congress re-assembling, after the usual processions and songs, the President moved a resolution.

On the motion of Moulana Mahomed Ali the Congress passed the resolution calling upon its Working Committee to prepare and submit at as early a date as possible, to the All-India Congress Committee for its consideration, a scheme of organisation of separate Congress Departments for more efficiently, expeditiously and uninterruptedly carrying out the various items of the programme of Constructive Work under its supervision and control. The Working Committee should also submit a scheme of national corps of paid workers who would carry out the work of the various departments and provide adequate and efficient help to the Central and Provincial Secretaries and local office establishments.

The Das-Achariyar Compromise Resolution

Sjt. C. Rajagopalachariar, then moved the compromise resolution. In moving his resolution in the open Congress, he said:

> Mr. President, Sisters and Brothers, I place before you a proposition which I want you to carefully consider and accept in case it meet your approval. The first thing that we have to settle in this Congress what is to be our future work. We all know that the Congress as a whole is determined upon non-co-operation. But we have to decide what part of non-co-operation and in what manner we shall work during the ensuing year, in what manner we have to act under the leadership of Maulana Mohammed Ali during the next 12 months. We all know what Maulana Mohammed Ali wants to do so far as he himself is concerned. He has told you already and it is that we must concentrate on the constructive Programme adopted at Bardoli not merely in policy, but day to day work and with strenuous and concentrated effort. I, therefore, want you to accept that pro-

gramme of work and if you do that, one part of the proposition that I place before you must be approved by you. You must decide upon carrying out the constructive work which is part of the non-co-operation programme.

Another part of the resolution which I place before you is a declaration that we still adhere to the principle and the policy of the triple boycott. I shall be brief and therefore straight and to the point. I want you to adopt the principle and the policy of the Triple Boycott as inaugurated and enforced by Mahatma Gandhi. I do not want you by this resolution to adopt the Triple Boycott by going to platforms and immediately and aggressively enforcing the programme of calling off the lawyers, school boys and the Councillors. We must keep that principle as insisted and enforced by Mahatma Gandhi before us; for we want to carry out the constructive programme without disturbing the atmosphere prevailing in the country and getting the concentrated effort of the people. This formulation of the Constructive Programme is necessary because I feel that the atmosphere in the country has been disturbed by what we have been talking and doing regarding the Councils. That declaration of policy is the re-affirmation of the Congress policy as inaugurated by Mahatma Gandhi and forms the second part of the resolution. Another part of the programme is a clear expression of our determination not to undo what we did at Delhi or to disturb those who acted under the Delhi decision. It does not mean that we adopt that policy for the future. It only means that we do not disturb what has already been done. These are the three things that form this resolution.

AVOID THE AFTER-MATH OF WAR

I have given them to you in the order of importance according to my opinion. Another important consideration I must place before you for adopting this resolution in the form in which I have placed it. The most important consideration why you should adopt this in the from in which I have placed it before you is that this resolution will be supported by Desabandhu Das and his friends from whom we have had the misfortune to differ up till now. (Hear, hear). Why does he give its support? It is because he does not want battle now, but simply wants you to accept the facts as they are and we want him to accept the facts as they are. On our part, we should not disturb what has been done at Delhi and on the other part he should not divide this House again over the programme which to him appears right and which the Congress has hitherto failed to accept. But he does not want you again either to adopt his programme here or to reject it. I recognise the fact that the Congress has the same policy to-day which it had before. I do not think I need add anything more to this except that, if an alternative were before you, whether you want a stronger resolution after a battle with all its consequences or whether you have this resolution which contains the substance of what we want, without the evil effects of the battle and a war, I would certainly prefer the latter. I want you, men who agree with me in the policy with which my name has been always mentioned up till now, I want you to rely upon yourselves and not rely upon the services of others except in so far as they are pleased to give it. Every man and woman must depend upon himself or herself. At the same time, he ought not to do anything to prevent other people from assisting him. You might take it from me that even where union is not possible we might at least avoid the aftermath of a bitter war. But if we proceed with work and forget the passions for war, we might get union even. I shall not detain you further, but proceed to read the resolution which is as follows. Mr. Konda Venkatappiah will follow me later on and will read the resolution in Telugu. But you will pardon me therefore if I stop reading only in English and allowing time to other speakers. What my friend said must be enough for all those who do not know English. (This is a reference to the translation of his speech into Telugu made by Mr. D. Gopalakrishniah). Those who know English might like to know every word of the resolution and therefore I read it.

THE RESOLUTION

"This Congress reaffirms the Non-co-operation resolutions adopted at Calcutta, Nagpur, Ahmedabad, Gaya and Delhi.

"Since doubts have been raised by reason of the Non-co-operation resolution adopted at Delhi with regard to Council entry, whether there has been any change in the policy of the Congress regarding the Triple Boycott, this Congress affirms that the principle and policy of that Boycott remain unaltered.

"This Congress further declares that the said principle and policy form the foundation of constructive work and appeals to the nation to carry out the programme of constructive work as adopted at Bardoli and prepare for the adoption of Civil Disobedience. This Congress calls upon every Provincial Congress Committees to take immediate steps in this behalf with a view to the speedy attainment of our goal."

Continuing, Mr. Rajagopalachariar said: I do not place before you a more complete and detailed programme of constructive work because in the present state of want of homogeneity each Provincial Congress Committee will have to consider what particular items are more urgent and necessary and possible and therefore will have to be considered. That programme will have to be considered by the executive of the Congress in consultation with each particular province.

But one thing is clear: that we give a mandate to our executive to concentrate on constructive work. Details with reference to the propriety of words and phrases in this resolution have been thoroughly threshed in your Subjects Committee and the Subjects Committee has recommended to you this resolution in the form I proposed it. I want you, therefore, as a National Assembly, of men intent on business, to accept this resolution without further doubt or discussion. We don't want to ask those who have entered councils to come out. The fact that we gave them permission at Delhi continues and we don't alter that permission. What was decided at Delhi remains without being extended by a single inch or fraction of an inch. Know also that it is not reduced by a single inch. That is all that I have to say (cheers).

MR. C. R. DAS

Mr. C. R. Das who was cheered as he ascended the rostrum to speak, contrary to expectations made on speech, and said: Gentlemen, I have great pleasure in seconding this resolution. I do so formally now and reserve my speech if there is any necessity for it later on.

SHYAM SUNDER CHAKRAVARTI'S AMENDMENT

Mr. Shyam Sundar Chakravarti moved his amendment. It reiterated the non-co-operation and triple boycott without making any mention of Delhi compromise. It runs as follows:

> "This Congress re-affirms its adherence to the programme of non-violent non-co-operation including the Triple Boycott as inaugurated by Mahatma Gandhi as the only means of attaining Swarajya and calls upon the people to take further steps towards the fulfilment of the programme by (1) mobilising the public life of the country through the Congress so as to increase its hold on the people and mantaining an attitude of dissociation from the legislatures, (2) establishing Panchayats for the private settlement of all disputes and by refraining from having recourse to Government courts, (3) by organising national institutions for the education of the youth of the country and dissuading attendance at schools and colleges run under Government auspices, (4) by increasing the production and use of Khaddar, (5) by abolishing the sin of untouchability and, (6) by achieving national solidarity by strict adherence to the principle of non-violence in all matters of intercommunal relationship and producing the spirit of brotherliness between the Hindu, Musalman, Christian Parsee, Sikh and other inhabitants of

the country."

Babu Shyam Sunder Chakravarti in moving his amendment said that under the resolution of Sj. Rajagopalachari the non-co-operation movement was greatly affected. He would have no quarrel with the Swaraj party if they would do constructive work. But so long as it was destructive work, this Congress which was intent upon constructive work alone must not allow the Swarajist to identify themselves with the Congress. If they did the Congress would become the butt end of ridicule.

MR. JAGAT NARAIN LAL

Mr. Jagat Narain Lal in submitting another amendment to Sj. Rajagopalachariar's resolution urged the deletion of the word 'Delhi.' He said that while he did not suggest that they should rescind the Delhi resolution, they must not re-affirm it. Mr. Haradayal Nag supported him.

Mr. Vallabhbhai Patel said that the Delhi resolution was on accomplished fact and to go back upon it now would be dishonourable. The Swarajists had secored victories with the support and in some cases with the sympathy of the Congress voters. Mr. Rajagopalachari's resolution, therefore, gave them the maximum possible in the circumstances. It pledged the Swarajists to give the non-co-operators facilities for constructive work and would enable them to go to the country and tell them that they must not expect any result from the Councils. He added that constructive work required great political sentiment to make it successful. The psychological moment for them would arise when either the Swarajists failed to get any thing as the result of capturing the Council or when they broke their pledges to the electorate. Then would be the opportunity for the Congress to disown them or their programme. But at present they must leave them alone and in the meantime carry out the constructive programme on the basis of Mr. Rajagopalachariar's resolution.

Mr. Azad Sobhani in his characteristic solemn style supported the amendment of Mr. Chakravarti. He said that three years' achievements since 1920 were due out and out to Non-Co-operation programme while since they had begun to entertain compromises their work had come to a stand still.

DR. PATTABHI SITARAMIAH

Dr. B. Pattabhi Sitaramiah, whose speech was perhaps the best in the Congress, opposing the resolution said in support of the amendment:

> Refferring to the amendment, namely that the word 'non-co-operation' should be deleted from the words 'non co-operation resolution of Delhi.', he said : Now if you look at the paper you will find altogether a new import and a new significance attached to the non-co-operation resolution at Delhi. It says in Mr. Rajagopalachariar's proposition—"since doubts have been raised by reason of the non-co-operation resolution adopted at Delhi with regard to Council Entry". Now this Congress for the first time in the history of the Congress ratifies the idea that the resolution at Delhi is a non-co-operation resolution in respect of Council Entry. (Hear, hear). This is a position to which you are unwittingly and insidiously. I beg your pardon, imperceptibly being committed. I tell you it is a most dangerous and pernicious position to take up in the Congress. (Hear, hear). For the first time you are putting your seal upon the proposition that non-violent Non-co-operation has got two aspects, has got two strings to the bow,—one string which will work from within the Councils and another one which will work from outside the Councils. I challenge any one to deny that the language will bear this interpretation that I have given. That is why Babu Hardyal Nag has asked to delete that expression. But I am not satisfied with it. I want you to go further and examine the position and the conditions in the land; to see whether, after we have been in Delhi, we wish it is not our duty to say definitely and once for all what should be our attitude towards the political problems in this ancient land, whether we should achieve

our salvation through the Councils by a process of boycott from within or apart from the Councils and irrespective of the Councils by a process of non-co-operation from without, by a process of mobilisition of public life through the Congress institutions, having nothing to do with the Councils. I honestly feel that just as at Nagpur after Calcutta you said that people should come out of the Councils, so having regard to the conditions of the present day to the antecedent circumstances of the present hour, it is your duty, certainly, not to ask for the withdrawal of candidates, but to say that the Congress has, apart from the political questions of the country, nothing to do with these Councils. (Hear, hear). Will you or will you not make that position clear? But I have had one difficulty in the matter.

The language which has been adopted in the resolution has been misinterpreted in certain quarters as mea ning that dis-association from legislatures signifies and includes disassociation form the Council party. I say, I repudiate such interpretation altogether. This Congress repudiates all association with, and all connection with, and all hope through, the Legislative Councils in so far as its emancipation is concerned and yet reserves a most hospitable, a most respectable, a most well-deserved corner of this Mandap for Desabandhu Das and Pundit Motilalji and all his noble comrades who are striving to the best of their lights for the emancipation of the country also, (Hear, hear). Therefore if anybody comes and tells you this evening that you are dis-associating yourself from the Council Party by this amendment, I ask you not to accept that proposition (Hear, hear). I have described to you the nature of compromise that has been entered into. It is painful to me, it is presumptuous on my part to stand on this pulpit and say that I have the audacity, the courage, the duty to differ from men like Rajagopalachariar and Vallabhbhai. But, gentlemen, we have to do our duty here. It is not a question of personalities. We feel honestly that we are war-wearied and that the leaders having fought and fought again feel that the time has come to call for a truce. So they have adopted this for an armed neutrality for the present (applause). And, this compromise like the after-math of war in all arbitrements of international fight bears in itself the future dissensions, the seeds of controversy, and contains ample, abundant and exciting material for interpretation, misinterpretation and mal-interpretation of the resolution, each according to his tastes, his abilities and his lights. Is that a compromise ? Do you in the name of compromise want to adopt a formula in respect of the interpretation in which already there have been differences. One does not know whether the word 'forthcoming' in the Delhi resolution is an expression which included only those foregone elections or as the forthcoming elections, in the next six months, one year, three years, twenty years, hundred years. (Laughter). Mind, we are not undoing Delhi. No sensible man would address himself to such a fatuous and foolish task. Delhi is there writ large like those Empires of Delhi that lived and vanished in the past. The Delhi resolution also lived through and perished. There is an end of the matter. We cannot undo it. We cannot repeat it. We cannot confirm it. It is an fatuitous to try to repeat it as to reaffirm it. That is our objection to the inclusion of the word 'Delhi,' however simple, however beautiful it may look for the suggestion that the word 'Delhi' should be deleted. This removal is not a simple matter. It goes to the heart of the compromise. It goes to the very root of the adjustments that have been made between the parties. Therefore I do not think that you can readily delete the word unless you delete the whole paragraph. But my contention is not merely to delete this paragraph or to delete that. But that if a vicious scheme or a vicious resolution has been formulated it is your duty to delete through and through and replace it altogether by a different resolution namely, that which has been sponsored by Babu Syam Sunder Chakravarthi. The purpose is compromised. The nature I have explained. At Allahabad we entered into a compromise. Nobody came to our help in making the Gaya collections or even carrying on the Gaya programme. The purpose was compromised. At Bombay the No-vote campaign was abandoned. It was always a policy of 'you give and I take.'

Nobody came to our help with regard to the collections of money for the Tilak Swaraj Fund that we advertised so widely, so nobly, as having been promised or collected. They vanished the moment the compromise was settled. Again we had a compromise at Nagpur. Later we had a compromise at Waltair and the greater compromise at Delhi. These compromises have never helped us. It is a compromise between parties who are looking in two different directions without a state of common bond. No doubt our pathways are divergent and one looks at the Council work for the emancipation of the country. And there are as many interpretations in regard to the conduct of the people that have entered the Councils as there are in regard to Non-co-operation itself. This interpretation has differed from 148 Russa Road to Bandra, Bombay (Laughter), and these interpretations will go on multiplying and multiplying. What replies have been given ? All in the name of Non-co-operation (Laughter), and of non-violent character.

As regards the recent shump in the constructive movement, the speaker said : Political tides have always their ebb and flow. The flow of this tide was at Ahmedabad, we are now in the ebb. Are we to be stranded on the beach and say that this tide will recede for ever and will not take us into the bosom of the ocean, or are we to bide only time and catch the Government at its weakest moment and then mobilise the whole country in such a manner as it can respond ? (hear, hear). Or, are we to adopt two views of non-co-operation, one view formulated by Gandhiji based upon the doctrine of self-purification, based upon the doctrine of suffering, based too upon the vital and noble principle: do not resist evil but overcome it with good. The other based upon the doctrine of retaliation,—a tooth for a tooth, a nail for a nail, a shot for a shot, a blow for a blow. Go to the Councils and wreck them to the best and throw them into the Bay of Bengal. In your ways create quarrels, make life inpossible for Governors and Governors-General, dictate terms to them from your palaces and then win Swaraj from your own home. These two views have been explained and formulated in the country. Which view, you gentlemen, who represent the vast masses of India, are you going to take ? Are you going to take the compromise in which all the sophistries and all the palpable fallacies and all the tortuous intricacies of the human intellect have been grouped and formulated. (Cries of 'No no). Or will you ask plain, honest, straight-forward questions and expect straight replies ?

It was never he said, contemplated in the history of Non-Co-operation, that the Delhi resolution was a non-co-operation resolution in respect of Council entry. I tell you the whole seat of danger lies there. And to-morrow it will be open to our friends, notwithstanding any assurances that may come from this platform, that deadlocks are permitted by this resolution, and I challenge the whole intellectual world of this country to deny that to go into Councils and invoke the authority of the Indian National Congress for the formation of deadlocks is contained in this resolution. (Cheers.)

SJT. T. PRAKASAM.

Sit. T. Prakasam in supporting the compromise resolution said:

I oppose the amendment so ably moved by Babu Shyam Sundar Chakravarti and supported by Dr. Pattabhi Sitaramiah. This is an amendment which re-affirms the Triple Boycott in express terms. The object of the amendment is to solidify the nation and to promote national unity amongst ourselves. I will ask you to consider what the first clause of this amendment says, whether the means suggested is not one which would destroy every chance of solidifying the nation (Hear hear.) You consider for one moment, my friends, dispassionately what is it that is proposed now, this amendment—to carry on propaganda from this day forward—when you pass this amendment in the House—to carry on propoganda to the country, to every village and to every home in the country, and that to the effect calling upon the people to dis-associate themselves from the legislatures. What are these legislatures? Does that expression mean the Councils or the persons who go there to represent the voters who sent them there? (hear, hear). Dis-association—if it is dis-association from the bricks or from the mud walls of the Legislative Councils, I have no objection. But if it is dis-association from friends who had entered the Council halls just a few weeks ago, I will ask you to consider what you are doing. Three months ago in Delhi, in all seriousness, you passed a resolution stating that those persons and friends who have no religious or conscientious objection had the liberty to enter the Councils, to give their names as candidates. Those who have no such objection are at liberty to give their votes to such candidates.

Now what had happened during the last elections? How many of the no-changers and how many of us voted at the elections. How many of us sent these friends into the Councils, relying upon the permission given under the resolution. I admit there is no mandate. Now, in three months, you turn round and tell your workers to go to the country and tell those very people, that those who have gone to the Councils are undesirable people, dis-associate yourselves from those persons. It is nothing short of treachery and betrayal (shame). Secondly, the resolution says, 'the object is to achieve national solidarity by strict adherence to the principle of non-violence in all matters of in ercommunal relationship and promoting a spirit of brotherliness'—Does this propaganda create a spirit of brotherliness at all if you go and preach against those very friends whom you permitted to enter the Councils? Does it not create bitterness, hatred and ill-will which we all noticed in the past—an impasse which made it impossible for us to go forward with our constructive programme?

Sj. Prakasam proceeding continued: Have we not found the position more difficult every month as we went out into the country, on account of wrangling, on account of controversy, and the quarrel amongst the leaders? The country was looking agnast all the time at what has been happening in this world of ours. Mr. Muhammed Ali had the courage at Delhi to take his heart in both his hands and face the situation in the same manner in which Mahatma Gandhi faced it when he recorded the Bardoli decision (Hear, hear). When he cried halt at Bardoli, Mahatma Gandhi, the author of the movement, himself was not spared by all of you (Hear, here). The last words which Mahtma Gandhi gave us when he went to jail were—'Carry on the Constructive Programme I have given you. All the political prisoners will be released and you will be able to establish Swaraj without anything else if you carry on the Constructive Programme.'

Don't commit yourselves, he said, to an untrue position created by the amendment of Shyam Babu. The resolution of Sj. Rajagopalachariar lays down that the principle and policy of triple boycott is maintained. Accept that and reject the amendment (Applause).

Dr. Kitchlew said that the resolution put it clearly that the Congress policy in respect of Councils remained unaltered and that if any Swarajist, in his election campaign, has given a wrong version, the main resolution before them should clear it.

MR. RAJAGOPALACHARI'S REPLY

After all the numerous speeches Mr. C. Rajagopalachari, replying to the debate said that he did not at all agree with the view that dissociation from Legislature would mean dissociation from their friends in the Legislatures. They had, under this resolution, every right if they felt necessary to say that they had nothing to do with the Legislatures and that they should not look to them, but it was not right to say that they dissociated from persons in the Legislatures, including Govt. members. Not only did they claim the right of dissociation from Legislatures, but also dissociation from Courts and Schools. But it was quite another thing to decide whether they would take an aggressive propaganda or not in future. He could not accept the amendment of Mr. Shyam Sundar Chakravarti, because it gave the go-bye to the Delhi resolution. They should not ignore what was done at Delhi. If the Delhi resolution was not a Non-Co-operation resolution, then why should some people bother about it. But if it was a Non-Co-operation resolution why should they not say so and declare their policy as before. They could not undo what they had done at Delhi with open eyes, without affecting the prestige and integrity of the Congress. They could do so if the people were prepared for aggressive triple boycott. But what they wanted was foundation for constructive work. In this resolution there was Non-Co-operation in all its force and there was an authority and mandate for constructive work for the next year, 1924.

THE VOTING—AMENDMENT LOST

After a prolonged debate in which some 20 members, including Mr. Shaukat Ali and others took part the counter-proposal of Mr. Shyam Sundar Chakravarti was put the vote and declared lost. On a poll being demanded, the house divided, with the result that the proposal was lost, 413 voting for and 703 against it. The original resolution of Mr. Rajagopalachari was then put and carried.

The Wrangle in the Subjects Committee

As this compromise resolution, the only non-co-operation resolution of this Congress, was the most contentions of all matters discussed, below is given an account of what happened behind the Congress, in the Subjects Committee, and the delegates' meetings.

The Ali Brothers were, ever since their release, trying to bring about an union between the two parties into which the Gaya Congress was split. At Delhi a compromise was patched up and at Cocanada this was sought to be confirmed. This gave occasion for all the old party squabbles once more to raise their heads. The Cocanada compromise, according to Sreejut Rajagopalachari, is not equivocal. He admitted the Delhi Compromise resolution as a Non-co-operation resolution on prudential grounds and gave it a touch of ratification on the ground of expediency. He surrendered Non-co-operation orthodoxy a bit for the sake of consistency. It is to be remembered that he did not or could not attend the Delhi special session. He sent a wire, when the compromise resolution was being discussed, asking his colleagues Vallabhbhai Patel, Jamnalal Bajaj, Deshpande and others to abide by the decision of Maulana Mahomed Ali and by doing so, he made himself indirectly, if not directly, responsible for the compromise resolution adopted at Delhi. That being his position he and his colleagues who directly or indirectly supported Maulana Mahomed Ali at Delhi could not consistently throw him overboard at Cocanada. When Sjt. Rajagopalachari spoke at Bijapur he seemed to have struggled once more against the Delhi resolution. But when Maulana Mahomed Ali and he met shortly before the Coconada Congress and the Maulana presented his case before him, he had no other alternative than capitulate Maulana Mahomed Ali, however, admits that the compromise resolution adopted at Cocanada is capable of more than one interpretation and that is necessary for the purpose of pleasing both the parties for the sake of peace; he refuses to resile from the position he took at Delhi before a reasonable lapse of time. Those of the orthodox Non-co-operators again, who were directly or indirectly parties to the Delhi resolution could not accept the compromise. So opposition to the compromise resolution was decided upon. Sj. Shyam Sundar Chakrabarty gave notice of his resolution which was eventually treated as an amendment. Mr. Hardayal Nag gave notice of an amendment for the deletion of the words "and Delhi" in the first clause and the word "Non-co-operation" in the second clause. Negotiations went on to make the compromise resolution acceptable to all and the discussion on the subject was put off from day to day. In the meantime other resolution were dealt with.

Negotiations for bringing all the parties to a common understanding falling, Mr. Rajagopalachari's compromise resolution with Pandit Syamsundar Chakravarty's counter-resolution as amendment and all other amendments were duly placed before the Subjects Committee. In Rajagopalachari's resolution Mr. Das's name was put down as seconder, but he did not turn up in the Subjects Committee after his defeat in the open Congress on the Bengal Pact. Speculation was rife that he will leave the Congress the very day. Mr. Motilal acted as his substitute in a later stage of the proceedings. Pandit Syamsundar Chakravarty made a splendid speech. Mr. Vijayraghavachari also made an excellent speech in support of his amendment in which he bitterly criticised the language of the compromise resolution. Pandit Motilal Nehru made a strong personal attack upon Mr. Vijayraghavachari directly, and severely criticised his reversion to legal practice. Mr. Vijayraghavachari retaliated and the matter became an incident of mutual personal recrimination between two ex-Presidents of the Congress, much to the shame of all. When all the amendments were lost and Rajagopalachari's resolution was carried, the President made an appeal not to carry the amendment to the open House. But Syam Babu immediately gave notice that he would move his amendment in the open House. Srijut Jagat Narain of Behar placed a written notice of moving Mr. Nag's amendment in the open House. A rumour spread in the Congress that the Ali Brothers would leave the Congress if Rajagopalachari's compromise resolution was defeated. A very strong feeling was created in favour of the two Moulanas who strongly declared themselves in favour of the Triple Boycott, but at the same time they were unwilling to be a party to the wholesale rejection of the Delhi compromise, Srijut Rajagopalachari spared no literary skill to make the draft of the compromise resolution acceptable to the othodox No-changers and the Swarajists. That the Swarajists were not fully satisfied with the draft appeared from the speech of Pandit Motilal Nehru in support of the resolution. Mr. Das also took the same attitude when he rose to second the resolution in the open Congress. His seconding without any speech meant nothing but want of whole-hearted support. In answer to a straight question whether the Swarajists would interpret the Cocanada compromise as extending the Delhi permission to coming bye-elections, the Pandit said that Sj. Rajagopalachari's resolution was a compromise resolution and that it meant perpetuation of the Delhi permission. He said. "we say, we are Congress, you say, you are Congress"—this was a serious position and it appeared as if small parties were again to devote themselves only to capture the Congress. Maulana Mahomed Ali's skilful handling however averted this and he was especially glad that after the final settlement each party could interpret the resolution in its own way.

The Civil Disobedience Committee

In pursuance of these resolutions the famous Civil Disobedience Enquiry Committee was next formed. The Committee appointed by the Congress consisted of Hakim Ajmal Khan, Pt. Motilal Nehru, Messrs Rajagopalachariar, Vithalbhai Patel, Seth Chottani, Seth Jamnalal Bajaj and Dr. Ansari. The Khilafatists appointed another Committee consisting of Seth Chottani as president, and M. Abdul Majid, S. Sulaiman Nadvi, M. Abdul Kadir, M. Tassadaq Ahmed, Mr. Moazzam Ali and Mr. Zahoor Ahmed as members. This Committee was to co-operate with and accompany the Congress Committee of Enquiry.

The Congress Enquiry Committee began its work on July 1st. On June 30th a preliminary meeting was held at Delhi to settle the programme. Mrs. Naidu and Mr. Bajaj, however, could not join the Committee, the former owing to illness, and the latter because of his pre-occupation with the All-India Khadi organisation. Seth Chottani also was unable to take part in the proceedings. The late Mr. Kasturiranga Aiyengar of the *Hindu* of Madras was elected in their place. A list of questionnaires was issued and intending witnesses in the different provinces were asked to supply the informations in writing. The questionnaire included a wide range of subjects and ran as follows:

Constructive Programme Generally

1. Do you agree that at present the constructive programme is to be worked to the extent necessary for strengthening and disciplining the Congress organisations so as to make them efficient and non-violent for civil disobedience?

2. Do you agree that the completion of the constructive programme is a question of years and that we shall have to continue to work that programme even after we get Swaraj?

3. Do you accept the view that as there is nothing of Non-co-operation in any of the items of the constructive programme, all parties in the country can unite in working it?

4. Do you agree that a Non-co-operator can work the constructive programme somewhat more effectively, particularly such items as national education, boycott of liquor, Khaddar and the like by entering the Councils and thus prepare the country earlier for civil disobedience and non-payment of taxes?

Swadeshi

1. (a) How many Charkas are working in this Province? (b) How many are worked under private enterprise, how many under the Congress and how many as cottage industry?

2. How does the Congress supervise private enterprise and cottage industry?

3. How much yarn is produced monthly and of what qualities?

4. Are there any organisations for selling yan; if so, are they private or Congress, if both give numbers of each?

5. Does the Province export or import yarn? How much and why?

6. How many Karghas for hand-looms are used in the Province?

7. How many weaving organisations are there in the Province? How are they controlled?

8. What is the monthly output of Khaddar and how is it sold? Is the Khaddar produced of pure hand-spun yarn or of mixed yarn?

9. Does the Province export Khaddar? Give approximate monthly yardage and the cost.

10. Is Khaddar popular in the Province? if not why? What is the percentage of Khaddar-wearing persons?

11. How does the price of Khaddar compare with that of rough mill cloth, Indian or foreign? If the price Khaddar is high, what are the causes? Would you suggest some means of bringing down the prices?

12. How far has Khaddar progressed as compared with latter Indian mill-made cloth and foreign cloth?

13. Is the use of Khaddar or increasing or decreasing; if why and how can it be remedied?

14. Compare this year with the last year with regard to the use of Khaddar—if it compare unfavourable, why?

15. How is your propaganda against foreign cloth going on and with what results?

16. Have you got any suggestions to make with regard to popularising Khaddar?

17. Have you got anything to say with regard to Khaddar as an item of the constructive programme?

18. How many institutions are there for teaching spinning and weaving and how are they controlled?

N.B. Khaddar includes hand-spun hand-woven cloth made of cotton, silk, wool or fabric produced in India.

Congress Members

1. What is the number of Congress members in the Province and what percentage of the population does this number represent?

2. How does the present year compare with the last so far as this item is concerned? If unfavourably, what are the causes? Suggest remedies.

3. Is the enrolment made after fully explaining the Congress creed to the members or not?

Volunteers

1. (a) What is the number of volunteers in the Province.
   (b) How many are in and how many out of jail?
   (c) How many of them have tendered apology?

2. How does the volunteer movement in this year compare with that in the first; if unfavourably, give causes and suggest remedies.

3. Have you got any suggestions to make with regard to: (a) enrolment; (b) volunteer pledge; (c) organization.

Finances

1. How much money has the Province collected for the Tilak Swaraj Fund and how much as the membership fees? Give figures for 1921 and 1922. If the present year collections are less, why? 2. Give the chief items of expenditure for the last year. 3. Have the accounts been kept according to the

forms prescribed by the Working Committee and have they been audited? 4. What improvements and alterations would you suggest as regards the collecting, distributing and control of accounts?

Education

1. How many national institutions are there in the Province and of what grades;

2. How do they stand financially and what are the sources of income?

3. What is the number of students and teachers in each grade?

4. How does national education this year compare with the last? If unfavourably, why? Suggest remedies.

5. Have you got any suggestions to make with regard to this item?

Panchayats

1. How many lawyers have suspended their practices?

2. What is the number of Panchayat Courts in the Province?

3. Are the Courts popular or not, if not why? Suggest remedies.

Untouchability and Anti-drink Campaign

1. How far have untouchability and drink been eliminated from the social life of the Province? Is the rate of progress hopeful? What measure has the province adopted? What further means would you suggest?

Unity

1. How does your province stand with regard to inter-communal relations generally? 2. If there is any friction, what are the causes and remedies in your opinion?

Non-Violence

1. How far has the spirit of Non-violence progressed in the Province?

2. What is your opinion as regards the right of private defence in relation to this movement.

Civil Disobedience

1. Is your Province as a whole or in part ready to start Civil Disobedience; if so, whether individual or mass and defensive or aggressive?

2. If your province is ready for Civil Disobedience, can you say whether it is for Disobedience of every unmoral law or of some? If the latter, mention the particular laws.

3. What would be the effect on the general situation in the country if a province undertakes isolated action in regard to Civil Disobedience?

4. Do you think that the majority of the Provinces are ready to start Civil Disobedience simultaneously?

Repression

1. To what extent repression is practised in the Province?
2. Is terrorism also resorted to ? If so to what extent?
3. How are the political prisoners treated in jail?
4. What particular and peculiar forms of repression, if any, have been adopted in your province? What effect has repression produced on:—(a) masses, (b) workers, (c) spirit of Non-

violence.

General Situation

1. How has the movement of non-co-operation affected the general situation in the country?

2. How has the repression affected the movement of non-co-operation?

3. How have the Bardoli-Delhi resolutions affected the movement?

4. Is any change in the programme required? If so, in what direction?

5. Have you got any suggestions to make as regards making the movement more effective?

The Work of the Committee

The regular sittings of the Committee was started at Delhi on July 1st. The procedure followed in taking evidence was first to call for written answers and then to examine witnesses *viva voce*. 459 such written answers were received in the course of their sittings, and 366 witnesses were examined orally. The oral examination was held in camera in order to encourage witnesses to speak out their candid opinions without let or hindrance. The tour programme included the whole of British India, but in the end Sindh, Ajmer-Merwara, and Central India were omitted. The work of the Committee had to be finished before the 15th August as settled at Lucknow as the A.I.C.C. was to have met on this date. But by a circular issued by the Working Committee of the Congress this date was postponed and the A.I.C.C. meeting was timed to be held in November. Thus four months were given to the Committee and their report was issued on the 30th October. In the interim all Congress work remained suspended and gradually the whole Congress organisation in the Provinces, Districts, and Taluks simply crumbled away. The main rocommendations of the Committee were summarised by themeselves as follows:

1. Civil Disobedience:

(a) The country is not prepared at present to embark upon general Mass Civil Disobedience but in view of the fact that situation may arise in any part of the country demanding an immediate resort to Mass Civil Disobedience of a limited character e.g., the breaking of a particular law or the non-payment of a particular tax for which the people are ready, we recommend that Provincial Committees be authorised to sanction such limited Mass Civil Disobedience on their own responsibility if the conditions laid down by the All India Congress Committee in that behalf are fulfilled.

(b) We recommend the restoration of the resolution No. 2 passed by the All India Congress Committee at Delhi on the 4th—5th November which gives Provincial Committees all the powers necessary to determine upon a resort to Civil Disobedience of any kind whatever, by cancelling Resolution I. cl. 1. passed on the 24th—25th February to the extent it conflicts with that resolution; provided that general Mass Civil Disobedience is not permissible.

(Unanimous)

2. Entry into Legislative Council:

(A) The Congress and the Khilafat at their Gaya Session should declare that in view of the fact that the working of the Legislative Councils during their first terms has, besides proving a great obstacle to the redress of the Khilafat and Punjab wrongs and the speedy attainment of Swarajya, caused great misery and hardship to the people, it is desirable that the following steps should be taken in strict accordance with the principles of non-violent non-co-operation to aviod the recurrence of the evil:

1. Non-co-operators should contest the election on the issue of the redress of the Punjab and Khilafat wrongs and immediate Swarajya, and make every endeavour to be returned in a majority.

2. If the non-co-operators are returned in a majority large enough to prevent a quorum, they should after taking their seates leave the Council Chamber in a body and take no part in the proceedings for the rest of the term. They should attend the Council occasionally only for the purpose of preventing vacancies.

3. If non-co-operators are returned in a majority which is not large enough to prevent a quorum, they should oppose every measure of the Government including the budget and only move resolutions for the redress of the aforesaid wrongs and the immediate attainment of Swarajya.

4. If the non-co-operators are returned in a minority they should act as pointed out in No. 2, and thus materially reduce the strength of the Council.

As the new Councils will not assemble till January, 1924, we further propose that the Congress Session of 1923 be held during the first instead of the last week of December and the matter be again brought up for the issue of a final mandate by the Congress in view of the election.

Recommended by
Hakim Ajmal Khan,
Pandit Motilal Nehru,
Sjt. V.J. Patel.

(B) There should be no change of the Congress programme in respect of the boycott of Councils.

By Dr. M.A. Ansari.
Syt. C. Rajagopalachari.
Syt. S. Kasturiranga Iyengar.

3. Local Bodies

We recommend that in order to clear the position it should be declared that it is desirable for Non-co-operators to seek election to Municipalities and District or Local Boards with a view to facilitate the working of the constructive programme, but that no hard and fast rules be at present laid down to regulate or restrict the activities Non-co-operating members beyond advising them to act in harmony with local or provincial Congress organisations. (Unanimous)

4. Boycott of Government educational Institutions

We recommend a strict adherence to the Bardoli resolution in regard to these by suspending for the present active propaganda calling upon boys to come out of schools and colleges. As required by that resolution reliance should be placed upon superiority of National schools for drawing scholars from Government Institutions and not upon picketting or other aggressive propaganda. (Unanimous)

5. Boycott of Law Courts by Litigants and Lawyers

Effort should be concentrated on the establishment of panchayats and cultivation of a strong public opinion in their favour. We further recommend that all existing disqualifications imposed on practising lawyers should be removed.

(Unanimous)

6. Organisation of Labour

Resolution No. 8 passed by the Nagpur should be carried out without further delay. (Unanimous)

7. Right of Private Defence

(A) We recommend that individuals should be given full freedom to exercise the right within the limits defined by law except when carrying on Congress work or on occasions directly arising therefrom subject always to the condition that it is not likely to lead to a general outburst of violence.

Using force in private defence in gross cases, such as insults to religion, outrages on modesty of women or indecent assaults on boys and men is not prohibited under any circumstances. (All members except Syt. V.J. Patel.)

(B) Full freedom to exercise the right within the limits defined by law should be reserved to non-co-operators subject only to the condition that it is not likely to lead to a general outbrust of violence, and to no further conditions.

(Syt. V.J. Patel.)

8. Boycott of British Goods

(A) We accept the principle and recommend that the whole question be referred to a Committee of experts for a full report to be submitted before the next Congress meets.

(All members except Syt. C. Rajagopalachari.)

(B) There is no objection to the collection and examination of facts by experts, but the acceptance of the principles by the All-India Congress Committee would mislead the nation and injure the movement. (Syt. C. Rajagopalachari.)

Moulana Azad's Efforts for Re-union

Meanwhile efforts were made by Maulana Abul Kalam Azad to settle the differences between the new party and the Congress. First he managed to secure a meeting of the Working Committee of the Congress at Bombay in the last week of January and proposed to it the following scheme of settlement :

"1. That both parties should whole-heartedly unite to work the Gaya Congress Programme for the next three months. 2. That there should be no propaganda or talk about any change of the programme relating to the Councils during that period or the formation of a New Party. 3. That if at the end of that period Civil Disobedience was decided upon, both parties should continue to work for it. 4. That if on the other hand no such step was found possible, a Special Session of the Congress should be held in June to consider the situation. 5. That for one month before the Special Congress both parties should be free to educate public opinion according to their views. 6. That the decision of the Congress should be carried out by both sides without forming separate parties."

After some discussion the above terms were unanimously agreed to by the Working Committee, and the Maulana Saheb was requested to place the matter before Mr. Das for the acceptance of himself and his party. Mr. Das however could not accept them *in toto*. The members of the Working Committee also met Mr. Das and had a discussion with him. He expressed his inability to accept the Maulana's scheme of settlement, but proposed other terms which involved the suspension of the boycott of Council propaganda at once and without reference to any Special Congress. The Working Committee considered this proposal but found it impossible to accept. Maulana Abul Kalam Azad, however, undertook to press his own scheme again on the leaders of the new party. As a result of his further efforts he was able to bring over Hakim Ajmal Khan and Pandit Motial Nehru to his point of view and they whole-heartedly accepted his terms. A message to this effect was issued on the 12th of February. He then proceeded to Calcutta to discuss matters again with Mr. Das. After further consultation and discussion with the Maulana Saheb and Pandit Motilal Mr. Das re-drafted the Maulana's terms with the addition of a clause regarding election machinery for the special session of the Congress. The terms of his draft and his letter annexed are given beolw :

1. A meeting of the All-India Congress Committee will be called without delay with a view to summon a Special Session of the Congress about the middle of June. 2. In

case a Special Session of the Congress is summoned by the All-India Congress Committee as stated above, both parties while adhering to their respective opinions agree to suspend their differences and jointly work the programme as laid down at Gaya till the end of April. 3. There should be no propaganda by either party concerning Council elections till the end of April. 4. The All-India Congress Committee will meet in the first week of May, and if in view of the situation at the time it decides to undertake immediate Civil Disobedience generally throughout the country (i.e. in the majority of the Congress Provinces), both parties will join in such Civil Disobedience and there will be no session of the Congress. 5. If, however, the All-India Congress Committee declares against such Civil Disobedience, both parties will thereafter be free to educate public opinion according to their views. 6. Further, if the A. I. C. C. in May declares against such Civil Disobedience, arrangements will be made in all the Provinces, as early as possible, in order to enable the election of delegates to take place on fair and impartial lines. 7. The decision of the Special Session will be binding on both parties. 8. The Compromise shall cease to have effect (any binding force on the Parties) in case the existing Councils are dissolved by the Government before the expiry of the full terms for which they have been constituted.

Mr. C. R. Das's Letter to M. Azad.

Mr. Das wrote at the same time:

"Dear Maulana Sahib,—The accompanying draft expresses the terms upon which I am prepared to enter into a compromise with the Majority Party. This will not prevent my Party from raising funds, without making and propaganda on the question of Councils, from those who are willing to trust to the judgment of the members of our Party as to the ways which such funds are to be spent. I undertake not to call any meetings to raise such funds.

"It is understood that to give effect to term No. 6 the

following or a similar arrangement to my satisfaction must be accepted:

"(a) For every constituency (district or local) returning delegates to the Special Congress an additional Secretary will be appointed belonging to the Party to which the existing Secretary is oppend. (b) In the Provincial Congress Committees, too, the same arrangement will be made (c) There will be two returning officers for each constituency, one belonging to each Party. (d) There will be an election board in each province, consisting of two members, one to be nominated by each Party. These two members will decide a third person to whom all election disputes will be referred in case of difference.

"This Board will be at liberty to modify the existing election rules to suit the circumstances of the Special Congress and for such purpose the powers of the Provincial Congress Committee will vest in them. This Board will in all matters be responsible for conducting the election of delegates.

"I further desire to make it clear that my acceptance of the terms mentioned is subject to the approval of our party."

The safeguards mentioned showed with what great suspicion the Congress organisation was looked upon by the new party. Obviously no compromise with such a background of suspicion was possible, and it seemed that the efforts of the peace-makers were only bringing up to the surface the worst features of our National character.

Meeting of February 20th

The new party met at Allahabad on February 20th and appointed a special committee with authority to agree on their behalf to such terms of settlement as they might approve after discussion with the Working Committee which was to meet at Allahabad on February 26th. Fcur sets of proposals were considered during the conversations at Allahabad between the

Working Committee and the new party's special committee. Two of them implied suspension of the resolution regarding the boycott of the Council elections without reference to any fresh Congress Session. Of the other two, one was Maulana Azad's proposal as modified and added to by Das and the other was the following:

> 1. Suspension of Council propaganda on both sides till the 30th of April. 2. Both parties to be at liberty to work in the remaining items of their respective programme in the interval without interfering with each other. 3. Each party to adopt such course after the 30th April as it may be advised. 4. No Special Congress.

The new party, however, made all the four proposals subject to the following condition :

> "Every proposal is subject to the condition that there is no dissolution of the existing Councils in any Provinces before the expiry of the full term for which they have been constituted."

The Working Committee decided against accepting any of the two proposals that involved a reversal of the resolution regarding Council boycott without reference to the Congress. They decided to accept either of the two sets of proposals but modified the terms drafted by Mr. C. R. Das in some particulars and by substituting for the special election machinery proposed by him a clause that the All-India Congress Committee should provide at its meeting in May a satisfactory machinery for the disposal of disputes regarding election of delegates to the Special Congress in a fair and impartial manner. To the other alternative proposal, the Working Committee added terms to secure co-operation in the collection of funds and the enlistment of workers. The two sets of proposals, either of which the Working Committee agreed to accept, were in short as follows:

I. AZAD-DAS DRAFT AS AMENDED BY THE WORKING COMMITTEE

1. Both parties, while adhering to their respective opinions, agree to suspend their differences and jointly work the Programme as laid down at Gaya.

2. There should be no propaganda by either Party concerning Council election till the end of April.

3. The All-India Congress Committee will meet before the end of May, and in view of the situation at the time, it decides to undertake individual Civil Disobedience on a large scale, both Parties will join in such Civil Disobedience and there will be no Special Session of the Congress.

4. If, however, the A.I.C.C. declare against such Civil Disobedience, both Parties will thereafter be free to educate public opinion according to their views.

5. If the A.I.C.C. to be convened before the 31st May declares against such Civil Disobedience, a Special Session of the Congress should meet about the end of June.

6. The A.I.C.C. meeting in May will provide satisfactory machinery for the disposal of disputes regarding election of delegates in a fair and impartial manner.

7. The decision of the Special Session will be loyally carried out by all parties and there will be no separate organisations for taking action contrary to that decision.

II. THE ALTERNATIVE PROPOSAL

1. Suspension of Council propaganda on both sides till the 30th April.

2. Both Parties to be at liberty to work the remaining items of their respective programmes in the interval without

interfering with each other.

3. The Majority Party will be at liberty to carry on their propaganda in accordance with the Gaya programme about money and volunteers.

4. The Minority Party will co-operate with the Majority Party in appealing for and raising such funds and enlisting such workers as may be necessary for the Constructive Programme and also in working the Constructive Programme and other common matters.

5. Each Party to adopt such course after the 30th April as it may be advised.

The Working Committee left these two proposals with the committee of the new party for the latter to decide whichever they might accept after consultation among themselves ; the latter intimated their acceptance of the terms of scheme No. II which were accordingly placed before the All-India Congress Committee at its meeting of the 27th and confirmed.

THE NO-CHANGERS' MANIFESTO

Mr. C. Rajagopalachariar, leader of the No-changers, also promptly issued the following manifesto :

With the 30th of April ends the truce entered into with the leaders of the New Party at Allahabad. They have declared their intention to call upon the people to participate in the coming Council elections and return the nominees of their party in preference to other candidates. On the other hand our duty according to the resolution of the Gaya Congress is to carry out the boycott of elections. It is hoped that we will be able to perform this duty without friction and with mutual good understanding. Though the suspension of controversy ended with the 30th of April and both parties are from that date free to carry on their respective propaganda, we should remember that the first and foremost duty now of all Congress Workers who stand by the resolutions of the Gaya Congress is to go on with the programme of collections and enlistment until the All-India Congress Committee meeting on 25th of May at Bombay. Every committee as well as individual worker should realise the supreme importance of putting forth during the next three weeks the maximum effort possible towards fulfilment of the resolutions regarding men and money. Against all kinds of difficulties a few faithful workers have fought with manful perseverence and achieved enough to show to ourselves if not to others that the national cause is bound in the end to triumph.

At the A.I.C.C. meeting we shall consider and decide upon civil disobedience. It should be remembered that the undertaking of individual civil resistance does not depend on the liberal fulfilment of the quota of men or money. I would advise my friends to undertake individual suffering even though the volunteers enrolled fall short of the number fixed and even if the money collected is below the programme. It is clear that without suffering, our apathy and our dissensions will not cease; while on the one hand our wrongs are increasing, the capital and fundamental evil of subjection to irresponsible foreign rule is killing our life, and our aparthy and dissensions are increasing and smothering our efforts at self-help and emancipation. It is clear that without a programme of suffering all these difficulties will become harder and harder everyday to overcome. On the other hand the challenges of the Government and the wrongs inflicted by it call for manly answer and resistance.

The manner in which civil resistance is to be offered and suffering undertaken will be decided at the A.I.C.C. meeting. If Congressmen undertake, as I want, a programme of intense suffering, there may be no need whatever to have any special propaganda for boycott of Councils. There is no need to go further than stating our position clearly to the people as to their duty to abstain from all participation in the Council election and its preliminaries. Let us not lose ourselves in controversy for which happily there is not much need now. The certification of the salt tax just on the eve of the elections is a calculated insult to the self-respect of the nation and betrays the Government's reliance on our weakness. The camouflage of the Reformed Councils has been so clearly exposed that a large statement of the case ought to be enough to induce not only Non-co-operators but even the Moderates to refuse to participate in the elections of this year. If however the issue becomes clouded and active propaganda becomes necessary, we have to undertake it, for which there is plenty of time yet.

The issue of these manifestoes in which the spirit of compromise was absolutely lacking served however to bring about a reshuffling amongst the supporters. The Bombay No-change leaders resented the tone of Mr. Rajagopalachariar and an attempt was made to remove him from the party-leadership. His plan of individual civil resistance was taken to mean a confession of weakness amongst the great majority of Congressmen, who were now charged by their opponents as having neither the courage to undertake mass-action nor the candour to confess their inability. Not all No-changers could attach the same mystic value to individual suffering as their leader seemed to emphasise. Suffering for a common national cause was intelligible but abstract suffering without any earthly objective did not for all its beatitude appeal to all. The failure of the No-change programme was due to the same cause that led to the split at Gaya. With the miasma of a lofty ideal the mass of men could not be moved for any length of time. As Pundit Motilal Nehru said, the method advocated by the majority party could not bring them the desired success even within 30 years. "It is useless to talk of Satyagraha until and unless that spirit and desire was created within the people which would prompt them to think that they should either get Swaraj or die for it." No doubt there were some in the country whose national consciousness was so far advanced that even in normal conditions, without the stimulus of hatred or injury received, they felt it intolerable that Indians were not masters in their own land. But such a consciousness must permeate the masses, must become so all-peryading as to dominate all class, caste and communal consciousness, before the adoption of a policy of Satyagraha could be even thought of. But the conditions in the country were different. There were Hindu-Moslem riots, and more than that the communal dissensions in the Punjab (see *poste*) and the U. P. were entering into Congress politics even. The Moderates were reeling under severe bureaucratic blows in the Councils. Angora's triumph had drawn the Moslem mind away from home affairs. Civil disobedience on abstract principles was already a lost cause. A hand to hand fight with the Government was a proposition which had more points of contact with the actualities of the situation. So the Das-Nehru party gained in strength, and by the time that the All-India Congress Committee met in May, the moral victory was already theirs.

BOYCOTT OF BRITISH GOODS

I have to express my respectful dissent from the opinions recorded by my colleagues about boycott of British goods.

It is needless to point out that so long as we seek to achieve our goal by the means planned by Mahatma Gandhi it would be the gravest mistake to introduce an addendum to his programme which according to his clear and repeatedly expressed opinion violates the basic principle of the programme. We are fighting a terrible and organised system of force with a new weapon conceived by Mahatmaji; and so long as we adhere to his scheme, it is fair neither to him nor to ourselves to tamper with the integrity and purity of his scheme in a matter considered by him as of essential importance. It would be a fatal mistake to accept. Dr. Lister's assurance that we can safely cut and chop the living human body, if we do not strictly follow his advice and see that our instruments are clean and absolutely free from poisonous germs. We are undertaking the most serious steps conceivable on the basis of Mahatmaji's doctrine of freedom from hatred and it would be safe only so long as we keep that essential condition intact. But if we add any item to his programme which has to be carried out by intense and widespread propaganda necessarily based on a clear emphasis of the principle of retaliation, we create an atmosphere fatal to the preparation of the people for the further steps of non-violent disobedience or non payment of taxes and for the suffering contemplated in our programme. It would be much better to give up Mahatmaji's programme altogether than to attempt to carry it out, disregarding his most insistent advice and creating an unsuitable and fatal atmosphere.

NO CHANGE IN MAHATMAJI'S ABSENCE

The proposal to boycott British goods as such is not a new one. Ever since Mahatmaji's guidance was accepted by us, this proposal was pressed on him again and again but was condemned and rejected by him. If his objections could be met properly, the leaders who now support the proposal had occassion and ample opportunity to convince him, or at least obtain his permission to add the item though it might not have his active support. But in view of its essential inconsistency with the basic principles of the main part of our programme, and the atmosphere of hatred which it would create and thereby render the rest of our programme impossible he never gave quarter to the proposal. It would be most unwise to push the proposal through now and obtain the endorsement of the National Congress to it, during the absence of our great leader and without bearing him, that is, if we do not set aside his principles altogether and proceed on totally different lines.

The great movement initiated by Mahatma Gandhi has appealed forcibly to the genius of the nation and obtained loyal attachment from the millions of our people by reason of its spiritual appeal more than anything else. It has similarly extorted the admiration of the world including the best minds even among those ranged against us, for that same reason. We cannot afford to tamper with that spiritual cleanliness of the programme whatever seeming advantage we might imagine that we shall obtain thereby.

MORE ABOUT HATRED

The arguments advanced by my colleagues, I have to say with the greatest respect, are based on an ambiguous use of the term 'punishment.' We may cause great loss to restaurant proprietors by cooking our food in our own houses but there would be no punishment or hatred in it, but to resolve to resort to all restaurants except one is quite a different thing and the feeling of hatred in that case should be obvious. By carrying out one's own duties to oneself or one's family or nation, one may cause injury, pain or loss to others, but it is neither punishment nor ill-will; but to prefer all others to one particular nation, for no reason of gratitude towards the former for any services rendered, or on account of any other bond of affection or attachment, and without any fulfilment of one's own duties is sheer hatred. To say that to obtain our birth-right of Swaraj we so prefer others to the nation that holds us in bondage is to beg the question, *viz*, whether the means suggested is consistent with the principle of non-violence adopted by us for the attainment of Swaraj. To make our own goods, to abstain from luxuries, to avoid buying needless British goods and to prefer Indian-made goods to British goods are always-recommended. These are not what is meant by boycott of British goods. The latter means setting up an agitation that the nation should favour buying the goods of non-British nations in preference to British. This is what has been repeatedly condemned and ruled out by Mahatmaji as contrary to his principles.

KHADDAR IN JEOPARDY

My esteemed colleagues make it clear that in approving of a policy of boycott of British goods, they do not intend that the Shuddha Swadeshi character of the cloth programme should be relaxed. They mean that we should adhere to Khaddar and not buy Japanese, or other non-British yarn or cloth. This may be the intention but I am certain that no intense propaganda can be carried on for boycott of British goods without affecting the mentality of people in respect of the cloth question also. We cannot in dealing with the millions of our countrymen make such reservations. Effects will be produced in a general way and not according to the rule and line we draw. The non-British foreign yarn and cloth merchants and the Indian Mill-owners using foreign yarn and the numerous middle-men depending on these capitalists will take every advantage of the new policy. The present difficulties of the Khaddar campaign will be increased ten-fold.

What has so far achieved the most striking results is the concentrated Khaddar idea. This concentration we lose if we take up a programme covering all sorts of goods, while yet there is a very great deal remaining to be done even in respect of Khaddar. Nothing can be achieved, even if it were right, by merely passing a resolution of boycott of all or such and such British goods. It must, if seriouly intended to be pressed, be followed up by intense propaganda; and this is sure to interfere with the concentration of effort over the cloth boycott which is admittedly the most important.

I concede that we may not succeed in weaning all people from hatred and ill-will towards a people that refuse freedom to us and are the cause of oppression and tyranny, and to delimit men's anger to the system and the tyranny and hold it back from the people that are responsible for the wrongs. But it is one thing to be unable to prevent a thing, quite a different thing to appeal to and encourage that very feeling.

A close and careful consideration of events will make it clear how Mahatmaji disarmed all open opposition to the Khaddar campaign by the elimination of boycott of British goods and by strict adherence to pure Swadeshi and yet at the same time succeeded in bringing about the most effective economic boycott. The disarming of opposition and the securing of moral advantage in the midst of the severest conflict is the peculiar strength and beauty of Mahatmaji's plans and are a result of the strict adherence to the principle of avoidance of hatred. It would be a mistake to deviate from this policy.

NO OBJECTION TO EXPERT COMMITTEE IF PRINCIPLE NOT CONCEDED

There is no objection to the collection and examination of facts by experts in any matter, but the acceptance of the principle by the All-India Congress Committee would mislead the nation and injury the movement. Even making people await the report of a committee expecting some great results and new proposals is mischievous, in as much as to that extent it encourages slackening of effort in one thing needed now, the completing of the cloth boycott. **C. Rajagopalachariar**

Rajaji did not favour the Council-entry programme. To mobilise the people of his region, he established an *Ashram* at Tiruchengode in Salem district in 1925. The railway station was at a distance of about 12 miles. His ideas was to carry on the constructive programme for the welfare of the villagers. The land was donated by a local zamindars. Many huts sprang up in the *Ashram*. Spinning was the main programme. A dispensary was also established to provide medical aid to the villagers. Rajaji asked several Harijans to join the *Ashram*.

The *Ashram* published two magazines; one was Vimochanam (Liberation) in Tamil and the other was Prohibition in English. These magazines dealt with several problems of the villagers. Besides attention was paid to the adult education. The inmates were also made busy in the manufacturing of soap, oils, quality seeds and several other works having deep linkage with the economic needs of a common man.

Thus with the sincere efforts of Rajaji khadi and village industries received a big boost not only in the *Ashram* but in the villages nearby. Very often they were advised by Rajaji and his associates to shun the habit of drinking.

In 1930, after the Lahore Congress, Mahatma Gandhi

commenced the Dandi March along with 78 satyagrahis chosen from all the regions of India. It was a symbolic protect against the Salt Law of the Raj. A distance of 241 miles was covered in 24 days, from Sabarmati Ashram to Dandi. The Salt Law was broken at Dandi and Sarojini Naidu hailed Mahatma Gandhi as Deliverer.

In Madras Rajaji selected a band of one hundred satyagrahis who marched from Tiruchi to Vedaranyam on 13 April 1930. The idea was to break the salt law as Gandhi had done at Dandi. The District Collector had sternly warned the people of the region not to join Rajaji's protest march. The march, however, continued for 16 days. As soon as the broke the salt law, they were asserted. Rajaji was sentenced to six months' rigorous imprisonment. He was fined Rs. two hundred and if he refused to pay the fine, he would spend another term of three months in jail. He heard the sentence like a well-disciplined soldier of the Congress and with a smile on his face he said that he would spend three months more in the jail. Other satyagrahis were also arrested and convicted. Rajaji and several others were detained at the Vellore jail.

At this point of time, thousands of other satyagrahis thronged to Vedaranyam and broke the salt law. They were lathi-charged by the police, were arrested and lodged in jails. It several leaders paid rich tributes to Rajaji on his remarkable and historic march, with a grand purpose, from Tiruchi to Vedaranyam.

For Rajaji jail life was a new experience. But it was not dull and drab. He made it interesting and fruitful. He advised the satyagrahis to observe the Gandhian principles in the best possible way. In a study circle, which he organised in a moderate way, he reminded them of the philosophy of Ruskin, Socrates, Thoreau, Tolstoy and other great philosophers. Besides *Gita* and its philosophy were discussed to achieve sublimeness in one's life. Marx and Engels were also discussed in these academic meetings. Thus the main idea of these discussions was to generate the spirit of sacrifice in a disciplined way for the great cause of freedom launched day Mahatma Gandhi.

At this point of time, when thousands of satyagrahis were lodged in jails, Ramsay MacDonald, the British Prime Minister and Lord Irwin felt much concern over the prevailing political situation. To ease the situation, the First Round Table Conference was convened in London in November 1930. The Congress refused to join. The prominent persons like Jinnah, Srinivasa Sastri, the Maharaja of Bikaner and others attended the Round Table Conference but it lacked its representative character on account of the absence of the leadership of the Congress.

Thereafter, Gandhi was released and his talks with Lord Irwin began on 17 February 1931 and ended on 5 March 1931. As a result of these talks the Gandhi Irwin Pact was signed. It was agreed to call off the Civil Disobedience Movement. The political prisoners were to be released. The Congress agreed to attend the Seeond Round Table Conference. Salt could be manufactured on the coastal areas. Property confiscated was to be restored. There was, however, no promise of granting Dominion Status of India.

Its aftermath was the Second Round Table Conference in which Gandhi represented the Congress. The Conference did not yield any result as the sectional interests dominated the national interests. Everyone echoed feelings for separate electorates. As a result thereof, Mahatma Gandhi who sensed the policy of 'Divide and Rule' on the part of the Raj, returned to India empty-handed. Soon after Gandhi and several other leaders were put behind the bars. The second phase of the movement continued for more than two years, when it was suspended in 1934.

After a span of three years when elections were held, the Congress leadership decided to contest and as a result thereof, the Congress could from ministries in sin provinces, Rajaji assumed the office of the Premier of the Madras province on

14 July 1937. It was indeed a challenging position and Rajaji performed his administrative functions with efficiency in all walks of life. He maintained cordial relationship with the British bureaucracy and assigned them official duties which had deep linkage with the developmental activities of the province. He introduced prohibition in Salem, Cuddapah and Chittoor districts. He attended to the development of industry, education, irrigation, roads and several other areas for the welfare of the people. For the proper functioning of various department, he always sought the coperation and goodwill of the State Governor, Erskine.

His temple entry programme was taken with much interest and enthusiasm. He sought the support of the progressive people in this regard. To overcome caste prejudices, he inducted a Harijan as a member in his cabinet. In this way he tried to raise the standard of the Harijans by affording the basic facilities having linkage with their socio-economic life. Besides his Debt Relief Act was a socio-economic measure for the weaker sections of the society.

On the formation of the ministry. The *Hindu* Commented thus:

Madras, 27 March 1937.

Conversations between H.E., the Governor and Mr. C. Rajagopalachari, Leader of the Congress Party in the Madras Assembly, have broken down and Mr. Rajagopalachari in his interview with His Excellency declined the invitation to form a Ministry.

Mr. C. Rajagopalachari drove to the Government House before time (3 pm.) and the interview with His Excellency ended in less than ten minutes.

From the Government House, Mr. Rajagopalachari proceeded to Mambalam where he reported to Mahatma Gandhi his final interview with H.E. the Governor.

"I regret to say that beyond the general offer of good will and co-operation. His Excellency has refused to assist me with any assurace of non-interference, formal or informal. I had, therefore, no option but to express my inability to take up office under these conditions, and respectfully to decline the invitation to form a Ministry", declared Mr. Rajagopalachari in a statement to the Press, soon aftre he returned from Government House.

Mr. C. Rajagopalachari, it is understood, discussed with Mahatma Gandhi yesterday evening the position with reference to his conversations with H.E. the Governor on the question of assurances.

After consultations with Gandhiji Mr. C Rajagopalachari went over to the Government House and continued the discussions for about half an hour.

Mr. Rajagopalachari met Gandhiji in the night and to-day also before he proceeded to the Government House this afternoon.

Congress Executive Committee Meeting

By the time the Executive of the Congress Party assembled at Congress House, it was becoming known that the conversations between Mr. C. Rajagopalachari and H.E. the Governor had almost reached a breaking point. H.E. the Governor having expressed his inability to give an assurance in terms of the A.I.C.C. resolution, it only remained for Mr. Rajagopalachari to state whether he agreed to form the Ministry or not.

The meeting of the Party Executive lasted for less than an hour. All the members excepting two were present; and the proceedings were conducted within closed doors.

Mr. Rajagopalachari is reported to have made a bried statement to them regarding the conversations that were proceeding between him and the Governor on the question of assurances.

At the close of the meeting, the following information was furnished to the Press by the Chief Whip of the Party.

"After a statement by the Leader of the Party that conversations with His Excellency are still proceedings, it was decided to meet again tomorrow at 9 a.m. at the Congress House.

Draft Rules of the Party were circulated to the members and they will be considered at the next meeting of the Committee.

Some funds were raised for the initial expenses of the office of the Party."

Mr. Rajgaopalachari Interviewed

Madras, 27 March 1937.

Soon after his statement to the Press, Mr. C. Rajagopalachari was met by The Hindu and was requested to answer one or two questions arising from his decling to form a Ministry.

"What is the secret of this refusal of your reasonable claim as you put it?" asked The Hindu representative.

"The secret is only this," declared Mr. Rajagopalachari with emphasis. "The people have not yet shown to the Government how much they stand behind the Congress. The votes have gone a long way; but much has more to be done to give that irresistible strength to the Congress which would automatically result in the acceptance of the Congress position by the Government.

"For instance," explained, Mr. Rajagopalachari, if after the elections, His Excellency the Governor of Madras had seen khaddar on the back of every one of the people that he saw, he dare not have refused to give me the assurance that I asked."

"What are your plans now," queried The Hindu representative.

Our plans are there, "observed Mr. Rajagopalachari," "in

the resolutions adopted at Wardha. National issues can never be treated as closed, as long as they are not solved. Settled facts are bound to be unsettled so long as they have not been properly settled. And the present is an instance.

"I do not know whether His Exceelency's advisers will have the courage to face the Assembly or can carry on without calling the members to meet. We shall have plans to suit either contingency," concluded Mr. Rajagopalachari.

Mr. C. Rajagopalachari's Statement

The following is the text of Mr. C. Rajagopalachari's statement:

"Having been called by H.E. the Governor of Maras to form a ministry for the province, I submitted to His Exceelency the condition on which I could take up the responsibility, and discussed the matter with him on 25th, 26th and 27th instant. I explained that I and my cabinet should be given the fullest freedom of action inside the scope of the provincial autonomy said to be given under the Government of India Act and that while we remain in office and undertake the responsibility of the Government of the province His Excellency should assure us that he will not use his special powers of interference or set aside the advire of ministers. I regret to say that beyond the general offer of good-will and cooperation, His Excellency has refused to assist me with any assurance of non-interference, formal or informal. I had, therefore, no option but to express my inability to take up office under these conditions, and respectfully to decline the invitation to form a ministry.

"In the course of my conversations with His Excellency I explained the position as clearly as I could, I pointed out that what we wanted as a condition precedent to the undertaking of responsibility was not an amendment of the Statute now and here, or any extension of the very limited scope of provinical autonomy, but that even while safeguards remained intact as regard possible interference, from the Secretary of State and the Viceroy, we should have a gentleman's agreement between His Excellency and me whom he has called, that his own discretionary powers of interference as provincial Governor should not be put in motion. I explained that when the provincial Governor invites me on the basis of the verdict of the electorate to form a government and undertake the responsibility, he has the right under the Act to give me the assurance of non-interference that we felt as necessary for the efficient discharge of that responsibility. If it be true that a real discretion is given to the Governor of the province, it must be within his power to use it or not to use, and if he is convinced that we can get the atmosphere and the psychology necessary for the efficient discharge of Cabinet responsibility only by ossuring non-interference, he could use his discretion best only by such non-use. To deny that right to the Governor of the province is a denial of provincial autonomy. It amounts to seeking to govern India from Downing Street through the old bureaucracy in spite of the forms of the new Government of India Act.

"If it is remembered that our party has been returned in this province by an overwhelming majority of 159 in a house of 215 in spite of the communal and special reservations of all kinds imposed on us, and that our party has been returned in a majority even to the Upper House, the refusal of the gentleman's agreement that we demanded within the framework of the Act is a denial of the claim solemnly made that the Governors' provinces will be constituted on a basis of full responsibility, and that we could achieve progress and full freedom through the exercise of provincial autonomy. It would be impossible for us to undertake the governance of the province after the distroy of antagonism through which we have passed unless at the outset we were expressly assured of such treatment as Ministers were entitled to under the Parliamentary system of popular government and of unqualified loyalty of the permanent service, which is impossible if the officials of the departments should be looking to the Governor for the exercise of special powers of interference at any and every stage press assurance could have dispelled the natural fears and apprehensions arising out of the history of case. To undertake responsibility without such previous assurance, and to depend on our breaking off as and when occasion arose, would not have been either an impossible position. The experiment was worth trying only if there was a clear indication on the other side of the readiness to party with power at least in the sphere of the province and the refusal of this at the threshold is better for the nation than a break-down after passing through humiliating conditions suffered in silence.

"The six million voters of the province returned us by majorities that left not a shadow of doubt as to the mind of the people. We tried to deserve the confidence thus expressed by seeking to utilise the victory not for getting our own party into places of power and position which we could easily have done but for improving the status of the nation. Office was there for us to pick up if we just chose, but we preferred rather to use that power for the permanent benefit improve the constitution from within. The Civil Service mast have resisted this and brought about a uniform policy in all the provinces, of refusing to give any assurance beyond repeating the old platitudes.

"Our path is clear,—the path of self-reliance. The naked power of force is there for the British Government to carry on without any constitution. Section 93 of the Government of India Act "provides" for this termination of constitutional pretence, and the dictatorship of the Governor, i.e., of the bureaucracy.

"I owe it to His Excellency to say that our conversations were throughout marked by utmost courtesy and friendliness on his part and the break-off is due not to any lack of patience or of personal good-will and I believe we both greatly regret that we could not arrive at a different and more happy conclusion.

"I appeal to the people of the province to realise that no power on earth can much longer stand between us and our birth right of freedom. We have had an ocular demonstration of the unshakeable strengh of the Congress. The dis-interestedness of its leadership has been proved by this episode so as not even its worst detractors can question it. May God give us yet greater strength of resolve and lead us to our goal.

"I have no doubt attempts will be made to demonstrate that the people can be ruled just as firmly as ever before. As an off-set against the break-down of the constitution surpluses will be utilised. I have no doubt, to give some relief to the peasants. Whatever the motive, we shall be glad if substantial measures of relief be underkaken during the dictatorship of the bureaucracy. We do not mind it if we are not in office, if our being out of office spurs the bureaucracy and its allies to greater efforts for a juster utilisation of the revenues of the province and the reduction of the burden of debt and taxation. We do not believe that the electorate can be decieved as to wherefrom really these springs of relief issue. Not the hand that distributes, but the strength of the Congress is what they should yet further strengthen, not only for immediate small reliefs, but for the final goal of national honour and independence."

"Declines to Accept"

Mr. Elwin Breaks News to Press

"Mr. Rajagopalachariar has declined to accept office. A communique is being issued," Mr. D.H. Elwin, Private Secretary to the Governor, informed the waiting Pressmen, on returning in his room from His Excellency's Chamber, "I have however, nothing, further to add to it," Mr. Elwin said.

A few minutes elaped before the Communique was got ready and handed to the press.

Official Communique

The following is the text of the Communique:

On the 25th March His Excellency the Governor invited Mr. C. Rajagopalachariar, the leader of the Congress Party in

Madras Legislature, to assist him in forming a Ministry, Mr. Rajagopalachariar at his first interview intimated that be could not accept the invitation unless an assurance was given by the Governor that he would not use his special powers or exercise the functions which are by law left to his discretion or individual judgment. His Excellency replied that it was impracticable for constitutional reasons for him to divest himself of the responsibilities and duties which have been placed upon his shoulders by Parliament, and that it was therefore not within his power to give any such guarantee. At the same time His Excellency intimated that Mr. Rajagopalachariar could rely upon receiving all possible help, sympathy and co-operation in the event of his forming a Ministry. After a series of very amicable conversations Mr. Rajagopalachariar has, while expressing appreciation of His Excellency's assurances, finally intimated to-day that he is unable to accept the invitation to assist in forming a Ministry.

His Excellency, while greatly regretting this outcome of the discussions, wishes to make it plain to the public that the decision is that of the Congress Party themselves, that the terms of the Statute are mandatory, and that the obligations imposed by the Act and by the Instrument of Instructions on Governors in respect of the use of special powers are of such a nature that, even if he wished to relieve himself of them, it would not be in his power to do so.

On the other hand, His Excellency wishes to state that as the representative of the King-Emperor in this Presidency, he is above party politics altogether, and that within the four corners of the Goverment of India Act he will always be willing and indeed anxious to extend the utmost Ministry, from whatever section of Ministry, from whatever section of political opinion it may be drawn.

At the present juncture His Excellency believe that time should be given for a reconsideration of the position. An interim Ministry will therefore be formed at once in order that the King-Emerpor's Government may be carried on. And His Ecellency hopes that, by this providing a period for such reconsideration, it will eventually be found possible to form a Ministry which will command the confidence of the present Legislature.

DRAFT THESIS ON CONGRESS MINISTRIES AND OUR TASKS

1. The crux of the controversy on the issue of the acceptance of office was that it was a question of struggle between two tendencies within the national front, between Reformism and Revolution.

The Right wing which dominates the leadership of the INC wanted to accept offiice with a view to canalise the forces of mass-struggle into the blind alley of pure parliamentarism. But under the pressure of the growing strength of the forces of anti-Imperialist mass struggle, under the influence of the Left which was being felt in the top leadership as well as at the base among the rank and file, it sought to cover its retreat by phrases about the wrecking of the Constitution, about developing mass sanctions to enforce its fairly extensive election programme.

The acceptance of office was fought because of these dangers. What was being fought was the tendency to nurture parliamentary illusions in the masses, the attempt to divert the masses from the path of anti-imperialist struggle to that of passive faith in the ministries.

2. With the acceptance of office our task was to see to it that ministries were being used for the purpose of widening the democratic liberties with a view to strengthening the forces of struggle against the Constitution. We wanted the masses to keep the ministries ever marching forward in the task of implementing the Congress programme. Widening civil liberties, creating bigger and broader opportunities for the organisation of workers and peasants, for increasing the striking force of the National front against the Constitution.

We put forward the slogan—"Fulfil the Election Programme or resign". The slogan is of course meant to hold good for the whole period of ministries. The period of Congress ministries must be utilised to quicken the tempo of struggle on all Fronts. That was the general task outlined.

3. What have been the main results achieved during the first four months of the ministries?

(A) During the first four months of the Congress ministries the tempo of the struggle of workers and peasants and of anti-imperialist struggle in general which had quickened since the election campaign rose steadily. The coming of Congress ministries and the few early concessions, the general change in the attitude of the petty official in the village served to draw in the masses of backward population into the struggle.

(B) Mass campaigns launched mostly under the leadership of the Lefts for the release of political prisoners, removal of restrictions, for the granting of immediate relief to workers and peasants by passing executive orders on debt moratorium, remissions, stay of legal proceedings in rent and debt suits against peasants etc. have been successful. (a) They have mobilised vast masses of the people, workers and peasants and given a fillip to organisation and struggle. (b) They have succeeded in making the ministers to move on, to take a stand, though not yet a firm one, against the vested interests. (c) This partial success is further galvanising the struggle. (d) During the course of these campaigns an unofficial united front is being built between certain local Congress organisations headed by the Left groups, and Labour and Kisan organisations (notable instances in Cawnpore, Behar, Orissa and Maharashtra).

(C) As a result of these developments the riting wave of strikes, and peasant militancy, the growing will of the masses to see that the Congress programme is fully implemented, the resistance of the vested interests is growing. Imperialism alaramed by these developments is instigating the vested interests to greater resistance and goading the Congress ministers to use repressive measures against this rising tide of militancy. As the movement is all unofficial the agents of Imperialism are trying to paint it as a Bed Communist movement and isolate it from the democratic masses under the Congress and crush it singly. Their aim is to split the Naiional Front, to isolate the left within the-INC.

4. The Congress ministers and the Right wing are equally alarmed and are attempting to put a brake upon the developing forces of mass struggle, by using the apparatus of repression in the name of creating non-violent atmosphere, (frequent use of 144 against strikers, the use of Cr. Law Amendment Act in Ahmedabad and Sholapur, the launching of sedition cases against Batliwalla in Madras, gagging orders on labour leaders in Cawnpore) are hindering the growth of the United Front movement by issuing instructions to the local Congress organisations to refrain from what they call hostile agitation and criticism (Gandhijee's Harijan article on the A.I.C.C., Pt. Nehru's last statement, Mr. Satyamurthy's threats). This tendency which is being greeted by Imperialists as a "realistic approach" cannot but prove disastrous to the growth of our National struggle.

5. Under these circumstances the tasks of the Lefts in general must be determined by the following considerations: (a) that inspite of the acts of commission and ommission of the Congress ministries which run counter to the letter and spirit of the election pledges, these ministries still enjoy the confidence of the vast masses especially the backward sections; (b) that these ministries being Congress ministries can persist in these acts only in so far as they are able to mobilise the support of the majority of the vocal political opinion under the influence of the Congress; (c) that these ministries have proved themselves to a certain degree responsive to public opinion and pressure.

6. The need to counteract the reformist and anti-struggle trend is as great as ever. But this struggle cannot be conducted on the assumption that the ministers have merged or are fast merging into the apparatus of Imperialism. However, the ministers are showing such a trend and it must be fought by mobilising pressure inside the Congress organisations as well as through the independent actions of workers and peasants.

We say that the ministers are pledged to carry out the spirit andl etter of the Election Manifesto and if they fail, the Congress organisations and members must always join up in protest with workers' and peasants' organisations. Such protests must be organised in various ways, through M.L A.s, through the press, through demonstrations, deputations, marches to the Secretariat.

7. The positive concessions won must be actually realised. It is necessary to acquaint the people with these concessions and the resistance, if any, of local bureaucracy or vested interests against their being put into practice, must be exposed and nullified. This work must be done through Congress Committees, Kisan Sabhas and T.U.s.

8. It is necessary to plan out practical pieces of legislation within the frame work of the Election Manifesto and place them before the legislatures, popularise them through Trade Unions and Kisan Sabhas to obtain for them the support of Congress Committees and M.L.A.s. The legislation proposed by the ministers must be properly studied and amendments suggested, which are practicable at the expense of the vested interests and the state and which fall within the I.N.C. programme. The Amendments or Bills must not be proposed just with the object of exposing the ministries, but must be such as are immediately practicable. All such Bills and amendments must be popularised by well planned out broad mass campaigns. What the ministries think impractical must be made practicable by creating the pressure of mass struggle and agitation to counteract the influence of the bureaucracy and vested interests.

9. Some reactionary anti-Congress interests are now using Left phrases and making a show as if they are fighting the ministry from the platform of the left. These elements are not only fighting the ministries but fighting the Congress organisations as well. We can have nothing in common with them. We are not out to wreck the Congress ministries; on the other hand we are out to prevent the ministries from wrecking the Congress programme and thus harming the prestige and the

unity of the Congress and of the National Anti-Imperialist Front. In our criticism against the ministers which must be sharp, we must never lump the Congress ministers and the Congress organisations together. We must not ascribe the mainifestations of the reactionary tendencies of the ministers shown in their individual actions and utterances to the Congress organisation as a whole. By our hard work within and with Congress organisations we must create a public opinion within Congress ranks which will make such actions on the part of the ministers impossible.

10. With every advance of the organisation and struggle of the masses, with every new and powerful offensive launched by workers and peasants, the ministers, infected by the panic of the bureaucracy and the antinational vested interests, are attempting to use repressive measures, and attempt to isolate the leadership, by damning it as communist or socialist, from the masses of Congressmen and the public. Every such attack (like the one against the workers at Ahmedabad and Sholapur) must be bitterly fought our by mobilising the Congress rank and file against the repressive measures, by exposing these measures as anti-Congress, as directed against the right of of strike and organisation and as dictated by bureaucracy and the vested interests. It may even be essential at times to defy these gag measures utilising at such moments the anti-police and anti-bureaucracy sentiments of the Congress minded public, and always enlisting the sympathy of the Congress rank and file in these actions. In this way every advance made under the ministries, however small, must be made irrevocable, and a base for further advance.

11. The failure of the Socialists, in effectively checking the disastrous policy of the Congress ministries, and in counteracting the growing aggressiveness of the fight in support of repressi (Tamilnad and Gujerat) is due to the lack of unity among the Left, the inability of the Socialists to influence the basic organisations of the Congress, to link up the labour and peasant struggles which they lead with day to day work in and with Congress organisations. These failings must be rapidly

liquidated and we must counteract this capitulatory tendency of the ministers by raising the demand to recall these ministers who are violating the spirit and letter of the Congress programme and replace them by others who will carry it out more loyally. In the measure, the Socialists are able to rally the Congress rank and file and the basic Congress organisations in support of the growing mass struggle for democratic rights and civil liberties both in British India and in the states, in defence of the workers' and peasants' fight for their minimum demands for the right to strike and to organise, and against the repression which is being instigated by Imperialism, bureaucracy and the antinational vested interests, in the measure they are able to unmask the shibboleth of non-violence which is being used by Right wing Congressmen to justify this repression, in that measure will they succeed in preventing the present ministers themselves from deviating from the anti-Imperialist programme of the Congress, in preserving the unity of the National front of the struggle and strengthening it so as to launch and successfully carry through the mass struggle against the Federation and the hated Constitution as a whole.

See *The New Age*, January, 1938, pp. 351-54.

IMMEDIATE ISSUES

Labour

Struggles for the restoration of wagecuts, and recognition of Unions are in progress. Enquiry Committees have been appointed. Further struggles are ahead, because of the resistance of the Capitalists. We must succeed in mobilising the entire mass of public opinion to support these demands and struggles and must strive to enlist the support of the Congress rank and file and other organisations. These struggles must be so conducted that the attempted isolation is sucessfully prevented and the demands won.

On the basis of this victory, on these immediate issues we must advance to struggle for a Minimum wage legislation and a legislation for Social Insurance and against the anti-working class Acts on the statute book.

Peasantry

The first stage of struggle was the fight for remission in rents and taxes, abolition of grazing fees, stay of proceedings in rent-suits, agitation for debt Moratorium and the fight to see that these concessions were realised in practice.

The next phase is the fight for actual legislations—far reaching. Tenancy reform, statutory lowering of rents, halving of Land revenue, Debt legislation. It is necessary to study the official Bills and to plan amendments which would be the basis of the next phase of agitation and struggle.

Civil Liberties

We should concentrate on repealing all extra-ordinary legislation, Press Act, Emergency Powers Act, Criminal Law Amendment Act and demand the lifting of the ban on the Communist Party. There should be for sedition no more prosecutions.

In 1939, the clouds of the second global war which engulfed our sub-continent as well were irksome for the Congress leadership. At this point of time there was no hope left to expect any kind of self-government from the Raj. The Congress working Committee decided that the Congress ministries should quit their offices. Rajaji moved a resolution in the Madras Legislative Assembly condemning the unilateral action of the British government by involving India in the war. The Soon after the Congress ministries resigned in the six provinces.

The period between 1939-47 was the most crucial in the history of Indian National Congress. Besides the global war, serious doubts began to lurk in the minds of its leadership, Muslim League and the Raj. In October 1940, Gandhi decided to launch the Individual Satyagraha. Several leaders were arrested. Rajaji was also arrested and detained at Tiruchi Jail. When the leaders were released they had to face the British Commission headed by stafford Cripps. His recommendations were rejected by the Congress and the talkes failed.

In April 1942 Rajaji with the support of several members of the Madras Legislature recommended to the Congress leadership that they should acknowledge the 'Muslim Leagues' claim for separation in order to install a national Government to meet the emergency'. Sardar Patel and other leaders did not approve of the idea in the AICC session held at Allahabad on 29 Arpil 1942. On account of opposition to him, Gandhi advised Rajaji to resign from the Congress. He obeyed the High Command's verdict.

The Quit India Movement launched in August 1942 led to the arrests and convictions of thousands of Congress leaders and satyagrahis, Rajaji did not join the movement. He, however, did not sit quiet and pleaded the case for India's freedom through his speeches, writings and personal contacts with the people. His plan was discussed with Gandhi and was published on 10 July 1944. Its main provisions were as follows. The Muslim League would endorse the demand for independence for the transitional period. At the end of the war, a Commission would demarcate those contiguous areas in North-West and North-East in which Muslims were in an absolute majority, and in those areas a plebisite all the inhabitants would decide whether or not they should be separated from Hindustan. (c) In the event of a separation, agreement would be made for Defence, Commerce, Communications and other essential purposes. (d) The terms would be binding only in case of transfer by the British of full power and responsibility to the Government of India. Later on, meetings between Gandhi and Jinnah did not bring forth any results.

Gandhi requested Rajaji to rejoin the Congress and he did so, like a disciplined worker, in August 1945. Whereas Gandhi called Rajaji a great social reformer, who was imbued with much political wisdom and integrity of the highest degree,

Sardar Patel enlogised his talents by calling him an international figure.

In the subsequent years, Rajaji held several offices of high position under the Government of India. He was in the Interim Government, the Governor of West Bengal, the Governor-General of India, and the Chief Minister of Madras province for the second time. Later on, he founded the Swatantra Party. Thus in every walk of life he served the people of India throughout the long-drawn political struggle for independence.

5

The Assessment

C. Rajagopalachari was a remarkable personality who held several offices in his own province as well as in the central government. In whatever capacity he served, he showed much success in every phase of the administration. He was mainly worried about the socio-economic development of the people of India. To achieve this end, he worked with zeal and strength during all the movements launched by Mahatma Gandhi.

His first meeting with Mahatma Gandhi moulded the political programme of his life. Gandhi stayed with Rajaji in Madras in March 1919. They were attracted to each other after some argument about political developments in our country. Since that day he began to carry on the non-violent political programme of Gandhi in a disciplined way.

He indeed was very hard working and pain staking. He considered no task below his dignity. Work was thus a kind of worship for him. He formed this habit as a young lawyer when he had to struggle hard to earn his livelihood. Even as a Congress worker, he worked consistently and completed the even the most arduous job assigned to him.

He always showed his done and affection for the poor peasantry of India. He felt unhappy to listen to their several economic problems and tried to solve them in every possible way.

As Premier of Madras he always showed much consideration to their economic needs and helped them in several ways.

V.V. Giri opined, 'A great personage that he was he played a crucial role in India's freedom movement and he was indeed a farsighted statesman, he like of whom we will not be able to see for generations. We have lost an elder statesman who had adorned many positions in our national life with dignity and distinction.

C. Rajagopalachari, he first Indian Governor-General and one who dominated the Indian political scene for over half a century, died in the general hospital Madras on 25 December 1972. He was ninety four and was the recepient of the Bharat Ratna. One of the last vanguards of Indian freedom, he was described by Mahatma Gandhi as his conscience-keeper.

The elder statesman of the country was often described as the great dissenter of Indian politics. He had the courage of his convictions, was intrepid at all times and in his fights he shared none.

Smt. Indira Gandhi, started that in the passing away of Mr. Rajagopalachari, Indira has best a sage, indeed a force. 'Shri Rajagopalachari was one of the makers of new India, a sincere patriot, a man whose penetrating intellect and moral sense added depth to national affairs. His analysis, his anticipation, his administrative acumer and his courage to steer an unpopular course if he felt the need marked him as a statesman and made an impact on national history at several crucial junctures. He had held the highest positions and lent distinction to every office.

'Politics could not contain his diverse gifts. He was a major figure also in the world of philosophy and literature'.

Jagjivan Ram opined thus. 'We have best an outstanding intellect, able administrator, renowned politician and unfaltering patriot'.

K. Kamaraj stated, 'Rajaji was a national leader of stature next only to Gandhiji and his life was interwoven with the history of our country during the last seventy years'.

Besides rich tributes were paid to him by other prominent Indians like Dr. Shankar Dayal Sharma, Y.B. Chawan, S. Radhakrishnan, G.S. Pathak, K.K. Shah, A.K. Gopalan, Devaraj Urs, E.V. Ramaswami Naicker, P.C. Sen and Several others.

An ageless fighter against the establishment, Rajaji's campaign's ranged from those against the B.C.G. vaccination to leading a three—member delegation to the United States, Britain and Italy in 1962 to convass support for prohibition of nuclear tests.

Rajaji's views on the manufacture and use of the nuclear weapons are well-known. Through his speeches and writings, he was much critical of the big powers which possessed these weapons. Besides his opinion about the national language and the development of education had innovations for the national cause.

NUCLEAR WEAPONS

It pains me very much to feel that the Western powers are going wrong in what they are doing and that it has fallen to my lot to be pointing it out in unequivocal terms. I would have left far happier perhaps if it had been the other way about and I had to point out only the faults of another party. I have said at another meeting how greatly we are bounden to America and I need not repeat the reason here. It is however good that I repeat my hope that what I say should be interpreted as the anxious thoughts of a friend and not as a carping criticism from one who is not concerned with the welfare of America or the other Western powers.

So much has recently appeared in the daily press about nuclear weapons that everyone now knows quite a deal about them. It is possible to know a lot in a vague way and yet not have it all in order in the mind so as to be able to come to reasoned conclusions. The papers daily bring fresh news of what is done and said about these nuclear weapons. We may thus, by verbal familiarity and repetition, even lose the sense of danger about them. This is the reason why I am before you to attempt to explain the points involved.

Much has been said in defence of science in general as I science itself stood accused and we were in need of being told about the advantages of scientific knowledge and progress. I am completely in favour of the search for truth that is called science, lead it where it may. I do not, for a moment, support State or Church control over knowledge. It is impossible and undesirable to put restraints on the search for truth, but it is desirable and possible to put restraints on the application of what we unravel out of the mysteries of Nature. If we control our *application* of knowledge, there is no danger in knowledge itself. The responsibility lies with those, who rule the affairs of men not to misuse science, or employ men of science for wicked purposes.

There is a spate of written and spoken matter concerning the constructive uses for atomic knowledge. Most of this comes from Governments and Government agencies, not the Scientists or Industrialists. The industrial use of Atomic Energy is not likely to spring out of Government hand-outs. It is all totally irrelevant for my plea which is that we should prohibit the production and the use of nuclear weapons and that we should stop the test explosions which are being carried out and so contaminate the atmosphere and waters of the world and endanger present life and the normality of the human species for future generations. I can see no relevancy in these political tributes to Atomic Energy unless the Governments, that want to keep nuclear weapons going, wish to confuse the public mind.

Who hates or disrespect science? Who disbelieves in the power of knowledge as capable of being used for good purposes? How does the possibility of using Atomic Energy for good objects justify the present use of nuclear weapons for indiscriminate mass destruction and injury to future generations with all the incidence of cowardly assassination? Everything in the world can be put both to good and bad uses and atomic energy is not an exception to this rule. The good use need not be called up to confuse a calm examination of the bad uses of the prohibition thereof. If it is proposed to poison the wells of enemy countries, and some people object to such methods of warfare, is it relevant to talk of the excellent medical uses to which arsenic can be put? It is not intended or proposed as possible that we should speedily use up all the nuclear material available so as to starve out the military requirements. On the contrary, it is proposed to use mostly the waste by products of the regular military use of such material.

Those borderland days, when old theories of science were put to severe trials, were truly great days. Soon came thereafter the break-up of the whole atomic theory and I knew enough, even after I left college, to follow what was going on in the world of science which brought matter and energy together into one equation. I do not hate science or its wonders. But I wish to warn those who examine the issues of disarmament and prohibition of anti-civilisation weapons of the irrelevancy of all this talk of the blessings of the atom. One should love science but we should hate the manufacture of nuclear weapons for cowardly mass destruction leading to the annihilation of the civilisation that man has achieved.

Disarmament does not mean an end to scientific progress. The prohibition of nuclear weapons for purposes of war does not mean the closing-down of laboratories or research in the field of fundamental or applied science for the good of mankind. On the contrary, she prohibition of nuclear weapons for war would mean the release of the monopoly of governments and the abolition of secrecy which comes into operation to prevent the spread of knowledge when anything is held for war purposes. The present military use of atomic science, in fact, prevents the free exchange of knowledge which is necessary for the progress of science and its beneficient application. What I plead for is the emancipation of science from the trammels of war.

When in fear and trouble, men's brains like those of the other animals are sharpened. It is true that war and its fears and hatreds quicken the brains of the men of science engaged by governments. War is said to be the mother of inventions. What a mother! Let us not fall in love with war because some clever things are discovered in time of war. Secrecy goes with the work of science in war and secrecy impedes science. It is reported that a very eminent Cambridge scientist who wished to go to America was refused permission to do so. I read that a broadcast proposed by an eminent scientist in America was recently prohibited and he had to restrict his talk to subject-matter already widely known. I believe that the most valuable report of an important commission was delayed by an order of the American government and only published when government policy demanded it later.

Before going in to the question of the prohibition of nuclear weapons and the issue of disarmament which has been mixed up with it, I should like to point out, indeed I should like to emphasise, that the most urgent matter is the immediate prohibition by International authority of the test explosions which are going on in spite of every protest. It will not do to suppress only the bang as Churchill indicated with his flare for taming democracy. What is demanded is to stop both loud or silent radio-active poisoning of the world atmosphere and of of the clouds from which comes the rain for men, beasts and plants. The world has some rights in spite of the fears of one great power of aggression by another and their mutual dislikes. It is truly scandalous that these tests should be going on when eminent men of science, one after another, have pointed out the grave danger to world health and to future generations, in the clearest possible language that men of science can command. I cannot believe that any civilised nation can ignore the evidence which has been adduced and which is accumulating every day. The *News Chronicle* (March 24), which gave information on the effects of nuclear radiation, quotes: "Professor Rotblat, an experienced and responsible nuclear scientist, says in an article in the Atomic Scientists' Journal published this morning that it is imperative that data on the dose of radiation we have all received from nuclear tests up-to-date, and the rate at which this does is increasing, shall be known to the Government and published.

"Would 75 H-bomb tests over the next 30 years bring everyone in the world to the point where many children might be born mentally or physically deformed in generations to come? Professor Rotblat thinks it may be so. The Federation of American Scientists is similarly alarmed over possible genetic disasters of the future. But, on both sides of the Atlantic, the Governments utter soothing and reassuring statements." No government can decently claim the benefit of doubt in such a case in its own favour as lawyers do in criminal cases. Where danger to humanity is apprehended by men of science, the thing should not be done.

It was reported that an attempt was made on behalf of India at the recent Commonwealth Conference of Premiers to get an international agreement immediately that all these test explosions should be stopped but the attempt did not go through. Surely, when the West has more than enough of these nuclear weapons, further production and test explosions might as well be stopped at once. I am aware that the strategy of nuclear weapons requires a lot more testing. Indeed, I would grant that testing in the actual battle-field will soon become necessary as no amount of parade drill is equivalent to battle practice! Tests may be necessary even to reduce the intensity or the area of destruction so as to conventionalise the new weapons. Whatever be the motive or necessity, the cold war Powers have no right to disregard the right of the world to continue in good health and in the prospect of successive uncontaminated generations of men and women being born.

There are people in the world with a troubled conscience.

There are others who do not suffer at all in this way. The bombing of Japan at the close of the last world war is troubling the conscience of America. The point is irrelevant for the present issues. Indeed, all matters relating to past history, where men and rulers have committed mistakes, are irrelevant when we propose to do something to correct all those errors and to avoid future calamities. All the same, America is proud of her ideals, past and present, and anything that leads to the detriment of her moral position has a tendency to cause pain. Let me dwell on it for a moment. There is no question about the fact that the use of the atom bomb over Japan followed closely upon a successful test in a desert and that two bombs were burst one after another with only a very short interval, August 6 and August 9 of 1945. About the advisability of this atomic bombing, there was just an exchange of information in an informal way between the President of America and Mr. Churchill. Stalin was kept uninformed till the last moment. It was felt that something should be mentioned to Stalin. This was perhaps done but nothing was conveyed beyond a vague and incomprehensible hint. One could understand this because the American Government at that time was not sure whether such valuable, secret and dangerous progress in military science could safely be conveyed to Russia even though at that moment she happened to be an honoured ally.

It does not matter, however, whether it was the entire responsibility of America or it was shared by others. The moral issue is not altered on that account. So far as we are concerned, if it was wrong, it was wrong, whether it was done by one or more than one or by all of them. The crime of Japan was that she was on the wrong side during this war. A further crime in the opinion of the West was that although Germany had been completely crushed by that time, Japan's courage could not be overwhelmed by defeat and that some groups of the Japanese nation were prepared for mass suicide rather than for unconditional surrender. This was called fanaticism and so, any new monstrous weapon could be permitted by Christian morality. More American lives could not be sacrified to meet this fanacticism although all power had been knocked out of

Japan by that time. It is best I refer to Churchill's narrative and as far as possible in his own words.

"A more intricate question was what to tell Stalin. The President and I no longer felt that we needed his aid to conquer Japan. A devastating attack on Japan had continued from the air and the sea. Among the principal targets were the remnants of the Japanese fleet now dispersed for shelter in the inland sea. One by one, big ships were picked out and by the end of July, the Japanese navy had completely ceased to exist. The homeland of Japan was in chaos and on the verge of collapse. The professional diplomats of Japan were convinced that only immediate surrender under the authority of the Emperor could save Japan from complete annihilation. The only point the Japanese were particular about was saving of the Emperor's honour. This was known to the allies. A message had been sent by the Emperor to Stalin. It had not been addressed, probably because it was clear to the Japanese then to whom the Emperor's letter should properly be addressed; but Stalin knew what it contained and it had been delivered by the Japanese Ambassador. It was meant either for Stalin or the President of the U.S.S.R. It stated that Japan could not agree to what was than called "unconditional surrender" which included the handing over of the Emperor as a war criminal but Japan was prepared for admission of defeat and cessation of war. It was decided by the allied authorities not to recognise this appeal and to give an ultimatum calling for an immediate "unconditional surrender". This was published on July 26th. By that time terrific air bombing of cities had already become familiar to the world and leaflet-throwing was also a familiar process. A large number of leaflets were thus thrown over Japan warning her not of the atom bomb but of destruction by bombing. In fact, as I have already stated, even Stalin was very imperfectly informed and deliberately kept out of any information beyond this that a novel weapon had been got ready and tried and would be used. He was not told about radio-active or atom action. The two bombs were thrown on August 6th and August 9th. We know the rest."

It would be a mistake to suppress, writes Churchill, that the fate of Japan was settled by the atomic bomb. Her defeat was certain before the first bomb fell and was brought about by overwhelming maritime power. Her metropolitan army had capitulated without striking a blow. Her shipping had been destroyed.

Now, Churchill is not a negligible authority. These are the circumstances under which I believe one is entitled to say that there was no real necessity to use the atom bombs and the unnecessary use was due to either of two causes : (1) That although Japan was crushed completely, it was intended to save wasteful sacrifice of American lives in street and house-to-house fighting before she could be reduced to complete enemy possession and therefore the new weapon and its horrors had to be exhibited, or (2) the irresponsible urge of science to demonstrate itself when the ground for the demonstration was all clear. My own view is that the second cause prevailed and the political authorities of America were induced to accept the decision to use the bomb by reason of this urge operating on those who were working on military science. Those who have lived and worked for science and research in the machanical arts can understand the intensity of the urge to which I refer. Progress in science is based on the natural force called curiosity. There is an equal and obverse force operating in science, the hunger for demonstration of what has been discovered. But again I wish to remind you that this is irrelevant for the present discussion of policy. One who believes in the Law of Karma may well attribute the present tension and the pain and anxiety now suffered by all the victorious allies to the moral consequence of crimes committed by the triumphant allies. Triumph leads to delusion and error. As a result of that American use of the Atom Bomb and following it, science has progressed, but equally rapidly has the Law of *karma* pursued those who triumphed. Little consolation it is for those who do not believe in the Law of *karma* to be told all this; and perhaps it may even hurt.

Leaving the Law of *karma* aside, the use of the Bomb had

its immediate effect on Russia, between whom and the other two victorious allies there was already growing up fear and suspicion as to the future. It is a matter for surprise that the inevitable result was a quickening of Russian scientific research to meet the newly demonstration power of America; and we have what we now have. We need not give the name of *karma* to this; but it is in accordance with the permanent pattern of human affairs.

My earnest plea that nuclear weapons should be done away with can be justified entirely on reasons of pure military strategy and commonsense. Apart from any question of ethics or the future of civilization, I am convinced that it is good for America and for all the Western nations that these weapons be given up boldly, openly and as soon as possible, if only from the point of view of their own self-preservation and future safety. My advice for unilateral action apart, we have now a definitely clear and reiterated proposal of the readiness on the part of the U.S.S.R. that all nuclear weapons should be destroyed immediately and no more of them should be made. Here then is a splendid opportunity for the West to accept the position without putting forward any further conditions. Let us not try to find and attribute this to base motives or fear. This proposal, unfortunately, is strenuously opposed by America. And Britain supports the American unwillingness and the machinery of political parties and the press have been successfully roped in.

Here is an incubus sitting on the world. Everybody really wants to get rid of the incubus. "But", says America, "the world is not yet free from fear. We suspect, we distrust, we fear aggression. This is the only thing that enables us to feel strong. We cannot drop it." Now one can understand this, if this new weapon had been only in America's possession. Unfortunately it is now with the other party and, as Churchill put it very graphically and very correctly, it is no use relying merely on keeping ahead in the race. The other side's capacity for destruction, however much less than what is ours, is yet so great this the difference is irrelevant. In this admitted circumstances of extreme danger, if the other side definitely offers that the new weapons should unconditionally be given up by all parties, is it not time that we accept that offer even though America might reject the proposal that she should act in the unilateral, Christian, Gandhian way ? It would be wisdom to show at least relative courage if not the absolute kind of faith that is required for unilateral action.

In spite of this, what does America say ? "Set the balance right in regard to strength in conventional weapons and man-power before we deal with nuclear weapons." She asks for a favourable balance in conventional weapons and man-power or at least equality before she can give up nuclear weapons. This is neither wise nor reasonable. There is no reality in the idea of equalisation of strength in conventional warfare. One can understand the ideal of total disarmament. But there is no meaning in asking for equalisation. Equalisation between whom ? It is a wrong assumption that the world must, for purposes of war appraisement, be divided solely on the issue of communism and anti-communism. The pattern of international grouping cannot be assumed always to remain what it is at present. Whatever arrangement we make for equalisation of conventional arms on the basis of the present pattern of friendship, it would be of no avail if the pattern alters. Russia was with the West against Hitler. Indeed, she fought all the time in a manner which drew the admiration of the world. America came to help Russia and the Yalta papers show that Roosevelt was quite fond of Stalin and his people. We cannot rely on any particular pattern of likes and dislikes or alliances in assessing dangers and safeguards. It is only those who lived in the days of Hitler who can realise the intensity of hatred which had developed against Germany and the German people as a whole. The entire nation to a man was behind Hitler and his atrocious ways. But now the world is ready and eager to put Germany on her feet, arm her and trust her. It is a hopeful turn in the affairs of man, and we should welcome the fact that so much hatred and fear can be forgotten by men as if it were just an ugly dream. But it also proves the folly of relying on any particular international pattern as a permanent thing.

Again, apart from the pattern of international grouping, is there any commonsense behind the demand for an assessment of strength in conventional warfare ? Would anybody believe that much time would be lost in adding to conventional strength in equipment and man-power if the necessity arose ? Again, although it is a matter of faith and not of reason or argument, let me say I am fully convinced that the power of the West is quite sufficient even if nuclear weapons are out of the field and so there is no cause for fear. A great issue is involved, in solving which we should set aside all other considerations. It is not right, therefore, that the acceptance of the Russian proposal entirely to abolish nuclear weapons by international agreement should be delayed on grounds based on the relative strength in conventional arms. The world would hail a decision on the part of the Western powers if the offer of the U.S.S.R. in this respect stands accepted by the West and the great incubus is removed. Let us not revert to the feeling that Russia has made this offer because she is weaker in nuclear weapons. Let us remember what Churchill has stated on this point which I have already quoted. Weaker she may be today but she has enough to destroy Western civilization if she makes up her mind. Why did Churchill fear the Japanese suicide men ? When a certain point of desperation is reached, there is no question of deterrence through self-interest. Mad courage takes the place of calculation and history has recorded many instances of this.

When once this nuclear incubus is removed by solemn international agreement, it will not be easy for many reasons to revert to it suddenly by a party guilty of aggression. The time lag necessarily operates. It is no reason for not doing the right thing now.

If the world is freed from this incubus of nuclear weapons, is there much ground to fear aggression and a new world-war with conventional weapons ? A set of people will tell us to be afraid. But let us remember that the results, positive and negative, of war are much better understood now than ever before. International negotiations will have a much better change in the present world than they ever had before. It is therefore not reasonable to demand what is called balanced disarmament and make it a previous condition for doing anything on the nuclear weapon issue.

We were told the other day that both America and India have the common goal of peace before us. This is true, but we should not forget that means are as important as ends. The great difference between America and India is that the means America is adopting for establishing peace on earth do not appeal to India. The *Daily Telegraph* wrote on March 21 : "The pace of nuclear rearmament is getting faster. Can it avoid becoming furious ? Can the pacific *end* prevail over the warlike *means* ?" The Avadi Congress passed the following resolution : "The ominous developments in respect of atomic and hydrogen bombs are a menace, not only to world peace but to civilization itself. Even the experiments of the hydrogen bombs, if continued, threaten the entire world by their far-reaching and unascertained effects, which may lead to grave and permanent damage to human life and civilization. The total prohibition of the manufacture and use of atomic and hydrogen bombs and other weapons of mass destruction is imperative if civilization is to be saved from destruction. This Congress earnestly requests all concerned to bring about a cessation of the experiments and the immediate consideration of this matter by the Disarmament Commission of the United Nations." This is the Indian position. It is no use confusing our Prime Minister with the Commonwealth policy on nuclear weapons.

U.S.A. does not accept this, and this is, the issue I am dealing with. The free world, according to American opinion, must demand 'balanced disarmament' in respect of all weapons, and meanwhile, till an agreement is reached on balanced disarmament, she must continue to make test and stock nuclear weapons. What is the atmosphere likely to result from the U.S.A. continuing to manufacture these weapons and making the necessary tests, and in order that they may have the necessary deterrant effect, to announce from time to time her increasing and accumulating strength ? This process would necessarily develop a certain climate, a climate of increasing fear and distrust. Can any agreement towards disarmament grow or be given effect to in this climate ? Can any plant of peace but fail to wither in this scorching condition?

It is simple logic that if America and the Western powers cannot agree to disarmament in respect of nuclear weapons wherein they are superior, much less could it be expected that the other party would agree to disarmament of conventional weapons. Stopping of future nuclear production is not an adequate offer when you have an established present superiority. The idea that it is easier to obtain general disarmament than to give up nuclear weapons is based on the belief that the terror of nuclear weapons would induce people, by nature wicked, to do the right thing at once. The more I examine the position, the more nonsensical it seems to me. These ideas remind one of the country behind Alice's looking glass in Lewis Carrol's book where, if you ran in the opposite direction, you got more quickly to where you wished to go.

Distrust and fear are at the root of the present international malaise. If we desire to change the situation, we should do something to remove the causes of fear and distrust. May be, it is a vicious circle but we should cut it somewhere and in any case, the opposite, viz., doing what will creat more distrust and fear is no remedy. But that is exactly what we are doing through nuclear weapons and by the stand we are making in respect of them. We are told that war is the real enemy and not the nuclear weapons and we should, therefore, all try to prevent war and, meanwhile, both sides should go on making nuclear weapons and rattling the sword and use the possession of nuclear weapons as an instrument of terror in order that men may agree to end war. Clement Attlee wrote in an article in the *Daily Mirror* in the first week of March: "Proposals for banning weapons of mass destruction get us nowhere. War cannot be regulated like a football game. It cannot be humanised. It must be abolished. Delay increases the danger that some spark may set the world ablaze."

Is it not absolutely absurd that we could abolish war in such a hurry? We are asked to believe that it is impossible to give up these weapons which, instead of helping to win wars, certainly lead to bringing an end to civilisation. Yet, we are asked to believe that we can get war abolished straightaway. The testimony of history is contrary to this.

My plea is that, instead of talking of what is impossible in the present climate and so deceiving ourselves and deceiving others, we shoul take up the lesser issue of the removal of nuclear weapons because they threaten mankind in general and not one warring nation or another and its interests or peace of mind. The Western thesis is that we are arming to disarm, obtaining peace through terror, etc. Attractive epigrammatic forms of speech, they will not help to make what is psychologically impossible into a possibility. And we forget continually that the instrument of terror is possessed by both sides and there is enough of it on either side although one may have more of it than the other. Winston Churchill spoke the truth the other day that "it is no use relying on keeping ahead in the race of nuclear weapons. The production is rapidly reaching the point of no return when the other side's capacity for destruction, however much less than ours, will be so great that the difference will be irrelevant."

The British war-norse has understood the position. Yet, he wants Britain to make more H-bombs as if America has not enough already.

We were told the other day that the disarmament talks have made some progress; I should be every glad if, even beginning at the wrong end, disarmament in the true sense became a reality. Whether they begin with nuclear weapons as I want or with conventional weapons as America desires, as long as a satisfactory situation is reached, we shall all be glad.

My view that they should begin with nuclear weapons is not a religious dogma to which I hold fast even if the other way about succeeded. But let me read the *Daily Telegraph* of

March 21: "Disarmament is a monstrous paradox. It becomes more necessary as the Powers move farther away from it. The bigger the hydrogen bombs we build, the more urgent becomes the need to control their production and prohibit their use. Certainly, the current disarmament talks in London, which apparently have reached a deadlock, give no cause for hope." *The Times* of March 21 said: "The London talks have achieved nothing, and there is no sign that the Soviet Government thinks of them as more than an opportunity to divide opinion." *The News Chronicle* of March 21 wrote: "Mr. Eisenhower observes that the current United Nations meeting on disarmament has got nowhere." After these concurrent expressions of opinion on the part of important London papers, it is difficult to believe that anything has been or will be achieved beginning with conventional weapons, keeping nuclear weapons going.

There is a report that Harold Stassen has been appointed to a newly created post, namely an Assistant Secretaryship for disarmament. Much hope has been expressed over this gesture. But an important British paper has expatiated on this appointment in a way which leads one to think that it is just a budgetary job to reduce unnecessary and overlapping expenditure. Since, according to American policy, nuclear weapons have come to stay, much expenditure on the old fashioned weapons could be cut out and so, some-one has to work on this! Does this lead to any hope? Disarmament in one direction plus rearmament in another and worse direction is not much of an improvement.

The Archbishop of York, Dr. Garbett, made a tremendous speech in support of the British H-bomb programme. He repeated the American thesis that the nuclear weapons will provide a good umbrella beneath which the work of peace-making can be continued. I am afraid that this thesis has found a great deal of hasty acceptance in British thought, in spite of previous doubts and native commonsense. The leaders of all the political parties in Britain have rallied together over this policy of Peace through terror with remarkable unanimity. The fear of a world-war starting with aggression by the

U.S.S.R. has seized the Western mind and is leading it blindly into very erroneous policies which takes it in a direction contrary to where civilisation has to go. We have a repetition of Hitler's days when the fear of Jewish conspiracies was responsile for a calamitous situation.

In order to support the thesis of apprehended aggression and the consequent need for going on with nuclear weapons as a deterrent force, we are referred to three grounds.

The Western Nations have had the experience, they say, of what happens when they are weak. They have seen, they say, how their weakness tempted Hitler to aggression. Secondly, they refer to the temporary unpreparedness of America which led to the Northern attack on Korea. Thirdly, they point out how Czechoslovakian freedom was trampled upon by Soviet Russia.

As this fear of aggression is at the root of the unwillingness to give up nuclear weapons, it is important, though unpleasant, to analyse the position in respect of these three grounds. First about Hitler. Would it not be better to agree completely to forget those days? Have not all nations, including Russia, learnt lessons from Hitler and from the war against Hitler? Is it sensible to assume that the U.S.S.R. will repeat the errors of Hitler? The history of no nation is so clean as to enable us to refer to past history for present purposes. Indeed, I would suggest that the policy of hugging nuclear weapons is itself a dangerous copy of Hitler's vast errors.

Next, as regards Korea, is it so completely clear that the partition of Korea into North and South was so good and permanent that we should consider any attempted unification to be aggression? Of course, all violent efforts are to be condemned but can we maintain that the use of violence to unify Korea should be deemed a proof of unalterable Communist aggressive spirit? I think it is unfair to use what happened in Korea as a ground for holding on to these new dreadful weapons.

The third ground for apprehending Communist aggression is what happened to Czechoslovakia. Even before the war came to a conclusion, soon after the Allies smelt victory, there was a deplorable competition among the powers whose coalition had been only for the purpose of defeating Germany and was not rooted deep. There was a race between Britain and America on one side and Russia on the other to occupy ground with their armies which they respectively believed to be either their just reward for sacrifices suffered or necessary for national security. Czechoslovakia was, all through that period, assumed to fall within the Soviet zone. Czechoslovakia was, at the very outset, taken under Soviet control. What happened subsequently is not relevant. Czechoslovakia was 'liberated' but the earliest opportunity was taken by Soviet Russia to regain what she felt to be her own. I am not taking sides. I wish nobody played with the freedom of nations in the manner in which it has been done. My only point is, what happened in Czechoslovakia is not adequate reason to feel that the moment nuclear weapons are given up, Soviet Russia will start aggression again against the West and will not abstain from throwing the world into a fresh world war.

The narrative of events and politics given by Churchill in the last volume of his History of the War, which he most appropriately calls Triumph and Tragedy, should be read before anyone judges Russia about Czechoslovakia. Written in 1953, the two chapters "Western Strategic Divergences" and "Growing Friction with Russia," chapters 27 and 29 respectively, throw a lucid light on the motives and strategies followed by the Allied powers *as against each other* while they were completing the campaign against Hitler. It may be truly said that long before March 1945, the war was silently waged by Britain against Russia more than against Hitler. Britain's leader felt that America did not understand the real issue in Europe. According to him, "the indispensable political direction was lacking at the moment it was most needed" and it therefore became Britain's duty like a good shepherd to guard the sheep against the wolves that were about.

Churchill categorically states that the points of strategy and policy as he saw sometime before Germany fell. Soviet Russia had become a mortal danger; a new front must be immediately created against her onward sweep; this front in Europe should be as far East as possible; the entry into Prague of American troops was of high consequence; a settlement must be reached on all major issues between the West and the East in Europe before the armies of democracy melted. In May 1945 Churchill wrote to Truman: "We should hold firmly to the existing position obtained or being obtained by our armies in Yugoslavia. In Austria, in Czechoslovakia on the front reaching up to Labeck.

Churchill confesses in his vivid story: "While the conference at San Francisco was agreeably planning the foundations of a future free civilised and united world, and while the rejoicings in our victory over Hitler and the Nazi tyranny transported the peoples of the Grand Alliance, my mind was oppressed with the new and even greater peril which was swiftly unfolding itself to my gaze."

One has to read these two chopters of Churchill's story written entirely from the point of view of Britain's hopes and fears to guess what must have been the corresponding feelings on the other side, and to judge whether the Russian moves in Czechoslovakia and the other border areas was aggression pure and simple or just the same security strategy as on the other side the West sought to carry out.

Past history in respect of Czechoslovakia connot, therefore, help us to come to correct conclusions as to what we should now do to save civilization. The Yalta disclosures have served, if nothing else, one good purpose—that we should not now rake up what was thought or decided upon or done in the flush of victory, in those ugly days of ambition, hatred and folly. I have no objection to reasonable suspicion, and reasonable vigilance. But I object to the misanthropy of unalterable distrust and uncontrolled, unreasoned fear. These are our real dangers and real enemies. We should not allow worry and suspicion to develop into madness and anti-civilizationist folly. I have no objection to defence plans. But I object to blind faith in retaliation as an effective form of defence or 'deterrence' as now intimidation is renamed. Retaliation has been sufficiently demonstrated to be no defence.

We cannot assume, at one and the same time, contrary psychologies in our enemy. We believe that he is so madly aggressive that he will forget all lessons of history and create a new world war. At the same time, and contrarily, we believe that talk about total destruction will deter him. Deterrence requires occasional use of the boms and that is fatal.

I object to anybody assuming that the U.S.S.R. will proceed beyond her present boundaries and start a world war even if we, by international agreements, drop all nuclear weapons on both sides. I want nations to pursue the path of friendship, to be cautious but to be friendly, to watch each step and go forward in the path of trust and friendship. I want nations not to go the contrary way, viv., to create terror, hoping it will deter the enemy from doing what is wrong. I do not want nations to announce and rehearse preparations to evacuate cities when nuclear attack is threatened. All this does not create an atmosphere for friendliness to grow. I do not believe that there is any danger so great as to bring about a feeling of desperation. The weaker party is always likely to get this feeling and then he will not mind the consequences and may do what we just do not want him to do.

I do not want government departments to be talking about the vast power that lies in the Atom to do good when it is irrelevant and premature and is just counter propaganda against the growing world opinion that it is cowardly to be occupied in producing instruments for mass killing by pressing a button without even the compensation of personal sacrifice and risk which go with conventional weapons.

No one hates nuclear *energy* as such; no one hates atomic power or constructive uses thereof when such uses are ready to be brought into operation. But the talk of such matters undertaken by the political and military arms of a government serve only as propaganda.

I do not approve of people talking about the 'atomic age' having arrived and to believe and make others believe that there is no escape from it. I am wholly against men throwing the blame on abstract phrases when what counts is human action or human forbearance. The atomic age comes through the activities of men, not by itself. We want it to come in one way and not in another way. I do not approve of people accept nuclear weapon policy. It is our business to see that the atomic age in this sense does *not* come. Such talk is a form of escapism, throwing the blame on the age, as if we are compelled to it by some superior natural agency. We should not develop akindly attitude towards evil saying that evil has come to stay.

An incidental matter is that the preparation of nuclear weapons by the great powers leads to a considerable quantity by-products which are most deleterious to local health. A lot of these by-products are accumulating in the nuclear weapon manufacturing countries and have to be got rid of. They carry radio-activitiy. It is possible to utilise them to good purposes abroad. Now, what happens if we buy such stuff? We get radio-active energy but we co-operate with the manufacture of nuclear weapons by the cold war nations, which is bad. I would rather prefer waiting to manufacture radio-active material ourselves without co-operating with evil.

If any official reports lead people in America to think that there is in India a want of goodwill for America, it is entirely due to the stupidity or impatience of those impression gatherers. There is deep-rooted respect and gratitude and even partiality for America among intelligent sections in India. Indeed, they are unwilling to do anything that is likely to give the impression of antipathy to America.

"I do not think", wrote Bertrand Russell in a recent book,

"that the sum of human misery has ever in the past been as great as during the last 25 years", and the reviewer of Russell's books adds, "with the latest advance in technique, it looks as if we might surpass even that achievement. It is literally true that, if the species were to exploit to the full the resources of destruction now at its disposal, it would be the end of humanity as we know it".

There is irremediable catastrophe facing the world. Yet, the "realists" will not listen to Bertrand Russell or the evidence of the greatest men of science or even to smaller men of the world among whom I claim to be one. Is America to be the nation Providence has chosen for melancholy task, to perfect and use this last weapon of destruction and bring about the supreme climax in the brilliant play of civilization that man, born out of the ape, had in his foolish conceit started enacting?

Again and again comes up the question of realism. Can there be anything more unrealistic, I ask, than this notion that we can defend ourselves through retaliation when we know that there is enough and more of these weapons on both sides? Which master strategist will arrange the sequence of retaliatory measures so as to prevent, one after another, American civilization from being utterly destroyed, British civilization from being utterly destroyed, Russia from being utterly destroyed and all hope of civilisation in Asia from being similarly destroyed? Captain Liddel Hart, one of Britain's most eminent experts on war, has roundly condemned all these defence plans as absurd, insane and lunatic. "After devoting forty years to the study of warfare", says Captain Liddel Hart, he has now to face up to the fact that "this accumulated knowledge has become useless, that any war in the atomic age would lead to the destruction of all the nations concerned". Now, this conclusion should not be used by either side merely to threaten the other side. It should be utilised to come only one conclusion, that this new defence scheme of retaliatory use of nuclear weapons should be given up. The way should be shown in this abnegation of fully as soon as possible while still it can be shown. It should be obvious to those conversant with war psychology that, as soon as the lunacy begins to take concrete shape, the weaker will be much more desparately inclined to make an anticipatory attack than those who believe they are stronger. Here lies the greatest danger for the democratic world. Safety does not lie through preparation for retaliation as far as nuclear weapons are concerned.

This last Christmas the "comfortable words" were spoken from Cathedral Hill and James Reston commented on it that "for all its bickerings and divisions, Washington has sought in these past ten years to carry the message of Christmas into its foreign policy", and that "it has striven to carry the Commandments into its relations with other nations". So it is that I have dared to persists as I am doing, though it may look strange for an individual like myself to play the part of adviser to great and powerful nations. I know that there are many hearts in America and Britain and France beating in sympathy with what I say although they dare not express their views in America lest they be thought Communist at heart. I believe there is a fundamental loyalty to the word of Christ in America as such there is not in other places and on which Humanity's fate hangs.

Brotherhood Week was celebrated according to a 21 years' custom in the United States and Canada in the last week of February and Dwight Eisenhower, who was chairman of the 1955 Brotherhood Campaign, sent a message which contained these words: "In the face of forces which work to lock each man within the prison of his own mind, which make friend distrust friend, nation distrust nation, it is imperative that we heroically, by word and deed, give voice to our faith; that every man is indeed his brother's keeper, that no human being in the world can escape his spiritual involvement in what happens to any other human being, that no man in the troubled sea of mankind can be an island".

NATIONAL LANGUAGE

You see I am talking in English. This is both an apology

and a warning to boys. If boys do not care to learn the *rashtrabhasha* when it is easy for them to learn, like me, they will grow too old to learn it afterwards. I hope that Hindustani will be taken up. not only by those boys of this institution whose mother tongue it is, but by those whose mother tongue it is not. In Bengal, the primary medium of instruction must be Bengali, but in cities like Calcutta there are quite a number of people whose only possible medium can be Hindustani. For such people, schools that work through the medium of Hindustani are absolutely necessary.

Children must receive education through their respective mother tongue. In fact, their education must be a family affair, whereby character is formed and culture shaped. This means, too, that the greatest amount of personal attention is necessary. But as, nowadays, our families are not capable of taking charge of the education of their own children, their co-operation is needed for the running of schools which may have the appearance of being communal institutions. These are necessary in cities such as Calcutta. This being a Hindustani school, it serves the incidental purpose of popularising the national language of the country.

The adoption of Hindustani as our national language does not imply that it is superior to other languages Hindustani has been selected as the national language because it is spoken by nearly everyone in nearly all places. I have noticed a strong tendency on the part of those whose mother tongue is Hindustani to push its claims for attention with a kind of arrongance. This is not a wise attitude. Consideration for others is necessary in all directions. I lay stress on this, because it is very effective propaganda for the national language in Calcutta and elsewhere. We should remember that those whose mother tongue is Hindustani get an adventitious advantage. They should therefore show great consideration when approaching those whose mother tongue is not Hindustani. Not only must you be careful, but in the beginning you must also bear the burden to a certain extent.

EDUCATION THROUGH WORK

I must, at the outset, appeal to you all to listen carefully to the several arguments advanced in support of the new scheme of education and give it a fair trial. The matter is complicated. It is unfortunate that small matters should have become so complicated. Big questions get through without any trouble or complication but, sometimes, small matters are not easily understood. This appears to be a natural phenomenon. We all readily understand that a stone is dangerous. But we do not easily understand the potentialities of the air with which we are surrounded. I would compare elementary education to the wind; we should realise it is powerful. It will sometimes blow off trees. Like the wind, elementary education should be spread all over without being noticeable. I will even call elementary education "Life's breath".

It is, indeed, regrettable that it should be said that there is a big conspiracy behind the new scheme. Probably, because I am its author, some people suspect that there is something behind it. If some other person would have done it, by God's grace, every one might have accepted it and the scheme might have worked successfully. I made similar suggestions over 30 years ago. I thought that somebody would do it but ultimately no one took it up. I myself did not take up this question in the past. In my old age I thought that I should put it through. People may ask why I am keen on implementing this scheme and not pass it off to a better person. That is one side of the question. On the other hand, I have left this undone all these years and feel that I should attempt it at least now. For some time people might abuse me and then there will be an end to it.

I cannot understand why there should be so much agitation over this simple issue. There have been many occasions in the history of this country when several changes have taken place in the field of education and no one has protested. It was said in olden days that Indian History should be studied. Later, the order was changed and there was a ban on its study.

Nobody protested then. Similarly, study of English History was made compulsory and subsequently this order was rescinded. Then again there was no protest. Similar treatment was given to the subject of Physiology. There was no reference to it at all either in the newspapers or elsewhere. People in olden days were fortunate but I am unfortunate because, for the small change I am introducing, there is so much protest.

As I was sitting at the meeting here today, it struck me what could have been the reason for the opposition. I would like to share with you what has occurred to be as a possible reason. Caste differences were there for a long time and I cannot say whether it is wrong to observe them. Inter-dining and inter-marriage have for ages been confined to various communities. A weaver confined his social activities to his own community. So also a washerman and those engaged in other professions. This compartmentalisation did not allow the people to mix with each other freely. The Englishmen who came in opened up schools, wanted all those who desired an education to come and join the schools. You should not mix up the system of education prevailing then with the modified system of education which we are introducing. Sometimes fees were levied in those schools and on other occasions not. The management was entrusted to the municipalities. Whosoever found it convenient sent their children to school and the number of those attending schools increased because the recipients of this education were provided with jobs, big or small. Those who got jobs drew salaries without much effort. A stage has now been reached when there is unemployment among this class of educated people. These people feel the same disappointment which those who lose in the race feel. In a horse race everyone cannot draw a prize and those who win are very pleased. Others mourn their loss and even go to the extent of asking why the Government do not abolish racing. This attitude is not adopted by the losers when they first go in for betting. Everyone cannot get jobs, just as all who bet cannot draw prizes in the horse race. If that happens, then there would be a heavy collection of taxes. Otherwise, it will not be possible to pay salaries to all. People have also come to realise that all those who are educated cannot be given salaries by the Government. The result is that there is unemployment of the educated class. I am not saying this as applying to Brahmins. Whoever gets himself educated is not sure to get a job and that is the position.

Already there are signs that students are not enthusiastic about continuing their studies after the intermediate class and perhaps after some time they will feel the same way after passing the S.S.L.C. To my mind, the confusion that is created in the minds of the people and the mistaken nation that education gets employment is the canse of what I call the disease.

Owing to this background, the word 'education' has acquired a wrong connotation. Its real meaning is "learning". It does not mean bookish education. That is the reason for the confusion. Criticism is made and fear expressed that the full period of education under the new scheme has been reduced by half and it is said that a full meal has been cut half. This is a mistaken notion and there is no substance in this fear. What is required is that everybody should know how to read and write. Everybody without distinction of caste or creed or profession should acquire this knowledge as life's breath. People should discern the difference between this system of education and the one that prevailed during the days of British rule. The question is whether it is reasonable to see that every one is taught to read and write, whether he is a labourer, a rickshaw puller or a washerman. It would be a good thing for every one of them to be educated. How this is to be achieved is the question. There are some who want to produce specialists. The job of the Government, however, is to see that every one receives some education. There is no connection between education and getting employment. If we realise the truth of this, the implications of the new scheme will be clearly understood.

A small change introduced under the new scheme is that the duration of instruction in schools is reduced from five to three hours. I have the authority of educationists to say that three hours are sufficient to teach the students to read, write and learn arithmetic, allowing for festival and other holidays. If it is possible to impart education in three hours, why should children be troubled for five hours. Some people criticise that if a child is left alone, he will climb a tree or somehow idle away his time. This class of objectors seem to say that they have entrusted their children to the teachers to be looked after all through the day and that they are disappointed that their children are being sent back to their care much earlier. I only pity those who raise such objections.

The real question is how the leisure hours can be utilised by the children. It is enough if the children spend the time in play and also incidentally learn with interest and pleasure some vocation. The thrill that children get from flying a kite can be appreciated; children learn a lot by flying kites. When I was a student, I was very much attracted by the potter's wheel and used to run up to watch the potter at work. This was a great experience for me. Can boys of the S.S.L.C. standard make pots? I am sure these boys will not be able to understand the technique of pot-maker. If the children watch the pot-maker, then they will learn the technique of it. Similarly, children can watch the mason and other craftsmen at work. It was suggested that these crafts can be taught by trained teachers within the school. This suggestion canot be accepted because our past experience with these teachers has not been very encouraging. Further, this requires buildings, equipment and finance.

Another criticism is that there are no industries in the villages. There are many industries in the villages. Only people must have eyes to see. Wherefrom do you get all the articles you find in the market? Have all the potters perished? In spite of the lorries, the bullock carts still exist and are rendering great service. These carts must have been made in the villages by the village artisan. Are they not village industries? Construction of houses is going on in the villages. There is so much of interesting work in this sphere. There is no point in saying that the artisan should be brought to the school. Where is the danger in the children going to the artisans?

Details in working out the scheme can always be discussed and examined. The scheme will be successful only if there is a change in the attitude of the people. Schools in village remain isloated from the people. This situation must change and the whole village should be converted into a polytechnic. I want everyone to learn a craft. People who oppose the new scheme, I am forced to say, are really opposed to vocational education. Everyone should be trained to use his hands and an interest in this direction should be created in the early years of life This will certainly contribute to the prosperity of the country. The modified system also gives plenty of scope for higher studies. If we do not put our limbs to use, we will be like a hen which, in spite of possessing two wings, is unable to fly. My idea is that if you are not able to get a job, you should be able to use your hands and so earn a giving. Some people suggest that we might have education first and later on learn some vocation. This does not recommend itself to me because I am of the view that everything should be learned when we are at an impressionable age. I would appeal to the people and, in particular, to the villagers to support this scheme. I want at least one person in each village to guide the children. If more men are forthcoming, we can even have a *sangham*. It does not matter if the guide is uneducated. I have no doubt that after five years of elementary education, with three hours schooling every day, the children will have learnt to use their head and their hands as well.

SATYAGRAHA IN TAMIL NAD

How Rajaji was arrested

The Tamil Nad Satyagraha Publicity Department has sent a report of the Vedaranyam Salt Satyagraha under Sjt. C. Rajagopalachar of which the following is a condensation :

The first batch of 100 Tamil Nad volunteers under Sjt. C.

Rajagopalachar set out for Trichinopoli to offer Salt Satyagraha at Vedaranyam on the morning of March 13th.

The receptions on the way in the Trichinopoly District were enthusiastic. They entered into the Tanjore District at Koviladi. Their entry was marked by the promulgation by the District Magistrate of Tanjore of a circular in Tamil to terrorise the people, of which the following is an English rendering.

> "It is understood that a batch of people intend to start from Trichinopoly on the 13th inst. to reach Vedaranyam *via* Tanjore and Mannargudi with a view to commit offences under the Madras Salt Act. Under Sections 141 I.P.C. this assembly will constitute an unlawful assembly. Whoever harbours, receives or assembles in any house or premises in his occupation or charge under his control any persons who have been hired or otherwise engaged for joining an unlawful assembly or who are members of an unlawful assembly, knowing that such persons have been so engaged or are members of such an assembly, will be liable to be punished with imprisonment for a term of six months and fine.
>
> "This gathering includes men belonging to other districts. With their object, which is to violate the law, the people of Tanjore have no sympathy. There is no reason why persons from other districts should come to this district, break the law and cause trouble to the people of this district. Therefore it is the duty of every one to discourage this band and withhold from them money, suplies and other help. Whoever acts in this manner in contravention of the provisions of Section 157 of the I.P.C. will be prosecuted."

To make matter sure the District Magistrate of Tanjore had sent the Deputy Collector, Tahsaildar, Magistrate & Police Officers with a battalion of constables in uniform and mufty to the village of Koviladi. They intimidated the Trustee of a big Chatram from giving accommodation to the Satyagrahis and camped themselves on the verandah of the Chatram. The whole village however assembled to a man and offered a cheering reception to the party led by Stj. C.R. with music, and a huge meeting was addressed by Sjt. C.R.

The first village in Tanjore district having thus successfully disobeyed the District Magistrate's order the subsequent march of the Satyagrahis was a triumphant procession. Sjt. Achariar and party reached Kumbakonam on the 20th morning and were accommodated in the house of Sjt. V. Panthulu Iyer a leading and influential Mirasdar, staunch Congressman, ex-M.L.C., and member of the Working Committee of the Tamil Nadu P.C.C. The Tahsildar of the place had been to him two days earlier (18th April) to warn him under threat of prosecution against giving accomodation and food to the Satyagrahis. Sjt. Iyer, an ardent supporter of the N.C.O. movement from the days of 1920, who had already signed the Satyagraha pledge and was ready to break the Salt Law spurned the warning with the remark that he was prepared to suffer imprisonment cheerfully for performing the *dharma* of feeling his guests. Sjt. Panthulu Iyer has since been convicted to six weeks simple imprisonment under Section 157 I.P.C. for harbouring members of an unlawful association. He was sentenced in the first instance to pay a fine Rs. 100 and in default to 6 weeks simple imprisonment Sjt. Iyer did not participate in the proceedings of the court. The offer of some of his relatives to pay the fine was resented by him strongly.

Another leading Mirasdar of Kumbakonam, Sjt. Rajagopala Iyer, a non-Congressman has been summoned to answer a similar charge under Section 157.

The party reached Tiruthuraipundi, a place 22 miles distance from Vedarayan, on the 25th evening. The arrangements for reception, lodging and boarding were made by one Sjt. Ramachandra Naidu, a wealthy and influential landlord of the place. The campaign of repression began that day dramatically, the police officer arresting Sjt. Ramachandra Naidu in full view of the audience while C.R. was in the middle of his speech. He has since been released on bail and is defending the charge against him under Section 157 I.P.C. as he is not a Satyagrahi. After the arrest and release on bail of Sjt. Ramachandra Naidu a meeting was held in the Bazzar Street of Tiruthuraipundi when merchants came one after another and publicly entertained the party. The provocative arrest of Sjt. Ramachandra Naidu only served to awaken the people and to strengthen the campaign considerably.

C.R. and party reached Vedaranyam on the 28th evening. The 29th was observed as a day of fast and prayer. On the 29th night C.R. sent a letter to the Sub-Divisional Magistrate of Mannargudi who was camping at Vedaranyam informing him that he and 16 volunteers would commence breaking the Salt Law at 6 A.M. on the 30th. The salt swamps were being vigilantly guarded by the police and excise officers. Early the next morning Sjt. C.R. with 16 volunteers proceeded to the salt swamp and broke the salt law. The Superintendent of Police with his subordinates and about 50 constables as well as the Assistant Commissioner of salt had stationed themselves on the road to another swamp with a view to prevent C.R.'s party from proceeding further. They were not aware of the direction in which the party had gone and did not know that the volunteers had broken the salt law until information was sent to them through one of the volunteers by C.R. himself. Immediately the officers came to the scene and the D.S.P. arrested C.R. at about 8 A.M. for breaking the salt law and for leading an unlawful assembly. The volunteers were not arrested but were asked to surrender the salt they had picked up. This they refused to do and returned to the camp with the salt they had collected. The trial took place before the Sub-Divisional Magistrate of Mannargudi who was camping in the premises of the office of the Asst. Inspector of Salt, and was finished in a few minutes. Achariar did not participate in the proceedings beyond pleading guilty and stating that everything necessary has been said by his leader Mahatma Gandhi. He was convicted to pay a fine of Rs. 200/or in default to undergo simple imprisonment for 3 months for the offence under Section 74 of the Salt Act. He was also sentenced to 6 months simple imprisonment for the offence under Section 145 I.P.C.

The Magistrate in the course of the judgment recommended C.R. to be treated as an A class prisoner. On hearing that C.R. said that he did not want any special treatment. The Magistrate replied that he was bound to do his duty.

The news of C.R.'s arrest and conviction spread like wild fire and Vedaranyam observed a complete *hartal*. It must also be noted that they had already given effect to their determination of social boycott of Government servants on account of which the officials on duty had to find their food at a place two miles distant from Vedaranyam. C.R. was taken the same day in 2nd class carriage to the Golden Rock Junction from where he was led to the Central Jail, Trichinopoly at about 9.30 in the night.

All the telegrams that were sent by the Satyagraha Camp from Vedaranyam about the arrest and conviction of C.R. were delayed by the telegraph office and were released for publication only after C.R.'s train had reached Golden Rock. Trichinopoly received the news at about 10 in the night and next day there was *hartal*. Shrirangam observed a complete and thorough *hartal*. At the meeting in the evening which numbered over 10,000, Dr. Rajan and a Musalman friend spoke on the significance of C.R.'s conviction. There was a huge bonfire of foreign cloth at the end of the meeting.

C.R. has nominated Sjt. K. Santanam to be in charge of Satyagraha Camp in Vedaranyam and in his letter to the volunteers he has exhorted them to maintain perfect discipline and brotherhood and has enjoined them to observe absolute non-violence in word, deed and thought. In his message to Mahatma Gandhi he has said that he has overtaken him in the race by a few days.

On 1-5-30, the day after C.R.'s conviction, two batches were sent to two salt swamps. One batch had a hard struggle with the police in bringing the salt they had collected. The other batch returned with about a maund of fine white natural salt. The police had evidently no scent of the excursion of this batch. On 2-5-30 two more batches were sent out.

Sjt. M. Arunachala Mudaliar, Karnam village officer of a village in Tanjore District, has sent in his resignation on account of the Satyagraha movement. In reply the Tahsildar of the place has stated that his resignation will not be accepted and that he will be recommended for dismissal. The ex-Karnam has signed the Satyagraha pledge and has been taken for the second batch. Sjt. Chidumbara Iyer, Assistant Station Master of Tiruppur, who gove up his job, has joined the first batch.

At Vedaranyam on May 3rd a party of police arrived at the camp a little after ten headed by the Deputy Superintendent of Police with search warrant authorising the party to search and take any contraband salt in the camp. The police surrounded the Camp. The D.S.P. asked for the surrender of the salt. Sjt. Santanam said it was their duty to defend it The volunteers formed a close and compact cordon round the salt. At a word from the D.S.P. the entire police force flung themselves on the volunteers. The attack lasted nearly for an hour. The police in fives and sixes caught hold of each volunteer by any part of his body that was easily available for a grasp and by sheer force wrenched him away and flung him apart. Those who were thus separated from the men were surrounded by the police and detained outside. Sjt. Santanam was dragged away twice, and returned a third time to share the brunt of the attack. The last few volunteers offered such stubborn resistance that when finally the cordon was broken six of them had fainted and yet held the salt tightly in their clenched fists. Volunteer Viraswami of Madura recovered consciousness after half an hour, and all the time salt was held tightly in his fist. Krishnaswami of Bombay also recovered only after a while. Raju of Coimbatore, who was the last to be lifted away, fainted immediately and has severe pain on the chest. Though the police employed maximum muscular force there was no attempt on their part to cause hurt or injury. The Deputy Collector visited the camp to enquire after the volunteers. He congratulated Sjt. Santanam on the wonderful discipline and non-violence of his volunteers.

A DANGER TO PEACE

All over India, and for a considerable time past, the national flag has been hoisted without any interference on the part of Government. The recent change in the design of the flag was, it is now well known, intended to remove the communal significance that was read in the colours. It was not intended to denote any change in the creed, or the policy, in regard to the legitimate and peaceful means to be adopted for the attainment of the Congress objective. The new flag, therefore, ought not to be treaded differently from the old flag by officials responsible for peace and order. Last week's newspapers showed, that in accordance with the instructions of the Congress Working Committee, the new flag was hoisted at almost every place in the country without untoward incident or interference on the part of Government. In Madas, in the District of Chittoor, however, several prohibitory orders were issued by local magistrates, all couched in identical terms as follows :

> "Whereas it has been reported to me by the Police, that the Congress party intends to hold functions all over the country and in particular in the Taluk of Kangundi for hoisting and saluting a new Congress Flag on the morning of Sunday August 30th; and whereas it has been published in reputable newspapers on or about August 20th, 1931 that a fundamental principle of the Congress creed is that the Congress must be recognised as intermediary between the people and the Government, and whereas the display of an alleged new "National" Flag by the Congress party in these circumstances is likely to give colour to the above false claim, and to deceive the public into thinking that the Congress assumed Governmental authority, and that the public can approach Government only through the Congress, and that they owe allegiance to the Congress party rather than to the King Emperor; and whereas, so gross and mis-

chievous a deception is likely to occasion confusion in the public mind, disobedience to constituted authority, and is a grave menace to the peace of this taluk; I, R.N. Ethirajulu Naidu, Sub-Magistrate, Kuppam, hereby direct you and all other supporters and adherents of the Congress party and all volunteers and paid employees of the same to abstain from holding, organising or attending any such function within my jurisdiction, from displaying in any public place any so called National Flag or emblem except the Union Jack for a period of 15 days from this date.

"The order is passed ex-parte in view of the urgency of the situation which does not admit of service of notice."

It will be noticed, that apart from the usual general incantation, no specific allegation is made, and no specific circumstances referred to, in order to justify an apprehension of a breach of the peace. The whole order rests on the ground, that the display of the national flag is likely to give colour to the "false claim" of the Congress to be recognised as intermediary between the people and the Government, and will deceive the public into thinking, that the Congress assumed Governmental authority. Such an argument, if admitted, would bar the flag all over India and for all time, and not only in Chittoor District or for 15 days, a *reductio ad absurdum.*

The orders were issued about the time of the Simla talks between Gandhiji and the Government of India. This may explain, but cannot justify the whimsical grounds for the prohibition. As usual a wrong step under Section 144 leads to a wide and sweeping interference larger in its scope than the intention with which magistrates start. Chittoor magistrates have promulgated additional orders so as to prohibit not only the hoisting of the flag, but also holding of or attending any meeting 'in support of the Congress party or creed.'

It is hardly necessary to say, that these orders are a clear breach of the Delhi Settlement, under which it was expressly conceded, that the Congress should not be put under any ban, and clearly, though implicitly, agreed, that there shall be no interference with its normal work.

Objections and considerations arising out of all this allegiance of the people to Congress authority as symbolised by the flag, and the threats to the sovereignty of the British Indian Government therein involved were wholly irrelevant ground for the magistrate, whose emergency powers under the Section are limited to preserving the peace and not to protecting the sovereignty As for questions connected with the sovereignty of the Government of India as at present constituted, everything is in the melting pot, and the magistrate cannot deal with them in this manner without hurting the cause of peace during Gandhiji's absence. A policy on the part of district officers, such as has been followed in the Chittoor District, is certain to lead to a most difficult situation which, we would like to believe, is not the desire of provincial Governments to develop.

MAGNA CHARTA

"I shall strive for a constitution, which will release India from all thraldom and patronage, and give her, it need be, the right to sin. I shall work for an India in which the poorest shall feel that it is their country in whose making they have an effective voice; an India in which there shall be no high class and low class of people; an India in which all communities shall live in perfect harmony. There can be no room in such India for the curse of untouchability, or the curse of intoxicating drinks and drugs. Women will enjoy the same rights as men. Since we shall be at peace with all the rest of the world, neither exploiting, nor being exploited, we should have the smallest army imaginable. All interests not in conflict with the interests of the dumb millions will be scrupulously respected, whether foreign or indigenous. Personally, I hate distinction between foreign and indigenous. This is the India of my dreams, for which I shall struggle at the next Round Table Conference. I may fail, but if I am to deserve the confidence of the Congress, my principals, I shall be satisfied with nothing less."

Thus has Gandhiji in a few simple ringing words told the world what the Indian National Congress wants. All-wise God has conceded man, his creation, freedom to err. Less cannot be conceded by one nation to another. This is Gandhiji's simple counter-claim in answer to all those claims for safeguard, which, in the interest of India, Britain seeks to impose on India. The poorest shall feel that it is their country. This is the charter for adult suffrage and equality of law and removal of all disabilities by reason of sex and caste. Gandhiji has reiterated the promise of the Congress to do away with the drink traffic. Swaraj for India means and includes the end of drink. The Indian National Congress is under promise to the women and the children of India, that the day we get self-government, prohibition will be decreed. This is why we cannot accept any terms from the British Government that do not permit us to dispense with the drink revenue. We cannot maintain the present army, nor can we concede the Britain the control over our military expenditure, disabling us from doing away with the drink and drug revenue. Our international policy is peace, and the smallest army of defence is all we need to keep. 'I hate distinction between foreign and indigenous:' this is the most characteristic article of Gandhiji's charter, and only this can be in accordance with the tradition and genius of India. The only safeguard is that the interests of the dumb millions should be respected : otherwise India shall belong to the world, and does not want to live for herself. Herein has Gandhiji explained the purpose, the aim, as well as the limitation of true Swadeshi.

SECTION 144 IN MYSORE

Gandhiji has tendered congratulations to the Mysore Government on many an occasion, among other things, for the noteworthy support it is giving to the hand-spinning movement. It has set a valuable example to other administrations in the acceptance of the scheme suggested by the Spinners'

Association, and by financing and managing through its own Department of Industries the village home industry of hand-spinning in certain areas in Mysore. At its Badanval centre the production had gradually progressed to Rs. five thousand a month worth of Khadi. It is unfortunate, however, in regard to the drink evil, that there is nothing similarly to say in favour of Mysore as compared with the British provinces. Even though the right of peaceful picketing now recognised as legitimate under the Gandhi-Irwin Settlement, it has been prohibited where it was sought to be exercised in certain places in the state of Mysore.

The right of picketing arises out of the ordinary law which is the same in Mysore as in British India. If it was a right that could not be denied in British India, it follows that it must be easily conceded in Mysore state. Yet we find, that the following prohibitory order has been passed by the District Magistrate of Kolar, and served on prominent workers and publicly promulgated in several places in his district. The prohibition order is framed so comprehensively that not only picketing but any kind of propaganda for temperance is effectively barred:

"Whereas from the reports laid before me by the police inspector of . . . Taluk, it appears to me necessary to prohibit the public utterance of cries, the singing of songs, the playing of music, the delivery of harangues and the use of gestures or mimetic representations and the preparation for exhibition or the dissemination of pictures, symbols and placards connected with the picketing of liquor and drug shops, as these will, in my opinion, probably incite to the commission of an offence or lead to a disturbance of public peace, in the municipal limits of . . . . and its neighbourhood, I, A. V. Ramanathan, District Magistrate, Kolar District, do, hereby, prohibit the public generally, and the undermentioned persons in particular, from the public utterance of cries, the singing of songs, the playing of music, the delivery of harangues and the use of gestures, mimetic representations, and making preparation for exhibition, or the dissemination of pictures, symbols, placards connected with the picketing of liquor and drug shops within the municipal limits of the town and a distance of two miles all round such limits, for a period of six months from this date."

The picketing, it need hardly be pointed out, is now nothing but the right of persuasion which any one may exercise wherever a wrong thing is about to be done by a brother citizen. It is a fundamental right, which, like all other liberties, is limited only by other people's liberties. It is not a concession of the Government of India, or a democratic advance, which the Mysore Government feels, it must take some more time to follow. Both in British India and in Mysore it is there unless taken away by law.

AMENDED PRESS BILL

The Press Bill, as amended by the Select Committee, has been published but amendments cannot set right a thing wholly illconceived. The ostensible object of the measure is to prevent the encourangement of political violence. Existing law amply provides scope for prosecuting and securing the punishment of persons guilty of acts of this nature. If it is felt that certain types of encouragement escape existing definitions of abetement such acts should be defined and passed through the Legislative Assembly as newly defined offences.

Instead of this straight forward course, which could secure the stated object, it is sought under the cover of preventive legislation and it makes liberty of the press a fiction by putting all newspapers under security for good behaviour. To enact a measure like the one proposed and to claim that the press is left free is as absurd as to put all citizens under Section 108 Cr. P. C. and claim that citizenship is still intact. A measure of this kind cannot be made right by amendments, either in the Select Committee or in the Assembly. It is not the fangs only but the very breath that poisons.

Not all the fangs have, however, been touched in the

amendments. Under the bill no new press could come to be, except, ordinarily, after giving security. The amendments provided no change in this, but makes the security refundable after three months probation. The ticket of leave habit generated during three months period may be expected to last, otherwise, there is the operative clause for all presses whenever local Government puts it in motion.

The amended bill is limited to incitements to murder and cognizable offences involving violence. It is not a very large class of allegations that are excluded by chance, as may be seen by a perusal of the schedule of the criminal procedure code. Most offences, even of a triffling sort, are cognizable. Any allegation that the police may take cognizance of is cognizable. Even criminal tresspass is cognizable. The picketers in Sembian, (Madras Presidency) who "trespassed" into the large cocoanut grove to picket a toddy shop situated therein are prosecuted for a cognizable offence, namely, an entry into a garden against the will of the owner. Any report or comment that may be alleged to have a tendency to encourage such or any other cognizable offence is enough to justify application of the act.

Sir Lawrence Jenkins' caustic irony in the Comrade Case has had some effect on the Select Committee. Absurd phrases of nervous amplification are omitted from clause 4, but omission does not restrict the scope of the clause in any wise. What is gained is brevity. The content is not lost, instead of exhibiting a full ugly surface it is put sideways to hide the ugliness.

The explanation that no expression of admiration made historical by literary work shall be a ground for action, unless, it tends to encourage crime, does not put one at ease. On the contrary, that such an explanation was found necessary by those responsible for the bill is sufficient proof of its danger. Far from putting one at case it indicates its possible scope.

The amended bill provides for an appeal to the High Court, whenever security is demanded. This was not formerly there but appeals could be made only against a forfeiture order. Dissenting members of the Select Committee recommend that, even when demanding a security the magistrate should hold a judicial, though summary, enquiry. It seems to us, however, this amendment does not visualise the realities of the case. A man has to be adjudged a criminal before he commits an offence. What sort of a summary judicial enquiry can be held ? The purpose of the issue before the magistrate, or in case of appeal, before the High Court, cannot be any offence already committed but the issue can only be the desirability or not of securing previous guarantee for the future good conduct. There can be no definite allegation that can be met. The issue must be largely over matters of prejudice and an enquiry under no conditions can be satisfactory. We hope that the Assembly, even constituted as it is, will refuse to pass a measure whose whole frame work is inconsistent with freedom of the press or contemplated transfer of responsibility for Law and Order to the people.

INDIRECT ELECTION

Gandhiji has disturbed the unanimous trend of public opinion in favour of direct election, which as against the report of the Simon Commission, Government of India supported. It is not easy to understand things from a great distance without the aid or elucidatory questions and answers.

The issue of direct or indirect election may be understood and considered from two aspects, one general, and the other, a particular application. Usualy it is in latter sense that the pros and cons of the two methods of election have been considered, namely, whether the Central Legislature should be a Federal Assembly of members, chosen by votes of the constituent provincial legislatures, or by direct election by primary votes spread all over India. In the other sense, the question is one of general application and not concerning only the Central Legislature. Indirect election, in the general sense, means that the voters will choose their representatives for local affairs in the first stage and these representatives will choose men to deal with wider affairs who again will have the authority to elect representatives to deal with more central affairs, and so on, right up to the top. In this sense, even the provincial legislatures may consist of members chosen, not by all the voters directly, but elected by a body of representatives, themselves elected. There will thus be double and treble filtration of choices. It seems that it is in this general sense that Gandhiji supported the principle of indirect election in his speech at the Round Table Conference.

The acceptance of the method of indirect election does not mean that it must necessarily run through all the way up to the apex. It may be accepted only up to the point necessitated by the unwidely character of the electorate, or expediencies arising otherwise and replaced from that point by the direct method. It does not follow that, because, for instance, the primary voter does not elect representatives to the provincial legislature but does so only through the Taluka or District Councils, the Central Legislature also must be elected only indirectly by the provincial legislatures. Taluka Boards may directly elect the provincial legislature without the intermediary District Board. Similarly, Taluka or District Boards may or will elect members to the Central Legislature and not necessarily leave it to the members of provincial legislature though indirect election may be permitted. The principle of a relatively direct choice may be followed to stages where it may be overtaken. There is nothing incompatible in the mixture. Criticisms implying acceptance of the principle all through, or not at all, are therefore wide of the mark.

The first question is, shall we have adult suffrage and equality of voters for all, irrespective of sex and property. If this is accepted as an overriding principle there is consideration of the physical conditions of the country, and spread of population which must lead us to find practicable ways to express voters choice, which may or will be other than what the democracies in small compact countries of the West have experimented with. In no country has an electoral system yet been evolved which is not open to objections. Considering the size and conditions for counting, if we have to choose between giving up adult suffrage or permitting indirect election, we must certainly prefer the latter alternative with whatever imperfections it may involve. After all, if a nation has life and vigour every institution will shape itself as time goes on, just as the human body develop antidotes in its own blood for poisons that constantly invade it, national institutions will automatically develop immunities against evils and imperfections. No constitution can be constructed now, which can be relied on for all time as perfect. It must be open to the people of India to alter and amend it in every respect. What appears to be a perfect safeguard may fail later on and may even become a halter round the neck. The strongest point against indirect elections is the fear in most minds of improper methods and corrupt practices having an easier and securer play in the system of direct election than in the indirect election by large territorial electorates. But civic honesty is necessary whether elections be direct or indirect and where it is not present, institutions will break down whether elections be direct or indirect. We have to requicken our atrophy in several respects under Swaraj. We have to develop civic life, civic initiative, civic honesty and civic efficiency in order to cope with the responsibilities of actual Swaraj, if we wish to evaluate Swaraj in terms of general welfare.

As regards the particular question of Central Legislature, the strongest argument against indirect election is that whereas in practice direct election, that has prevailed hitherto, quickened sentiment of a unified India, the method of indirect election will stop the growth of national allegiance to the central and act as a growing centrifugal force. There will be altogether a too strongly provincialised atmosphere in an institution whose function will be the consideration of large questions of general interest. Again, if lifetime provincial councils differ from that of the Central Legislature, the members, later, may cease to feel responsible to any one and function like bureaucrats, responsible to no one. Those considerations are weighty but as pointed out already Gandhiji's support of the general principle of indirect election and his grounds for it, does not necessarily mean a support of the Simon Commission's proposal that both chambers of the Central Legislature should be elected by provincial legislature.

PUBLIC CENSURE OF OFFICIALS

It is a somewhat melancholy kind of satisfaction but at the same time quite true that from the faults of the present regime we can learn many a useful lesson for Swaraj, and save for ourselves a deal of error. If any official is found after a just and full enquiry to have gone wrong, there is a strong temptation to hush it up in the belief that the administration will suffer by a frank admission of the official's guilt. It is obvious that the prestige of the administration will on the whole gain and not be diminished by public censure. India's millions are but too easily governed by authority. The predominant instinct is for obedience. This is the case among all people with an ancient civilisation and a long history of ordered government. The need is all the greater for constantly emphasising the limits of authority. But what is happening in the present regime is that the limits of liberty are stressed on every possible publicity is given to infringements of the limits of authority. Officials, instead of being checked and kept within bounds, are thus encouraged to believe that they will rarely be found fault with and that even on those rare occasions they will be saved from public exposure.

In countries where law and order are but recent achievements, the state officials need protection and special treatment, but among people where obedience to organised authority is well established, it is the people that need protection, and the State officials need constant warning to keep within bounds. The following correspondence will serve to illustrate the point.

I

Gandhi Ashram,
Tiruchengodu, 22-7-1931

Dear Mr. Cotton,

I heard some time ago that the Sub-Inspector of Police of Kazhugumalai (Tinnevelly District, Madras Presidency) published a proclamation declaring the Congress to be illegal within his jurisdiction. I could not believe the story and wanted details and a definite statement from responsible people. I have now received a solemn statement signed by 24 respectable merchants of the place of various castes and communities to the effect that on 27th May the police sub-inspector of the place, Mr. A. S. Alwar Das, went to the Bazar of the place and addressed the merchants thus: "You shop-keeper fellows is your head turned ? Have you become so bold and impertinent as to give rice and things to Congress-fellows? Remember the police firing in Chintamani. I shall set fire to this town likewise". After this, the said sub-inspector went round the town accompanied by a number of well known rowdies, and himself with uniform on, had the following proclamation published with beat of drum : "Congress meetings are unlawful. People are prohibited from giving lodging or food or grain or other articles to Congress men. No one should attend meetings at which they make speeches nor should people follow them. All persons disobeying this will have to incur the penalties and trouble that will ensue". I do not believe that 24 respectable merchants would give in writing a solemn declaration to this effect if the sub-inspector had not done as alleged. The affair appeared in the press at the time and many complaints were brought to me. I therefore asked for a written statement from respectable witnesses so that I might place the matter before you.

In my humble opinion, the conduct of the sub-inspector of police is not only high-handed but shows grave lack of discipline. It was highly wrong on his part to have set aside the peace concluded between the Congress and the Government in this flagrant manner. I hope that you will take adequate notice of this official's conduct, if the facts stated by me are found by you to be correct.

I shall send you the original statement if wanted. You are aware that it is not easy to get merchants in rural parts to take the risk of making such complaints against local police officers.

I hope that this will not lead to further harassment of these people.

1. At Koilpatti, same District, I have received a list of 17 persons, almost all merchants, who were subjected to prosecution under the Town Nuisance Act and fined. It is not impossible to find technical and legal cause for prosecutions duner the Town Nuisance Act for one reason or another. But the feeling in the town is that this crop of cases has come up because of the assistance rendered by the local merchants to the Congress cause and in order to terrorise them.

2. There is yet another complaint. On 30-5-31, the Divisional officer of Koilpatti came to Kalugumalai, where there was picketing, and asked the volunteers to stand at a furlong's distance from the toddy shop. The volunteers did not agree. While they were marching back to their camp singing national songs, the Divisional officer got furious and directed the Inspector of Police to arrest the volunteers and take them into custody to the station.

Mr. L.R. Guruswami Naidu hearting this went to Kalugumalai the same night and early in the morning sent word to the police Circle Inspector of Sankarankoil who was camping there and sought an interview. After a couple of hours the Inspector sent for Mr. Guruswami Naidu who explained that the interference of the police and the Divisional Magistrate was unwarranted as the picketing was perfectly peaceful. Mr. Naidu was offering to furnish security to let the prisoners on bail. The inspector was pretending to let them on bail.

Meanwhile, the accused were taken to the local Sub-Registrar, Hon. Magistrate, and put on trial and sentenced to 7 days imprisonment on a Sunday (31-5-31) even though the accused wanted time for defence and examination of witnesses-on their side. Mr. Govindaswamier, Vakil later applied for copies of the judgment and records. But the application was returned without any endorsement. When the Vakil went in person, the Sub-Registrar said he could not grant copies because the records were sent to the Divisional Officer on an urgent letter from him. The application for copies was then presented to the Divisional Officer who said that the records had been sent to the District Magistrate. The Sub-Registrar recently informed the Vakil that the copy application had been sent to his office and that the copies would be granted on an early date as soon as the records were received from the Divisional Officer. I have only to add that on 14th July the copies had not yet been delivered.

I do not know if you consider that the 7 days' imprisonment on a charge of nuisance before an Honorary Magistrate was not an oppressive sentence even if the accused were guilty of any nuisance. But the circumstances under which, while bail was being offered, the case was proceeded with and concluded on a Sunday and thereafter the grant of copies were delayed in the manner set forth above are extremely ugly in my humble opinion. If the facts are not correct I shall gladly withdraw the language I am using. But if you find the facts to be correct, it is not merely a matter of judicial but one for you to take notice of in the interests of good administration and the prestige of the judiciary.

I am enclosing herewith a true copy of a solemnly affirmed statement of Mr. L.R. Guruswamie Naidu in support of these allegations.

Yours sincerely,
C. Rajagopalachar

C.W.E. Cotton, Esq., C.I.E.,
Chief Secretary to the Government of Madras.

II

Fort St. George,
Dated 22nd September, 1931.

Dear Sir,

Police and the Magistracy-Kazhugumalai and Koilpatty-allegations against-continuation of Mr. Williams' demi-official No. 3747-3 Public (General) dated 8th August, 1931.

I am directed to say that the Government have investigated the allegations made in your letter of the 22nd July 1931 and are satisfied that the District authorities are doing their best to observe the terms of the Settlement of the 5th March 1931 in the face of considerable difficulties and provocative action.

I am to suggest that in future cases of alleged irregularities by subordinate officials, the persons aggrieved should, in the first instance, approach the District Magistrate concerned for redress.

Your sincerely,
G.T. II, Bracken, 23-9-31.

M.R. Ry C. Rajagopalachar Avl.,
Gandhi Ashram, Tiruchengodu.

III

Gandhi Ashram,
Tiruchengodu, 25th September, 31.

Dear Sir,

I enclose herein a copy of my letter addressed to the Chief Secretary on 22nd July and his reply thereto dated 22nd September. I am so deeply disappointed by the reply of Government, that I cannot believe that His Excellency's attention had been drawn to the case, and I deem it my duty to bring it to his personal notice before concluding that we are left remedyless in a matter arising out of the Truce.

If I had hoped in any case that Government would unmistakeably express their severe displeasure of the conduct of any official, I did so in the two cases contained in paragraph 1 and 3 of my letter to the late Mr. Cotton, enclosed herein. The Chief Secretary's reply dated 22nd September does not make it clear whether Government found upon investigation that the facts were different from my allegations in regard either to the Sub-Inspector's case, or the trial and sentence of the volunteers on Sunday. If the facts were not found inaccurate, as I guess from the absence of any contradiction of them in the Chief Secretary's letter, it is most disappointing that Government have not thought it fit to express their censure of the conduct of the officials concerned.

I must be forgiven for saying that the reply of Government that District authorities are doing their best to observe the terms of the Settlement in the face of considerable difficulties and provocative action is entirely beside the mark. My complaint was that the Sub-Inspector of police published a proclamation that totally misrepresented the Government's policy and attitude towards Congress under the Settlement and aimed at misleading and terrorising the citizens. Such a misrepresentation of Government policy should at least be disowned, even if the officer was not to be censured. In the other matter, may complaint was about what I deem to be most oppressive and illegal procedure on the part of the Sub-Registrar Magistrate at the instance of the police, such as would bring discredit to the administration.

The prestige of the administration would be enhanced, not diminished, by the censure of such officials. To say in answer to all this, without contradicting the facts or alleging that they were overstated, that the District authorities have done their best is a most disappointing disposal of my complaint.

I request you to place this before His Excellency and to crave his forgiveness on my behalf for troubling him so often.

Yours sincerely,
C. Rajagopalachar

A. D. Crombie, Esq., I. C. S.,
Private Secretary to H.E. The Governor of Madras.

IV

Government house,
Obtacamaund, 5th October, 1931.

Dear Mr. Rajagopalachari,

In reply to your letter of September 25th, I am directed to say that His Excellency has seen the case to which you refer and is satisfied that the District Magistrate of Tinnevelly is doing his best to observe the terms of the Pact and to set right any irregularies commited by his subordinates. His Excellency has the more reason to think so because, so far as His Excellency is aware, there have been no complaints of any breach of the Pact from Tinnevelly since June. I am to add that the Government do not propose to communicate to you any disciplinary action they may think fit to take in regard to individual officers.

Yours sincerely,
A.D. Crombie

REAL MINORITY PROTECTION

I venture to think that common people, both Hindus and Muslims, do not understand the exact difference between joint and separate electorates. Hardly nine out of ten Mussalmans that gather to hear questions discussed may know what joint electorates with reservations and what separate electorates for allotted seats would respectively mean. Questioned about it they would, in most cases, give their reason that joint electorates would lead to only Hindus being returned and to the exclusion of Muslims, whereas separate electorates would ensure the return of at least a few Muslims.

It is not widely understood among the common people that in both cases the return of Mussalmans is assured, and that the difference is that in the one case, only the Mussalmans choose the Mussalman representatives, and the Hindus choose the Hindu representatives; whereas in the other, Hindus and Mussalmans combine and choose so many Mussalmans and so many Hindus. Ask any group of assembled people, would you like the Mussalman representative to be chosen by and to have the authority and the backing of all the people, Hindus as well as Mussalmans, or would you like the Mussalman representative to be chosen by the few Mussalmans, to represent his own people and be looked upon as an outsider by the Hindu representatives? If the question is clearly put, I venture to think that they would give an answer decisively in favour of the former alternative. For, much as they would like good men of their own community to be in the councils, they would prefer them to have the full authority of the people and not represent only a section; carrying ever the badge of minority on their delegation ticket.

What is said with reference to Mussalmans applies also to other minorities apprehensive of the tyranny of the majority. It is not generally explained or sufficiently impressed on them that in the system, of joint electorates a certain number of their people will necessarily find places, either because those places are definitely reserved for men of their community, or because in certain localities they are themselves a majority and must be presumed to act for their own benefit. Common people are led to think that a joint and national electorate may wipe them out of all representation. It is not made clear to them that reservation is conceded whenever a minority has reasons to ask for it.

Repetition often achieves the semblance and force of

truth. But at certain stages it is necessary to analyse things and sift the true from the untrue. What is the true meaning of protection of minorities ? What are the limits of such protection consistent with democracy ?

Minorities have existed among all nations. Any group of people with a strong conviction in matters affecting their lives, which differs from the opinion of the majority is a minority needing protection. It is not only the castes and religions of Hindustan that make up minorities. The need for the protection of groups and individuals against the main current has always been felt, wherever the principle of democracy has been accepted in Government. But it was never thought in those countries that it involved Government under a constitution based on separate electorates.

Democracy must necessarily mean rule by the majority. So long as we want democracy, we cannot but consent to be governed by the majority. Minorities must at some stage accept the commands of the majority, if they wish to form one community and one State with the majority.

Successful Democracy not only means rule by majority, but involves the providing of suitable machinery for initiation of measures, prompt decision and effective action by the majority. We cannot be safe under a democracy that is unable to do any of these things. It is not enough to produce an absolutely faithful reflection of the hetrogeneity of nation in the national government. For Government is intended not to be a pretty and a faithful picture on the wall only, but to *act.* At some stage it is necessary to give shape to the will of the majority, and to ignore the dissentient vote. The further this is postponed, the greater the deadlocks and the inefficiency. Imagine for a moment that the Government of India were entrusted to a body like the minority Sub-committee of the Round Table Conference. Government would be impossible.

If democracy necessarily involves the effective rule of the

majority, then what is protection of minorities ? Is it simply a mirage, and a falsehood, just to lead the thirsty minority on with rest of the caravan ? Not at all. There is such a thing as protection in a real and admissible sense. In all good democracies there is a substantive measure of protection. But this protection consists first, in limiting the field of interference by the state in individual or minority group life; secondly, in providing for initiation of measures necessary for the welfare of smaller or weaker groups, and for the effective representation of their grievances; and lastly, in the equality of law and the removal of disabilities. It does not consist in incapacitating the majority to rule.

The history of the British constitution has been most remarkable for the manner in which the liberty of the subject has been guarded against infringement by the state beyond the necessary minimum. In no country in the world is there the feeling of individual liberty in the measure which one feels when one puts his foot on British soil. In other countries democracy has meant the tyranny of majority rule, but in England the principle of Liberty has been worked into a strong and durable tradition. This it is which affords protection to all minorities in England. But these minorities do not seek to get separate electorates and to fill Parliament with sectional delegates, so as to offer the largest possible resistance to majority rule. They are satisfied with effectively limiting the authority of Government, that is, the field of majority rule. You are larger in number and must therefore rule, but in what ? Thus far and no further. This is the true protection of minorities.

Minority groups may have disabilities born of past history. These must be removed. They may have been oppressed by the strong. The law must be made equal and available to all. Their welfare has not been the concern of the powerful. The majority may not concern itself about them. So adequate scope must be provided for effective representation of grievances and for initiation of measures necessary for removing their grievances and promoting their welfare.

This brings us to the proposal that there may be separate group electorates for a second chamber. If the second chamber is not to have powers of creating a deadlock in majority rule, but constituted so as to provide for ventilation of grievances with powers of initiating measures, it would be a proper step to create such a second chamber, and give all minority groups, and special interests representation in that chamber through separate electorates if desired. It would be a place where grievances and minority view points can be brought out, and special measures initiated to meet special wants, which would otherwise the forgotten or find no adequate advocacy in the democratic chamber.

Representatives clected from separate electorates would there ventilate their complaints and initiate special measures. But the right of final decision and the responsibility for good government will rest with the chamber that is elected on the fundamental principle of democracy viz., rule by majority, which must be single in aim and purpose, and capable of prompt action. No nation can govern itself unless the majority is truly and effectively liberated.

The minorities have every right to ask for protection in the Constitution. But they should seek this protection in the article guaranteeing the liberties of the people, not in the chapter constituting the assemblies. Any other claim is inconsistent wiih democracy. The history of England is an ample and an impressive proof of the far greater efficacy and importance of the laws guaranteeing individual and group liberties than mere electoral arrangements.

But beyond even laws guaranteeing the fundamental liberties of individuals and minority groups, there is a greater protection which the whole nation has been taught to realise and effectively use; this is the inalienable right to resist through Satyagraha.

THOSE PICTURES

A crore and a quarter of rupees gone according to a computation in the Madras Secretariat based on receipts for April and May of this year, compared with the same months in the previous year. This was enough to meke any Finance Member fret and fume. On the top of it came the dismal results of the toddy license auctions in August and September enough to drive any bureaucracy mad. Before the middle of September, that is, before the secret "tender" and confirmation dates for all licences that could not be disposed of, something must be done to create confidence in the minds of the Liquor-trade men. All departments are busy finding out means somehow to create this confidence. The Picketing activity of the Congress has acted as a nucleus and a creative agent of a wonderful deal of energy all over the country. Man, woman and child in remotest hamlet sing anti-drink songs. The resolve to do away with the curse has spread like a prairie-fire, I shall not grudge other organisations some share in this great revolution. Even the Madras Government's Temperance Propaganda last year—they spent many lakhs on it—could not have been all for nothing. It must have contributed its share to the development of popular feeling.

So, all castes and communities are busy adopting Total Abstinence. "If the Brahmin need not drink, if the other high castes do not waste their earning on the Toddy shop, why should we not also try. After all 'high' and 'low' can be got over with a well filled purse. If we get over poverty, we have done half the hurdles in life's race." So the "low castes" think, or have been taught to think. Is it impertinence or mischief to teach them to think this way and raise their status ? In India the vegetarian and the man who does not drink intoxicating liquor are automatically high caste. It may be all superstition but it is there.

Finance Department, therefore, has turned its angry eyes at caste organisations. "What are the magistrates doing ? Do they not know that there is a lot of coercion and intimidation and oppression in these caste panchayats ? Read your Penal Code please, and do your work !"

"But we have rarely interfered in such matters, and never without a complaint from aggrieved parties. They seem to be here submitting to be caste pressure." No, this will not do. The right to drink must be protected !

Alas that any honest government, be it our own or foreign, should thus lose its nerve. Dependence on an evil trade is a dreadful thing. Should any ruler be sad or ruffled because his people have reduced their consumption of alcoholic liquors ? It is a tragedy that instead of rejoicing on the reduction of an evil that saps body and soul, instead of lending a helping hand to the straggling man that walks up the steep slope, our government should have to deem it a misfortune and lose its equanimity. Pharaoh has hardened his heat indeed and the waters have been turned to blood.

A friend sent me two picture posters the other day. I don't know why he sent them. He has sent them without any covering letter. Both bore the artist's autograph and the seal of the Madras Government's defunct Central Propaganda Board. Beautiful powerful pictures both of them,—one represented the parting of the ways; to wife and children and domestic joy on the right, and to the toddy shop and crime on the left. The artist might have put the picketers at the gate of the shop and the Finance Member at the counter. But it was drawn on 28-1-30. The other picture also a double scene, shows how the highway man says "your money or your life; " But on the other hand, Drink takes money and life and soul, all together. Alas that a portion of the money must go to Government and thereby create a vested interest in this wicked business, and they must feel anger, instead of satisfaction that less liquor is consumed. This was drawn on 20-11-30. In 1931 August-September, such cartoons, with the seal of the Government on it, would be impossible. As Temperance has caused all this trouble of reduced income, first step in retrenchment off with the Temperance Board

The poor dumb pictures seem to complain. But the Finance Member, I can imagine, is enjoying the discomfiture of those undistributed pictures. You caused it all, so you must be cut out first. And the Madras Cabinet of members and ministers feel like having bound Samson with fetters of brass.

The Right of Peaceful Picketing

This right that was secured for us Sy Gandhiji in the Delhi Settlement has been vigorously and continuously exercised throughout the Southern provinces. In spite of all impediments and difficulties offered on the part of Government as well as the liquor dealers, the results have been most encouraging. The fall in rentals at the recent auctions is a measure of the liquor-dealers' estimate of future business. They are shrewd men and are able to sense the feeling in the country and their bids may therefore be taken as a reliable measure of the degree of success attained in our work.

Out of 9,000 toddy shops in the presidency of Madras, I was reliably informed, that about 3,000 were still unsold until the last week of September. 30 per cent of the shops in Tamil Nadu were not yet assigned to licensees. The shops that have been sold off so far have been given away for annual rentals totalling about Rs. 35 lakhs, that is to say, less than half of what the toddy licenses in Tamil Nadu were sold for in previous years. We should remember that this is the result of tremendous official activities. Taking sample districts, out of 560 toddy shops in Coimbatore as many as 260 remain yet unassigned. So also in North Arcot of 400 shops, more than 200 are yet unassigned. In South Arcot out of nearly 300 shops more than a hundred are still undisposed of. On the other hand, in Ramnad District though all the shops have been assigned, they have fetched only two lakhs annual rental as against an average of 4 lakhs in previous years.

The work has not been uniform all over. On the contrary, persistent effort in some places have resulted in the general atmosphere. If the active centres are separately taken we can see what can be achieved if men and women make up their minds. In a certain taluk only ten out of ninetyone toddy shops could be properly disposed of. In another taluk, there were no bids whatever for 16 out of 21 shops.

I calculate that with reduced tree-tax and reduced rentals, the total excise revenue will be affected so far as Tamil Nadu is concerned to the extent of from 75 lakhs to one crore under toddy alone.

THE OUTRAGES

On October 28th Mr. L. G. Durno, the District Magistrate of Dacca, was shot at and seriously injured. Close upon this came the news that on October 29 at Calcutta, Mr. E. Villiers, president of the European Association, was the victim of a revolver attack and narrowly escaped death. These outrages, it may be fairly assumed, are political in character. They are sad proof that the Congress has not only failed to convince the revolutionaries that their methods are wrong, but that at least some sections of these young men do not respect the Congress appeal for at least a suspension of activities. This is tragic beyond measure. If the revolutionaries imagine that they are helping the cause in their own way, they are much mistaken. Two opposities can not help each other. There can be no synthesis between non-violence and violence. Every outrage of this sort serves to undo what the Congress may have achieved.

If these young men have made up their minds that Congress and Gandhiji have had enough time and should be given no further chance they might indulge in these profitless outrages. But if they have not so made up their mind and would give Gandhiji and his programme a chance, it is unfair in the extreme to be indulging in these outrages at this time. The leaders of the Congress of all shades of opinion are convinced that these acts, not only do not serve any good purpose, but positively injure the cause we seek to serve. Let none of the revolutionaries imagine that any one among the Congress leaders is pleased with their activities. Every one, including those who fully appreciate the patriotic impulse behind such acts, feels that they are all so many revolver shots at the Congress and not only at Mr. Durno or Mr. Villiers. Both the victims have escaped death and so far it is a matter for congratulation. But while the shots have fortunately missed the work so far as the European victims go, they are unerring so for as the Congress prestige and the Congress plan are concerned. These are hit point blank.

All this has been put as from a lower plane of expediency, because we feel that any expression of moral revolt or a reiteration of the principles of non-violence will make no appeal to the young men that are entanglad in these plans of saving India through the Browning pistol, or are carried away by the tempting fallacies of political revenge.

We had hoped that the great campaign we were in, the great sacrifices that the nation underwent and is still to undergo according to the plan of non-violence, and the great hopes we raised not alone in India, but in the breasts of greatmen all over the world that India is on the point of solving the world's as well as her own problem of liberation from violence, might make their combined appeal to the young men who had put their trust in gun-powder, at least for a suspension of their contrary and incompatible plans. From what we have seen it appears as if these hopes cannot be fulfilled, or their patience has not stood the strain.

The Government know on their part only one patent remedy for all ills, that of arresting on suspicion and imprisoning people without trial. This patent remedy has been tried all along and has not succeeded. But this will not be admitted. It is ever believed that a stronger dose is all that is wanted, and they have lost no time to prescribe it.

Madura Lathi Charges

The peaceful picketing of liquor shops in Madura (Tamil Nad) was suddenly and without warning disturbed on the night of October 5th, by the police who attacked the volunteers with *Lathis* and the buttend of guns injuring several of them. The result of representations made to the Government of Madras has just been announced in the press. The Government have passed orders holding that the action of the Police was justified as the picketing was in contravention of the terms of the Delhi Pact. If the principles of natural justice are thrown to the winds, it is not difficult to arrive at any result that one may want. As soon as the news of the incident reached me, I telegraphed to H.E. the Governor challenging an enquiry, and agreed to abide by the decision of the President of the District Board of Madura as sole arbitrator. The President of the Madura District Board is a European gentleman, a zamindar, an old and experienced citizen of Madura, and a friend of the Government. The Government, however, did not choose to accept my suggestion but contented themselves with calling for a report from the District Magistrate. The District Magistrate, too, did not hold any enquiry of which the Congress or the public or the aggrieved volunteers had any notice or at which they were given any opportunity to represent facts or explain anything definitely urged against them.

When I heard that the Government had called for and were considering the *ex parte* report of the District Magistrate, I sent a further representation saying.

"I feel that if investigation means only getting the reports of the District Officers, and subjecting them to no further test or examination and accepting them as correct, unless on the face of them there are obvious difficults, such an investigation cannot satisfy any one except the District Officers concerned. It is not satisfactory from the point of view of the injured volunteers or the Congress or the public."

And I added that I still stood by my offer to submit to the decision of the European District Board President upon an open enquiry and urged on His Excellency the desirability of such an enquiry. But these representations were not heeded. Solely on the District Magistrate's *ex parte* report, and without giving any opportunity to the aggrieved party either in the first or in the later stage, to urge or to meet any points, the Government of Madras, have adjudged that the picketing was in contravention of the Delhi Pact terms and therefore, the Police Lathi charge was justified. This is a travesty of administrative Justice. It does not satisfy fundamental principle of fair play or natural Justice. If this is the interpretation that is to be given to the obligations arising out of the Delhi Settlement, it is tantamount to making, it a mere scrap of waste paper.

THE WAR AGAINST DRINK

Caste Panchayats

I

The end of the Drink traffic in India is very near. It is a matter for congratulation that among castes that hitherto permitted the use of spirituous liquors there is a strong movement to adopt the general rule in India against it, and in all parts of the country one community after another is pledging its members to total abstinence. The Congress programme of picketing has focussed attention and intensified public opinion against the evil. The campaign has become the daily absorbing thought of millions of men, women and children of all grades of society. In a land of illiterates, direct action is the only effective propaganda of education.

Reform in India has ever come about not so much by individual action as by group or caste activity. This is how vegetarianism and abstinence from spirituous liquors and all other movements of reform in personal habits have always spread in India in times past. It is consistent with our social organisation and civilisation. Individualism does not thrive in our country, whether it be for good or evil.

The movement of Total Abstinence is specially strong among those hitherto relegated to an inferior social status. Apart from the aga-long superstitions of caste gradation, and doubtful theories of race origins, their inferiority has been maintained by their hopeless poverty and indebtedness. These classes are naturally the greatest victims of the licensed traffic. The economic advantages of a strict adherence to Total Abstinence appeal most strongly to the leaders of these castes. No wonder that they have quickly responded to the movement and are most enthusiastically at work pledging their men to a taboo which will at once save them from moral and economic degradation and give them, according to Indian psychology, a higher social status.

Government, by reason of its financial entanglement in the Drink business, is, whatever its declared policy man be, in actual practice, opposed to any movement that will actually and at an inconveniently swift pace, reduce the consumption of spirituous liquors. This is specially unfortunate for the "lower" orders of our society. As long as the Temperance movement was a talking hobby of the upper classes, and did not effect any serious reduction in the actual use of intoxicating drinks and drugs, the Government patronised the reform propaganda. But when it took forms that threatened seriously to affect consumption and revenue, it quickly began to withdraw its patronage and approval, and be thought itself of restrictions and practical obstacles in its way.

When the Drink traffic is reinforced and backed up with Government control, and Government finance is mixed up with it, and licenses are sold by Government to the highest bidder, it is not easy to attack the Drink evil without attacking the Government. Government and government officials are moved by the stock Exchange psychology. Temperance propaganda easily becomes sedition, picketing becomes obstruction and group pledging and caste organisation become coercion and antimidation. Reformers actively working among classes, hitherto the unfailing customers in this business, become enemies to the Treasury and evil-minded disturbers of the King's peace. Make-believe reformers are extolled for their wisdom and moderation, but strenuous workers are asked to give security for good behaviour.

When once there is a great popular awakening, however, while individuals can be threatened or suspended into inaction, the tide of reform cannot be stemmed. Prohibition is in every one's mind and no Government can stop a process of purification.

Castes in India have been all along permitted by Government to exercise internal authority. If foolish Brahmins shave the heads of their girl-widows and prohibit re-marriage on pain of excommunication, Government keeps aloof. If untouchables are not allowed the use of common drinking water-sources, places of workship and sometimes even roads and schools, the Government does not feel called upon or entitled to interfere. Persons daring social intercourse with "untouchables" are visited with severe caste penalties, but the Government cannot and dare not attempt to interfere or protect the individual against the tyranny of the caste. But when "low" castes pledge themselves to total abstinence from sprituous liquors, copying the practice of "high" castes and adopt measures to raise themselves socially and economically, Government is anxious to safeguard individual liberty against what it deems to be caste coercion. The way in which our interests give a bias to our ideas is well known. An honest indignation, I can imagine, moves many a Government official when he sees that a door fellow is deprived of his drink on account of rules imposed by his people. It may be he does not think of the revenue. But introspection would show that, back of it all, the motive works unconsciously.

The law is well understood to be that, barring illegal or criminal conspiracies, castes and sub-castes as well as other institutions are entitled to regulate the conduct of their members. Fines and penalties levied as alternatives to expulsion from the caste are really voluntarily sumbitted to, so long as it is open to any offending member to choose to submit and remain in the group or prefer to leave it.

IS IT UNSOUND ECONOMICS

What cloth shall we buy? Foreign cloth is out of the question. No one would willingly help to drain out the country's gold. But as between 'Swadeshi' and 'Khadi' where should a wise and informed patriotism lead the choice ?

The question is, shall I contribute my mite towards the Mill-Magnates' profits and share-holders' dividends or, shall I pay a tax for the relief of nation-wide unemployment ? Swadeshi does the first, Khadi does the second.

In other civilised countries, now the people submit to compulsory taxation to enable the State to give doles to their unemployed. The Khadi plan for the relief of unemployment may also be described as a tax, but it is an indirect tax and a voluntary tax. The tax, is on an article of universal use, *viz.*, cloth, so that the burden is distributed fairly evenly. It is utilised, not to give doles, which is demoralising, but to give work, which adds to moral fibre and dignity.

Relief of nation-wide unemployment is a State duty. Khadi is the national solution of this Government neglected duty. Government wants money for its extravagant civil and military establishments and therefore, puts a duty on salt so that everyone may be indirectly made to pay towards the expenditure. It feels no compunction on the ground that salt is an article of universal use and that the tax makes it twenty times costlier than it should otherwise be to the poor man. For the purpose of supplementing the peasants' inadequate earnings and to relieve his unemployment during more than six months in the year, the Khadi plan is to levy a voluntary poll tax through cloth that all must use. This is the economics and the ethics of the extra price one has to pay for Khadi.

The Indian peasants' poverty is fairly widely known. But the burden of his indebtedness has now doubled on account of the fall in the prices of the commodities he is producing. His debts were incurred when the prices were twice as much. The interest he has to pay is calculated on a money basis. Taxes are levied on the old money basis, for even though the price of every other commodity has fallen more than fifty per cent, the price of the Government servants' labour alone is steady and refuses to go down. The Government is still spending extravagantly, still only talking of voluntary cuts of ten per cent, and the like, and has not reduced but increased taxation. Taking the present prices into account, we can easily see how the notoriously low average earnings of the Indian peasant have gone still lower. He is in dire distress and the only relief that can be said to be in operation on any large scale is the relief given through *Khadi*. It is, therefore, unpatriotic and selfish to shirk the *Khadi Tax*.

The use of Khaddar, in preference to all other cloth, will keep in circulation among the agriculturists all the money that the nation uses to buy its clothing. The least that may do to help the poor peasants is to keep the money we expend for our food and for our clothing in circulation among them. To buy mill-cloth is to obstruct and divert the flow of money to the villages and to refuse to relieve their distress.

There is glib talk of Khadi being an 'economically unsound' proposition. And the poor man who sees that the price of Khadi per yard is higher than that of foreign cloth, or of the Indian mill *dhoti*, takes this as expressing his own personal feeling in the matter, and feels consoled by science. One might as well say that the salt we buy is economically unsound because it is twenty times its natural price. The only difference is that for the taxed salt there is no substitute, whereas, for Khaddar there are many injurious substitutes and we are free to poison ourselves with them.

Minimum hands to be employed and maximum quantity to be produced; the formula of the machine, served well in the

West as long as foreign markets staved off the problem of unemployment. But when Railway extensions and exploitation of foreign nations reach their termination, the monster of large scale production has nothing to feed upon except itself. Competition Economics is in the throes of death. Investment and re-investment of surplus wealth for further increase must end in a deadlock. Capitalists have found themselves at the mercy of the machines that they believed they owned but which in reality owned them and economics is in the melting pot in the West. Khadi is, not only not economically unsound, but is based on a far sounder and stabler economics than the worn-out pseudo-science of that name that has broken down in the West.

THE STORY OF TWO VOLUNTEERS

Kasim : or Hope for Everybody

This is a true story. Not a word in it is fiction. Mahomed Kasim is a volunteer in the Namakal Picketing corps (Salem district, Tamilnad). All the members of the corps are honorary workers and so also is Mahomed Kasim. His history is a treasure-trove of Hope and I want to share it with everybody.

A butcher by profession, a powerfully built man, amateur wrestler and gymnast, and a heavy drinker for the last nine years, Kasim's name had been a word of terror to women and children in his street. He is now a total-abstainer, a simple fellow among the volunteers, and a favourite with everybody in the town !

He was three years old when his father, Chote Mian, a Court process-server died. He grew up under his maternal grand-father's care at Madura for some years and then lived with his sister's husband, Sarvar Sahib, who was a butcher in Namakal. When Kasim came of age, he opened his own meat-stall and did good business. He earned from three to four rupees every day like the other butchers in Namkal. He was married nine years ago and had a boy by that wife. She died two years ago and he took a second wife, his decreased wife's sister.

One day, some ten years ago, when he was doing the "grand circle" in the private gymnasium that he and his friends had opened, he had a fall. Ever since he suffered from a pain in the abdomen. He tried several medicines but the pain persisted. A dismissed police constable who was practising as a quack doctor gave him a purgative pill for the ailment. He had three or four motions in the quack's house at once ! But even that did not cure him. Then a peasant told him that if he took a little toddy everyday, drawn from the same tree, he would be curred. This single-tree-toddy cure is a popular superstition and is prescribed for all sorts of ailments among ignorant and helpless folk.

Kasim tried this for a fortnight. He felt relieved for a few hours each time he drank the toddy, but the pain would revert again. All the same he got used to the toddy all right, and he drank more and more every day. Soon he gave up the single tree and began to visit the toddy shop. Then he passed through the common history of every victim.

Kasim's stomach pain disappeared in course of time, but he became a hardened toper. He used to stay in the tavern from morning ten to eight in the night, drinking all the time. He would consume there all that he earned from his meat-shop. His wife and child were no longer any care of his. He would come home drunk and beat them everyday. When he came home at night, his wife used to hide under a cot. His little son would show courage and intercede when he beat his wife. As he passed down the street, the women and children used to say "Kasim has come !" and bolt their doors in fear. He was arrested twice and fined by the Magistrates, and he paid the fines by instalments. His business was gone very soon after he took to drink. His brother-in-law was looking after his family. He used to get so drunk that he lost all sense of decency.

A month ago, when picketing was going on, there was a meeting of the Musalmans of Namakal at the Masjid when they all talked about taking the pledge. There were nearly sixty Musalman habitual drinkers. Many took the pledge, but some did not agree. The Chairman Sahib and another were very particular and convened another meeting a fortnight ago, and earnestly pleaded that not a single Musalman of Namakal should drink, and that it should be recognised as a crime, henceforth, if any of them visited the tavern. Kasim used to visit the shop though the picketing was going on. But at this second meeting, Kasim resolved to give it up. He made up his mind and he found it easy. No one can say what God may not do !

"When I took the pledge and signed, other hardened topers signed also. There is not now a single Musalman in Namakal drinking. I offered myself as a Congress volunteer that same day and I was taken. Ever since then I have been working under Congress. I do not care for drink at all now. I go to my house and eat my meals there. But even when eating I feel I must hurry back to the Congress office. I have a disgust for toddy now. I would hang myself and the rather than drink again. I was a terror to my wife and child and relatives. Now they are all so-happy."

"Do they pay you anything in the Congress ? Does your brother-in-law like your serving the Congress for nothing and doing no business for yourself ?"

"Oh, yes. He is delighted. He will do anything for my having been saved from the toddy shop. My wife is pleased that I am in Congress. I want no payment for Congress work. They will let me do anything. They don't object to my serving the Congress, full time, if only I don't drink."

Kasim assures me that he has never felt the craving since he took the pledge at the Musjid. Who may disbelieve him, for he has kept the pledge and his face is as bright and joyous as that of a life-long abstainer ? The blessing of the Almighty is upon him.

"Will you start business again ? Do you think you can do it if you have some little money ?"

"Of course. It is so easy. If I have twenty rupees now, I can start my meat-shop again. My brother-in-law will help me. Every one is willing to help. And now that I don't drink, I can make lots of money in no time. Within a year, I shall save a couple of hundred rupees easily."

"So you will never again drink ?"

"Never ! Why should I ? Every one was disgusted with me before. Now every one likes me. I feel nausea when I think of the toddy now."

Nallaswami : or How It Begins

Here is another story, also true in every detail. "My name is Nallaswami Pillai. I am now 23. In 1921, I began my life as a motor cleaner. My father was a clerk keeping accounts under Peer Patcha Sahib, who owned motor buses. I learnt motor-mechanics and became a first class fitter and driver.

"During the Mariamman festival at Namakal my friends enacted a play. My cousin Kumarasami Pillai took a leading part in it. This was in 1927. He as well as the other actors used to drink before acting. They said it was necessary for good acting. I had offered to join the troops and was taken. So my cousin pressed me during rehearsals to drink a little. The toddy was brought to the shed itself. I used to refuse. But one night he pressed me very much and forced quarter of a bottle into my mouth. I drank but I vomitted and felt uneasy. Again, on the second and third nights also, I drank under pressure. I was disgusted. I resolved to keep away. For a month I avoided my cousin's company. But after that, we became friends again. He used to send me to the tavern to bring him toddy. I did this and every time he used to press me to drink also. I resisted for some time but then yielded.

"I soon became a regular toper, and drank as much as ten to fifteen bottles a day. I was eating cakes and fried meat with the toddy and spent all my time in the tavern. I was not going home for meals except at night. Then too, if I was very drunk, I would not eat at home but simply lie down to sleep.

"It is now four years since I was married. There is no prohibition in my caste against drinking though it is not considered decent. But now there is a pledge and excommunication. I have taken the pledge. All my people have totally given up drink except my cousin, Kumarasami, who is still drinking. He is under ostracism. He does not visit my house now.

"I am a full time Congress picketer now. My mother buys unhusked rice, sets it husked and does business in it. She also keeps a couple of cows and sells the milk She earns enough to keep the family going. She is very happy, so also my wife, that I have joined the Congress. They are not anxious that I should earn money. When I was earning, I was spending all the money, at the toddy shop and causing trouble.

"I can stand 3 bottles of toddy easily. I used to drive the motor bus with that much inside. I am an expert driver and so I could do it. I have given up drink for ever now. I find no difficulty whatever."

Nallaswami is saved. But his story shows how the Devil finds his way and seizes souls.

CLAUSE 19 IN MADRAS

It is well known that one of the clauses of the Delhi Pact was the re-instatement of village officials and other government servants. This was in consonance with the underlying principles of the Truce that as far as possible, the *status quo ante* should be restored and that no one should be the worse off on account of the campaign.

Only a very few cases up for relief in Tamil Nad under this clause of re-instatement of officials. People naturally respected that for this very reason the few cases would be liberaly dealt with. Clause 19 of the Settlement expressly stated that local governments "will pursue a liberal policy in regard to the reappointment of government servants and village officials who apply for re-instatement."

But all expectations have been sadly disappointed. The cases that were sent up were the following:

1. Tyagaraja Tevar, a village karnam in Mannargudi Division, lost his post because he sold fourteen cents of land to a Congressman who used it as a camping ground for some of the salt satyagrahis, at Vedaranyam. He not only lost his post but was permanently debarred from any future appointment.

2. Sivanataraja Tevar and his ancestors held the post of village headman of Vanganagar in Tanjore District for many decades. He resigned his post on 26th April 1930 in token of sympathy with the Salt Satyagraha on the day that the volunteers marched past his place. He was told that he stood dismissed and his heirs debarred from appointment.

3. Arunachala Mudaliar resigned his village karnam's post in Shiali Taluka. After the Truce he applied for re-instatement. He first got an order that his application would be considered, but later he was told he could not be re-instated.

4. Nagalingam Pillai, a village official of Mayavaram Division, was compelled to resign his post because he gave a

five rupee donation for salt Satyagraha.

5. Ramaswami Iyangar, an *Amin* of court at Kumbakonam, was dismissed because he gave water and refreshments to salt satyagrahis when they halted on their march.

Not one of these cases has been restored. Cover is taken behind the proviso that where the places have been "permanently filled" Government is not bound to re-instate the men. Clause 19 of the Settlement is said to have been "specifically designed" to protect the interests of those newly appointed. The clause as to re-instatement has thus been practically nullified. The proviso is found to cover every case, and the main clause has disappeared like a mirage.

Can if be contended that Government could not tell the new incumbents that no account of the Truce those who held the posts previously have to be restored, and that the services of those who were appointed during the campaign would, therefore, be dispensed with ? Would there be any right or claim on the part of these newly appointed men to hold the posts against the wishes of the government ? No undertakings were given to them by the local governments and no promises were made that the posts would be held on any tenure other than the ordinary one, namely, during the pleasure of the government. There is really no case of in-ability, which is the express word used in the Clause to denote the principle behind the proviso. On the other hand, there is a complete failure of the expectation raised in the Clause that the local governments would pursue a liberal policy in regard to re-appointments.

The fact seems to be, that though the Truce intended a liberal policy of 'forget' and 'forgive' on both side, and a reversion to the *statuquonte*, the local governments are unable to rise to that moral level. If they did, there was nothing to prevent them from thanking the new incumbents for their timely service during a critical time, and re-instating the old incumbents. This would have been no surprise to the former, and would have been truly in consonance with the spirit of a great Peace after a great Battle.

We must be thankful, however, for small mercies, and so I have to inform the public that as a result of some correspondence on the subject, I am in receipt of a letter from the Chief Secretary that "the Government have issued general instructions to the effect that when the only reason for not reinstating a village officer with reference the Clause 19 of the Settlement with the Congress, dated 5th March 1931, is that the post has been permanently filled, he and his heirs should not be debarred from other employment under the Government and that the bar order in such a case should be withdrawn."

REPRESSION IN MYSORE

It is a laudable desire on the part of the Government of Mysore that there should be no conflicts between Capital and Labour within its borders and that order and peace should prevail. This, however, is not worth the attainment if it is to be secured by a suppression of the soul of Labour. One has a right to expect the Government of H.H. the Maharajah of Mysore to help the weak to get justice at the hands of the strong. If they would have it that Labour should get justice and fair treatment without the travail of conflict with Capital, they should take steps to pass laws for due recognition of Trade Unions, for compulsory arbitration of all disputes and for close supervision and due protection of labourers in factories. Before doing this to seek to suppress labour organisations is nothing short of tyranny and injustice.

Sjt. P.M. Rama Sarma, has been a resident of Banglore and a worker among the mill-hands in that city for five years past if not more. He as well as the labourers among whom he works, have been struggling hard all these years to maintain the claims and rights of Labour as against powerful employers, both Indian and British. On 21st July last, Sjt.

Sarma was served with an order which now, on 14th September, has been renewed for six months by the Government of H. H. the Maharajah of Mysore. This order prohibits him, though he is admitted to be the Vice-President of the Textile Labour Union, from even entering the labour area and gags him entirely within the Municipal limits :

> "In exercise of the powers conferred by sub-section 6 of Section 144 of the Code of Criminal Procedure 1904, the Government of His Highness the Maharaja of Mysore hereby direct that the order passed by the District Magistrate, Bangalore under the said section on the 21st July 1931 directing Mr. P.M. Rama Sarma, Vice President, Textile Labour Union and Congress Workers, Basavangudi, Bangalore City, not to enter the area in the Bangalore City included within the following boundaries—on the North by the Sampige Road, the Seshadri Road, on the South by the Sri Narasimharaja Road and the Mysore Road, on the West by the Mill Tank Bund Road and the Mysore—Bangalore—Madras Railway line and not to deliver any public speeches within the Municipal Limits of Bangalore City, shall remain in force for a period of six months from 21st September, 1931."

It is easy to be persuaded that a labour union worker is a danger to peace. In the opinion of some people, and a very large class of people, from which all government servants are recruited, every labour union may be a danger to peace. The preventive provisions of the Criminal Code place in the hands of the executive authorities very large powers which, if they are misused or applied for purposes beyond their legitimate sphere, are nothing short of engines of tyranny. There is little or no judicial check on the exercise of these powers and even when decisions come up for revision, the issues involved are vague and incapable of clear proof either way.

The management of the two or three mills that are carrying on business in Bangalore will no doubt be grateful to the Government of Mysore for thus depriving their workmen of their chief worker and union official. But it is a shortsighted policy unworthy of the pretetations of a model State. It is often urged on the part of Indian States that their subjects are not so advanced as those of British India and that, therefore, the time is not ripe within their borders for the liberties and institutions enjoyed or proposed in British India. The fact of the matter is that for this backward condition, if true, the Princes and their Governments are themselves responsible. Neither in education nor in natural gifts of character or intellect are the people of Mysore inferior to those of British India. There is no reason why they should not enjoy at least the same rights and liberties as the people in British India. No one but the Government is to blame if political progress is less in Mysore than in British India. Assuming, however, that there is no press or public to watch the interests of labourers adequately in Mysore on account of the backward political condition, the injustice is all the greater if poor workmen are deprived of their organisation and the service of their Trade Union officials, and they are thus left entirely to the mercy of their employers whose immediate interests lie in exploiting them.

This appeal may make no impression on the authorities of Mysore. The public spirited citizens of the State must rest content with the consolation that repression is the best school for the education of a subject people. The people of the State are no less endowed with qualities and resources for peaceful resistance than the people of British India. Repressive laws and measures have a definite place in the evolution of liberty.

MUNICIPAL SWEEPERS

In all our Municipalities there ore sweepers and scavengers, consigned to a standard or life too bad for description. But I am dealing only with one aspect of their life. Even a small municipality pays about six hundred to a thousand rupees a month tc these poor people. If we enquire as to what happens to the money on pay day, as I did at the Municipality of—, we shall learn that nearly the whole of it goes immediately to people who have lent them money at exorbitant interest and to the liquor shop. Even at the liquor shop the money goes partly for previous advances and only partly for current enjoyment. All rules against selling intoxicants on credit are in abeyance in regard to these unfortunate people and other habitual customers of that kind. The liquor-shop men have a feeling that the pay of these scavengers stands mortgaged to them.

Why should not the municipalities themselves run the liquor shop for these sweepers and scavengers? If a thing can be tolerated, it is more straighthforward to take it over under direct management. Let me assure municipalities that they will not lose by it. There is good enough business in it.

Another alternative would be to farm out the scavenging work on a contact to the toddy-shop renter himself. Let him take so much per month and his business will be to get the sweeping and scavenging of the town done properly. He has his gang of scavengers, and they work under him and satisfy the municipality. He gets the payment in lump and deals with his gang, giving them liquor and money for foodstuffs. Even this would not be bad from the point of view of sound management, At present, the scavengers do not do the work properly, and these men also do not get their money's worth of liquor; for no purchaser on credit and running account ever gets full value.

If it is thought it would be improper to do either of these alternatives, it is equally improper to allow the present state of things to go on. What is very wrong is, if done by a public body, also indecent.

Must scavengers and sweepers be consigned always to hell ? There are sweepers and scavengers even in England. During work they put on uniforms and do their task. When it is finished, every one takes a bath for which soap and towels and conveniences are provided. He puts his coat on; brushes his hair before a mirror and goes into the specially provided buffet where he gets healthy refreshments and soft drinks at concession rates. After feeding, he walks out with a smile on his face and like any other gentlemen.

What is possible in one country is quite possible in another. These conveniences do not depend on the climate. They depend upon people's resolution of purpose, people's sense of duty. Let no one think that England was always like this, either in sanitation or in other respects, far in advance of us.

In the year 1290, the monks of Whitefriars complained that the stench from the London drainage was so bad that "it even occasioned the death of some of the brethren." An official report of the year 1540 tells us thet "even in well-to-do houses, rushes covered the earthern floors and got saturated with scraps of fool which remained to putrify under a new layer of rushes scattered over it; so that periodically 'Petremen' came to dig salt-petre out of the floors." An Act of 1539 discribes the streets of London as "very full and full of pits and sloughs very perilous for King's subjects on horseback or on foot." A Commission reported in 1844 that "it was not customary to provide 'sanitary' accommodation for poor dwellings under £ 10 annual rental. Thus use had to be made of streets fos this purpose. The courts were the receptacles for human excreta and filth. One part of London had 645 houses with only 33 privies. In Liverpool, 20,000 persons lived in cellars with no privies whatever. The overflow liquid from cess pools, of which there were large numbers frequently inside houses, was not allowed to drain into the sewers and had to soak away into the soil and often into the wells. To avoid the expense of them cess pools were made as large as possible and of such depth that liquid would flow from them through water-bearingstrata into drinking wells. The gasses and effluvia poisoned the air in every direction."

If this was so in 1844 in London, why should we lose hope to achive improvement in our own country if we put our shoulders to the wheel ?

In 1461, barbers who practised surgery were incorporated by the King of England into a barber-doctor's association. In 1540, again. We read of an Incorporated Barbers and Surgeons Company. No one need laugh at our barber mid-wives or refuse to recognise their services throughout the country, or, give up hopes of improving and incorporating them.

Talking of civilization, very few people probably know that it was only in 1362, that the French language was substituted by English in the Law Court of England. In 1401, heretics, that is, those who did not accept all the delails of the Church creed, were convicted in a spiritual court and committed to the secular authorities and publicly burnt alive under Statute. We read that in 1416, witchraft and necromancy were rampant in England. Under an Act passed in 1661, no dissenters could hold office even in municipalities. This would be something like a Vaishnava Ministry passing an act of the legislature that no persons dissenting from the Vaishnava doctrines and following Shankaracharya could hold any public appointment even in municipalities and taluka boards. In 1673, under an Act of Parliament, every Government servant was 'tested' and rejected if he was a Dissenter. It was only in 1829 that an act was passcd by which Roman Catholic citizens of England were emancipated.

Why should we be hopeless in our country where Akbar ruled in 1600, gave posts of honour and power to Rajput Princes and other Hindus both in the Army and the Civil government, was delighted to bear Brahmins and Buddhists, Parsees and Jesuit Fathers, deliver discourses on religion and philosophy, and tried to teach his subjects that there was a measure of Truth in all religions.

During Queen Anne's time in the seventeenth century,

women were put in stocks in England, if they were considered as "scolds." Ducking stools were also provided as a deterrent for such people. We read that in 1695, the heads of executed traitors were exhibited on Temple Bar. This beautiful practice of adorning public places with the heads of executed offenders was indulged in even in 1776 when London Bridge gate was adorned with the heads of Scottish rebels upon pikes. We read again that even in 1740, there was neither infirmary nor doctor in prisons all prisoners were incarcerated together. In fact, prisons were owned by the Jailor and managed by him for his own benefit. The safe custody of the inmates was his sole public responsibility Horace Walpole describes the country of that time as "One great shambles" and the jail as the "high school of crime."

We all know that British people abolished salverv. They did this in 1833. But we read that in 1760, 50,000 slaves were carried yearly in British ships. An artificial ventilator was invented in order to prevent the slaves dying of suffocation in the ships. They were chained to the floor within 18 inches of one another. The ventilator is reported to have reduced mortality from 50 per cent to 10 per cent of the victims.

If within a wonderfully short period of time, England could emerge from these terrible conditions all round into the present clean and civilised life, let us also take courage and make up our minds that with faith, hope and work we can make our land also a land of cleanliness and happiness and civilisation.

Our Heritage

[While in Bellary Jail last year, Sjt. Rajagopalachar engaged his fellow-prisoners with talks on all sorts of subjects. The following is one on Karma.]

Whatever else I have read or studied, I have not studied books on our religion. My religion I have learnt only from my mother. I did not learn it from any book or under any Guru. What I lernt from my mother has not been contradicted by anything that I learnt afterwards.

A little knowledge of science unsettles our ideas regarding Religion. But a deeper study of Western sciences will enable us the better to understand Religion especially Hindu religion. There are many discoveries of modern science at which we wonder. We admire the railway, the telegraph, the air-ship and the wireless, but the greatest wonder is the Unity and the infinity that pervade the whole Universe. Even the smallest thing is as difficult to be comprehended completely as God Himself. We cannot understand the very word "complete". When I was a child and learnt 1, 2, 3, I thought at some point the numbers would end, where I could stop. Later I understood that they end nowhere. Whatever the number may be I could add one to it. They cannot be carried to the farthest limit. It is infinite. Not only have we no end counting upwards, but what is more wonderful you are in an infinite maze even if you count downwards by dividing and again dividing. The smallest thing can yet be divided, just as the biggest thing can be multiplied. Where is this thing to end? So that, on a state with the help of a pencil, you can see the infinity of God.

If you look at the sky without telescope. The Universe as a whole, and every part of it, is infinite. The greatest knowledge is the discovery that we cannot understand anything. Nothing can be completely understood, you can only understand it as a whole and in a rough way. If you go deep the simplest thing becomes a secret and a mystery.

You I now that there was a wise man called Socratery, in Greece. He insisted again and again that we cannot know things, so that however learned we may be, our first duty is to be humble. Just as Grandhiji is in politics to us, so Newton is in the world of science. Newton even now is considered to be the greatest man of science of all time, and he said that our knowledge and researches are like picking shells on the sands of the ocean. So much of the ocean is there vast and unknown. After picking a few shells thrown here and there upon the beach, we imagine that we have learnt all about the ocean. We must approach knowledge with a due sense of humility and reverence like Newton. It is only if we are humble that we can known things.

The modern discoveries of Science do not at all contradict Religion. I look upon both as the same sort of thing and, therefore, I see no contradiction in them. Do not imagine that to marry a girl at the age of ten is Hinduism or to shave the head of a widow of sixteen is Hinduism. Don't imagine that to put a triple strand of handspun thread on your shoulders is Hinduism or that to paint your forehead in a variety of ways is Hinduism. These customs are like the waves on the surface of the Ocean of Hinduism. Don't imagine that only the waves constitute the ocean. The waves may shift or stop but the ocean remains. Even if you changed all your customs you would still be Hindu, you would not become a Mussalman of Christian or an Athiest.

You see a man, Rama. What is it that we call and recognise as Rama? Rama is not his hands, feet or head. Even if smallpox attacked him and his face were disfigured; even if he should lose his feet or eyes or if any other changes take place in his body we have the same love and respect or aversion or hatred towards him. The man, we may say, consists of a group of feelings, thoughts and ideas; he is not the body. Even if the thoughts change, even if his character should change, we hold on to the man, his personality. He is, therefore, not even in the thoughts; he is somewhere behind the thoughts. It is he that thinks, speaks, moves and acts. This is the fundamental of all religion.

If you put a stone in water you will find the water ripple, that ripple will produce another ripple, that again will produce a third and so on, and we may say not even God can stop it. If you add two and two it becomes four, can God change it? It is only if you understand this that you can understand what I consider the essential of Hinduism.

Every bad thought in our mind is a painful ripple in the Universal spirit, or put in a different way is a stap in the heart of God, and that is why sages imagine that God is shedding tears whenever we think any bad thought. Just as we do not see but know how "wireless" vibrations started in America can be received here even if there is no wire, across the "either," we may assume that there is an all-pervading substance which receives the shock of every bad thought though we may not see it. Do not imagine that 'wireless' waves are a peculiar invention of some European called Marconi. It is only a discovery of what was going on from time immemorial. The vibrations were going on from eternal time back, and men of Science just discovered them one day.

Imagine a deaf man who sees the whole beautiful world but hears nothing. He suddenly discovers his ears. He finds vast noise all over the world and he did not hear it at all so long. Similarly, there is a deafness of the soul which disables us from perceiving the vibrations of good and bad thoughts. If we were relieved of this deafness of the soul and suddenly begin to feel the vibration of thoughts pervading the whole world we would, then wonder how there was so much evil going on in the world and we did not prevent it. Just as sleep is a blessing,—when we are tired we go to sleep and are happy for ten or twelve hours though we may have many reasons for unhappiness during the other twelve hours,—we may say that God has blessed us with this deafness, so that we may live in peace in this world which is full of evil thoughts.

As there are some people who light a lamp and read in the night, when all the world is asleep and when they should sleep also,—there are a few mad people who want to find the truth of soul vibrations, even though God has blessed us with a useful deafness in that respect. This is religious speculation and philosophy. Follow the same mad fellow who lights his lamp at night. He reads for some time, then he grows tired of the whole business, puts out the lamp and goes to sleep. Similarly, a men may grow tired of religion and go to sleep. But there are a few people like those who rang the Upanishads, and like those who are carrying on scientific researches in the

West as well as here. Both belong to the class of madmen, who light their lamps at night and go on bothering with knowledge and dying for it. It is their work that we call Religion, their work that we call Science.

Just as the very simple idea of universal natural attraction called by Newton, Gravitation, was the basis of all the complicated calculations and theories of science until recently, so also the Karmic doctrine is an extremely simple thing to under-stand and yet is the basis of all the complicated ideas of Hindu Religion. It is only very simple truths that are the foundation of all things. The doctrine of Karma is that whatever we do, immediately an effect is produced. We cannot escape it. Not that we will be punished later on or get heaven or hell, but an effect is immediately produced.

Action includes thought and word, as well as as what we ordinarily call action. For instance, if I see somebody possess a thing and feel jealous, think how nice it would be if I got it, it is a kind of theft. Just as there are robbery, burglary and different kinds of theft, so also this thought is one kind of theft.

There was a French philosopher who wrote, imagine that a man residing some where in France could get the property of a wealthy man in China, who was not a relation or a friend or even known to him at all,—and to kill him needed no effort but to press a button in France, and there was a guarantee that nobody could know anything about it, it would be absolutely secret, yet certain to produce the result. Who was there, the French philosopher asked, who would not press that button and get that inheritance? Through strikingly put, this was a wrong view. Another French philosopher immediately wrote in anewer to it that even under such circumstances a wise and good man would not press the button and kill the man. The mind which is our most valuable possession would be spoiled that very thought of killinght the man in China, and not all the wealth would be compensation enough. Even though nobody

nobody need know it and no physical harm will come to you, still your most beautiful and precious possession is ruined by an evil thought like a stain on a fine picture, and therefore you abstain from it.

It is well-known that if we misbehave in respect of women, we are likely to catch disease. The doctrine of Karma says, "Even though you do not catch syphilis or any other disease, there is a disease which you unfailingly catch by your bad action. What is that disease? When we do a thing we are inclined to do it again. We prepare and shape ourselves more easily and readily to do it again. Whatever thought or action we go through once, it gets a title for easy reoccupation. I do not use-I find it difficult to use,—foul language; but once I use it, the second time it becomes easy for me. I fear to go in the dark; once I go, the second time it becomes easy. There is not child but if it does a thing once, it is easy for it to do it a second time. Once I think a bad thought or utter a bad word, or do a bad action, my character, more delicate than a waxen image, whose shape the slightest touch spoils, has been altered, to that extent. Our character is a delicate living thing. It grows through eternity. Once you do anything it receives and retains the impression at once. The slightest evil that you do leaves its ugly and indelible impression behind. You cannot go back on what you have thought or done.

But this unchangable law of cause and effect is not a law of hopelessness. You cannot withdraw effect from cause, but you are free to think and act again and beat your character into shape again. This is the true freedom of action contained in Karma. It is not fatalism.

Death is not a wiping off of the slate so that we end there or begin anew. After death we continue as with an opening balance. This is the Hindu belief. The shape which one has given to oneself in this life is the start with which the soul proceeds on the next journey. Our character as we build it with our thoughts and actions is not only our present greatest possession, but it is also our inalienable inheritance. We live for all time, every one of us. We close our account now and then but then, the balance is carried forward to the next page.

Some of you are Mussalmans. I want Mussalmans too to understand Hindu religion correctly, and even to be proud of Hinduism in a way, as the great religion of the land of their birth. If I were a Hindu born in Arabia I would be proud of Mohomed and of Islam. I would be angry with anybody who spoke ill of Mohomed. I would consider it my duty to study Islam, my first duty, if I were a Hindu born in Arabia. Similarly, if I were a Hindu born in Palestine, I would consider the religion of Christ one of the first things to be understood and respected, and I would give my vote to spend large sums of money in order to protect the churches of Christ, just as today you find the civilised Britishers spending large sums of money to protect Hindu and Moghul monuments and temples. I want you all therefore to understand the doctrine of Karma in Hinduism. Even Christians and Mussalmans should understand it, as I said, provided they are Indians.

The Finance Bill

"The big financial effects are in the lower salaries. Officers at the top have been subjected to an additional heavy income-tax. In view of this and other factors, the Government have come to the conclusion that it is not fair to ask the higher grades to be subjected to more than a total ten per cent cut in their pay." This is what Sir George Schuster said in defence of a flat cut in all salaries down to Rs. 40 per month as against the proposals for enhanced cuts in higher salaries. It is a brutally frank statement, but not more convincing on that account.

Sir George said that a ten per cent flat cut would bring in more money than a graduated scale rising to 20 per cent for higher salaries, because salaries above Rs. 1,800 per month were only about rupees two crores. Why should we stop at 20 per cent? Why should not these be subjected to a 50 per cent cut for that matter, and a saving of a crore effected? It is not as if the officer cannot live decently on Rs. 900 a month. There is nothing impossible or improper in a step of this kind when the Government is faced by insolvency. More revolutionary economies are generally effected when an officer retires on pension, or when trouble has to be faced in private life. Economies in public finance ought to be no less courageously undertaken than in private life.

Referring to the notorious Lee Concessions, Sir George Schuster said that "Government must definitely set their face" against any withdrawal of them. Sir, George had the audacity to say that the removal of these concessions regarding free passages from India to England and back for European officers and their families, and bearing travelling expenses incurred by European officers and their families, for high class medical treatment and such like, would be "discriminatory action of a most unfair kind." Strange indeed are the uses of the phrase 'discriminatory.' He similarly urged specious arguments against income-tax being levied on interest paid on sterling securities, on pensions, leave-pay and allowances paid out of Indian revenues to persons living abroad. He urged a deal of bad law as well as bad reasoning.

Sir George instituted a comparison of his own present economies as against reductions of expenditure previously achieved and claimed that the present proposals were more daring, being about 16 per cent of the "controllable" expenditure in various services. The measure of his daring, is however, far more obvious in the percentage of increase in the burden of taxation.

WHAT THE MILLIONS WANT

Mr. E. Villiers' pronouncements have acquired additional and adventitious importance on account of the recent attempt on his life. At a meeting of one of the branches of the European Association, he gave out that in spite of everything that has happened, he was one of those who still believed that Lord Irwin's policy of peace with the Congress was the right policy. "In saying this, I am not unmindful" Mr. Villiers said, "of the tremendous difficulties consequent on that policy or of the heavy price that his policy has entailed." Mr. Villiers made some interesting comparisons of the effectiveness of terrorist activities with that of the civil disobedience campaign. Referring to the former, he said, "it is not one tithe of the politial significance of the latter. Terrorism is not the real challenge to the Government. The real challenge has been and may again be civil disobedience." Of course Mr. Villiers proceeds to describe the remedy, namely, "unhesitating speed and ruthless strength."

Mr. Villiers is near the mark when he says that the real challenge to the Government is civil disobedience. But, if he had dived deeper, he could have seen that the real challenge is that of truth and justice as against falsehood and exploitation. It is the moral justification that is, on the one hand, the source of strength and the secret of calm suffering offered by the oppressed in resistance, and on the other hand, the cause of fear and agitation and the consequent strong language to cover that agitation on the part of the exploiter.

Mr. Villiers stands up still for peace with Congress. It is well known to us that the British Commercial exploitation has no objection to any political concessions or any truce or policy of peace, provided the even course of his exploitation is guaranteed its undisturbed continuation. If this is endangered, he stands up for ruthless strength and unhesitating speed.

Mr. Villiers assures all those whom it may concern, that, if the Government are prompt and strong the untold millions in this country, who ask nothing better than that they should be allowed to live their daily lives in peace, will reassert their loyalty to the crown and flock to the standard of Government. The millions according to the President of the European Association are only dying to form an undisturbed market for British over-production, and will be happy only if half-starved.

The conscience of Britain was given a great shaking last

year. It seemed for some time there was repentance and the birth of a new thought. But the traditional fear of idealism has seized Britain again. Britain is under the sway of caste, no less than long suffering India. The ruling caste of Britain has reasserted its authority and is again in possession of power and office. Gandhiji always knew that it was useless to depend upon the vague promises of other parties and preferred to treat with those who could deliver the goods on behalf of England. He is doing all he can to get the Conservatives who are the British ruling caste to make up and tell him their mind in the matter, so that India may make up her own mind as to what she should do.

This is the critical week in the London programme for India One of three things may happen. We may have honourable terms and assurances such as Gandhiji will ask us to accept and live in peace with Britain. Or we shall have a resumption of the conflict between people and Government. Or the whole matter will still be left undecided and the present armistice may continue.

Whatever be the event, our immediate duty is certain in one respect, the duty of eschewing foreign cloth. Freedom is so much a part of the natural law of the world, that simple economic considerations lead to the same conclusions as the political motive for emancipation from foreign rule. This convergence of economics and politics should not be cause for inaction or hesitation on account of the holding up of political issues. The economic exploitation of the nation should be stopped as it lies in our power and at any cost, Nation-wide unemployment is not a thing that can wait for politics. There is no other course open to us to solve the problem of our poverty, than that Indian industry must be converted into Indian cloth. Otherwise, our people will be workless, and living death will be the chronic state of the nation. If we wish really to live, we must refuse to take foreign cloth.

Just as we breath without stop or interval for keeping up the individual life, industry is the breath of national life.

Every one of us, whatever be our walk of life, must now be incessantly giving this message against foreign cloth throughout the length and breadth of the land, as the necessary first aid to recover healthy national life. Let no one imagine that he must wait for a declaration of war for this.

THE BENGAL ORDINANCE

The Congress is against violent crime. Violence huts Congress more than it hurts Government. Violent crimes demand measures of suppression. But crime does not justify madness.

Honest fighting either of external foes or of internal sedition is one thing. But it is a sign of a confused state of mind to forget civilisation and allow fighting to degenerate into brutal cruelty or regardlessness of consequences to innocent people. Frightfulness may have its value in dealing with a situation where entire populations have revolted or are assisting rebels. But dealing with the plots and crimes and abetments of a few people working secretly and unknown to others among whom they are living, a Government policy of putting innocent men in risk of punishment without proof and of infliction of hardship on inhabitants of a whole area carries not one iota more of deterrent terror or punishment to the real criminal. It succeeds, however, in adding to the plotters' satisfaction. These men are incensed at the indifference of people, and would derive some satisfaction from the prospect of widespread and unthinking infliction of trouble on all alike as a result of their own activities. They would look upon miscarriage of justice and ruthless military rule as a just punishment for those who have been guilty of apathy.

There is no need to go through the agony of an analysis of the provisions of the new Bengal Ordinance promulgated on 30th November. It can be expressed briefly as a complete withdrawal of the protection of the Law and of legal procedure, and the substitution of pure military government. Practically any criminal trial, can, by order of the District Magistrate, be transferred to a special magistrate under the Ordinance, and thereby all important and well known provisions associated in civilised countries with judical procedure to ensure just and impartial trials and to save the innocent and those about whom there may be a reasonable doubt, are at an end.

Panic is written in every line of the Ordinance. It must be admitted that cause has been given for this panic, and the occasion is favourable for exaggeration and distortion. Rulers and ruled being of different races without the bond of blood or kinship, Authority does not feel called upon to observe such restraints as it would have felt, had it to deal with men and women of its own face under similar circumstances. Anger and revenge take frightful shapes when accentuated by a difference of race. If I am worried with ants or flies, I strike out wildly, not discriminating or choosing. This is the spirit in which the recent outrages in Bengal are avenged by the new Ordinance in the name of protection. The theory is that ninetynine men may be hurt if the hundredth man cannot be punished otherwise, just the opposite of a principle which was the glory of British jurisprudence and a proof of British courage. But courage has yielded to panic.

It is not only the law of Criminal Procedure and Evidence that is repealed by the Ordinance. It establishes a state of things as on the invasion of an enemy—power or an armed and open rebellion. Property, moveable and immoveable, can be commandeered. Men and women may be stopped and arrested anywhere, and, on no proved or stated ground except mere suspicion, detained. Any one's services may be requisitioned by officials, that is to say, personal liberty is at an end. Communications, private and public conveyances and means of transport may be restricted and altogether denied to any one. Whole villages may be collectively fined by an army Captain or a Police official and the monies recovered by imprisonment as well as ordinary processes of coercion. Indeed, short of express provision to kill at sight and burn villages, a state of war has been declared.

It is not, however, to be thought that without the promulgation of an ordinance of this kind, the police and the magistracy have not been doing all or most of these things. Wherever anything has been done to make them angry, or nervous, the authorities have never stayed their hands by reason of want of legal authority. Wherever they felt inclined to take such measures, they have done it in advance of Ordinances, and the Government has never found itself strong enough or willing enough to find fault with them. The Ordinance puts down on paper not anything new which the people have not already suffered, it gives no new machinery which the Bureaucracy had not been already fully using. It only serves to record the immediate plan and policy of Executive authority. Were not men detained on mere suspicion hitherto for more than twenty-four hours? Is not any property commandeered even now, law or no law? Are not the military and semi-military called in now? Is not access to public buildings fully controlled even now by police and magistracy? Do they not commandeer, restrict, intimidate, prohibit and do anything they like in regard to means of conveyance, and private and public transport? Again, do magistrates feel free and independent to do just what they like in political cases? Is there any real confidence in Law Courts, Original or Appellate, in such cases? Do not people feel that the result in these cases is ever foregone? There is no new law here in the Ordinance, but only a promulgation of executive policy and a notice of a free hand to local officials, and a direction for large-scale activity. It is needless, therefore, to subject the terms of the Ordinance to juristic criticism. Sir Stanley Jackson's statement, his post-prandial cricketing figures of speech and the reported elaborate preparations of civil and military authorities for a midnight round-up, these are more relevant.

The charge that there have been outrages of violence cannot be denied. That the Government is entitled to take adequate measures to put this down must also be admitted. But the Government does not claim that there has been an armed revolt in Chittagong District. They do not contend that the inhabitants of the district or of any place, town or village, have risen in open rebellion. A man going about in the district before the Ordinance did not see War or Rebellion. He saw ordinary peaceful life, civil trade, business and avocation. Secret crime there may have been. It may have been not merely stray crimes, it may have been even organised crime. But villages did not rebel. There was no mass movement of violence. All the provisions of the new Ordinance are such as to be conceived only if there were an armed revolt or mass organisation of violence. We have, therefore, no hesitation in characterising the Ordinance as a wholly unjustifiable plan of revenge and frightfulness against undetected individual crime. There is no garndener so foolish as would, because there are some deadly snakes in the garden, call in the aid of fire and sword and a regiment or two of soldiers to destroy the snakes and the garden. But than gardeners are interested in the garden.

THE SHRADDHANAND BALIDAN

By this week it will be five years since Swami Shraddhanand passed away from us like ghee in the sacrificial fire. Let us now during Christmas 1931 call to memory that great sacrifice and once more offer it from our hearts to quench Anger and Ignorance. Let us pray to the Universal Spirit to try us no more, but to give us the peace and the joy of love and concord and united national life.

We have a festering sore in our body-politic known by the ugly name of Untouchability. The thing itself is much uglier than the name. It generates continual deadly poison that makes healthy national life and work and progress impossible. Swami Shraddhanand's life was devoted to the healing of this canker and the purification of Hindu society. May his undying spirit still help us in the work until it is accomplished.

With this gangrenous ulcer in our body how can we have peace or progrees ? The Nation is not a mere congregation of individuals or of groups, even as a single living being is not a mere congregation of living cells. The vital sap, the sensitive nerves of pain and pleasure and activity, make the countless cells and parts of the body all into one beautiful living crystal. With a magnifying glass you could see those individual cells, all separate and living as if each for itself. But there is a unity of purpose, and a single life behind the million seemingly separate lives that are built into one individual body. Each cell struggles and lives for itself, but they all together make up the tissues and organs, and render homage and obedience to the law of the life of the higher organism of which they are components. The remotest nail and seemingly unessential part lives, works and dies for the common life. The seemingly separate growth, struggle for existence and death of every cell is a part of the life of the whole.

So, also, the Nation is not a mere conglomeration of individuals or even of groups. Individuals and groups may seem to struggle and live each for itself. But the nation has a great and a single and an indivisible life. Its life-blood, and its sensory and motor nerves run through and through, and make it all one delicate living organism. Individuals and groups may seem to be struggling and tumbling one against another, as if living in a mad intoxication of utter selfishness but the life behind binds them all together without their knowing it. The national life is one and indivisible, and hence suffers terribly if there is a cut or a wound or a sore. Untouchability is a terrible sore, and must be healed if we should live.

You cannot have a festering store, and live in peace by mere flapping. The flies will be on it so long as the sore is not healed and the skin has not covered it, making the spot a part of the whole. You cannot quarrel if Christians or Musalmans or Government hover over the untouchables and seek to suck food or draw strength or support from these people whom Hindu society does not cover with its protecting skin and make them part of itself. They are part of Hindu society, no doubt, even as the sore is part of living body. The pain is felf by you, unmistakeably, and not by any one else proving that the sore is yours and no one else's. The untouchables are Hindus, no doubt, for no one else feels the pain or suffers by it. But the sore has to be healed.

Let us remember that if the Christians, the Musalmans, or the Government are at the Untouchables, whatever be their motives, their interference is the result of the Law of Nature and the Humanity bedind that Law of Nature. Nature drives them, may be through selfish motives, to help the Untouchables, out of their unfortunate condition. This causes pain to the Hindus, even as the flies on the sore. But that, too, is to rouse Hinduism to an inflammation so that it may absorb the sore and the poisons that are generated, and heal it and cover it so that not even a scar may be seen. Hinduism has enough vitality in its bood to heal this canker.

Swami Shraddhanand's life was devoted to this healing process. May his memory be preserved for all time, and inspire us.

THE UNTENABLE CLAIM

Gandhiji put two clinching questions to convict Britain of unfitness to hold the trusteeship of India.

'Is it or is it not a fact that India today is the poorest country in the world, wherein millions of people are condemned to unemployment for six months in the year?'

'Is it or is it not a fact that India has been emasculated not only by compulsory deprivation of arms but also through being denied so many opportunities that members of a free nation enjoy ?

These were the two tests applied by Gandhiji. Yet the so-called safeguards, to which the non-Congress delegates at the London Conference would seem to agree, will on examination be found calculated to preserve for the discredited trustee the opportunity to continue just these two great delinquencies of his. The restrictions sought to be imposed on popular control over finance render it impossible for India to emerge from her poverty. The unimpaired continuance of British control over Defence will serve to prevent India from recovering her manliness which is the spring and secret of all freedom.

No one will deny that obligations incurred by the Government of India which are found at the settlement to be binding on the people of India must be borne and discharged in full. Even Reform may be postponed for that reason. The discharge of Debt is a part of the ancient and unbroken culture of India. But what is plain now is to hold India in possessory mortgage for these obligations. This amounts to a charge of insolvency or fraudulent intent which India must indignantly deny. To hold possession of national assets is a claim that is not ordinarily put forward in the case of debts among nations, for it would be a contradiction of the very term freedom. International obligations, even when entered into by contract, are not guaranteed or claimed to be secured by possession of assets and by control over internal administration. How then can it be justly claimed that Indian revenues should be held in possessory mortgage by or on behalf of England for obligations imposed on her without consent or contract but in the exercise of trusteeship? To talk of self-Government, at the same time imposing a usufructuary mortgage on revenues and on the internal administration of the country, is a contradiction in terms and reduces freedom to an unreality.

This claim to hold possession in order that Debts may be duly discharged is wrong enough. But the further claim in respect of salaries and pensions payable to men of British extraction employed in the internal administration of the country is outrageous. If India were at once declared to be on the verge of bankruptcy, one could understand Britain's anxiety to seek to hold possession for Debts and obligations. But this admission would be nothing short of a confession of a capital offence on the part of the socalled trustee. If India can bear the burden of the obligations claimed to have been incurred on her behalf, then it is unreasonable and against all international precedent to claim, at the time of constituting responsible government, to hold possession of and control over all or any part of the revenues and the administration of the country. If the smallest nations of Europe can borrow and remain in debt without transferring possession of customs, railways, or services to the creditor-government, Indian obligations certainly can stand admitted without a transfer of control or possession of finance or administration.

The control of Defence is a fundamental of freedom and cannot be separated and transferred to an external authority without rendering freedom totally illusory. Those Indian Liberals who imagine that we can throw off the sense of slavery by taking over Civil government without responsibility for Defence are grievously mistaken. To divide responsibility along the dividing line between civil and military affairs is fatal to the development of citizenship, freedom, or national economy. If the cleft between Civil and Defence administration is left yawning, no progress towards freedom or responsibility is possible. To submit to this arrangement and yet to strive for real freedom and national independence is to programme for a deadlock and a conflict.

Not only is Defence at the root of real responsibility, but in the present state of India it is inextricably mixed up with civil progress. It is impossible for India to order her own affairs and emerge from the slough of poverty unless he is free to prune and settle her own Defence estimates. Government without the freedom to do this would end in a miserable failure to justify itself before the people.

The constitution proposed at the termination of the London Conference can be no more sucessful than the provincial Diarchy that was tried and which has served only to prove the uselessness of such an attempt to bifurcate government. Self-government is an organic whole, one and indivisible, and cannot be divided without killing the life. India cannot consent to the status of a glorified municipality or Local Board. The size of it does not improve the status, but only makes it impossible.

Rajaji on Handloom Fund

Shri Rajaji, in the course of his reply to a debate in the Madras Legislative Assembly, incidentally referred to the Handloom Fund proposed to be created by the Union Government. The occasion was the Government resolution for a demand for restricting the production of *Dhotis* and *Saris* solely to the handloom. The demand calls for basic reorientation of our textile policy. It is asking our mills to subserve one of our greatest cottage-industries by supplying its yarn need and not to compete with it as they have been doing till now. It is in relation to this that Shri Rajaji's following remarks (as reported by *The Hindu* of 6-11-'52) are worthy of our attention :

> " 'The offer of money bonus or stipends is in the air,' Mr. Rajagopalachari said and added, 'Anything is welcome. If money is given, it is not for us to say 'no." The Government of India would tell them what to do with it usually. But he could not imagine what he could do with the share of Madras. It might be one crore. The question was how they should help the handlooms. He was unable to think what they should do with the three pies cess which they got from the mills which were to him the 'throttling' agency. 'We should not', the Chief Minister declared, 'get into the danger of earning some money from that which is going to throttle us to the extent we earn money. It is just like trying to use the drink money for propaganda against drink.' Unless the cess was a deterrent one, it was of no advantage. The cess proposed on mills was a mild one. It would just tickle the mill-owners to pay it for the handloom weavers. It would serve no other purpose whatsoever."

Glossary

Ahimsa	non-violence
Ashram	home for community living
Bania	member of the commercial community
Bapu	Father, often used in respect for Mahatma Gandhi
Bhandar	store
Bharat	India
Charkha	spinning-wheel
Chamar	a leather worker
Dal	association
Darshan	glimpse
Dharna	a sit-down strike
Firangi	a term used for the British
Ghat	bank of a river
Harijan	a name given by Mahatma Gandhi for an untouchable. The idea was to raise his social status in our society
Hartal	strike; stoppage of work and business.
Hakumat	rule
Himsa	violence
Inquilab	revolution; a slogan often raised by the of India against the *Raj*
Istri	people a woman
Jai	victory
Jatha	numerous persons
Khadi	hand-spun cloth
Khaddar	hand-spun cloth
Khilafat	the line of succession to the Prophet Muhammad
Kisan	peasant
Lathi	stick

Mahatma	a high-souled person; used for M.K. Gandhi as a mark of respect for him
Mahila	a woman
Murdabad	down with
Nari	a woman
Parbhat Pheri	a peaceful march early in the morning
Purdah	veil
Purna Swaraj	complete independence; demand of the Indian National Congress at the Lahore session presided over by Jawaharlal Nehru in 1929
Raj	government; often used for British Government in India
Sari	a long piece of cloth worn by Indian women
Satyagraha	truth-force or soul-force
Satya	truth
Satyagrahi	one who practises satyagraha in a non-violent way
Swarajya	independence or self-rule
Swadeshi	an article produced in one's own country
Takli	twirligig used for spinning cotton or wool
Taluka	revenue division
Thana	police station; normally a Sub-Inspector of Police was the incharge of a police station
Toddy	Juice of the palm tree
Vidyapith	university, an institution of higher learning. A chain of Vidyapiths was opened in various regions of India by the Congress in 1920s and 1930s. The idea was to boycott the government institutions
Vakil	lawyer
Zalim	cruel
Zamindar	landlord
Zindabad	victor
Zulum	oppression.

Chronology

1878	(10 December) Birth
1889	Leaves Hosur Scoool
1897	Passed B.A. Examination
1898	Marriage
1899	Passed Law Degree
1900	Began legal practice at Salem
1906	Attended the Calcutta Congress as a delegate
1907	Attended the Surat Congress
1911	Member, Salem Municipal Council
1915	Wife's death
1917-19	Chairman, Salem Municipal Council
1920	Joins the Non-Cooperation Movement
1921	First imprisonment
1922	Editor, "Young India"
1924	Attended the Belgaum Congress
1925-29	Busy in constructive work
1930	Vedaranyam march; sentenced for nine months
1932	Engaged in Temple entry movement
1937-39	Premier, Madras Province
1939	The second global war; resignation of office
1942	Differences with Congress on 'Quit India' issue; resigns
1946	Taken back into Congress working Committee; Joins the Interim Government
1947	Governor of Bengal
1948	Governor-General of India

1950	Joins as Member, Central Government
1952	Chief Minister, Madras State
1954	Bharat Ratna
1959	Founded Swatantra Party
1962	Anti-nuclear Mission
1972	(25 December) Death

Bibliography

Primary Sources

Speeches of C. Rajagopalachari
AICC Papers
The Collected Works of Mahatma Gandhi
Indian Annual Register by H.N. Mitra

Journals and Newspapers

The Modern Review Harijan
The Hindu
The Hindustan Times

Secondary Works

Azad, Abul Kalam, *India Wins Freedom*, Bombay, 1959.
Brecher, M., Nehru: *A Political Biography*, Oxford, 1959.
Chatterjee, Bimanesh, *Thousand Days with Rajaji*, Delhi, 1973.
Copley, A.R.H., *The Political Career of C. Rajagopalachari, 1937-1954*: *A Moralist in Politics*, Delhi, 1978.
Felton, Monica, *I meet Rajaji*, London, 1962.
Gandhi, M.K., *An Autobiography*, Ahmedabad, 1963.
Hodson, H.V., *The Great Divide*, London, 1969.
Iyengar, Masti Venkatesa, *Rajaji*: *A Study of His Personality*, Vols. I and II, Bangalore, 1975.
Menon, V.P., *The Transfer of Power in India*, Bombay. 1957.
Murti, R.K., *Rajaji*: *Life and Work*, New Delhi, 1979.

Nehru, Jawaharlal, *Autobiography*, Delhi, 1962.
Perumal, N., *Rajaji*, Calcutta, 1948.
Prasad, Rajendra, *Autobiography*, Bombay, 1957.
Rajaji's Speeches, Delhi, 1948.
Rajmohan Gandhi, *The Rajaji Story*, Vols. I and II.
Ranga, N.G., *Fight for Freedom*, New Delhi, 1968.
Tahmankar, D.V., *Sardar Patel*, London, 1970.
Woodruff, Philip, *The Men Who Ruled India*, London, 1954.

Index